PROTEUS
UNMASKED

PROTEUS UNMASKED

Sixteenth-Century Rhetoric and the Art of Shakespeare

Trevor McNeely

Lehigh
University
Press

Bethlehem: Lehigh University Press
London: Associated University Presses

Associated University Presses
2010 Eastpark Boulevard
Cranbury, NJ 08512

Associated University Presses
Unit 304, The Chandlery
50 Westminster Bridge Road
London SE1 7QY, England

Associated University Presses
P.O. Box 338, Port Credit
Mississauga, Ontario
Canada L5G 4L8

The paper used in this publication meets the requirements of the American National Standard for Permanence of Paper for Printed Library Materials Z39.48-1984.

Library of Congress Cataloging-in-Publication Data

McNeely, Trevor, 1934–
    Proteus unmasked : sixteenth-century rhetoric and the art of
Shakespeare / Trevor McNeely.
        p. cm.
Includes bibliographical references and index.
    ISBN 0-934223-74-2 (alk. paper)
1. Shakespeare, William, 1564–1616—Technique. 2. English
language—Early modern, 1500–1700—Rhetoric. 3. Rhetoric—History—16th
century. 4. Drama—Technique. I. Title.
    PR2995.M325 2004
    822.3'3—dc21

                                                        2003008433

PRINTED IN THE UNITED STATES OF AMERICA

*To Shirley for her
love and support, and
never forgetting her patience!*

Contents

Preface

T he following study is neither a history of sixteenth-century
rhetoric, nor a systematic survey of either terminology or
taste, but an attempt to build on, rather than merely supple-
ment, previous scholarship on the subject of the relationship
of Shakespeare to the rhetorical tradition. Its thesis is multi-
faceted, and sufficiently expansive that some initial guidance,
with an over-view of the whole, will be useful to the reader
before plunging directly *in medias res*. The thesis is developed
cumulatively over four chapters, each stage linked to the one
preceding, moving from the general picture of the role of rhetoric
in sixteenth-century English culture, through its contribution to
the rise of Elizabethan drama, and culminating in its specific
application to the interpretation of Shakespeare. Recognizing
the thesis's challenge to critical orthodoxy, both traditional and
contemporary, in all of these areas, its development proceeds
with full discussion and deliberation at every stage, citing a
broad range of sixteenth-century as well as Classical rhetorical
materials to justify a radically subversive reinterpretation of
their thrust.

The study's claims rest on two central and closely related
premises, both of which are in one sense quite conventional, but
in another much more radical. The first premise is that "rhetoric," in the primary sense of that term, "the art of using language so as to persuade or influence others," in the words of the
OED, is *the* integrating principle behind the Renaissance revolution both in Italy and England, the essential element that
holds tenuously together a universe threatening momentarily to
lapse into incoherence and chaos. The second premise, depen-

dent on the first, is that the heart and soul of the art of rhetoric lies in the principle of persuasion, that it is in persuasion rather than in precept that rhetoric has its essential being.

The cultural implications of these premises are explored in detail in chapter 1, demonstrating that the surface manifestations of the cult of rhetoric in the Elizabethan period—its central role in education and the universal adulation its professors enjoyed—mask profound insecurities in the culture, a fear of rhetoric in its untrammeled use that acts to undermine the very stability that in its surface features the cult strives to support. The tensions within the subject are epitomized in the contradictory visions of rhetoric that flourish side by side in the period —the mainstream Aristotelian tradition, in which rhetoric has a natural alignment with truth, and the more marginal declamatory tradition, in which its function is simply to persuade. A symptom of these tensions appears in the uneasy awareness, occasionally acknowledged, that rhetoric in theory, as taught in the academy, and in practice, as applied every day in the world of affairs, are often profoundly at odds. The product of these tensions is a kind of collective cultural neurosis, one that, like all neuroses, requires an outlet, a means of expression that can provide a harmless sublimation of these potentially crippling anxieties. Elizabethan society discovers its outlet in theater.

Chapter 2 takes up, as its first point, the many close affinities between rhetoric and theater, noted from classical times, though largely ignored in modern commentaries on the development of Elizabethan drama. In this omission modern scholarship simply follows the lead of the period itself, which is constrained from explicitly acknowledging any link, as to do so could compromise its carefully constructed defenses against direct recognition of rhetoric's darker powers. Theater can nonetheless act as an escape valve for these psychological pressures, mirroring, in the form of mere entertainment or "fiction," the actuality of a society held together by the most ephemeral, yet at the same time magically impenetrable, of rhetorico/theatrical illusions, "the illusion of power," in Stephen Orgel's phrase. Several of the popular courtesy texts of the period are cited for evidence of the implicit overlap of the courtly and theatrical milieus, while the pretense of a separation between authenticity and "art" is at all times strictly maintained, in conformity with society's psychological needs. Shakespeare makes his entrance into the discussion at this point by way of an implicit connection to the most characteristic and best of the Elizabethan courtesy texts, Puttenham's *The Art of English Poesie.*

Taking rhetoric's power of persuasion as its essential force, and thus the key to successful courtiership, Puttenham moves closer than any of his peers to an explicit linking of politics and art in his thesis that poetry is the ultimate rhetoric, "a kind of super rhetoric," as Brian Vickers calls it, possessing the power to actually take over the mind of its hearer. That Shakespeare is aware of this viewpoint, and subscribes to it, is then postulated and illustrated by many well-known, and some lesser-known, references in several of the plays that affirm exactly that principle.

Extrapolating from this postulate, chapter 3 advances the claim, much the boldest of the whole study, that Shakespeare is at all times a fully conscious artist, and specifically that he is conscious of the role of rhetoric in the culture in the manner that chapters 1 and 2 have described. The claim is bold because while no one who studies Shakespeare can be unaware of how almost laughably far short of the mark all the superlatives of praise like "prodigy" and "genius" are when applied to him, criticism has traditionally been reluctant to accede him full credit for his achievement. From Ben Jonson forward, it has been the implicit view, based largely on the "naturalness" of Shakespeare's portrayals, that his artistry is somehow innate, like that of the child Mozart, rather than in any way externally acquired. The thesis of this chapter is that this view is wrong. Both the educational and courtly literature, as well as the universal cultural norms of the period, give evidence that "nature," as the hallmark of Shakespeare's work, is precisely an illusion. Like the "hidden" personality of the man himself, it is an artful and consciously created product of these background influences. He has achieved the rhetorician's ideal of making his *art* invisible, of separating his speech from his own personality, as if he himself did not exist.

Chapter 4 takes up the question of the rhetorical mastery that has achieved such a coup, going back first to the general rhetorical background of the period, and considering the antithetical aims of rhetoric in the two different contexts in which it is employed, the academic and the political. In the academic context, where the focus is on teaching, the aim is visibility, to display one's mastery of the art in the variety and originality of the figures one has the skills to employ. Outside the academy, on the other hand, while the skill required must be at least as great, the aim becomes in a way the opposite, not to dazzle and call attention to oneself, but simply to be effective, to persuade. Making one's art visible would be in this context a hindrance rather than a help, because the hearer may be placed on guard, moved to skepticism in his view of the speaker. Working both sides of this visible/invisible dialectic with supreme skill through the speeches of his characters, Shakespeare *himself* now opens up a third way in which his rhetoric may be viewed, one in a sense combining the other two, here designated the allegorical or philosophical.

While the medieval tradition of allegory was still very much alive in the Elizabethan period, the Renaissance, stimulated by the Classical revival, had extended the term's application. It was now understood to apply to any subject on which a writer might wish to make a forceful and, for personal or political reasons, *partially concealed* statement. In addition, in line with the new humanistic perspective characteristic of the age, the focus of allegory now shifts to the human dimension, away from the wholly Christian or even the more broadly spiritual, becoming "none other than the Glass and Figure of Humane Life," in Tasso's words. Out of this evolving intellectual milieu emerges the allegory in Shakespeare's plays, an "allegory of rhetoric," an occult commentary on the centrality of persuasive rhetoric in the culture of his day, where language and style take on the creative power of life itself, in their capacity not merely to influence, but actually to create our vision of the world. "The medium is the message," McLuhan said; but Shakespeare anticipated him by 350 years, using theater as both the medium and the message of his allegory, that "reality" and theater are one and the same. On the stage rhetoric is applied imaginatively (i.e. poetically), with calculated art creating a world that is an imitation of reality; in the "real" world rhetoric is applied politically, with artifice equally deliberate (if sometimes less conscious), creating a world that is an imitation of the stage.

Chapter 5 begins the exploration of Shakespeare's plays with an overview to show how the allegory of rhetoric as now laid out is manifest in his work. Separate chapters on five of the plays as representative examples of his rhetorical philosophy follow this introduction, providing a new view of Shakespeare as artist, and inviting a similar approach to the interpretation of other plays in the canon.

Acknowledgments

I would like to acknowledge the kind cooperation of several other libraries in addition to Brandon University's, of whose resources I have made generous use in researching this book, first among them the University of Alberta, as well as the universities of Manitoba, Toronto, and Calgary, and the Folger Library.

Special thanks go to Jan Mahoney, tireless, enthusiastic, secretary *extraordinaire.*

PROTEUS
UNMASKED

1

Introduction:
The Culture Connection

The starting point of this study must be the distinction, cited in the Preface, between the conventional and radical aspects of the two premises relating to rhetoric on which it is based. Of the first premise, the conventional aspect is largely self-evident, both in the literature of the Renaissance itself, and perhaps even more so in the picture of the period that twentieth-century scholarship has given us, where "rhetoric" clearly figures as, if not absolutely the dominant element in Renaissance thought, then certainly as one of its most prominent features. Illustrations of this thesis abound in both contemporary and Renaissance writings: Hannah H. Gray, for example, writing on "Renaissance Humanism [as] The Pursuit of Eloquence," and citing a large number of both modern and fifteenth-century Italian sources, informs us that "the humanists' stand on eloquence implied an almost incredible faith in the power of the word";[1] and for Remigio Sabbadini likewise, *"il Rinascimento e il trionfo dell'eloquenza."*[2] The claims of rhetorical preeminence made on behalf of the English Renaissance are no less comprehensive: rhetoric is "the darling of humanity," says C. S. Lewis, that "rides the *renascentia . . . like* [a] wave";[3] and J. W. H. Atkins, citing the "inspiration" of Cicero and Quintilian in the sixteenth-century revival of rhetoric, calls rhetoric "the queen of the literary 'kinds'," and accords it "the leading place among intellectual studies."[4] And if the twentieth century recognizes the ascendancy of rhetoric in the Renaissance, it was in the great awakening itself that tributes to its power rose to truly lofty heights: in dicta that were the current coin of both educators and educated in what Elizabeth J. Sweeting, speaking of its "intoxication with linguistic power," calls "the full Elizabethan period,"[5] rapturous tribute is over and over paid to the "powre above powres, . . . heauenly *Eloquence*," as Samuel Daniel[6] termed it; or, in the equally inflated words of Thomas Wilson in *The Arte of Rhetorique* (a work which was reprinted seven times between 1553 and 1600), "what is he at whom all men wonder and stande in a maze, . . . whom do we moste reverence, and compt half a God emong men—: Even suche a one assuredly, that can . . . utter both wordes and matter, and in his talke use suche composition, that he . . . keep an uniformitee, and (as I might say) a nomber in the uttering of his sentence."[7]

Thus frequently exalted as a near-divine art at what one might call the "imaginative" end of the intellectual spectrum, rhetoric is equally touted at the other or "practical" end as an indispensable utilitarian skill of universal applicability. Leonard Cox, who wrote the first English textbook on rhetoric in 1530, justified his work on the grounds that "the right pleasant and persuadible art of Rhetorique . . . is very necessary to all such as will be either advocates . . . of the law, . . . sent in Princes Ambassades . . . or techers of goddes worde";[8] and "Lazarus Piot" (Anthony Munday), writing sixty years later, defended his translation of a French text titled *The Orator* on almost the identical utilitarian basis: "If thou study laws [these orations] may help thy pleadings, or if divinity . . . they may perfect thy persuasions. In reasoning of private debates, here maiest thou find apt metaphors, in incouraging thy souldiours fit motives. Fathers here have good arguments to moue affections in their children, and children vertuous reconcilements to satisfie their displeased fathers."[9] Sir Walter Raleigh, in his introduction to the modern edition of the Hoby translation of *The Courtier* of Castiglione, sums up the Renaissance attitude to rhetoric when he suggests that it is classical oratorical training that personifies the Renaissance man: "The Courtier was the embodiment and type of the civilization of the Renaissance, as the Orator was . . . of ancient Rome. And the treatises of Cicero and Quintilian, wherein is set forth the character of the perfect orator, have their exact counterpart in the books written by the Italians of the Sixteenth Century for the instruction of the Perfect Courtier."[10]

If the above very briefly conveys something of the conventional view of the central position of rhetoric in the Renaissance, the radical half of the equation is likely to prove more controversial. One might begin, however, by observing that even in the minute excerpts quoted above, an apparent discrepancy exists between the passion with which the cult of eloquence was embraced in the Renaissance, and the body of precepts to which this passion is ostensibly referred. If this statement sounds enigmatic I might clarify it by relating it to a particular well-known twentieth-century commentary on Shakespeare, one with which most readers are doubtless familiar, T. S. Eliot's famous essay on *Hamlet*. This is the essay in which the theory of the "objective correlative" is outlined, and in which Hamlet's failure to act is attributed to his inability to find an "adequate equivalent" in the "external facts" for the passion that consumes him, a passion which is therefore "inexpressible, because it is in excess of the facts as they appear."[11] I bring this analogy in to illustrate the problem the Renaissance faced in finding an "objective correlative" of its struggle for expression, and suggest that the canons of classical rhetoric, however tirelessly and with fanatical intensity extolled, pored over, rehearsed, and regurgitated they were in the sixteenth century, remain essentially lifeless in that role. Admittedly this postulate is merely intuitive at this stage, but it does not take either especially wide reading or unusual powers of perception to sense that there is indeed something in it. Eliot found in *Hamlet* something "inexpressibly horrible," "some stuff that the writer could not drag to light, contemplate, or manipulate into art"; and something of the same "stuff" may lurk within the confused conceptions of Renaissance rhetoricians, "stuff" which it is the chief objective of this study, focusing on Shakespeare, as representative of, though far transcending his age, to "drag to light."

A short excursion into some of the mysteries hinted at in the last paragraph is necessary at this point; and it may begin, as just suggested, in the realm of the commonplace. In considering the near-universal adulation accorded the study of rhetoric, and particularly the classical rhetoric of Cicero and Quintilian, in sixteenth-century England, a number of possible reasons for this obsession spring immediately to mind. The mainstream classical revival, first, the original Renaissance impulse, which by the beginning of the sixteenth century had arrived in England, is obviously a primary contributing factor. It brought about a total revitalization of the educational system along classical lines, and even among the phlegmatic English fostered an interest in things classical that has already been described as fanatical. It is not necessary to recount in detail the tributes to "luminar[ies]" like Pliny, Cicero, and other "such exalted writer[s]" that dot the works of Tudor educators like G. R. M. Ward,[12] but Roger Ascham's testimonial to the Erasmian ideal that "almost everything worth learning is set forth in [the] two languages[.] ... — Greek, of course, and Latin"[13] speaks plainly for them all: "The providence of God hath left unto us in no other tongue, save only in the Greek and Latin tongue the true precepts and perfect examples of eloquence, therefore must we seek in the authors only of those two tongues the true pattern of eloquence."[14]

A less obvious factor perhaps in causative terms, but one which is unquestionably linked to the phenomenon of the worship of classical rhetoric, is the spectacular developments that were taking place in the vernacular language during precisely the same period. That this link, though seemingly paradoxical, is not coincidental, is attested to by the fact that parallel developments and their corresponding classical countermovements had previously taken place in Italy decades earlier and were taking place contemporaneously with England in the other cultures that were touched by the Renaissance, particularly that of France.[15] I use the term *classical countermovement* to indicate the nature of the link between the two phenomena; because one of the principal impulses behind Renaissance classicism is a kind of neomedievalist conservatism, which attempts to place limits on the explosive development of the vernacular, controlling and guiding it in acceptable traditional channels. Not to go into the cultural psychological implications of these contradictory forces for the moment, one can demonstrate that a link does exist by looking once again briefly at some contemporary statements on the subject. Richard Foster Jones's fine book *The Triumph of the English Language* chronicles very fully, first, the rise of the vernacular from a limbo-like state of self-conscious provincial isolation at the beginning of the sixteenth century to the highest levels of literary achievement by the end. Most earlier references to the vernacular as a literary medium Jones cites are highly disparaging. Typical is Henry Bradshaw's 1521 apology for the "rudeness all derke" of his English translation of a saint's life, contrasting it with its Latin original, "flourisshyng in the flouers of glorious eloquence."[16] Among the more famous users of the vernacular at this period, who like many others deplored its crudity even as he used it, was Sir Thomas Elyot, in his influential *Boke Named the Governour* (1531), who says at one point that poets who write in Latin "do expresse them [good ideas] incomparably with more grace and delectation to the reder, than our englyssh tonge may yet comprehend."[17] Invidious comparisons with the Latin continue until well into mid-century, such as the following example from as late as 1560 in the translation of Seneca's *Oedipus* by Alexander Neville: "In fine I beseech all . . . to beare with my rudenes, and consider the grosenes of our owne countrey language, which cã by no means aspire to the high lofty Latinists stile."[18] By the 1590s, this attitude has entirely changed, and tributes fully as brave are now extended not to Latin but to English, as many examples could be adduced to show. Daniels's "heavenly eloquence," for example, comes from a nationalistic paean of 1599 called *Musophilus*:

> Should we this ornament of glorie then
>   As th' vnmaterial fruits of shades, neglect?
> Or should we carelesse come behind the rest
>   In powre of wordes, that go before in worth
>   When as our accents equall to the best
> Is able greater wonders to bring forth:
> When all that euer hotter spirits exprest
> Comes bettered by the patience of the North?[19]

And his contemporary Puttenham likewise refuses to let English take a back seat to Latin and Greek, "our language being no less pithie and significative," and "admitting no fewer rules and nice diversities than theirs."[20]

It is the spirit implied in expressions like these latter that justifies my contention that classical rhetoric is inadequate to contain the vernacular explosion in sixteenth-century England. The development of a staggeringly complex theoretical foundation for an elaborate artificial style, based principally on Cicero and Quintilian, exactly parallels the movement toward vernacular expression, a movement in its very nature spontaneous, free, and beyond the control of any rhetorical system whatsoever. That the two movements are, like Prometheus and his vulture, related, is once again demonstrable by the fact that they exactly chronologically coincide. The earliest statements on rhetoric in English, including those of Caxton (1481), Hawes (1517), and Cox (1530), give no special emphasis to *Elocutio* or style, noting it as but one of the five classical divisions of rhetoric.[21] The same balanced approach is found in the popular early Tudor educational program outlined by Erasmus in his *De ratione studii* (1511–12), where authors are to be studied "with a view to content rather than to style,"[22] though it should be noted that this had reference strictly to writings in Greek and Latin.[23] By the time of the publication of Sherry's *Treatise of Schemes and Tropes* in 1550, however, a radical shift in emphasis has clearly taken place, and questions of style have become, as they remained for the rest of the century and well into the next one, the paramount concern.

If Erasmus's *De ratione studii* represents the typical early Tudor guide to the acquisition of letters, Ascham's *The Schoolmaster* of 1570 may be taken as the corresponding Elizabethan prototype; and the contrast the two texts make in terms of stylistic emphases is striking. Ben Jonson may have tempered his admiration of Shakespeare to keep it "this side idolatry," but Ascham clearly had no such scruples as regards his devotion to his "Master Cicero," who, when he "doth set up his sail of eloquence in some broad, deep argument, carried with full tide and wind of his wit and learning, all other may rather stand and look after him than hope to overtake him."[24] *The Schoolmaster* as it stands is not a manual of style, as most of the popular rhetorics were, but it is also an incomplete work,[25] and certainly quite enough of Ascham's methodological biases emerge in the book as to leave no doubt where his stylistic sympathies lie. *The Schoolmaster* is chiefly known today for two things: Ascham's humane pedagogical technique, which advocates "cheerful admonishing" over "beating and driving" (16, 24) as a spur to laggard scholars; and, most importantly, his method of "double translation" as the most "ready way to the Latin tongue," a method which if its ideal could ever have been achieved would have had its practitioners producing not merely Ciceronian Latin (and English as well, as an incidental accomplishment), but Cicero's actual words, in a kind of sixteenth-century approximation to programmed learning (80, 87).

The significant point about Ascham's method, however, and it is a point that all the other educational literature, and indeed the whole rhetorical bias of Elizabethan culture reinforces, is that it represents a systematic attempt to control the use of language, and to confine that use to rigidly prescribed and historically sanctioned classical forms. Walter Ong sees this educational movement as a response to the instabilities with which the Renaissance was assaulted, that "style was to be controlled by modes of speech fixed in writing and thus freed of the transiency of the present time."[26] That these attempts at control failed we need hardly point out, having the unparalleled achievements of Elizabethan vernacular literature, climaxed by Shakespeare, to testify, but the really significant thing in this context to note is that this spectacular achievement takes place against the background of a culture dedicated in many ways to resisting it. Stephen Cohen refers to "the anarchic malleability of language of which the plays, and the sociopolitical structures they depict, are composed," encapsulating in that expression his thesis that instability, linguistic and social, was both the hallmark of the age and at the same time its greatest fear.[27]

It is in this meeting between doctrinaire rigidity on the one side and creative innovation on the other that the gap between the professed adulation of eloquence and the sterile taxonomical apparatus of *Elocutio* and *Amplificatio* to which it is constantly referred back in the Elizabethan period stands out clearly. If Elizabethan eloquence at its best is "the applause, delight! the wonder of [the world]" (to slant Jonson slightly), Elizabethan *books* on eloquence come closer for the most part to the summary description Lee A. Sonnino's *Handbook to Sixteenth-Century Rhetoric* gives of the "book which," she says, "stands at the apex of the tendency towards ridiculous detail [,] . . . the almost unreadable *De universa ratione elocutionis rhetoricae* of Joannes Sturm, a monument to remorseless pedantry and tireless industry."[28] This is the same Sturm, incidentally, who was Ascham's mentor and close collaborator through most of his professional career.[29] I would maintain that this description fits not only the texts used by Elizabethan educators, but the teaching method such texts necessarily entail, a method based exclusively on rote learning and endless repetition of the "figures" of rhetoric, gleaned with tireless assiduity from the writings of Tully and Quintilian by two generations of schoolmasters. As there is no doubt that this was the principal method for inculcating knowledge of the principles of language in the sixteenth century, so there can be no more doubt that for the true genius of language to assert itself in such an atmosphere it could only be done through a kind of hidden opposition to the stifling constraints on

the development of language such methods impose. Ascham may
have been a humane schoolmaster (as tutor to Henry VIII's children he could hardly have been otherwise!), but he was in this
clearly the exception rather than the rule. Elizabethan schoolboys may indeed have grown up "in a world of 'prettie epanortho-
sis', paronomasia, *isocolon*, and *similiter cadentia,*" as C. S.
Lewis says (adapting Spenser's E. K.), but that they "adored
sweet Tully and were as concerned about asyndeton and chias-
mus as a modern schoolboy is about county cricketers or types of
aeroplane,"[30] one may be permitted to doubt.

Much more plausible as a general picture of Elizabethan
classrooms is Brian Vickers's observation that "the whole Renaissance school-system was built around an extraordinarily
thorough process of learning by rote, . . . enforced by espionage
and beating."[31] The very fact that Ascham feels compelled to condemn "butcherly fear"[32] as a means of enforcing learning is a
clear signal that such means were the norm in his day. And it
should scarcely need saying that the kind of writing such methods would be almost guaranteed to produce would be stilted,
stylized, constrained, and lifeless in the extreme—in effect, a
mirror image of the methods themselves. T. W. Baldwin has
given us an excellent illustration of this very point, from the
career as it happens of Roger Ascham, in an exercise in translation that he may have assigned to the Princess Elizabeth, an
exercise which its modern editor can scarcely read without chok-
ing:

> In order to render the pedantic jargon of this periphrastic version
> a little more intelligible, the original Latin is here annexed, [.] . . .
> On the whole, . . . this royal translation is certainly a curious
> piece of pedantry; albeit, if we could raise maister Puttenham and
> the other court critics of Elizabeth's age, from their tombs, they
> would be driven to a nonplus to defend this Euphuistic labour of
> their virgin queen from the charge of vying with the fustian of an-
> cient Pistol.[33]

We come, indeed, in anecdotes like the above, closer to the
true spirit of sixteenth-century rhetoric than whole shelves of
textbooks and critical analysis can ever bring us. I have said that
the system of rhetoric as elaborated *ad nauseam* in the sixteenth
century is inadequate as an objective correlative of the vernacular explosion that took place in England in the same period. In

fact that system, an academic exercise from start to finish, is but the shadow of a linguistic revolution that took place, not in the schoolroom, but in the corridors of politics and power. And it is at this point that the "primary" definition of rhetoric as "the art of using language to persuade or influence others" comes critically to bear. For they mistake the idea of *rhetoric* who apply the term *mainly*, as most of both its sixteenth-century students and their twentieth-century expositors do, to the development of an elaborate theoretical system for the classifying and analyzing of oratory.[34] For such systems are always secondary to the practical use of rhetorical skill as a technique of manipulation in the real world of human affairs. Shakespeare says this himself, "that the art and practice part of life / Must be the mistress to this theoric." (*Henry V*, 1, 1.51–52). At most the "theoric" can do no more than inspire the apt pupil to discover his own rhetorical ability, at worst it may inhibit the development of whatever potential as a creative user of language the student may actually have. Certain it is at any rate that the only lasting value the formal training may have is to foster the development of the skill in the users of language that enable them to transcend it, as Shakespeare and many of his contemporaries, to their endless credit, were able to do.

If it is true that the real story of sixteenth-century rhetoric is told in the vernacular, and that the whole garguantuan edifice of academic rhetoric was finally nothing more than a huge quixotic crusade in defense of an illusion, the question remains as to why anything so manifestly (as I would claim) beside the point was so influential, so widespread, and so dominant a cultural force for so long. The roots of this enigma lie deep in sixteenth-century culture, deeper certainly than the men of the period were themselves fully aware (with perhaps one notable exception, in the subject of this study) but deeper also, I would suggest, than modern scholarship has so far penetrated. Focusing on rhetoric primarily as an intellectual "system," a "discipline," and a tradition from the ancients, both periods' scholars miss the essential driving force behind the rhetorical revolution, namely, the principle per se of persuasive speech and the power potential therein implied. On the surface a complex system of controls to guide the development and use of language, academic rhetoric on a deeper level is a largely unconscious smokescreen behind which the real rhetorical revolution, the revolution of power, can carry on unhindered and undetected. It is both the inadvertent and indispensable means to that revolution taking place.

We come at this point to one of the most elementary, but at the same time most difficult-to-grasp aspects of the whole question of rhetoric, particularly of its sixteenth-century form. This is the self-evident yet perhaps profound revelation that rhetoric in its general definition is inseparable from the act of speech itself; that is, every speech act, even a "yes" or "no," is an attempt to persuade, and must perforce use rhetorical techniques, whether the user has names for the techniques he is using or not, or whether he has even so much as heard of the art of rhetoric at all. This is an absolutely essential point, however infrequently noted by students of the art, because it has the effect of adding an unavoidable dimension of ambiguity to everything that is said by anyone *on the subject* of rhetoric, and regardless of whether that person intends to be ambiguous or no. And it is a particularly important point in respect of sixteenth-century rhetoric, because, remarkably in a century so hyper-attuned to every nuance of speech and its delivery, apparently no student of the dozens who wrote on the subject and were endlessly studied and discussed, picked up on this dimension of ambiguity that is built in to rhetorical discussion. It is my contention that, given the unique circumstance of the intensely rhetorical focus of sixteenth-century thought generally, that this omission cannot be entirely accidental. This is not to say that it is precisely intentional either, but that students of the art as steeped in its subtler possibilities as, say, Gabriel Harvey, George Puttenham, or Francis Bacon, could have been totally unaware of these darker aspects of rhetoric even as they exploited them, asks a suspension of disbelief that might well give pause even to a Coleridge.

Considered from the somewhat altered perspective that these possibilities place on the subject, certain characteristic features of sixteenth-century rhetorical theory change their orientation quite radically, and tend in fact to reinforce the view that there is considerably more going on below the surface of that theory than conventional interpretations have been aware of. One feature that stands out as possibly questionable, for example, is the axiomatic assumption among all rhetoricians that their art serves the cause of reason or truth. This truth may be Christian, or it may be more broadly humanist; it may be expounded at length or left simply as an inference; but whatever its form, it is present in the attitudes of all rhetoricians.[35] A brief sampling may again quickly confirm the extent to which sixteenth-century rhetoric stands on this assumption. In Wilson's *Arte*, for example, we find:

> Therefore even nowe when man was thus paste all hope of amendemente, God . . . stirred up his faythfull and elect, *to persuade with reason*, all men to societye . . . and also graunted them *the gift of utterance that they myghte wyth ease wynne folk at their will, and frame them by reason to all good order.*

Peacham:

> By the benefit of this excellent gift, (I meane of apt speech given by nature, and guided by Art) wisdome appeareth in her beautie, sheweth her maiestie, and exerciseth her power. . . both for the search of truth and for the direction of humane life.

Bacon, in a well-known passage:

> The duty and office of rhetoric is to apply reason to imagination for the better moving of the will. . . . [I]f the affections were . . . obedient to reason, . . . there should be no great use of persuasions . . . more than of naked proposition and proofs; but in regard of the continual mutinees . . . of the affections, . . . reason would become captive and servile, if eloquence of persuasions did not practice and win the imagination from the affections' part, and contract a confederacy between the reason and imagination against the affections.[36]

Like the emphasis on *elocutio* or style in Elizabethan rhetorical theory, an extrapolation from classical rhetorical principles that evokes an idealized image of Ciceronian/Caesarian Rome, the moral/rational bias seen in these examples conforms to the same idealized social vision. Both reflect the dream of a perfect society, and underlying both is the assumption that as power over language is the source of civilization, so will rhetorical power both preserve that civilization and lead it to ever greater heights of self-realization through self-expression. It is a wholly positive image, and while it recognizes the contribution of rhetoric to the birth of modern consciousness, the very zeal with which the *morality* of rhetoric is insisted on suggests another side to that vision—an unacknowledged fear of that same power in its unbridled or unscrupulous use. It is exactly this fear that I suggest is also betrayed by the total absence in the writings of sixteenth-century rhetoricians of any direct acknowledgment of the ambiguities inherent in the use of eloquence as an instrument. It is a paradoxical dilemma, and only a partially conscious one, in which the exponents and teachers of the art in the sixteenth century are caught. Political realities are such that the use of rhetorical skill to practice deception–to lead the mighty by flattering them–is mandatory, but at the same time the accomplishment of the rhetorician's end, *even when that end is altruistic*, is directly dependent on the deception's not being seen, or at least on its not being acknowledged as being seen.

There is nothing new or startling in this revelation, of course; indeed it requires no special perception to make. But what is of significance is the proposition that it represents not merely a subversive, but a potentially disastrous threat to the whole edifice of Elizabethan rhetoric, that edifice so painstakingly constructed by two generations of Tudor educators, and then reconstructed by their twentieth-century peers. I called it a "paradoxical dilemma" in which the exponents of rhetoric in the sixteenth century find themselves, and no expression more accurately reflects the spirit of the confrontation between the academy and the political arena in the Renaissance world than that. The art of rhetoric stands, in fact, exactly in the middle in this confrontation. For within the academic context, to which formal rhetoric is rigidly confined—to which it must be confined if it is to be developed without constraint—it is a highly structured, highly abstract, and intellectually challenging discipline. It is also, and this is of at least equal importance in the development and transmission of the art, touted as being politically as well as morally, not merely neutral, but impeccable. These are the qualities that render it both legitimate and safe, and allow it to perform its function in the educational field. It is a part of academic rhetoric too, however, to recognize that the value and in fact the point of rhetoric as a discipline is in its application in the world of affairs, and here once again is where we approach the rhetorician's dilemma. Indeed, as an axiom among all rhetoricians, this particular point is a classic illustration of just how rhetoric straddles that border between politics and art. Thus, the point that rhetoric has its application in the real world is a point that *must be made* by exponents of the art: truth demands it; but on the other hand it is not a point that can be emphasized in any way, for to do so would be to approach much too close to the dangerous shoals of politics, where rhetoric can become quite literally a question of life and death. The autonomy of the academy is thus protected by the avoidance of this question in all but the most cursory way, while the real work of manipulative politics carries on unimpeded, *ex obliquo*, in Bacon's phrase,[37] at the same time.

The kind of token acknowledgment of the practicality of rhetoric I am referring to would be the type of thing quoted earlier from Leonard Cox, and many similar examples could be cited from other works: Abraham Fleming's *A Panoplie of Epistles* (1576), for example, is described on its title page as "conteyning a perfecte plattforme of inditing letters of all sorts, to persons of al estates and degrees, as well our superiors, as to our equalls and inferiours"; while with a more subtle awareness of political reality it further notes its special value to "the unlearned," "that [their] wants and imperfections of Art and cunning may be supplied." A similar emphasis appears in another epistolary guide of the same period, William Fullwood's *The Enemy of Idlenesse*. When writing to "our superiors," says Fulwood, "we must warily take heed that we exalt them not too much and more than reason would permit, for so might we be noted of flatterie and adulation, and they themselves also might therewithall bee offended."[38] Or Anthony Munday, in the dedication to his *Defence of Contraries*,[39] "Paradoxes against Common opinions" of 1593, is even more coy, in proportion as his material is potentially more subversive, noting that he can draw no censure from the learned for his declamations, since they are only "exercise of wit."

The archetype of all such subtlety, and undoubtedly partly for this reason the universal Renaissance courtesy text, is Castiglione's *The Courtier*. With an unerring instinct for style and a delicacy of touch that approaches magic, Castiglione manages repeatedly throughout his text to achieve the seemingly impossible—to condemn flattery even as he flatters, insinuate unpalatable truth through the medium of attractive lies, and in general work a mystical transformation of sycophancy into statesmanship:

> In this wise maye [the Courtier] leade [the Prince] throughe the
> way of vertue (as it were) deckynge yt about with boowes to shad-
> owe yt and strawinge it over wyth sightlye floures, to ease the

greefe of the peinfull journey in hym that is but of a weake force.
And . . . continuallye keepe that mynde of his occupyed in honest
pleasure [,] . . . beeguilinge him with a holsome craft, as the warie
phisitiens do, who manye times whan they minister to yonge and
tender children in ther sickenesse, a medicine of a bitter taste,
annoint the cupp about the brimm with some sweete licour.[40]

It is in textbook examples like these of the use of the rhetorical figures *suavitas* and *charientismos*[41] that the claim made initially here that rhetoric "holds tenuously together a universe
threatening momentarily to lapse into incoherence and chaos"
begins to take on meaning. And it is in the same rhetorical context again in which Castiglione is admired that his opposite
number, Machiavelli, is hysterically condemned, as he was certainly in England. As Castiglione is admired for successfully
bridging the gap between political reality and the utopian political dream, Machiavelli is pilloried correspondingly for ripping
the mask from the utopian dream altogether. Thus, while it was
permissible, even obligatory, that a rhetorician condemn flattery,
it made both scholars and courtiers tremble to see it condemned
in Machiavelli's way:

> Courts are always full of flatterers; men take such pleasure in
> their own concerns, and are so easily deceived about them, that
> this plague of flattery is hard to escape. Besides, in defending
> against flattery, one runs the further risk of incurring contempt.
> For there is no way to protect yourself from flattery except by let-
> ting men know that you will not be offended at being told the
> truth. But when anyone can tell you the truth, you will not have
> much respect. Hence a prudent prince should adopt a third course,
> bringing wise men into his council and giving them alone free li-
> cense to speak the truth—and only on those points where the
> prince asks for it, not on others.[42]

In keeping with the extraordinary care with which the art of
rhetoric must therefore tread in the Renaissance, there develops
an unspoken duality from top to bottom of the structure of academic rhetoric. While in its formal aspects, based on the study
and imitation of the classics, it is irreproachable, the informal
result of that very discipline is, in the gifted student, exactly the
opposite of an academic exercise—to instill an instinct for
rhetoric that in the right hands becomes a political instrument
as powerful as that of Cicero himself. For the ear that is tuned to

nuances, the informal aspect of this duality is readily visible between the lines of much of the educational literature of the period. William Kempe's *The Education of Children* of 1588, for example, contains the following typical advice for the more advanced classes:

> And . . . he must observe in authors all the use of the Artes[—]
> the axiom, wherein every argument is disposed; the syllogisme,
> whereby it is concluded[.] . . . Agayne, he shall observe not only
> every trope, every figure, as well of words as of sentences; but also
> the Rhetoricall pronounciation and gesture fit for every word,
> sentence, and affection.[43]

The whole question of the relations of the arts of logic and rhetoric in the sixteenth century partakes of the same ambiguity. While the universal assumption, as Kempe implies, is that they are closely allied, the hidden fear, indeed the hidden truth, is that this alliance is by no means so innocuous (or logically sound) as the conventional statements of it suggest. Once again statements proclaiming both the uprightness and the legitimacy of this alliance abound: one of the most frequently cited is Zeno's famous analogy, as framed by Richard Rainolde in 1563:

> *Zeno* the Philosopher comparing *Rhetorike* and *Logike*, doeth as-
> similate and liken them to the hand of man. *Logike* is like saith he
> to the fiste, for euen as the fiste closeth and shutteth into one, the
> iointes and partes of the hande, . . . [s]o *Logike* for the deepe and
> profounde knowlege, that is reposed and buried in it[.] . . . *Rhe-*
> *torike* is like to the hand set at large, wherein euery part and ioint
> is manifeste[.] . . . So of like sorte, *Rhetorike* in moste ample . . .
> maner, dilateth and setteth out . . . woordes, . . . with soche abound-
> aunce and plentuousnes, . . . that the moste stonie and hard hartes,
> can not but bee incensed, inflamed, and moued thereto.[44]

What this analogy fails conspicuously to bring out, however, is that though rhetoric *can* be a support to logic—that it can, as Bacon says, draw the affections in to the support of the reason; yet things can also work the other way, and *logic* be used in the support of *rhetoric*—to make persuasion, that is, by a show of reason, that much more effective. Adding to the unspoken ambiguity of all such arguments, of course, is the fact that the logic of a conclusion has nothing to do with its truth in any case, logic being a matter purely of abstract method, and independent of the truth of the premises to which the method is applied.[45] Howell, in his account of Wilson's *Rule of Reason*, makes this point very explicit in discussing Wilson's treatment of the sensitive question of priestly celibacy in the sixteenth century. What Wilson sets out (and succeeds to his own satisfaction) to "prove," is that it is "logical" for priests to marry![46]

A question which must arise out of the considerations being discussed here, but which in the nature of things does not admit of being entirely satisfactorily answered, is naturally the question of *consciousness* on the part of those who deal with such slippery issues in such manifestly slippery ways. Perhaps the best illustration of both the question itself and of the difficulty of satisfactorily resolving it is found in the example of probably the most eminent Elizabethan writer on the subject of rhetoric, who is also recognized as the period's greatest philosopher, Francis Bacon. While there are no ambiguous inferences in Bacon that are not found in the other rhetoricians as well, or that are not found for that matter in all the Elizabethan writers who depended on patronage to survive and who dedicated their works to great men, there is at the same time no other writer whose insights and whose statements on the subject of rhetoric are more penetrating, or in whom the contradictions latent in such insights stand out more prominently. One may say that if Bacon was not fully aware of what he was actually saying at critical moments in his writing, then it is not only possible but probable that the others were equally so. His was the brilliant mind that, even as it worked out the tightly structured theory of rhetoric as an aid to reason that we have quoted from, could also write that

> the very styles and forms of utterance are so many characters of imposture, some choosing a style of pugnacity and contention, some of satire and reprehension, some of plausible and tempting similitudes and examples, some of great words and high discourse, some of short and dark sentences, some of exactness of method, all of positive affirmation, without disclosing the true motives and proofs of their opinions, or free confessing their ignorance and doubte, except it be now and then for a grace, and in cunning to win the more credit for the rest, and not in good faith.[47]

These are striking observations, to say the least, when contrasted with Bacon's assertions of the integrity of rhetoric cited earlier. And when further considered in the light of his own rhetorical practices, in certain notorious instances particularly, such as his whitewash of the Essex trial and his obsequious praise of the king in the dedication to *The Advancement of Learning*, their implications must indeed bring him close to an irredeemable intellectual damnation.[48]

There is a further argument for unconsciousness, on the part of its students, in the unique power that the art of rhetoric is perceived in the sixteenth century as possessing, tied as that perception is to the obscure inner workings of politics and power. The adulation of eloquence so characteristic of the writings of the century conveys unmistakably the sense of the period that the power of eloquence is in its effect virtually an earthly analogy of the creative power of God. This view is clearly an aspect of Renaissance Platonism, allied to, though presumably not derived from, the more familiar Platonic love idealism of Castiglione and Spenser. That the two forms of Platonism are not directly related is inferred from the fact that Plato occupies a somewhat paradoxical position in the Renaissance where the subject of rhetoric is concerned, because of his well known strictures against rhetoric as taught in Athenian schools in certain of the dialogues. The name of Plato is in fact rarely mentioned in a rhetorical connection in the Renaissance, even though his attitude to rhetoric must certainly have been well-known to scholars.[49] I suggest that it is another of the anomalies of the period that while Plato's theory of ideas is both adaptable and adapted to the Renaissance view of rhetoric, that Plato's own more negative view of rhetoric is in general passed over in silence by his Elizabethan admirers. It is an anomaly that bespeaks again not merely a conscious/unconscious insecurity concerning the real nature of that power so extravagantly lauded and so strenuously pursued, but the deeper, and correspondingly more threatening, hidden emotion of fear.

The necessity of such a fear may be inferred in several different ways from the surface attitudes displayed by Elizabethan commentators. We might, for example, using the familiar analogy of a coin, suggest that if eloquence is seen on one side as embodying the creative power of God, it may equally well be feared on the other as potentially embodying the destructive power of Satan. The operative word in this analogy, from the same standpoint, is no longer the word *creative* but the word *power*. If rhetoric is seen first as power, and only secondarily as truth, as this "underground" perspective would suggest, this perception alters radically the *real* meaning of those value-oriented apologies for the art that are so frequent in the literature of the period. For it has the effect of reversing the apparent meaning or apparent order of such apologies, of placing *fear* in the foreground, in the realm of the actual, while *hope*, on the other hand (morality, truth, historical integrity, classical discipline, and so on), recedes into the background, as a dream of what should be, in contrast to the nightmare of what is. And it is in direct ratio to the depth of this hidden fear, then, that the height of the virtues claimed for the discipline of rhetoric must therefore rise, in compensation, as it were, for the magnitude of a horror that only the most lofty of Platonic visions can override. One can take really any of these tributes to eloquence that dot the writings of Elizabeth's contemporaries and read through them to the hidden potential for devilish deception that they contain. Richard Sherry's prescription for what he calls "the great, the noble, the mighty, and the ful kind of endighting [i.e. writing]" is a clear instance, describing a style that "with an incredible, and a certain divine power of oratiõ is used in weighty causes, for it hath with an ample majesty, very garnished words: . . . And they that use this kind be vehement, various, . . . and thoroughly appointed to move and turne men to their purpose."[50]

The relevant phrase in this panegyric, from the underground standpoint, would be the words "to move and turn men to their purpose," words which, while they complement the "divine power" of oration, also clearly contain the unspoken implication that "purposes" may be other than divine. Indeed, the semi-divine powers ascribed to eloquence in the Renaissance cannot but contain the seeds of their own destruction, a proposition that can be confirmed in many ways. The famous image of Protean man, for example, first articulated by Pico della Mirandola and recognized universally as an archetype of their age by his contemporaries, has explicit associations with the diabolical potential of eloquence that go all the way back to Plato. In an excellent article on the Protean archetype in Renaissance literature, A. Bartlett Giamatti spells out this association in terms that focus both on the ambiguities inherent in language as a medium of communication and on the magical powers that are never far removed from discussions of rhetoric in the Renaissance period:

In the Renaissance, the power to manipulate words carried awesome responsibilities. As words could create, imitate, and ennoble, they could also falsify and deceive, projecting illusions which bore no necessary relation to actuality. . . .Words as a medium for illusion . . . found their proper counterpart in Proteus, who was archetypally both deceitful in his various disguises and the very quintessence of change.

. . . .

    The link between the darker elements in Proteus and in words is magic. As Proteus' role as *vates* had allied him with the beneficent figure of the poet, it also associated him with the often sinister *magus* or magician. In his *Oratio,* Pico had distinguished two kinds of magic. He referred to both kinds as "artes" but says one is the most deceitful of arts, the other the best; one makes man a slave of evil powers, the other makes him their lord and master.[51]

With the mention of "evil powers," the first Elizabethan exemplar that comes to mind is Christopher Marlowe (sometimes spelled *Merlin!*[52]) in his guise of Doctor Faustus, discussed in this connection in the Giamatti article. Christian zealots were quick to posit a diabolical connection between his bloody end and his blasphemous writings,[53] and could hardly fail to notice the special place the powers of language held in the whole notorious affair. As Faustus "forward and backward anagrammatiz'd" (1.3.10) the name of God to raise Mephistophilis, claiming "there's virtue in my heavenly words"; and "who would not be proficient in this art ?" (1.3.29–30),[54] so Marlowe himself reportedly had the dangerous ability to bend logic "to show more sound reasons for atheism than any divine in England is able to give to prove divinity."[55]. And while magic is one of the dangers in a rhetoric uncontrolled, clearly a more immediate one is in the realm of political diabolism, the sin of Tamburlaine, who began a "paltry Scythian" (1.1.53), but for whom "words are swords" (1.1.74), that ultimately carried him to "the ripest fruit of all," "the sweet fruition of an earthly crown" (2.5.67, 69). The political charge most often leveled against Marlowe was the crime of Machiavellianism, synonymous in England for the open espousal of what amounts to a sixteenth-century version of *real politik*. And among Machiavellianism's most notorious techniques was the cynical use of rhetoric to gild whatever horrors a regime might find necessary to maintain itself, or conversely, to manipulate both the public and the regime's own servants to the

actual commission of those horrors. As Machiavelli put it baldly
in *The Art of War*:

> Countless times situations arise in which an army will come to
> grief if the captain does not know how or does not speak to it. For
> such speech takes away fear, fires souls, increases determination,
> uncovers snares, promises rewards, . . . reproves, entreats, threat-
> ens, fills again with hope, praises, condemns, and does all those
> things by which human passions are allayed or incited.[56]

The threat of Machiavellianism was thus not so much that its
methods differed significantly from those actually followed by
Renaissance princes, including England's Elizabeth, but that in
laying out those methods stripped of their usual cloak of oratory,
it revealed (among other things) "the divinity doth hedge a king"
as the creation not of God at all really, but simply of policy, the
same "policy" in fact that Christopher Marlowe rashly attributed
to the ministers of religion, "affirming our Saviour to be but a deceiver, and Moses to be but a conjuror and seducer of the people,
and the holy Bible to be but vain and idle stories, and all religion
but a device of pollicie."[57]

It is not difficult to understand the threat to the status quo
latent in such ideas, nor the extraordinary rhetorical stratagems
that must be called upon in the sixteenth century to combat that
threat. Nor indeed is it a wonder, in this context, that rhetorical
power is so often cloaked with the trappings of divinity, for to
rhetoric almost exclusively is owed, in a period perhaps uniquely
disturbed and tumultuous in postclassical human history, not
only the sustaining of the fabric of the state, but very probably
the preserving of its collective sanity as well. Fraught with paradox and tension, beset with intellectual, moral, religious, and political challenges without parallel in history, it is to rhetoric the
age looks to lead it through modernity's maze, without losing
either its sense of continuity with the past or its belief in the legitimacy of both its actions and its institutions. And the indispensable function of academic rhetoric in particular in this
salvationist mission cannot be overemphasized. It is society's
matrix, "teaching," as Ralph Lever says, "a perfect way to argue
and dispute"[58]—"perfect," because in holding together the disciplines of logic and grammar inherited from the ancients, it
builds a structure of so-called truth that can sincerely claim to
be infallible and therefore proof against all assaults.

What matter that the foundation of this structure is rotten, that rhetoric in its underground hides diabolical manipulative skills and other potential evils too horrible to contemplate? In its attachment to the wellsprings of humanity rhetoric remains resourceful enough to stand proof against challenges as profound even as these. Through a never-relaxing vigilance, backed by a rigid classical structure providing constant discipline and control, and with its final polish imparted by an infinitely subtle awareness of the niceties of style, academic rhetoric holds its place in the center of Elizabethan culture; and the doubts of a Plato, like the machinations of a Marlowe or a Machiavelli, are as if they were not. It is in this dynamic duality of power and persuasion, of ancient languages and modern men, that our true "objective correlative" of the the Renaissance linguistic dilemma, the question with which this excursus began, finally consists. By an infinitely subtle application of what in bluntly Orwellian terms we may call "doublethink," and that Lever with delicate irony in the 1570s called "Witcraft"—a process combining essentially unconscious self-censorship and selective stupidity—the age defends its rhetorical integrity, justifies and stabilizes the status quo in all fields, while at the same time allowing itself the flexibility necessary to effect these complex maneuvers successfully. So subtle is this process, and so essential secrecy to its success, that though its operations are universal in the sixteenth century, so also is the silence that surrounds them. It is a silence never breached; and only adepts, and they only rarely, reach out to exchange signals of their craft before the very eyes of an uncomprehending world. The Masonic overtones here are deliberate, for they suggest just that combination of secrecy and illumination that these mysterious "signals," as I call them, contain—thinking of things like Bacon's "*ex obliquo*" term, or Lever's "witcraft" (a term that Thomas Wilson also uses)—expressions that say far more *ex obliquo* about the real inner workings of the arts of language in the sixteenth century than any but initiates into their mysteries could possibly be aware of.[59]

There is, of course, no area of sixteenth-century intellectual life more filled with thorns and thickets than the field of religion, and for this very reason no area in which the discrepancy between the overt and the hidden sides of the technique of rhetoric stands out more boldly. Religious polemics are characterized throughout the century by the same one-sided claims to

moral virtue, adherence to the laws of nature and reason, even
the same divine power and integrity that rhetorical apologists
claim for their discipline. But whereas rhetorical apologetics
tend to elevate either Cicero specifically or the Latin language
in general as their sacred *logos,* such uniformity is not for the
religionists, whose sectarian partisanship invariably narrows
"truth" down to whatever institutional dogmas a particular
writer supports, a process which accentuates the contradictions
in such rhetoric—its paranoid fear of devilish subversions, its selective forgetfulness, sophistry, and careful self-censorship. The
blatancy of these contradictions in religious rhetoric is in nothing more easily demonstrated than in the simple observation,
requiring neither dialectical nor theological sophistication to
make, that the arguments used against both Puritans and Cath-
olics by Elizabethan polemicists are virtually the identical arguments turned around as were used by Catholic apologists
against the Protestants forty years earlier during the reigns of
Henry VIII and Mary Tudor. And invariably the critical issue in
all such arguments is the egregiously self-contradictory one of
the sophistries and equivocations employed by the other side
in attempting to prove its case! Thus Stephen Gardiner, Mary
Tudor's chancellor, attacked the Protestants on these grounds in
his *A Detection of the Devil's Sophistrie* in 1546:

> But againste this truth, the devyll striveth, and fyghteth by his
> ministers, & lewde apostels, with sophistical devyses, wherewith
> he troubleth the grosse imaginacitiō of the symple people. . . .
> such as be thus overthrowen in their iudgement, and so blynded
> in themselfe, the devyll easely entangleth and byndeth fast to
> him, with carnal reasons, deceitfull expositiō, crooked argumentes,
> and counterfet cotradictiō, and therby leadeth them away, captive
> and thralde, from the true catholique byleefe.[60]

While in the anti-Catholic hysteria of Elizabeth's last years such
false persuasions are no longer the simple sophistries that Gardiner saw, but the calculated treasonable policies pursued by the
highly sophisticated Jesuits—"[the devil's] new Secte[,] hypo-
critically adorned with the name of Jesus, & furnished with
more shew of learning, holiness, & godliness, then . . . other
popish fraternities"—the hallmark of whose evangelism is "to
fayne and profess, as occasion serveth, any religion," and whose
chief means of persuasion is "their honied enticing and sugred

speach."[61] The cumulative effect of all such polemics, of course, is to render the sacred word of God ultimately as illusory as the phantom of academic rhetoric, a phantom of classical form, of truth, of tradition, of legitimacy, and of control, serving admirably as a blind behind which the machinations of power can operate in perfect freedom.

This is an appropriate point at which to shift the discussion to the second of the two basic premises concerning rhetoric that support this study, the premise that the essential concern of rhetoric is *persuasion,* a premise which the previous discussion should already have gone a long way towards establishing, but which draws additional support both from logic and from a rather rich historical tradition of its own. The essential concern of rhetoric being persuasion, a corollary is that in logical terms it is impossible for a rhetorician to be other than insincere when he claims that either logic or truth have any direct bearing on the aims of his art. That is to say, it is self-evidently impossible to speak without at the same time attempting to persuade, and this independently of whether the content of one's speech is truth or lies, fact or fiction. Here again we enter that strange realm of what might be called "categorical ambiguity," the intrinsic ambiguity that haunts all discussion on *the subject of rhetoric,* turning it into a kind of metalinguistic hall of mirrors: for to discuss rhetoric requires the use of rhetoric, and the use of rhetoric, whose sole aim is persuasion, automatically casts doubt on the validity of any claims the rhetorician makes or conclusions he seeks to establish. Thus the claim made by a rhetorician that his discipline is somehow allied to truth is in these terms by definition a rhetorical claim, introduced solely to give a color of legitimacy to his pleadings, and thereby make them more convincing not only to the hearer but perhaps even to the speaker himself.[62]

Two contradictory traditions of rhetoric in fact distinguish its development from the time of the Greeks, both of which traditions and their classical origins were known in Tudor England. Nancy S. Streuver, in a study of the historiographic heritage of the Renaissance, gives a concise account of what she calls "the strange double heritage of promise and decadence [in] the rhetorical tradition"[63] that comes down to the Renaissance from the Greeks. Citing numerous classical sources, including Plato extensively, as well as a couple of his rhetorical nemeses, the sophist Gorgias and Isocrates, Streuver shows clearly that the attempts which all the Greek rhetoricians made to redeem their discipline from charges of amorality and opportunism were doomed to failure by reason of the inner contradictions within the discipline itself. These contradictions, she says, have their roots in the rival ontologies of the Heraclitean and Socratic schools of philosophy, the Heraclitean viewing "the cosmos as flux," hence "relative, rather than final and absolute," the Socratic seeking through what it calls reason to transcend flux and enter "the sphere of the Eternally true" (6). Socrates saw the Sophistic rhetoric of Gorgias as based on Heraclitean relativity, and therefore in its nature both partial and partisan; while his own "philosophy," he claimed, was rather dialectical, examining its subject from all sides, and thus overcoming all errors of partiality or bias. As Streuver points out, however, this view is logically untenable, for while sophistic rhetoric is indeed "relativistic," its dialectical range is not axiomatically thereby limited (17, 18); and while Socrates (or Plato) *claims* that his dialogues are "philosophical," there is nothing in the final analysis to back that claim except Plato's word.[64]

The fact of an unavoidable inner contradiction within the art of rhetoric is demonstrable, again, in the development and continued great importance of the branch of rhetorical training known as *declamatio*, or the art of making speeches on hypothetical cases.[65] Aristotle himself tacitly acknowledged this tradition and the contradiction it implies in the opening pages of his *Rhetoric* when he noted that (in spite of "truth," apparently), an orator "ought to be able to persuade on opposite sides of a question."[66] The declamatory tradition, baldly contradicting rhetoric's simultaneous insistence that "truth" is its real aim, shows that claim up for the rhetorical ruse that it actually is, and while this fact does not in any way inhibit the practice of both branches of the art in the sixteenth century, it does effectively stifle all public comment on their incompatibility. It is not merely that there is nothing to say on the subject, for when indeed in human history was that ever a barrier to comment on any subject under the sun? Rather it is that any comment whatsoever can have only negative effects, further disturbing an already perilously fragile status quo. The political overtones in this remark are calculated, for silence on such a subject is as much political as it is intellectual, and shares a good deal with famous historical cases like that of Thomas More in his long struggle with absolute power, when he realized too late that total silence was his only hope. The rhetoricians' uncanny self-protective instincts fortunately curb their curiosity well before this point.

Two lines of argument in defense of *declamatio* are sanctioned by the unwritten code governing rhetorical discourse in the sixteenth century. One is essentially the same argument that is used to justify the study of sophistry; namely, that such studies teach one, in Wilson's words "to try the corn from the chaff," "by knitting together true Argumentes and untwining all knotty subtilties that are both false, and wrongly framed together."[67] The other, psychologically suggestive justification for *declamatio* is that it is not a serious matter anyway, but simply a *jeu d'esprit,* or a joke. This argument is actually the perfect defense of *declamatio,* for it neatly undercuts any criticism that "serious" rhetoric might be moved to bring against it, without at the same time in any way weakening the logical or satirical thrust or downgrading the inventive skill of the declamation itself. The most famous of all sixteenth-century declamations, Erasmus's *The Praise of Folly,* uses this defense, and there is evidence that among his contemporaries his disclaimers of seriousness were accepted at face value, in another amazing apparent triumph of the instinct of political survival over self-awareness and even common sense.[68]

In accordance with the convention of nonseriousness, by which a certain legitimacy is conceded, or at least an opening allowed, to *declamatio* in the sixteenth century, any declamation that acknowledges the convention may be published; but any which fails to make explicit acknowledgment will sink like a stone into the abyss of lost literatures, if indeed its perpetrator escapes with name and property intact at all. Such was the fate of the audacious *Oratio Contra Rhetoricam* of Bishop John Jewel, about which silence among contemporary intellectuals is so total as to lead Jewel's modern translator, Hoyt H. Hudson, to wonder whether the oration was ever actually given, in spite of the fact that its title reads "Delivered in the Hall of [Corpus Christi] College before All Members of the College."[69]

As has previously been noted, Anthony Munday as an exponent of declamation does acknowledge the convention of nonseriousness, and thereby escapes the censure of orthodoxy. So fulsome an acknowledgment does he give us, indeed, a point which makes it of some interest here, that it verges almost on parody—as witness, for example, the following from the title page of *The Defence of Contraries*:

THE DEFENCE OF CONTRARIES

> Paradoxes against common opinion, debated in form of declamations in place of public censure: *onlie to exercise yong wittes in difficulte matters.*
> Wherein is *no offense to God's honor,*
> *the estate of Princes, or private mens honest actions*
> *but pleasant recreation to beguile the iniquity of time.*
> (italics mine)

It is difficult to interpret such an effusion from a writer of some ability except as a calculated attempt to disarm in his reader a criticism of which he would appear to be fully (albeit perhaps unconsciously), cognizant in himself, the awareness, namely, of the extent of the challenge to orthodoxy in all fields that his declamations actually represent. For, like all declamations, indeed like the concept of *declamatio* per se, they are, if taken seriously, highly subversive. And they are subversive not only in the obvious political and even religious senses, but in philosophical senses profound enough to challenge meaning in life altogether. While by no means of the standard of the elder Seneca, Munday's declamations do, of course, use the tricks of rhetoric as they can to make their case; but it is not so much their rhetorical gilding that makes these arguments dangerous, rather it is the perverse strength of the arguments themselves, remote from reality and even absurd as some of them seem to be at first glance. They defend such propositions as "that it is better to be fowle than faire," "that ignorance is better than knowledge," and "that it is better to be a fool, than wise"; but the apparent silliness of such topics is not borne out by examination, for the plain if startling truth is that the conclusions of many are every bit as sound as their conventional antitheses.

In the oration on ugliness, for example, the argument is proposed that if chastity is a virtue, then to be ugly or "fowle" may well confer an advantage in living a virtuous life, as Touchstone's Audrey ingenuously also suggests.[70] In the oration on folly, reminiscent of Erasmus again, the thoughtful reader may find, if he will, enigmas to challenge an Oedipus: if, for example, a "meane and base" person in his folly imagines himself Pope or Emperor, is not this commendable? Is not such "folly" better than wisdom? And is it not also true that the reputed wise are very often the most foolish, as in the case of Solomon, with his worship of idols and his hordes of concubines—by what stretch of the imagination or judgment, Munday asks, is such behavior to be considered wise? The rhetorical figures—*interrogatio, exemplum*, and the like—are there in such speeches for all to see, problematic usage itself in a century in which academic rhetoric is one of convention's most substantial props; but the real force of *declamatio* and its threat far transends what would probably be rationalized in such cases as a mere warping of rhetoric's true purpose. For if such arguments can be made to seem true, a truly horrible specter is thereby raised over a society whose principal tenet is the sacredness of truth. It is the specter of intellectual anarchy, launching society first helplessly into a realm where one man's truth is as good as any other's, and shortly thereafter into a moral and political abyss in which the sole function of language is persuasion and its sole end power.

Munday, as stated previously, is emphatically not an Elder Seneca, nor is Elizabethan England imperial Rome, but the coupling of the names of these two practitioners of *declamatio* and the periods they represent is not without philosophical significance. For what the Elizabethan expresses indirectly and tentatively in the culture of his age, the Roman expresses starkly and in fact in the culture of his. Seneca Rhetor, as he was known, father of Roman declamation, lived in a period in Roman history recognized by both its own people and their Renaissance expositors as decadent, extending from the beginnings of the empire through to the increasingly flagrant degeneracies of the reigns of the later Tiberius and Caligula. Seneca himself said, ominously, that Roman rhetoric had reached its peak with Cicero, and had been in steady decline since,[71] and it requires little historical knowledge to observe the symptoms of that decline reflected in his declamations. Collected into ten books called *Controversiae*, in their combination of subject matter and treatment they form a case study for the possibilities of intellect and inhumanity that is probably unique in literature. Quintilian and other later Latin writers decried Seneca's sensational subject matter—preoccupied with "tyrannicides, . . . ravished maidens, or incests" in the words of Tacitus[72]—but the gratuitously decadent subject matter is less significant as an index of inhumanity in these controversies than is the detached and casual manner of treatment. For the humanities of the issues simply do not engage the author's mind; the arguments on one side of the question of, say, whether a rapist should be forced to marry his victim without a dowry or be put to death[73] are as skillful as those on the other; the victims and their sufferings are mere abstractions, their emotions nothing but rhetorical colors. As the revelation of both a mind and a culture these textbooks are the intellectual analogue of the Roman arena, contests of verbal gladiatorial skill in which the humanity, indeed the life and death of the participants are utterly inconsequential.

While declamation as a branch of rhetoric never reached the level of development or of detachment in Elizabethan England that it reached in imperial Rome, there are nonetheless a number of ways in which an awareness on the part of Elizabethan rhetoricians of the intrinsic relation between rhetorical skill and pure power (that is, power stripped of all moral encumbrances or constraints) may be inferred from this comparison of the two epochs. For what Seneca the Elder leaves to be inferred in his *Controversiae*, the younger Seneca his son it may be said exemplified in his life; and it is in no sense historical accident that this greatest Roman philosopher, rhetorician, and literary artist (as the Elizabethans considered him) of his generation was the most popular classical dramatist and probably the single most important influence in the development of the art of drama in the age of Elizabeth. It is one of the enigmas of that period for many modern scholars that of all the writers of the Silver Age it should have been Seneca who was upheld as its noblest representative—"a sage admired and venerated as an oracle of moral, even of Christian edification, a master of literary style and a model of the purest principles of dramatic art," in the words of E. F. Watling.[74] And while as a philosopher Seneca retains even for our age something of the nobility with which the Elizabethans so generously endowed him, on the question of his virtues as a dramatist, the achievement for which he was probably held in highest esteem by the Elizabethans, we are totally unable to see into our ancestors' hearts. For us his plays remain as Schlegel described them in 1815, as, "beyond all description bombastic and frigid, utterly devoid of nature in character and action, full of the most revolting violations of propriety, and . . . barren of all theatrical effect."[75] For the Elizabethans to have idolized such works, clearly deeper spiritual affinities must have existed between the two cultures than our modern interpretations have as yet given satisfactory account of. I submit that these affinities lie in a complex combination of rhetorical, political, moral, and literary factors in the life and work of Seneca that spoke profoundly, if only partially consciously, to the Elizabethan mind.

T. S. Eliot, in another of his very astute observations on the later English Renaissance, noted that it was characteristic of the mind of that period to tend to see things not in pieces but as wholes, and I believe the mystery of the Elizabethans' fascination with Seneca is solved by a return to that conception. On the one hand, the modern problem with understanding Seneca is precisely our inability to integrate the fragmented elements of character he presents; Professor Watling, for example, speaks of the "sense which all readers feel of an astonishing incongruity between the humanity and dignity of the prose works and the bombastic extravagance, the passionate yet artificial rhetoric, of the tragedies. And not less has been noticed, and frequently commented on, the discordance between the high moral principles professed by the philosopher and the cynical time-serving behavior of the emperor's adviser" (7). For our Elizabethan ancestors, on the other hand, not only were these incongruities not a problem, they were, on the contrary, just the feature of Seneca's life and work that spoke most profoundly to them. I suggested earlier that Seneca the younger exemplified in his life the moral lessons and attitudes that his father's *Controversiae* present as purely rhetorical problems. In the simplest sense this transition from the academic to the practical realm is shown in the younger Seneca's very prominent political role, first as tutor, then adviser, and then subsequently hatchet man for the emperor Nero, a role which required that he put into daily practice all the declamatory skills, with their accompanying inhumanities, that his father's preaching advocated. Certainly the epitome of all these double-dealing practices is the episode which ultimately cost Seneca his political reputation, and which stands as one of the most repellent chapters in the whole history of imperial politics, Seneca's drafting and presentation to the Senate of the letter which excused Nero for the murder of his equally ruthless

and psychotic mother.[76] But if politics is the simplest way in
which the amorality of the rhetorical tradition of the Silver Age
finds expression, the subtlest form of the same phenomenon in
the life of Seneca is found in the fact that he reserved his greatest declamatory efforts not for the academy like his father, not
for the forum like Cicero, but for the stage. I suggest that
Seneca's popularity as a dramatist in Elizabethan England
stems directly from the fact that the Elizabethans instinctively
recognized in his dramas the key not only to the unity of
Seneca's life, but, much more importantly, the key to the unity of
their own.

   This is a complex question, and obviously not one that can be
adequately addressed as just a final item of discussion in an introduction to a work on Shakespeare, but the paradox of Seneca
as a dramatist is also the paradox of drama as an artistic analogue and authentic revelation of Elizabethan culture. The
meaning of Seneca's life, first (as it is also of Cicero's and Castiglione's), is style. As a master rhetorician, he can don whatever
style or form of persuasion is required by the task in hand. It is
by virtue of style, thus, as the Elizabethans clearly sensed, that
Seneca can be at once the sublime moralist and stoic saint of the
philosophical writings, the thundering avenger of the tragedies,
and the venal and opportunistic politician of his public career,
with apparently no sense of impropriety or discontinuity among
the three. There is a reason also why I set the thundering
avenger of the tragedies between the other extremes in this description, because not only does Seneca's dramatic world medi-
ate between the seemingly impossibly contradictory "realities" of
his philosophic and his public careers, but only in the fictional
world of drama is it possible for Seneca to express freely the
hidden truths that are his source of life. It is for this reason that
the word *paradox,* used above in connection with both Senecan
and Elizabethan drama, is an appropriate word. The paradox
lies in the fact that *outside* the theater the true meaning of "life
as style," or "rhetoric as persuasion," can never be acknowledged
by Seneca or any other rhetorician. To do so, of course, is to destroy the illusion on which one's power over others directly depends. It would be to acknowledge, for example, exactly what
Cicero's well-known statement on the "noble ambition" of eloquence actually means: "nothing," he says, "seems to me a nobler
ambition than to be able to hold by your eloquence the minds of

men, to captivate their wills, to move them to and fro in whatever direction you please."[77] In the theater, however, which differs from the real world only by its renunciation of any claims to truth or even necessarily reason in its rhetoric, the dramatist is liberated from the necessity of maintaining his mask, and can express the underlying motives of both his own and his culture's life exactly as he sees them. And as Seneca reveals them in his dramas, they are, as might be expected, far from pleasant:

> Let loose the Furies on your impious house.
> Let evil vie with evil, sword with sword;
> Let anger be unchecked, repentance dumb.
> Spurred by insensate rage, let fathers' hate
> Live on, and the long heritage of sin
> Descend to their posterity. Leave none
> The respite for remorse; let crimes be born
> Ever anew and, in their punishment,
> Each single sin give birth to more than one.
> . . . .
> The high shall be brought low, the weak made strong,
> The kingdom tossed by ceaseless waves of chance.
> Let there be culprits banished for their crimes,
> And when restored, by mercy of the gods,
> Returning to their crimes, to make their names
> Hateful to all mankind and to themselves.
> Vengeance shall think no way forbidden her;
> Brother shall flee from brother, sire from son,
> And son from sire; children shall die in shames
> More shameful than their birth; revengeful wives
> Shall menace husbands, armies sail to war
> In lands across the sea, and every soil
> Be soaked with blood; the might of men of battle
> In all the mortal world shall be brought down
> By Lust triumphant.
>   (*Thyestes* [tr. Watling] ll. 23–33, 38–52)

While the Elizabethans quickly learned, in keeping with the somewhat softer truths of their own world as compared with that of Seneca, to mitigate the harshest images of power in their depictions of the world they lived in, inspired by Seneca nevertheless, their dramatists, and preeminently William Shakespeare, saw that world, for better or for worse, as one in which persuasive rhetoric is the key to power.

2
Rhetoric, Theater, Poetry, and Shakespeare

Not, as noted previously, a history of sixteenth-century rhetoric, neither is the present study a history of sixteenth-century drama, albeit one of its principal tenets is the existence of a direct developmental link between the two. In postulating such a connection we are on familiar ground; certainly no commentator on or student of sixteenth-century rhetoric, Shakespeare's contemporary or our own, can fail to note the many associations with drama and the manifest "theatricality" that rhetoric as a discipline has. Noting this association, most histories of Elizabethan drama do not, however, give it the emphasis in their discussions that I would suggest is legitimately its due. Where mentioned at all in historical discussions it is typically in passing, with the primary focus either on the continuity that Tudor drama has with the medieval folk drama, or simply on that drama itself, as virtually a Palladian birth in the reign of Elizabeth, fathered indeed by the great Zeus of the Renaissance, as most commentators recognize, but in whose original inspiration the contribution of the discipline of rhetoric specifically is not apparently of special moment.[1]

Given the long-established critical tradition of emphasizing the historical continuity of the Elizabethan drama with its predecessor English dramas, hints of a contribution from rhetoric and of a new rhetorical quality in the drama of that period are the best we can realistically hope for in commentaries on the subject. Scholars do, of course, note many new features of the drama of both earlier Tudor and particularly the Elizabethan epochs, though again not as a rule with the degree of awareness

of the real revolutionary *political* character of these developments that one might have expected. The shift of focus of Tudor
drama from the religious to the purely secular, for example, a
trend initiated in the reign of Henry VII and completed under
his son, along with the system of aristocratic patronage of the
drama that was firmly established by the time of Elizabeth's accession, gives a "politic" twist to everything that happens in the
field of drama in that epoch that has not been perhaps sufficiently remarked.[2] And if the realities of power in the Tudor era
express themselves indirectly but unmistakably through such
subtle changes as this alliance, other concurrent developments
are even more revealing of the way in which rhetorico/political
considerations decisively influenced drama in the sixteenth century. An example of such would be the significant fact that of the
new generation of artists who lit the spark, so to speak, of drama
in the 1540s and 1550s, all had either one or both of two critical
qualifications for their vocation: they were either courtiers or
schoolmasters.[3] The two plays in particular that literary historians consider largely to have ushered in the new era, the first
popular English imitations of, respectively, classical comedy and
classical tragedy, Udall's *Ralph Roister Doister* (1553) and Sackville and Norton's *Gorboduc* (1561), are both directly the product
of an academic environment, the one by a once and future headmaster of two eminent public schools, the other by two aspiring
courtiers, students, at the time of the play's composition, of the
Inner Temple.

The academic and particularly the rhetorical background of
not only these two plays but many other works of roughly the
same era is a profoundly significant indication of the extent to
which rhetorical considerations actually inspired the theatrical
revolution of the Elizabethan period. Typical of both plays is a
new fascination with "language for its own sake," as Parrott and
Ball appropriately express it,[4] in commenting on the appeal of
Seneca as a dramatist in the sixteenth century, an appeal which
is generally recognized as first and foremost rhetorical.[5] *Gorboduc* as an adaptation of a Senecan theme to an English historico/
mythological context is a unique revelation of Elizabethan sensibility in a number of ways. Commentators have noted first that
in tone it is political far beyond its original—that "the Senecan
interest in passion and suffering," as Palmer puts it, "is subordi-
nated to the oratory of debate and the rhetoric of the council

chamber."[6] This statement reinforces the point that, as a practical art, rhetoric is always political, that its position in society is therefore necessarily transitional between the academy and the seats of power, and that the sixteenth-century stage is uniquely the medium in which these hidden authentic features of the art can emerge. Udall's *Roister Doister* too is linguistically a significant expression in ways that take it far beyond mere entertainment. As a "word-farce," in Wilson Knight's term, whose "surges of doggerel absurdity ris[e] at high moments to nonsensical word-makings of rough syllabic music,"[7] it is less an acknowledgment of classical supremacy than another statement of English freedom, and represents a major victory in the vernacular wars that were to vanquish the Aschams and the Harveys and make both the *Gorboducs*, and, ultimately, the Shakespeares possible. It seems indeed in retrospect almost inevitable that the man who produced this innovative work should have been one of England's most prominent schoolmasters, author of a language text that was standard in its day, and a man with whom Shakespeare himself may even have had a significant if indirect educational connection.[8]

The extent to which the schools were the prime instigators of the rise of Elizabethan drama is shown again in the fact that the first established acting companies in the sixteenth century were composed of children from several famous schools, among them Udall's Eton and Westminster and Mulcaster's Merchant Taylors'.[9] Not only was playacting thus manifestly a product of the educational system, but an examination of both the educational prescriptions of the day and the classical texts from which they are derived reveals that fundamentally the very concept of acting, of rhetoric, and indeed of education itself, are synonomous in that age, and represent, in fact, in a revelation of the Renaissance of great profundity, variations on a single universal theme—the theme again of Protean Renaissance man. While to the sixteenth-century educator himself his theories are wholly classical, and indeed there is virtually nothing in the educational prescriptions of Erasmus or Vives that does not have its source in Cicero or another Latin author, yet it is another example of that same unconscious process discussed in the last chapter, the way in which these classical precedents mysteriously adapt themselves to reflect far less the character of either republican or imperial Rome, the milieu from which they came, than the quite different and unique character of Renaissance Europe. The primary influences in the rise of Elizabethan drama are thus simultaneously ancient, in the classical conceptions of the orator from Cicero and Quintilian, in which theatrical metaphors are encountered literally at every turn, and modern—in the political requirements of the Renaissance itself—in the burgeoning theatrical cult which these requirements fostered, and ultimately in that striking stage/reality identification that became the hallmark of the age. While the contribution of the Morality and the folk drama to the explosion of theater in Elizabethan England is not small, in comparison to this influence from the larger politico/linguistic sphere it is scarcely necessary; lacking it, England would simply have had to invent its theater, as for all practical purposes after 1553 it did.

It is not to be expected, of course, that any of these things can be presented exactly overtly in the literature of the period, educational or *belles lettres*. Once again for political reasons circumspection, caution, and delicacy are as essential in the development of these cultural features as they are second nature to the practitioners of all these rhetorically connected arts. While never acknowledged as such, the principles underlying education, politics, and theater in sixteenth-century England are all the same ones, with the linking motive in all three areas being rhetoric, and rhetoric in one specific aspect—the aspect of persuasion. The first English treatise on the education of a gentleman for public affairs, Sir Thomas Elyot's *The Booke Named the Governour*, for example, makes short but very pointed acknowledgment ("In good faythe to speake boldly that I think") of the fact that the aim of oratorical training is political power and persuasion its principal means: he distinguishes two approaches to the art; one, as he notes, for the amateur (the second sons, perhaps,) "that nedeth nat, or doth nat desire to be an exquisite oratour," for whose training in rhetoric, therefore, "the litle boke made by the famous Erasmus, . . . *Copiam Verborum et Rerum* . . . shall be sufficient[;]" and the other, his real target, the student destined for the greater role of counsellor to kings, to whom, "after that xiv. yeres be passed of [his] age, . . . the arte of Rhetorike wolde be semblably taught, either in greke, out of Hermogines, or of Quintilian in latine, begynnyng at the thirde boke, and instructing diligently the childe in *that parte of rhethorike, principally, which concerneth persuation: for as moche as it is most apte for consultations.*"[10]

An even more striking, though admittedly selective, illustration of the absolute dominance of the principle of persuasion in the educational thought of the sixteenth century may be found in Mulcaster's *Elementarie* of 1582 (a book that T. W. Baldwin allows "may . . . speak for [all] the schoolmasters"[11] of Shakespeare's day), in which the word *persuade*, or its cognates, is used as many as fifteen times in the first eight pages! Such striking usage, I would suggest, precisely exemplifies the hidden force of the concept in the author's (and his age's) mind: he says over and over that his book is written not only to prescribe a method and curriculum of elementary education, but to persuade of the utility of such an education as well, using the word *persuade* as virtually a touchstone, or piece of magic, an abstract principle of power whose relevance is universal—no more the province specifically of the discipline of education than of any other of society's functions:

> In persuading and admitting even the very best things, there be two other points, besides the pretended goodness in the thing, which they have still in eie, that ar to be persuaded. Whereof the one is, what coūtenaūce he carieth, which is the persuader, and what mean he useth to work his persuasion.[12]

Considering the more narrowly *dramatic* applications of the study of rhetoric as it relates to sixteenth-century education again, any number of forceful illustrations of my thesis may be found in both the classical rhetoricians themselves and in the special emphases that their Renaissance exponents gave to the study of the masters. Thus Juan Luis Vives, the great Spanish humanist and contemporary of Elyot's, who like Elyot enjoyed the patronage of the Tudor monarchs, was renowned for the stress that he gave to dramatic-style recitation in his educational theory. The bulk of books 3 and 4 of his five-book educational masterwork *De Tradendis Disciplina* (also 1531) is given over to the discussion of language teaching, in which the memorizing and practicing of declamations from Seneca Rhetor and Quintilian, and the imitation in both speech and writing of other classical authors, receives heavy emphasis.[13]

The classical rhetoricians themselves, and none more so than Cicero and Quintilian, Renaissance rhetorical superstars for just this reason, perhaps, assumed the virtual identity of rhetoric with theater in almost everything they say about oratorical technique. Vives does not distort Quintilian by making practice in declamation and imitation the core of his educational discipline, but rather follows the prescription of the master to the letter in fashioning that discipline on a foundation of performance. While Quintilian did object to the more sensational themes of some of Seneca's *Controversiae* as proper fare for young minds, he nevertheless accepted declamation as, in the words of M. L. Clarke, "by far the most valuable method of education, if properly used, and he certainly employed it himself in his teaching."[14]

B. L. Joseph, in his treatise on Elizabethan acting, attributes to Quintilian in fact probably the major role in forming an awareness of theatrical values among the educated elite of Tudor England. For Joseph, Quintilian's directions laid out in book 6, relating to the arousing of emotion in one's hearers, stand out as principles that his Elizabethan students would have applied directly to the art of acting:

> It is not generally realized that Quintilian actually advises his readers to evoke emotion truthfully within themselves by one of the methods taught by Stanislavski: that is by means of what are called 'private images' by some modern actors and teachers of acting:
>
> > But how are we to generate these emotions in ourselves, since emotion is not in our power? I will try to explain as best I may. There are certain experiences which the Greeks call $\phi\alpha\nu\tau\alpha\sigma\iota\alpha\iota$, and the Roman *visiones*, whereby things absent are presented to our imagination with such extreme vividness that they seem actually to be before our very eyes. It is the man who is really sensitive to such impressions who will have the greatest power over the emotions.
>
> Quintilian agrees with modern theorists . . . of acting that this "is a power which all may readily acquire if they will." He continues: "We must identify ourselves with the persons of whom we complain that they have suffered grievous, unmerited and bitter misfortune."[15]

As for Cicero's role in sharpening English sensibility in the sixteenth century toward the relationship of rhetoric and theater, this is if anything even more vital than Quintilian's. References to acting can be culled from almost anywhere in Cicero's theoretical writings, and always with the emphasis on how the

arts of oratory and theater parallel each other: "[O]f an orator,"
says Cicero, "we . . . demand . . . a diction almost poetic, a lawyer's
memory, a tragedian's voice, and the bearing . . . of the consummate actor. . . . Nothing is done without . . . charm, . . . and so as
to move and enchant."[16]

Unquestionably the key figure among classical authors, however, whose contribution to the development of Elizabethan
drama was in every way indispensable—the kernel around which
the crystal instantaneously forms—is still the moralist, tragedian, "vile politician" (as he actually was), and "flowre of all writers," as Jasper Heywood called him,[17] Seneca. It was in Seneca
more than any other author that the Elizabethans found the
synthesis of language and power that they recognized intuitively
as the engine that drove their own world. The word *instantaneously* in the sentence above, it might be noted, is more than
merely metaphoric, for it suggests something of the speed with
which Seneca conquered the English stage; from the publication
of the first English translation of the *Troas* in 1559, to the first
performance of *Gorboduc* before the queen at Whitehall in 1561,
"in three years, in Latin and English, in the theater and in the
press" as H. D. Charlton tells us, "Seneca . . . established himself."[18]

Two points about Seneca the dramatist's English popularity
stand out in the theme of this study as highly significant. The
first is that the real breakthrough for Seneca in England came
by way of English translation. In the context of the struggle between linguistic mutability and fixity, and the other elements of
power that are the underground theme of sixteenth-century culture, the creation of a vernacular version of Senecan tragedy—
"our Seneca," Ascham called him [129]—was a revolutionary
step. Charlton points out that there were actually two, or, better
perhaps, three, stages to Seneca's English triumph. The first we
may call a false start—a production in Latin of the *Troades* at
Trinity College, Cambridge, in 1551–52, an apparent nonevent
in literary circles that was followed by eight more years of silence. The real first stage, then, is Heywood's *Troas* translation
of 1559, which he followed shortly, perhaps because his first
effort was so well received, with two more works in 1560 and
1561, inspiring at the same time several academic imitations of
Seneca, including *Gorboduc,* all written by students of the Inns
of Court and all performed at Court (Charlton cxl–lii). The

decade of the 1570s saw a lull in the production of new Senecan-style material, but after simmering in the public mind for ten years, the year 1581, which saw the publication of Newton's *Seneca His Tenne Tragedies Translated into English*, ushered in the new age. Well before the end of that decade, with some help unquestionably from a vital native tradition of popular comedy, what we know as Elizabethan drama was born—a roster of names that includes Peele, Kyd, and Shakespeare as the "Senecans," along with Marlowe simply as himself—no longer the academic or courtly elite of the 1560s, but the spontaneous flowering of a culture in the process of discovering its own linguistic soul.

The second point of great significance about the Elizabethan "Senecan craze," as Schelling terms it, is that it took place initially almost entirely in an academic environment. The four principal translators—Jasper Heywood, Alexander Neville, John Studley, and Thomas Nuce—were all very young at the time they did their work, with the first three at least, the only ones of whom anything much is known, being directly university connected, Heywood as a twenty-four-year-old fellow of All Souls' Oxford, Neville and Studley as Cambridge undergraduates in their teens.[19] While neither their ages nor their educational links prove anything in themselves, they nevertheless suggest strongly that my thesis in this study has a basis—that the real place of rhetoric in the sixteenth century is precisely in that middle ground between the academy and the seats of power; and even more, perhaps, that theater is uniquely the medium to express this important concept. Part of the basis of this claim relates to the study specifically of Seneca in Elizabethan schools, and the peculiarities once again of his dramatic style. The key element of the Senecan style that demonstrates, first, his drama's *transitional* character—transitional, that is, between the academy of Seneca Rhetor and the forum of Cicero—and second, that it functioned as a free creative outlet for him in ways that his other careers could not, is its basis in oratory, or more specifically, in declamation. The plays *as plays* are indeed, just as Schlegel said, "bombastic and frigid, . . . devoid of . . . character and action, . . . and . . . barren of . . . theatrical effect," but what this means is not that they do not do their work effectively, indeed far from it, but that they draw their power wholly from the persuasive effects of brilliant speech. Since there is no action, and little more of individual character in any of them, clearly their appeal to the Elizabethan mind lay in the mesmerizing force of pure language, language pitched to the point that it begins, in the words of Pratt, to "seethe and boil":[20]

> The night is gone, and dreadful day begins at length t'appear;
> And Phoebus, all bedimmed with clouds, himself aloft doth rear,
>
> . . . .
>
> Now shall the houses void be seen, with plague devoured quite;
> And slaughter that the night hath made shall day bring forth to
>   light.
> Doth any man in princely throne rejoice? O brittle Joy,
> How many ills, how fair a face, and yet how much annoy
> In thee doth lurk, and hidden lies! what heaps of endless strife!
> They judge amiss, that deem the prince to have the happy life!
> For as the mountains huge and high the blust'ring winds with-
>   stand,
> And craggy rocks the belching floods do bash, and drive from land,
> Though that the seas in quiet are, and calm on every side:
> So kingdoms great all winds and waves of fortune must abide.[21]

What happens in these plays, I suggest, is that the gap is suddenly bridged between the academic world and real life. In the academy, rhetoric is always essentially empty, a laborious but ultimately sterile discipline, abstract in theory, swamped with memorization and drill in practice. In the councils and corridors of state, on the other hand, that same discipline becomes an instrument of awesome power—with amazing feats of philosophical, logical, and emotional verbal manipulation played for life-and-death stakes—a game that probably never in history has had more horrifying if melodramatic real-life consequences than those witnessed in the career of Seneca. But it is in theater alone, finally, that we have the perfect combination of these two functions—neither the sterile abstractions of the classroom nor the corrupt and venal survival tactic of the court, but simply pure linguistic creativity, inspired by emotions that are as real as imagination can make them, yet freed at the same time by their very inconsequentiality from the nightmare elements of self-interest and guilt that debase them in real life. The authenticity of *theatrical* rhetoric as compared to the other two is based on the paradoxical principle again of the separation of the tradition of rhetoric into two branches: Aristotle's "truth" branch, which postulates that rhetoric and reason are linked; and the "fictional" branch, represented in the academic history of rhetoric by the equally ancient practice of declamation. Seneca's dramas, then, are not only declamatory, and in fact they were used as exercises in declamation in Elizabethan schools[22]—but they are an actual development directly from the Roman declamatory tradition. As Pratt informs us, the practice of declamation had changed its orientation in the period after the accession of Augustus: with the decline of political oratory, the Senate having lost much of its power, rhetoric, and particularly declamation, previously confined almost completely to the schools as an exercise, had broadened its appeal: "[I]t continued to take place in the schools for the most part, but it was an activity not restricted to students and teachers. It became a public, intellectual, and even social function for students, their teachers, guests, other teachers, experienced amateurs like the elder Seneca, and others indulging in a fashionable pastime."[23] It was in this atmosphere of fashion that Seneca's dramas were conceived, as a natural extension of public declamation into a medium that gave fuller scope to creativity by freeing the author from the purely forensic traditions of the academy. Adapting declamation to the model of Greek tragedy which he had to hand, Seneca could use the theatrical medium to combine the two halves of academic rhetoric into one, and at the same time demonstrate exactly how rhetoric functions in the real world. The "truth" component of academic rhetoric is there in the plays, though not in its conventional form, but rather in the *guise* of fiction (the basis of declamation), in the ambitions, the jealous motives, the struggles between their lust and their honor that engage the characters; and with the whole thing directly transferable to the arena of real-life politics:

> O drowsy, dreaming, doting soul, what cometh in thy brain
> To seek about for thy defense what way thou may'st attain?
> . . . .
> Now nurture's lore neglected is, all right doth clean decay,
> Religion and dignity with faith are worn away.
> And ruddy shame with blushing cheeks, so far, God wot! is past
> That when it would it cannot come now home again at last.
> O let me now at random run with bridle at my will!
> The safest path to mischief is by mischief open still.[24]

In making Seneca theirs, in recreating him in their own language, as they had been trained to do in school, his Elizabethan devotees went through essentially the same process of discovery with respect to the role of rhetoric in their culture as Seneca had gone through with respect to the role of rhetoric in his, discovering that rhetoric is indeed transitional between the academy and the court, and that the stage is the mirror of the culture. Everything in the society, from the principles of education that it followed, to the model of courtly elegance, intellectual sophistication, and power toward which it aspired, contributed to the shaping of a cultural concept of which theater is the archetype. The classical rhetoricians establish the concept, the vernacular rhetorics popularize and extend it far beyond the school. As Wilson says,

> Firste nedefull it is that he, whiche desireth . . . to prove an eloquent man, must . . . to his boke, & learne to be well stored with knowledge, that he maie be able to minister matter, for all causes necessarie. The which when he hath gotte plentifully, he muste use muche exercise . . . [.] [W]hat maketh the lawyer to have such utterance? Practise, what maketh the preacher to speake so roũdly? . . . Marie practise I warrant you. . . . Now before we use either to write, or speake eloquently we must . . . follow the moste wise and learned menne, . . . [t]he whiche when we earnestly mynde to do, we cannot but in time appere somewhat like them.[25]

And in a complementary commentary on Shakespeare, Eileen Jorge Allman, after noting the extent to which sixteenth-century schoolmasters like Udall and Mulcaster used "playwriting, acting, and staging [as] part of the curriculum," observes that "this connection between education and drama [may have been] made for Shakespeare himself in his own early schooling,"[26] an observation to which I would give enthusiastic assent here.

It was arguably in England, as it happens, and especially England under Elizabeth, that the most deliberate, if not the most conscious exploitation of the theatrical potential of the political process of the whole European Renaissance took place. Diane Bornstein, in her book *Mirrors of Courtesy*, a discussion of the chivalric element in the English aristocratic code of the fifteenth and sixteenth centuries, observes typically that "[u]nder Elizabeth . . . [t]he English court was like a great theater. Elizabeth deeply believed in display, ceremony, decorum, and the whole theatrical apparatus of royal power."[27] The mythic dimensions of both her person and her reign were extensively cultivated by the queen, and in the romantically charged atmosphere of the period, her encouragement found a ready response among artists, poets, and artisans. Among literary practitioners of the cult Spenser and Raleigh are well known, but they were but two of a host of contemporary celebrities who contributed their share to the Platonizing process.[28] The queen herself, as suggested, was the foremost practitioner of the art of political theater: "Princes, I tell you, are set on stages,"[29] she is reported to have said on one occasion, and throughout her career she achieved a blend of actress and empress in her behavior that served, with a combination of instinct and skill worthy of a Burbage, to preserve, in Stephen Orgel's phrase, the "illusion of power."[30] Elizabeth and her establishment were "the centre of the national consciousness," G. K. Hunter tells us, and in that role were "neither natural nor free. [Court] ritual was artificial to the last degree[;] . . . [t]he sovereign was a painted idol rather than a person. . . . Yet this . . . artifice does not seem to have cut off the sovereign from her people, but on the contrary seems to have focussed more clearly what they wanted to see—a manifestation of Divine order on earth."[31] The critical point for our purposes in recalling these events is to note not just the theatrical atmosphere that imbued the court, but the central role of rhetoric both in creating and guiding these developments. A recent biographer of Elizabeth, Carolly Erickson, finds three elements combining in the young Elizabeth to make her, as Erickson paraphrases Ascham, "a marvel[:] political sophistication, . . . linguistic accomplishment and, inseparable from these, . . . oratorical skill";[32] a viewpoint that Stephen Greenblatt complements in words that bring us back to the point again at which this study began:

> The chief intellectual and linguistic tool in th[e] creation [of the "Renaissance mind"] was rhetoric, which held the central place in the humanist education to which most gentlemen were at least exposed. . . . It offered men the power to shape their worlds, and it implied that human character itself could be similarly fashioned, with an eye to audience and effect. Rhetoric served to theatricalize culture, or rather it was the instrument of a society which was already deeply theatrical.
>
> The manuals of court behavior which became popular in the sixteenth century are essentially handbooks for actors, practical

guides for a society whose members were nearly always on stage.
These books are closely related to the rhetorical handbooks that
were also in vogue—both essentially compilations of verbal strategies and both based upon the principle of imitation.[33]

Greenblatt's reference here to the close relations that obtain
between the rhetorical handbooks and the popular courtesy
books like Castiglione's *The Courtier* and Guazzo's *Civil Conversation* is a telling one, for it touches on a number of issues that
are central to the thesis of this study. That there is a close connection between the two genres is first of all patent, indeed obvious: theatrical display may contribute to the queen's mystique,
but as Ascham said, it is really "that excellency of learning, to
understand, speak, and write," that made the queen "the ultimate courtier," as Daniel Javitch modernizes Ascham's flattering
depiction.[34] Hoby, in introducing Castiglione to English readers,
makes sure they do not miss the connection, by making a
lengthy comparison between the Castiglione and Cicero himself:
"were it not that the auncientnesse of tyme, . . . and the eloquence of Latin stile in these our daies beare a great stroke, I
knowe not whether in the invention and disposition of the
matter, as Castilio hath followed Cicero, . . . so hee maye in . . .
lyke trade of writing, be compared to him: but well I wotte for
renowme among the Italians, he is not inferiour to him."[35]

One lesser known courtesy text Greenblatt mentions makes a
particularly good illustration of just how subtly ambiguous the
courtly art of rhetoric was capable of becoming in the 1570s.
This is *The Philosopher of the Court*, an English translation by
George North of a French original, a work that was apparently
completely forgotten until Daniel Javitch resurrected it for discussion in a 1971 article.[36] For Javitch the book's interest lies in
the fact that it was intended as satire, in the classical Lucianic
tradition of the "satirical eulogy,"[37] and was understood as such
in France, but that in England both its translator and presumably its readership as well missed the author's irony, taking the
work instead as, in Javitch's words, "a useful handbook of serious
intent."[38] The critical point this issue of differing interpretations
in England and France illustrates, however, is that there is a
genuine ambiguity in the whole concept of courtly philosophy
and the rhetoric that cloaks it, an ambiguity that makes it in the
final analysis impossible to establish a distinction between irony
and serious intent in any statement touching on these issues.

This is really the same question in "courtly" form as was discussed earlier in "rhetorical" form, and that touches on one of the central mysteries of the art of rhetoric, the question of the inherent duality in the use of eloquence as an instrument of persuasion. The implication is that since persuasion is the rhetorician/courtier's only real goal, irony, intentional or unintentional, is always a part of his pitch, and skepticism on the part of reader/hearer therefore always to some extent warranted. Without completely recapitulating the argument of this forgotten work, the principles of sixteenth-century thought that it reveals are extremely important, and considerably more complex than Javitch's interpretation would suggest. The general gist of the book is that courtly "philosophy" consists, not as Philosophy proper has traditionally been thought to do, in "the knowledge of secret and hidden causes," but rather in "certaine small humanities, and chiefly in outward appearances."[39] Success as a courtier, in other words, depends on one's *appearing* wise, witty, educated, and skilled in all the arts that mark the Castiglionian courtier. This is a straightforward position on the part of the author, clearly enough, but the question of the extent to which irony is operative in either his or his reader's grasp of the idea is by no means easily answered. And this is not the limit of our author's subtlety, for he goes on to say that, after all, appearance is not really enough—that to master courtly philosophy we cannot merely ape but must possess "the Artes and liberall Sciences, whereby we become right Courtiers: As of Musicike, . . . playing on the Lute, . . . the Arte to compose devices, . . . Songs, Sonets, . . . verse, or ryme" (29). I would suggest that the levels of irony in such a conception are finally impenetrable. It is a Machiavellian and a Castiglionian treatise once: satirizing the courtly ideal by showing it up as nothing but pretense, but sincerely extolling the beauty of the image it fosters in the same breath. One of the greatest of the courtly virtues, for example, we are told, is what the author calls "distributive justice" or liberality, a special virtue in courtly terms, because nothing so conduces to "the glorie and reputation of a man" than generosity—with such precepts thrown at them is it any wonder that English readers might be confused?

Not to spend too much time on Philbert's little text, the essential difference between it and other courtesy texts is really only the degree to which it places the rhetorical or "theatrical" element of courtly behavior in the foreground of its prescriptions rather than slipping it in by the back door, as it were, covered with a cloak of style. For Philbert, thus, dissembling is not only required in the courtly philosophy, it is wholly a good thing as well:

> It is therefore worthie great prayse to moderate our affections, that they appeare not any way to others and so to dissemble and accommodate oure selves to everie one: for this is an easie meane to wynne and drawe to us the good willes of all men, whereof cometh honor and reputation. (98)

As an example of rhetorical technique this statement is identical in form, though a reversal of the content, of what the conventional rhetorics do when they claim that rhetoric has a natural affinity for truth and is therefore wholly good—it uses rhetoric to hide rhetoric's own self-serving motives and its ultimate irrational basis. To present these things Philbert's way, however, to praise dissembling and take Proteus as the hero of one's philosophy[40] is at the very least a refreshing change in a society whose very soul is tied to the practice of dissimulation, but which must at all times maintain, as an essential part of that dissimulation, that truth, honor, and tradition are what really rule. Indeed such an avowal does more than merely reflect society's image; in a sense it liberates its soul. In a society driven by ambition and fear, the forces that now actually hold sway in men's hearts, however much the shell of the past in the form of both courtly and religious tradition still rules the imagination, dissimulation, and above all style, are the essential matrix that sustains the culture. And while the culture itself recognizes how essential that matrix is, as the proliferation of both the rhetorical and the courtly literature in Tudor England testifies, it remains part of the matrix itself that the mask of virtue be maintained, and the pretense to reason and truth be carried on. This necessity causes a contradiction in which all of the priests of culture are caught: while they are aware that deception and dissimulation are essential to society, they cannot appear to approve them, for to do so is to open the door to chaos. And this contradiction in turn provokes a standard response in the literature: acknowledgment, implicit or direct, that deceit *is* an essential part of the rhetorician's armament, accompanied by the excuse that only when it serves a "higher" end can it be justified.

Indeed the whole burden of both the rhetorical and the courtly arts in the Renaissance is found in those two ideas: the recognition that rhetoric (style) enables one to sway the minds of others by the arts that one employs, yet all the time insisting that those skills must (indeed *can*) only be employed in the behalf of right —a position that seems on the face of it to cover the question of deception very neatly, but that below that placid surface leaves the contradiction unresolved.

Thus Wilson, for example, firm partisan that he is of the rhetoric/reason alliance and who concludes his *Arte* with the pious exhortation "what needes wishying, seeying the good will not speake evill, and the wicked cannot speake well,"[41] in order to say such things at all, has had to swallow the many references in his own book to various kinds of "dissemblying[;]" viz.—"when twoo meetes together, and the one cannot well abyde the other: and yet they both outwardly strive to use pleasaunt behavior, and to show muche courtesie: yea to attende on both partes, whiche shoulde passe other in usyng of faire wordes, and makyng lively countenaunces: sekyng by dissemblyng the one to deceive the other."[42] Or again, browsing in Wilson's Index, I come upon an item under "M" that reads, "Matters harde to avoyde, should bee past over as though we sawe them not," itself an interesting example of the hidden contradiction that runs through his book, but more than that, in falling just where it happens to fall in that index—immediately preceding three separate entries under the heading "Memorie"—a revelation. It is a revelation because it reveals the true function of memory for the rhetorician. Memory, as every student of rhetoric knows, is one of the five classical divisions of rhetoric; perhaps the key division: Quintilian speaks rapturously of its "supernatural capacities," and of its being memory "which has brought oratory to its present position of glory."[43] Without disagreeing with the master we may nonetheless note, in the light of the contradictions found everywhere in rhetorical discussion, that there is more to the art of memory than its own students can ever acknowledge: like rhetoric itself it has two sides; it is not only the power to *retain* information and recall it at will, as conventionally assumed, but also its opposite—the power to suppress and reject inconvenient knowledge—in Wilson's words, an "arte of forgettinge"[44] as well as of remembering!

Returning to *The Philosopher of the Court* for a final moment, when it was suggested earlier that the value of a text like

Philbert's to a culture like the Elizabethan is that such texts help to "liberate its soul," what that hyperbolic pronouncement meant was that by extolling the virtue, indeed the necessity, of dissembling in a courtier, it acknowledges what is in fact true of the culture, but what in other, more conventional courtesy books and rhetorics, must be covered up. Suppressing these truths, however, creates psychological pressures of intolerable intensity in that culture, amounting indeed to a virtual collective neurosis, pressures for which books like Philbert's provide an essential outlet: in the guise of an irony which is in truth no irony at all, such works act as an escape valve, a literary mask which permits the whole truth at last to be expressed. And if Philbert's little *Philosopher* seems a very slight foundation on which to mount so vast a psychological design for society, as indeed it is, it should be emphasized that it is not the particular book that is important here, but rather the principle of Elizabethan society requiring such outlets, literary or social, owing to the unique psychological and political conditions that obtain in that period.

In fact there is another whole branch of literature that came into its own in this period as well, in response to the same pressures and serving the same function as that I have ascribed to Philibert, that it can be said without hyperbole is fully commensurate with the magnitude of the psychological dilemma we have described, that branch of literature being Elizabethan drama. Drama is essential to the culture precisely because it answers a psychological need: operating under the same laws as the culture itself does—the laws, that is, of rhetoric—with persuasion as the end, and style, linguistic and theatrical, the means, it glorifies the Protean impulse, and makes pretense openly and freely its goal, enabling society to admire without guilt the arts that shape its political life, but which it is constrained by the peculiar circumstances of the time from avowing in the arena in the "real" world. Barbara Hardy has coined a memorable phrase to express the satisfaction this outlet provides—"the warm liberating release of performance."[45] There is no other way, it seems to me, to account for what happened in English drama in the 1580s, when, almost literally out of nowhere, a new theatrical art, rich in a language that could only be English of a new and brilliant kind, emerges full blown from the mouths of a dozen practitioners almost simultaneously, at least one of whom, Shakespeare, as the remainder of this study will be dedicated to showing, is fully conscious of the exact nature of the impulse that drives both his culture and his own art.

The other topic in the chapter title, the views of the sixteenth century in general, and Shakespeare in particular, on the subject of the relationship of rhetoric to poetry, may be introduced by discussing briefly one more of those rhetoric-cum-courtesy (and in this case cum-poetry as well) texts so characteristic of the age, Puttenham's *The Arte of English Poesie* of 1589. The subject is an important one for obvious reasons in a study of Shakespeare as rhetorician, he being the supreme poet, yet working at the same time within an artistic convention in his plays to which the tradition of rhetoric contributes more than any other source. Puttenham's book, "with which Shakespeare was very familiar,"[46] is likewise an important one, not only as epitomizing the overlap between the courtly and the literary arts in the Elizabethan conception, but as containing principles of thought, relating to poetry in particular, to which Shakespeare unquestionably subscribes. Puttenham's monumental text is notably chauvinistic; in part a courtesy text like the others we have been discussing, it differs from these by its specifically English orientation—suggesting, for example, that manners in other European courts, particularly that of France, are by no means up to the English standard. While Puttenham is not the only English writer in the rhetorical line who has taken this slant, his use and praise of English models, both courtly, and especially literary, is unique, and marks his work a product of post-Armada English expansionism, as prideful and as confident in its kind as much of the drama with which it is contemporary. All of the elements of thought with which this chapter has dealt to this point come into play in Puttenham's book, and, in addition, its emphasis on poetry *as a form of rhetoric* introduces a new idea for this study, but one which was almost as important for the Renaissance as the study of rhetoric itself was.

While the nominal subject of Puttenham's book is poetry, with two hundred of its three hundred pages devoted to discussion of stylistic questions, poetic and rhetorical, a "courtesy" aura nevertheless invests the whole book by virtue of the author's directing it to a courtly audience, whose improvement in the language arts is said to be the book's principal objective:

And because our chiefe purpose herein is for the learning of . . .
idle Courtiers, . . . for their private recreation to make now & then
ditties of pleasure, thinking for our parte none other science so fit
for them & the place as that which teacheth *beau* semblant, the
chief professiõ as well of Courting as of poesie: since to such . . .
mindes nothing is more combersome then tedious . . . and schollarly methodes of discipline, we have in our owne conceit devised
a newe and strange modell of this arte, fitter to please the Court
then the schoole.[47]

The "*beau* semblant" or beautiful "seeming" idea here, Puttenham's version of the dissimulation motif that runs throughout
the courtesy literature, is the tie-in between the literary and
courtly elements of his book. By implication, the courtier's need
to put on a "*beau* semblant" is his justification for wishing to
master the rhetorico/poetic art. The "new and strange model" for
the teaching of the art of poetry of which he speaks refers to the
style of the book itself, which is of a quite charming lightness
and ease, successfully avoiding the "tedious . . . and schollarly
methodes of discipline" that mark the usual textbook treatment
of such subjects, and a model of the smooth sophistication of
which the "vulgar" tongue is capable in Puttenham's view, the
linguistic standard to which the modern English courtier may
now aspire. While no one would call Puttenham a Shakespeare,
in comparison to schoolmasters like Ascham and Mulcaster
there is a sureness, indeed a conviction, in his use of the English
that is still lacking in most Elizabethan scholarly writing, and
that, like the drama itself, marks the true coming of age of English as a literary language the equal of any:

Then when I say language, I mean the speach wherein the Poet or
maker writeth be it Greek or Latine, or as our case is the vulgar
English, & when it is peculiar unto a countrey it is called the
mother speach of that people: . . . so is ours at this day the
Norman English. . . . This part in our maker, or Poet must be
heedyly looked unto, that it be naturall, pure, and the most usual
of all his countrey: and for the same purpose rather that which is
spoken in the kings Court, or in the good townes and cities within
the land, then in the marches and frontiers, . . . or yet in Universities where Schollers vse much peevish affectation of words. . . ,
or finally, in any uplandish village or corner. . . , where is no resort
but of poore rusticall or vnciuill people: . . . for such persons do
abuse good speaches by strange accents or ill shapen soundes,
and false orthographie.[48]

The key concept in the book, from the standpoint of its "courtesy" function, is the concept of *decorum*—the rhetorical "figure of figures," as John Hoskins termed it.[49] An approximately fifty-page concluding section of the *Arte* is devoted to discussion of this important, indeed climactic subject, one which also unites the book's literary with its courtly or political objectives. The term *decorum* itself needs no definition; even in an Elizabethan context its application to the areas of behavior and speech is obvious, though, as becomes clear, more openly political in Puttenham's conception than modern usage connotes. While the term does mean "appropriate behavior" in exactly the modern sense in Puttenham, its basis is not, for him, as it would be for us, the behavior's own intrinsic "rightness" as it were, but rather its usefulness as a political strategy. Power, in other words, is still the name of the game, and "decorum," therefore, means the shaping of one's image accordingly: "[Is] it not . . . requisite," as Puttenham puts it, "our courtly Poet do dissemble not only his countenances & cõceits, but also his ordinary actions of behavior, . . . *whereby the better to winne his purposes and good advantages?*" (italics mine).[50] As the English equivalent of the Latin *decorum* he uses the word *decency*, and in all of his examples to illustrate the term what comes through most strongly is its political dimension—that the ultimate criterion of decency is in effect *deference*, or what a more Machiavellian thinker than Puttenham would probably call ingratiation:

> And there is a decencie, that every speech should be to the appetite and delight, or dignitie of the hearer & not for any respect arrogant or undutifull. (268)
>
> . . . .
>
> And in the vse of apparell there is no litle decency and vndecencie to be perceived, as well for the fashion as the stuffe, for it is comely that every estate and vocation should be knowen by the differences of their habit: a clarke from a lay man: a gentleman from a yeoman. a souldier from a citizen, and the chiefs of every degree frõ their inferiours, because in confusion and disorder there is no manner of decencie. (283)
>
> . . . .
>
> Right so in negotiating with Princes we ought to seeke their fauour by humilitie & not by sternnesse, nor to trafficke with them by way of indent or condition, but frankly and by manner of submission to their wils, for Princes may be lead but not driuen,

nor they are to be vanquisht by allegation, but must be suffred to haue the victorie and be relented vnto: . . . and in praysing them to their faces to do it very modestly: and in their commendations not to be excessiue for that is tedious, and alwayes sauours of suttelty more then of sincere loue. (293–94)

. . . .

Likewise in matter of aduise it is neither decent to flatter him for that is seruile, neither to be to rough or plaine with him, for that is daungerous, but truly to Counsell & to admonish, grauely not greuously, sincerely not sourely: which was the part that so greatly commended Cineas Counsellour to king Pirrhus, who kept that decencie in all his perswasions, that he euer preuailed in aduice, and carried the king which way he would. (295)

I have quoted at greater length from Puttenham's essay on decorum here, because the passages quoted reveal, I believe, more of the actual subtle workings of the Tudor political theater, with its carefully crafted roles for both monarch and subject, than probably three times as many words of commentary on the subject could do in their place. Again one of the most striking impressions one receives from reading these passages is of the extraordinarily delicate balance the author maintains between a full Machiavellian awareness of the realities of power on the one hand, and its exact opposite on the other—a sincere belief in and commitment to both the courtly "play" itself, and the role one is given to act within it. This is a book avowedly on the subject of language, and in its mastery of the courtly idiom it is itself the perfect example of precisely the skills it teaches—Montrose calls it a "*meta*courtly discourse"[51]—as with infinite delicacy it threads the shoals of politics by careful application of the guiding hand of art.[52]

A question that must come up in considering a book like Puttenham's, is again the question of the degree to which the writer is actually conscious of the politico/linguistic game he is playing here. In Puttenham's case, like Philbert's, he may be more conscious than many of his contemporaries. I say this because *The Arte*, while making use of all the same stylistic formulae as its conventional bretheren—Wilson, Sherry, Peacham, et al.—takes a different slant, from the very beginning, on the question of the purpose of these devices. By making poetry rather than rhetoric the basis of his theory, he takes his stand on *artificiality*, in effect deceit, as the first criterion of both the courtly and the linguistic arts, rather than reason or truth, as Aristotelean dogma maintains. As noted, the subject of the relationship of poetry and rhetoric is an important one in the Renaissance, but surrounding which considerable ambiguity, not to say confusion, exists. The confusion existed in the Renaissance, and in fact is part of the whole vexed question of the authentic definition of rhetoric in that period—whether it is allied to truth and reason, or whether, as we know is actually the case at the underground level, "the modes of persuasion are the only true constituents of the art" as Aristotle says, and high principles of any kind therefore ultimately irrelevant to it. In an introductory essay in their *The Great Critics* text, Smith and Parks point out that the original distinction between the two arts of poetry and rhetoric, both in classical times and in the Renaissance, is really the distinction between poetry and prose: the word *poetry* referring to imaginative writing generally—"*belles lettres*" is the term they use, while "oratory[,] . . . the only pure prose[,]" relates strictly to "the problems of [a] speaker."[53] Sidney has this distinction in mind when he defines poetry after Aristotle as "an arte of imitation, . . . a representing, counterfetting, or figuring forth"[54] and refers at the same time to "oratorie" having "persuasion," as its "chief mark," with "a plain sensibleness, [to] win credit of popular ears"[55] its most effective technique. The carryover of the one art to the other, then, and the mixing of the two that characterizes Renaissance criticism, comes from the fact that each may use the techniques of the other for its different purposes—imaginative illustration to bolster the orator's persuasiveness, the tricks of style to augment the poet's artistry or enhance his skills in depiction. Classical and Renaissance definitions of the two arts are close as well, and for the same reason, with three very familiar words in particular being associated in various combinations with both arts, the words *teach*, *delight*, and *persuade*. The terms were first used in this combination by Cicero to define the purpose of oratory, while Horace, the best-known classical theoretician of poetry in the Renaissance, applied the first two— "to instruct or to delight or to combine the two"—in his definition of the function of poetry. Among Italian Renaissance literary theoreticians, Scaliger (1561) and Minturno (1559) use the same terms again, as do Wilson and Sidney in England.[56]

For Puttenham, though teaching, delighting, and most importantly persuading, remain essential elements of his theory of

language, really the most fundamental principle of that theory is
the principle of *artificiality*, an idea that I do not believe any
other theorist of his day has, and one that makes explicit the
connections among language, politics, and theater that I have
said form the underlying structure of sixteenth-century society.
In a unique formula that brings together the concepts of art and
nature in a way that a modern linguist might ponder, Puttenham suggests that while "language is given by nature to man for
[inevitably!] perswasion of others, and aide of them selves," that
gift cannot be fully utilized, or it remains in an embryonic state
only, until the *arts* of speech, developed and refined through education and practice, release its authentic power. And it is the *artificiality* of speech, with all that term connotes of awareness on
the part of the speaker *of* that artificiality, and his corresponding
control over the manipulative potential of speech, that unlocks
the power of language: "For speech it selfe is artificiall and made
by man, and the more pleasing it is, the more it prevaileth to
such purpose as it is intended for."[57] Poetry and rhetoric are thus
not two studies for Puttenham, but one, which may be given the
generic name of *art*, and which is fundamentally poetic in Aristotle's terms—"an arte of imitation, . . . a representing, counterfetting, or figuring forth," as Sidney says, from which a quite
conscious use of imagination (read dissimulation) can never be
wholly absent. The primary purpose of speech art for Puttenham
is to deceive: the stylistic devices of rhetoric are geared to this
purpose:

> As figures be the instruments of ornament in every language, so
> be they also in a sort abuses or rather trespasses in speach, be-
> cause they passe the ordinary limits of common vtterance, and be
> occupied of purpose to deceive the eare and also the minde, draw-
> ing it from plainnesse and simplicitie to a certaine doublenesse,
> whereby our talke is the more guilefull & abusing, for what els is
> your *Metaphor* but an inversion of sense by transport; your *alle-
> gorie* but a duplicitie of meaning or dissimulation under covert
> and darke intendments[?] (154)

And the courtier-cum-poet for whom the *Arte* was written is
likewise before anything else a deceiver; Puttenham concludes
his work with an emphatic reiteration of this, his primary point:

> We have in our humble conceit sufficiently performed our prom-
> ise . . . in the description of this arte, so alwaies as we leave [the

poet/courtier] not unfurnisht of one peece that . . . may serve as a principall good lesson for al good makers to beare cõtinually in mind, . . . which is in plaine terms, cunningly to be able to dissemble. (299)

The final rhetorical touch, of course, would be lacking, were Puttenham not to add the mandatory proviso, that dissembling is only really permitted in the practice of the *poetic* art, not the art of life, wording his retraction in such a way, however, that the note we are left with is once again the note of categorical ambiguity:

therefore leaving these manner of dissimulations to all baseminded men, . . . we do allow our Courtly Poet to be a dissembler only in the subtilties of his art: that is, when he is most artificial, so to disguise and cloake it as it may not appeare, nor seeme to proceede from him by any studie or trade of rules, but to be his naturall. (302)

It might be noted that this description of the artist might have been written with Shakespeare in mind, so exactly does it conform to his rhetorical and poetic method. The other point on which Puttenham and Shakespeare entirely agree is that though the arts of rhetoric and poetry may in theory be separate, in practice they are essentially one, having as they do the same goal, to persuade. This statement is actually only a slight but again a very significant variation on the conventional interpretation of the relations between the two arts in the Renaissance. Traditionally, though scholars do note their many affinities, a theoretical distinction still remains between them, based again on taking at face value the Aristotelean "truth" bias that attaches to rhetoric in its academic guise, while poetry, in contrast, is an art of "imitation."[58] It does not need reiterating now, however, that the supposed alliance of rhetoric with truth is a mere tactic, part of the political game of rhetoric, and indeed recognized as such and therefore disregarded at the deeper level of practice by both politicians and wits alike in the Renaissance. And it is this deeper *identity* of the two arts at the practical level, then, that is the real basis of their overlapping in theory. Indeed, the only significant theoretical distinction that may remain between them, and it is one that some Renaissance theoreticians touch on, is a distinction not of kind, but merely of degree: since both are arts of deception, of imaginative and ma-

nipulative skill, the only real question is of their relative persuasive powers. And the answer to that question, for theorists whose
views emphasize the poetic rather than the rhetorical side of the
linguistic equation, at any rate, like Puttenham or John Rainolds, is that poetry gets the nod as the "supreme persuader," in
Sloane's paraphrase of Rainolds.[59] Brian Vickers, in a discussion
of Puttenham's *Arte*, calls poetry "a form of super-rhetoric"[60] for
Puttenham, and as a capsule commentary on Puttenham's view
of the genius of poetry the term is entirely appropriate. He represents essentially the culmination in the critical literature of
sixteenth-century England of the protoromantic tradition from
Petrarch to Boccaccio that elevates not the rhetorician but the
poet to the status of a god.[61] In a sense a rival tradition in the Renaissance to the rhetorician-as-god tradition, the poetic school of
criticism, absorbing the powers of rhetoric into poetry's own ar-
senal, confirms the status of poetry as the linguistic art of arts:

> It is therefore of poets thus to be conceived . . . as creating gods.[62]
>
> . . . .
>
> [T]hey were the first . . . Priests and ministers of the holy mister-
> ies[,] . . . the first Prophetes or seears, . . . the first lawmakers to
> the people, and the first polititiens[.] (7)
>
> . . . .
>
> Poets were also from the beginning the best perswaders and their
> eloquence the first Rethorique of the world. (8)

In discussing famous definitions of the functions respectively
of poetry and rhetoric earlier, I noted that Renaissance theoreticians of poetry for the most part follow Horace's "to teach and delight" formula, while the Ciceronians add the term "persuade" to
complete the list of rhetoric's functions. As these quotations from
Puttenham make clear, however, *persuasion* in the Ciceronian
sense is by no means absent from the mainstream view of
poetry's function in the Renaissance either. While as faithful Latinists the Renaissance theorists may hesitate to depart explicitly from Horace in their definitions, yet implicitly the awareness
of poetry's supreme persuasive powers informs every word they
write. Minturno actually has a third term in his definition of
poetry, one based directly on "Cicero's idea of oratorical persuasion," in the words of Smith and Parks, the term *to move*: the
poet's purpose is "so to speak in his verses that he may teach,

that he may delight, that he may move."[63] While the connotations
of the term *move* in English may differ somewhat from those of
the term *persuade*, it is an equally correct translation of the
Latin *permovere*; and indeed this shared Latin root suggests
both the common objective of the two terms, to win the hearer's
sympathy, and their common achievement as well—namely,
"emotional power," in Quintilian's words, "the form of eloquence
that is the queen of all."[64] Scaliger sees this power as poetry's
supreme attribute, and even suggests the direct link between
the drama and the arts of rhetoric and poetry that is the thesis
of this study:

> Now is there not one end, and one only, in philosophical exposi-
> tion, in oratory, and in the drama? Assuredly such is the case. All
> have one and the same end—persuasion.[65]
>
> . . . .
>
> But it is only poetry which includes everything of this kind ex-
> celling those other arts[;] . . . since poetry fashions images of those
> things which are not, as well as images more beautiful than life of
> those things which are, it seems unlike other literary forms, . . .
> and rather to be another god, and to create. (156–57)[66]

   Turning to Shakespeare, to the examination of whose rhetorico/
poetic practice all of the preceding is preliminary, while the sub-
tleties of his mind on all aspects of these questions are, as all
Shakespeareans will agree, of apparently inexhaustible depth,
an entrance as good as any into that daunting realm is provided
by the present subject. Accepting also what is surely the first
principle of Shakespeare criticism, that Shakespeare's own
views on any subject are problematic, accessible at best only by
inference in his works, and indeed that calling *any* opinion his in
most instances reveals more about the critic's own foolish temerity than it does of the mind of his subject; nevertheless as this is
the universal reality of Shakespeare criticism, so it is criticism's
universal failing to make such inferences anyway, with every
critic implying that his interpretation represents, if never the
whole, at least a significant part of Shakespeare's own thinking.
The method of such criticism is that suggested by Shakespeare
himself—"by indirections [to] find directions out"—on the basis
of hints and leads, reading both within and between his lines, to
fix on one or more of the myriad possibilities of meaning the

plays offer, as a legitimate reading of the author's own intentions. In terms of the present subject, for example, out of the
combination of his implied and stated views on the subject of the
persuasive powers of poetry, I offer the opinion that Shakespeare
does believe, with Puttenham and many others, that poetry is
the supreme persuasive art. The implied part of this interpretation, while problematic, is perhaps less so than a good many
other of the propositions that are sometimes offered about
Shakespeare, since the evidence to support it is so vast. What I
mean by this, is simply that his writings themselves are the testimony—both in terms of the mesmerizing effect that his poetry,
the heart of Shakespeare's artistic achievement, has had on
twenty generations of readers, and of the self-evident (I suggest)
fact that follows from this, namely, that Shakespeare himself is
fully conscious of the effect his work produces. In addition to the
indirect weight of general evidence in Shakespeare's poetry
itself of his views on the subject of the persuasive powers of that
art, there are a significant number of direct references in his
writings to this theme as well, references that clearly confirm
his *awareness*, at least, of the principle of poetry's special power,
if not necessarily his unqualified personal acceptance of it. Some
of these references are very well known, others much less so, and
they range as well from quite explicit statements of the Puttenham position in some cases—"Much is the force of heaven-bred
poesy[,]" for example, in *The Two Gentlemen of Verona*—to others
in which the interpretation may verge on the conjectural; but
with all of them suggesting a view of poetry that Puttenham
would clearly endorse. Indeed, idolizing English poetry as he did,
yet lacking the sublimest gifts of expression himself, Puttenham
would not only have endorsed but undoubtedly have envied the
language in which the greater artist expressed a view of poetry's
power that echoes his own. As it happens, in the play just cited is
found one of the best examples in all of Shakespeare's writing of
this view of poetry, the very well-known,

> For Orpheus' lute was strung with poets' sinews,
> Whose golden touch could soften steel and stones,
> Make tigers tame, and huge leviathans
> Forsake unsounded deeps to dance on sands[;][67]

while the character who speaks these lines, Proteus, is almost a
model, both for his name and for the manner in which Shake-

speare presents him, of Puttenham's (or for that matter, Castiglione's) courtier-wit: "As worthy for an empress' love, / As meet
to be an emperor's counsellor," he is master of both language and
decorum:

> Yet hath Sir Proteus, for that's his name,
> Made use and fair advantage of his days:
> His years but young, but his experience old;
> His head unmellowed, but his judgment ripe;
> And, in a word, for far behind his worth
> Comes all the praises that I now bestow,
> He is complete in feature and in mind,
> With all good grace to grace a gentleman.
>
> (2.4.63–70)

While it was more in Shakespeare's younger years that direct
statements about poetry's power found their way into his plays,
his later views on the subject do not change. As early as *The
Comedy of Errors*, for example, he clearly takes for granted, and
expects his audience to understand as well, that the sound and
rhythm of poetic speech, especially to the ears of love, have a
sovereign power:

> Teach me, dear creature, how to think and speak;
> . . . .
> Are you a god? Would you create me new?
> Transform me, then, and to your pow'r I'll yield.
> . . . .
> O, train me not, sweet mermaid, with thy note,
> To drown me in thy sister's flood of tears.
> Sing, siren, for thyself, and I will dote.
>
> (3.2.33, 39–40, 45–47)

The play which contains perhaps his best known explicit
statement about poetry, and is itself the classic example among
the early works of what Brandes called "absolutely poetical
poetry,"[68] is *A Midsummer Night's Dream*, and the lines,

> The poet's eye, in a fine frenzy rolling,
> Doth glance from heaven to earth, from earth to heaven;
> And as imagination bodies forth
> The forms of things unknown, the poet's pen
> Turns them to shapes, and gives to airy nothing
> A local habitation and a name.
>
> (5.1.12–17)

While this passage does not refer specifically to the *persuasive* powers of poetry, it does pay tribute to other traditional elements of the art—the power of the imagination to create, as well as the Brunian "frenzy" of creation,[69] but other lines in the same play do pick up the theme of the power of poetry to entrance and beguile, and in familiar terms:

> once I sat upon a promontory,
> And heard a mermaid on a dolphin's back
> Uttering such dulcet and harmonious breath
> That the rude sea grew civil at her song,
> And certain stars shot madly from their spheres
> To hear the sea-maid's music.
>
> (2.1.149–54)

The tradition of poetry as an art of deception, in the pejorative sense fixed on by Puritan polemecists like Gosson and Stubbes, was known to Shakespeare as well, and is alluded to at least three times in the plays. The first of these allusions, the exchange between Touchstone and his "poor thing" Audrey in *As You Like It*, almost seems to concede Gosson's point:

> *Touch.*   Truly, I would the gods had made thee poetical.
> *Aud.*   I do not know what "poetical" is. Is it honest in deed and word? Is it a true thing?
> *Touch.*   No, truly; for the truest poetry is the most feigning, and lovers are given to poetry; and what they swear in poetry may be said as lovers they do feign.
>
> (3.3.13–19)

The modified version of this idea that he throws into *Twelfth Night*, however, is much more subtle. On the surface the exchange sounds at first like the one in *As You Like It*, with Olivia rejecting Viola's rehearsed speech, the one that she "took great pains to study," on the grounds that since "'tis poetical," "it is the more like to be feigned." When this first conventional attempt at poetical persuasion fails, however, Viola is then cleverly allowed by her creator to substitute a "spontaneous" statement of "sincere" feeling whose irresistible poetic power leaves the hearer no defense. We have here a perfect example of the type of "dissembling"—knowing "when the naturall is more commendable than the artificiall," and "where arte ought to appeare, and where not,"[70] that Puttenham wrote his book to celebrate:

> *Vio.* If I did love you in my master's flame,
>   With such a suff'ring such a deadly life,
>   In your denial I would find no sense;
>   I would not understand it.
> *Oli.* Why, what would you?
> *Vio.* Make me a willow cabin at your gate,
>   And call upon my soul within the house,
>   Write loyal cantons of contemned love
>   And sing them loud even in the dead of night;
>   Halloo your name even to the reverberate hills,
>   And make the babbling gossip of the air
>   Cry out 'Olivia!' O, you should not rest
>   Between the elements of air and earth
>   But you should pity me!
>
> (1.5.248–60)

Finally, three separate tributes from early to late Shakespeare confirm that his views of the persuasive powers of poetry remain unchanged. As some of the material we have already looked at suggests, there is an abstract element of pure beauty in poetry, for Shakespeare, that is essentially independent of content, and is the element on which poetry's power depends, the quality, namely, of musical sound per se—Walter Pater's aesthetic philosophy, in effect, three hundred years before its time. The frequent coupling of the name of Orpheus with references to the art of poetry in Shakespeare establishes this link, and makes clear that as poetry approaches music, in Shakespeare's view, the power of the mind to resist its spell correspondingly declines. Lorenzo's panegyric to music in the earlier *The Merchant of Venice* is probably the best known of these tributes:

> *Jes.* I am never merry when I hear sweet music.
> *Lor.* The reason is your spirits are attentive;
>   For do but note a wild and wanton herd,
>   Or race of youthful and unhandled colts,
>   Fetching mad bounds, bellowing and neighing loud,
>   Which is the hot condition of their blood—
>   If they but hear perchance a trumpet sound,
>   Or any air of music touch their ears,
>   You shall perceive them make a mutual stand,
>   Their savage eyes turn'd to a modest gaze
>   By the sweet power of music. Therefore the poet
>   Did feign that Orpheus drew trees, stones, and floods;

Since nought so stockish, hard, and full of rage,
But music for the time doth change his nature.

(5.1.69–82)

There are at least two very significant implications in these
lines, one for its bearing on the subject at hand, the other for its
relation to another rhetorical theme central to this study. The
first is the opening reference in Lorenzo's speech to the "attentive" state of mind as making one less receptive to music's influence. The effect of music, in other words, is clearly to make one
less attentive, at least to oneself, to beguile and entrance, as the
dream the poet weaves, "inuegleth the judgment [,] ... [carrying]
opinion this way and that, whither soever the heart by impression of the eare shalbe most affectionately bent and directed."[71]
One is reminded also in this connection of Julius Caesar's similar reflection to Antony on the "attentive" Cassius:

He is a great observer, and he looks
Quite through the deeds of men. *He loves no plays,*
As thou dost, Antony; he hears no music.

(1.2.202–25, italics mine)

The second implication is more profound, perhaps, suggesting
that poetry has the power, while its influence lasts at any rate, to
turn lust to love—"the hot condition of [the] blood" to a "modest
gaze"—an implication that is clearly very important in terms of
the love theme in Shakespeare's own poetry, but whose political
ramifications may be even more important, touching as they do
again on the supreme question of Renaissance culture, the question of the power of speech art to mitigate a harsh reality, to turn
what is ugly in fact to what is beautiful in appearance, *persua-*
sion substituting for *power*, in Castiglione's classic formula. It is
perhaps this latter implication that was most in Shakespeare's
mind when he inserted a similar tribute to music's charm into a
poignant scene in the late play *Henry VIII*, as Queen Katherine
seeks diversion from "attentiveness" to her own unhappy fate:

Q. Kath. Take thy lute, wench. My soul grows sad with troubles;
Sing and disperse 'em, if thou canst. Leave working.

SONG

Orpheus with his lute made trees,
And the mountain tops that freeze,
Bow themselves when he did sing;

> To his music plants and flowers
> Ever spring, as sun and showers
>   There had made a lasting spring.
> Every thing that heard him play,
> Even the billows of the sea,
>   Hung their heads and then lay by.
> In sweet music is such art,
> Killing care and grief of heart[.]
>
> (3.1.1–13)

And Ferdinand, in *The Tempest*, finally, returning again to the theme of our first examples, is similarly prepared, by the influence of Ariel's music, for the sea-change that will transform him from a state of mourning to a state of perfect love:

> *Fer.* Sitting on a bank,
>   Weeping again the King my father's wreck,
>   This music crept by me upon the waters,
>   Allaying both their fury and my passion
>   With its sweet air; thence have I follow'd it,
>   Or it hath drawn me rather.
>
> (1.2.389–94)

As these examples suggest, and as the next chapter will attempt to demonstrate in detail, we are dealing in Shakespeare with an artist whose "art is of such pow'r" that it can command not only its own resources, but the resources, and indeed the mind, of the culture as a whole, all with full awareness, and all with equal ease.

3

Shakespeare's Conscious Art

The preceding chapters, and particularly the just-concluded brief survey of what I have suggested can be read as direct statements by Shakespeare of his convictions regarding the persuasive powers of poetry, bring us to what is probably the central conception of this study, the claim I wish to make that Shakespeare is a fully conscious artist. Among other things, what this principle means is that, for example, the subtle social and psychological nuances associated with the arts of rhetoric and drama in the later sixteenth century, as outlined in the preceding chapters, represent essentially Shakespeare's own understanding of these matters. Proof, or at least an attempt at proof, of this claim will follow, indeed it will constitute the whole remainder of this study, but a more extensive introduction to the principle itself is required first, as befitting the revolutionary (as I am tempted to term it) scope of the conception.

It is perhaps surprising, when one reflects on the matter, how little there is in Shakespearean criticism of direct discussion of what might be called the Shakespearean consciousness itself—and by this term is meant precisely the point that the paragraph above raises, the fundamental question again of the degree of control over his medium Shakespeare actually exercises and commands. The greatness of Shakespeare's poetic *gifts*, of course, like that of his thousandfold insights, no one ever denies; but on the matter of his "art" opinion over the centuries has been both less outspoken and, I would suggest, less secure. Taking our cue perhaps from Ben Jonson, we tend merely to accept, with few specifics, the contribution of "art" to Shakespeare's genius, while reserving our greatest admiration for the results rather than for the method of his work. Criticism, it is true, and especially in this century, nibbles, as it were, around the edges of Shakespeare's art from time to time, finding indeed many examples of almost superhuman subtlety and skill in choice and meaning of word or phrase; but of Shakespeare's overall, firm, and continuing *total* control over every nuance of his medium and his expression, no commentator has to my knowledge ever been so bold as to affirm with complete conviction. I should like to correct this omission by postulating without qualification a degree of conscious control and artistry that surpasses that of the only other writer in history who, in terms of this one special trait at least, may be mentioned in the same breath as Shakespeare, namely James Joyce. Jonson, in another famous judgment on Shakespeare, faulted him for a trait that, in Jonson's own words (and to his apparent surprise), "the Players . . . often mentioned as an honor to Shakespeare, . . . that in his writing (whatsoever he penn'd) he never blotted out a line."[1] I would add to this judgment, and in support of the Players' viewpoint, that if Shakespeare never blotted a line, he likewise never forgot a line that he had once written. The works themselves are the illustration of the categorical thesis I am asserting here, and a quick introduction to the kinds of data that they involve may be provided by a few select references to the writings at this point. I would propose, then, for example, that among the things to which the famous Sonnet 30, "When to the sessions of sweet silent thought," specifically refers, one unquestionably is to Shakespeare's own past writings, and his faculty of virtual total recall regarding them. Again, a key play from the standpoint of the rhetorical interpretation of Shakespeare's art, as we shall be seeing, is *Othello*; among whose many deliberate effects are several *direct* linguistic analogues with others of Shakespeare's writings—with the *Comedy of Errors*, for example, in something as trivial as the names of the inns in the two plays—the Centaur in one, the Saggitary in the other; or with the *Lucrece*, again, perhaps, in the bedroom scene in act 5 of *Othello*, where the picture in Shakespeare's mind, of an Othello eaten up with passion at the sight of Desdemona's alabaster flesh directly recreates a scene that he had written before, of Tarquin in the bedroom of Lucrece:

> Into the chamber wickedly he stalks,
> And gazeth on her yet unstained bed.
> The curtains being close, about he walks,
> Rolling his greedy eyeballs in his head.
>
> (365–68)

These are observations that no doubt any reader of Shakespeare might make—indeed I am not the first to make this particular one[2]—but the element of conscious awareness in Shakespeare's development of parallels like these has not received the emphasis hitherto in criticism that I believe it warrants. The parallel is not absolute in this instance, as motives (it will be said) quite obviously differ greatly between Tarquin and Othello; and yet even these differences are provided for too, in Shakespeare's imagination, as betrayed by other hints, in other works, of unmistakable corroborative intent to the ear that is tuned to their nuances. The following couplet from *Pericles*, for example, provides, with full awareness on Shakespeare's part I believe, an exact imaginative bridge between the passions of Tarquin and Othello:

> One sin, I know, another doth provoke:
> Murder's as near to lust as flame to smoke.
>
> (1.1.137–38)

And in a similar way, when Shakespeare flayed his Gertrude, in the closet scene of *Hamlet*, for her infidelity to the memory of her husband-king, he consciously anticipated both the idea and even some of the imagery of the murder that was to be committed three years hence in the play he would call *Othello*:

> Such an act
> . . . .
> Calls virtue hypocrite; takes off the rose
> From the fair forehead of an innocent love,
> And sets a blister there; makes marriage vows
> As false as dicers' oaths.
>
> (3.4.40–45)

Or the same observation could be made of *Macbeth*, where that play too picks up, recalls, and comments implicitly on ideas and themes that *Othello* had earlier explored: the catastrophic *speed* of *Othello*, for example (Iago's "Dull not device by coldness and delay"), appears again in Macbeth's "From this moment / The very firstlings of my heart shall be / The firstlings of my hand," (4.1.146–68) and ironically in Malcolm's "modest wisdom plucks me / From overcredulous haste" (4.3.119–20). The reference to *speed* here is a pointed reminder of a direct connection between *Othello* and *The Two Gentlemen of Verona* as well—in such plot elements, for example, as a planned elopement, which the Iago character, Sir Proteus, manages in the earlier play, however, to thwart. And do we not catch an echo again of that same Iago's plot in a reference in *The Winter's Tale* to a story told, like Iago's, at second hand, yet so convincingly, that "[t]hat which you hear [you] swear you see, there is such unity in the proofs" (5.2.30–32)? Similar citations could be made from end to end of Shakespeare.

Many well-known modern critics, H. C. Goddard is a good example, starting with the premise that "Shakespeare is one," take their critical stand on treating him "integrally," as Goddard says, considering his works "not separately[,] but as parts of a whole."[3] Or L. C. Knights, again, posits a similar critical objective in his *Some Shakespearean Themes*, "based on the belief," as he says, "that Shakespeare's plays form a coherent whole, . . . that they stem from and express a developing attitude to life."[4] Few critics, however, including both Goddard and Knights, succeed fully in this unifying aim, instead dissipating their integrated perspectives over and over in lengthy discussion of either individual characters or specific themes, and making few overt pretences in embarking on these excursions that an alert Shakespeare is still on their tenuous trail. One of the reasons that most attempts at an integrated vision of Shakespeare break down is precisely that their authors lack that essential sense of what I have called the Shakespearean consciousness—the clear sense that behind every character and word of the plays lies a continuing, a coherent, and a real human mind and heart. I should hasten to add, and this is again critical, that most of the difficulty critics have in keeping a grasp on the Shakespearean consciousness is difficulty that Shakespeare himself has put in our way; so chameleonlike are the myriad faces that greet us in the plays that the task of seeing behind them is made as formidable it almost seems as mapping the human genome, to decipher the code of life itself. This point is critical, because it is calculated on Shakespeare's part: it is precisely his technique, and a product not of magic or even particularly of "nature," but of art and skill, developed in youth in the course of a typical sixteenth-century education, honed and refined over a thirty-year professional career.

The word "nature" here raises a key issue that must be tackled in any discussion of Shakespeare. The "naturalness" of Shakespeare's writings has been a byword of criticism for centuries, as well as being probably the primary source of his appeal among ordinary readers and audiences. He said in *Hamlet*, in a famous phrase, that a player's greatest skill is "to hold as 'twere, the mirror up to nature," and no more apposite words than these to describe Shakespeare himself as a *writer* have yet been written—these and their expansion in the lines that follow: the ability "to show virtue her own feature, scorn her own image, and very age and body of the time his form and pressure." Here, in this consideration, we see another typical failing of our appreciation of Shakespeare's artistry, as well as another reason for the ease with which criticism loses sight again of the "Shakespearean consciousness." In acknowledging the supremacy of Shakespeare's imitation of nature we come too easily to identify him *with* nature; the imitation is at all times so skillful and so rich that absorption in the *image*—the poetry, the language itself—becomes total, while the man who created that image fades from sight, almost indeed into the realm of the nonexistent.

While this phenomenon of identifying Shakespeare with nature has been a feature of critical thought about him from the beginning, it has been accentuated since the nineteenth century and the Romantic movement. The supreme eminence that Shakespeare now enjoys among literary artists is directly a product of that movement's focus on nature as the fountainhead of truth in both art and life, and its simultaneous "discovery" of Shakespeare as the personification of that truth.[5]

Suggesting that the nineteenth century marks the high point of Shakespeare worship among the critics, as the epitome of nature, it may be noted as well that the reason he did not stand generally as high in critical esteem before the nineteenth century was in fact the same one—that as a *natural* genius he lacked both the purity and the artistic control that the classical discipline alone can impart. Placed by some neoclassical critics lower on the scale of achievement than Jonson and Fletcher, he is excused his lapses on the grounds, as Rowe said, of ignorance:

> If one took to examine [Shakespeare's tragedies] by those Rules which are establish'd by *Aristotle*, and taken from the model of the *Grecian* Stage, it would be no very hard Task to find a great many Faults: but as *Shakespeare* liv'd under a kind of mere Light of Nature, and had never been made acquainted with the Regularity of those written Precepts, so it would be hard to judge him by a Law he knew nothing of.[6]

Going back further yet, it was Jonson who first observed that Shakespeare "wanted art," and though this expression is usually given a neoclassical twist, as alluding to Shakespeare's unfamiliarity with classical dramatic theory, it should be remembered that by far the commoner sense of the term "art" when Jonson used it was still *rhetoric*—in fact style—style not, however, as a natural gift, of the sort that Jonson clearly believed flowed like a tap from Shakespeare, but as a cultivated and at all times conscious discipline, modeled on the classics, purified by practice, cooly shaped and formed, weighting every line. That Jonson could accuse Shakespeare of lacking this discipline marks him as the first, though far from the last, then, of that endless line of readers and critics whom Shakespeare hoodwinked—fooled deliberately: by a *conscious art* so superior to all their notions of the same that its methods remain *even yet* largely unknown and unseen, he has attained, for them at least, what Joyce described as the supreme artistic goal, when "[t]he artist, like the God of the creation, remains within or behind or above his handiwork, invisible, refined out of existence, paring his fingernails."[7]

In searching for the definitive link connecting Shakespeare's period, his art, and the man himself, some of Northrop Frye's perceptive comments in *The Anatomy of Criticism* on the Elizabethan drama may serve as a convenient starting point. What Frye calls the "high mimetic" fictional mode enjoyed its greatest development, he notes, during the Renaissance, and the terms in which he defines this "mode" make clear why this was so—because it is fundamentally theatrical in nature, related in obvious ways to Pico's vision of Protean man as the center, or, using Frye's word, the "cynosure" of creation:

> The central episodic theme of the high mimetic is the theme of cynosure or centripetal gaze, which, whether addressed to mistress, friend, or deity, seems to have something about it of the court gazing upon its sovereign, the courtroom gazing upon the orator, or the audience gazing upon the actor. For the high mimetic poet is pre-eminently a courtier, a counsellor, a preacher, a public orator or a master of decorum, and the high mimetic is the period in which the settled theater comes into its own as the chief medium of fictional forms.[8]

The proximity of this description to Puttenham's or Castiglione's conception of the courtier-cum-poet-cum-actor is patent, but Frye

makes a further observation about Shakespeare specifically as
the archetypal Renaissance artist that makes an especially significant point. He observes that "[i]n Shakespeare the control of
decorum is so great that his personality disappears behind it altogether." As a recognition of Shakespeare's supreme artistic
powers this matches Joyce's dictum about the artist; it also complements in obvious ways the "Shakespeare as nature" critical
tradition, in the sense that, with his representations of life being
so authentic, there is no need, as it were, to search for an author
behind them; but by introducing the idea of his "control of decorum" it gives us still another Shakespeare—the real one, finally,
I believe, whose art is *not* purely instinctive, and whose "disappearance" is therefore a contrivance as calculated and as finely
balanced as the concept of decorum itself.

   That concept in fact may provide one of our principal avenues
of approach for the exposure of Shakespeare the man and the
artist. Passage after passage from sixteenth-century writings
and textbooks on the subject of decorum and its relation with
rhetoric and poetry, give direct insight into both Shakespeare's
thinking and the methodology of his art. Decorum is primarily a
rhetorical term, but rhetorical in the broadest sense, embracing
not only comeliness in speech, but in dress and deportment as
well: As Puttenham says, "this comelyness resteth in the good
conformitie of many things and their sundry circumstances[.]" I
cite Puttenham here again for two special reasons, two ideas in
his treatment of the subject of decorum that are of particular
import; both are Renaissance commonplaces, and very familiar
to modern criticism, but, strangely, never applied, as far as I am
aware, to Shakespeare, the archetypal Renaissance artist. The
first is that the *model* of decorum is found, exactly as critical orthodoxy observes of Shakespeare's art, in nature: "This lovely
conformitie . . . between the sense and the sensible," Puttenham
says, "hath nature her selfe firste most carefully observed in all
her owne workes." The other, more important for our purposes, is
the view that the ablest practitioners of decorum are those most
skilled in the ways of art and artifice; "which sheweth," as Puttenham says, "that it resteth in the discerning part of the mind,
so as he who can make . . . the best and most . . . wittie distinction is . . . the fittest judge . . . of [*decencie*]. Such generally is the
discreetest man, . . . in any art the most skilful . . . , and . . . those
that be of much observation and greatest experience."[9] "The
meaning of . . . life," it will be remembered, "is style" in the Re-

naissance, but "style" in itself is an empty concept; to achieve its end, which is to persuade, it must *appear* to be grounded in the one thing still thought to lie outside style's aegis, namely "nature."

The most successful art is therefore precisely the art which seems most "natural," but which to achieve that natural illusion must of necessity be the most contrived and most conscious of all. Pope's succinct phrase hits it exactly—it is "nature methodized." There is an exact parallel between Shakespeare's method of achieving the illusion of nature in words, and Raphael's, Holbein's, or other Renaissance masters' achieving the same illusion in paint—with the critical difference that the one has been the subject of exhaustive analysis for centuries: treatises on perspective and other Renaissance artistic techniques that demonstrate the mathematical precision behind the naturalistic depictions of these great artists exist by the score; while the treatise that will do the same for the Shakespearean method has yet to be written. Despite the lack of an analytic key, however, the necessity of an equally exact method behind the Shakespearean facade may be taken as a fact.

On the subject of *decorum* as a key concept in the Renaissance, Annabel M. Patterson, in her book on the Greek rhetorician Hermogenes and his influence, *Hermogenes and the Renaissance: Seven Ideas of Style*, notes that the last of his seven "Ideas," *deinotês*, which the Renaissance "equated with decorum," was "the most important attribute of style." Hermogenes is much less studied by modern students of sixteenth-century rhetoric than are Cicero and Quintilian, probably because until very recently he had not been translated into English, but in the Renaissance itself, Patterson observes, his influence rivalled theirs. "Hermogenic Ideas" had a great "influence . . . on the . . . Renaissance," she says, filling "a great gap in the art, not of invention, but of *persuasion*." Puttenham's *decencie* has a Hermogenic twist, Patterson says, reconfirming its tie to nature in a manner that explains its importance to the Renaissance: "Puttenham regards decorum," she says,

> not only as an organic unity which gives aesthetic pleasure, but as part of the total mysterious pattern of the universe. . . . Decorum of style, then, is but one aspect of the whole "lovely conformitie," and to place the patterns of language within the larger patterns of the universe was in itself an act of "decency."[10]

Returning to Shakespeare and the question of the missing "analytic key" to his technique, were there such a key, an Elizabethan dramatic equivalent of, say, to continue the analogy with painting, Alberti's famous *Della Pittura* of 1436, a book that served as a guide to artistic method for painters and architects for centuries after its publication, the mystery of the man might well be less than it is—not the marvel, of course, any more than the marvel of a Leonardo is lessened by having access to his sketches and studies, but something at least of the mystery. As to why that analytic key does not exist one cannot say, but speculation leads one back again to the political and social circumstances that produced Elizabethan drama. The illusions of painting lie to some extent outside the daily workings of politics and culture; they are academic, somewhat in the manner of academic rhetoric (in fact the two are closely related);[11] in an analytic age they invite analysis; the illusions of theater, on the other hand, are sufficiently closer to the theatricality of social life itself that to approach them with too zealous an analytic gaze is again to risk exposing the workings of that life, thus threatening the delicate balance on which its continuation depends. The treatise which might do for Shakespeare what Alberti does for Michelangelo would be something like a combination of Machiavelli's *Prince* and Puttenham's *Arte*—the withering analytic gaze of the one, tempered by the subtlety and hypersensitivity to nuance of the other. No one in England, hardly surprisingly, produced such a treatise, though Shakespeare might have; it took fifty years of slow development of the European consciousness for it to reach the stage that Shakespeare reached in the 1580s, where it could articulate the actual inner workings of its own social machinery. The writer whose works actually *are* primers for the Shakespearean method is the Spanish Jesuit and rhetorician Baltasar Gracián, who in a series of texts written in the 1630s and 1640s provided most of the insights needed to understand the Shakespearean method, texts that are various combinations of rhetoric, poetic, courtesy, and philosophy, whose titles alone suggest a striking parallel between his mind and Shakespeare's—titles like *The Oracle* and *The Mind's Wit and Art*. Detailed discussion of Baltasar Gracián is not within the scope of this study, nor is it necessary; for my purposes his rhetorico/social theories have three essential points of comparison with Shakespeare: 1) his fundamental belief that style and wit are the keys both to knowledge and to life; 2) his view that genius is not a gift so much as a study, its acquisition a controlled and conscious process; and 3) that the ultimate goal of all social behavior is power, or, as Leonard Mades puts it, "that the only one who counts is the outstanding individual—the man who succeeds by using prudence and reason, who understands himself thoroughly and knows how to make all things work to his advantage."[12] Gracián himself may be quoted briefly on all of these subjects: on the question of the relations of academic rhetoric to artistry, for example, he introduces *The Mind's Wit and Art* by saying,

> [T]his [work] I am dedicating to the Imagination [*Ingenio*], to wit in art, a resplendent conception— . . . though some of its artifices glimmer in rhetoric's discipline, . . . they hardly approach a sparkle: orphan children adopted by Eloquence, . . . they don't know their true mother. Wit makes use of rhetorical figures and tropes as devices for elegantly expressing its concepts; but they [the rhetorical figures] contain . . . the material foundations of the nicety and, at best, the ornaments of thought.[13]

And on the absolute necessity of consciousness and method in artistic creation, from the same work:

> The ancients found a method for the syllogism and . . . the trope; but wit . . . they confined . . . to the mere swagger of the imagination. They were content to marvel[,] . . . but . . . never came to observe wit carefully, and so never found a system for it, much less perfection. . . . Conceits . . . used to be children of the brute force of the mind rather than of its cunning, . . . conceived . . . and brought to light without conscious mastery. . . . *But conscious craft cannot be denied where so much complexity reigns.* A syllogism is made with rules; with rules, then, let conceits be hammered out. Let . . . skill beg for instruction, all the more when it is a matter of subtleness of the imagination. (85–87, italics mine)

And, finally, on the hidden realities of rhetoric and appearance:

> *Know how to be all things to all men.* A discreet Proteus; a scholar among scholars, a saint among saints. That is the art, *par excellence*, of winning every one's regard, ... Take note of temperaments and adapt yourself to that of each person [you meet]; follow the lead of the serious and jovial in turn, changing your mood discreetly; an indispensable device for dependants. This high skill . . . demands great ability. (107)

. . . .

Always keep the ultimate tricks of your trade to yourself. This is [a device] of great masters, who make use of craft in the very act of teaching their own. You should always be on top, always the master. (211)

While nothing so straightforward appears in Elizabethan writings on the subject of style and method, whether theatrical or social, the materials out of which such theses might be formed—indeed were formed by Shakespeare into the mystery of his "hidden" personality—exist in abundance. While avoiding any direct engagement with the issue of Shakespeare's "art," no commentator would at the same time dream of suggesting that he is not an intelligent observer of society and student of rhetoric—attuned to the nuances of both with an acuteness that has no contemporary peer, indeed no peer at any time.

The shaping of the Shakespearean rhetorical consciousness goes back to his earliest education, and to prescriptions again like this of Quintilian's on the question of making one's art seem natural, from his introduction to the study of style:

[T]hose words are best which are least far-fetched and give the impression of simplicity and reality. For those words which are obviously the result of careful search and even seem to parade their self-conscious art, fail to attain the grace at which they aim and lose all appearance of sincerit[y].[14]

Not only is it child's play in effect, an inevitability virtually on the face of it, that a mind like Shakespeare's must translate words like these into a full conscious awareness of the social and literary implications of such formulae, but illustrations by the score might be cited from the plays to show that he in fact did so. Marion Trousdale, in her book *Shakespeare and the Rhetoricians*, takes the character of Iago as an illustration of the very passage quoted here from Quintilian, in order to demonstrate the extent to which Shakespeare absorbed its lessons;[15] or the exchange from *Twelfth Night* between Olivia and Viola that we looked at in the last chapter could illustrate the same point equally well. And if schooling alone were not sufficient training in such matters, the norms of social life itself, like the books and prescriptions on which these norms are based, continue the educational process: Castiglione, for example, refers to those "excellent Oratours, which among other their cares, enforced themselves to make

every man believe that they had no sight in letters, and dissem-
blinge their conning, made semblant their orations to be made
very simply, and rather as nature and truth lead them, then
study and art"[16]—as exact, if indirect, a description of Shakespeare's own creative method, I suggest, as will be found. Sir
Edward Sullivan, editor of George Pettie's *Guazzo*, makes the
case that much of Shakespeare's depiction of manners comes
from Guazzo, which may be true; if so he could equally well have
based much of his method of making an art of "nature" on the
same source. Guazzo's art/nature discourse contains passage
after passage of advice on the finer points of method of which
Shakespeare's full conscious absorption can hardly be in question:

> if you consider how in Villages, Hamlets [!], and fields, you shall
> find many men, who though they lead their life far distant from
> the Graces and Muses . . . yet are of good understanding, whereof
> they give sufficient testimonie by their wise and discreete talk:
> you cannot denie, but that nature hath given and sowed in us cer-
> taine seedes of Rhethorike and Philosophie. But . . . I would have
> him aide nature with . . . art but take heede least eloquence bee
> not counted natureal, . . . yea and it is much misliked of, when it
> swarveth from the common phrase and fourme of speech.[17]

And similar things can be done with any number of other contemporary writers on courtly and rhetorical subjects. The "Epistle Dedicatorie" of Peacham's 1593 *The Garden of Eloquence*
speaks of the "secret and mightie power of perswasion" in words
that evoke the "hidden" Shakespeare with uncanny aptness: it is
"by the commendable Art and use of eloquence" that "the secret
counsells & politicke considerations of wisedome" are "brought
into open light[;]" so that "he [the Orator] is in a manner the em-
perour of mens minds & affections, and next to the omnipotent
God in the power of persuasion."[18]

Even closer to home for Shakespeare than these common
courtly and rhetorical sources of insight are the literary ones,
whose references to style have a specifically linguistic application that speaks directly to his own practice. As one of those who
participated in the sonnet surge of 1590s, inspired by Sidney's
Astrophel and Stella, he can hardly have been unaware, for example, of that much admired gentleman's mastery of what Castiglione called *sprezzatura*, the affectation of ease, the pose, as

Kenneth Myrick says, "not of a dabbler or dilettante, but of a so-phisticated man of the world who has learned the art of conceal-ing art."[19] Sidney himself made an invidious direct comparison in his *Apologie* between the "professor of learning," who, "using Art to shew Art, and not to hide Art . . . , flyeth from nature, and in-deede abuseth Art"; and the courtier, who, "following that which . . . he findeth fittest to nature . . . doth according to Art, though not by Art."[20] As a student (admirer?) of Marlowe as well, Shake-speare would have been fully appreciative of the fact that his Tamburlaine, as Alvin Kernan says, "is as great a poet and orator as he is a warrior. To speak poorly in this play, as the weak Mycetes does, is to show inadequacy in all other areas; while to speak magnificently reflects and instruments all other kinds of power."[21]

While few commentators until very recently have been so bold as to speak directly of even an Elizabethan, let alone a Shake-spearean "consciousness," there have been those willing to assert the opposite of Shakespeare—that he could *not* have been fully cognizant of the riches he was pouring into his plays. A good ex-ample of this argument is found in Mable Bruland's important 1966 book on the use of "double-time" in Elizabethan drama, in which the case is made that Shakespeare's manipulations of time in his plays are just a natural [read "unconscious"] progres-sion from what had been the common practice before him; and, even acknowledging that Shakespeare does a number of things with time in his plays that are unique, still "it is probable," as she says, "that [he] never took the trouble to compute . . . the time,"[22] and "however much Shakespeare *became* aware of the . . . inconsistencies [in his time-schemes], the double-time move-ment . . . was unconscious in its origin."[23]

Two other more recent works take diametrically opposite views on the general question of artistic consciousness among Elizabethan writers, though the primary focus of both books is on Shakespeare. Jane Donawerth, defending the view that our twentieth-century linguistic approaches to Shakespeare are meaningless because anachronistic, states that Shakespeare's "age discouraged him from the self-consciousness about . . . lan-guage that we see everywhere in . . . our own age. In this connec-tion we must beware of seeing language as a major theme of the Elizabethan playwrights."[24] Marion Trousdale, on the other hand, demonstrates at length that in fact a highly analytic approach to language was as much an element of dramatic theory and practice in the sixteenth century as it was of rhetorical: "[T]he exercises that schoolboys performed, insofar as they grow out of certain beliefs about the nature of language, are not different in kind, although different in effect, from the exercises of the practicing dramatists."[25] Both are supported by a theory "of composition in which *the art as much as the matter* [is] seen as true, [with] that art . . . *made visible by . . . an analysis of its underlying frame*" (16, italics mine). She also cites with approval Ralph Lever's claim that his *The Art of Witcraft* "'doth not onely teach an order to reason wittily of doubtfull matters, . . . But . . . also yeldeth to them, that are cunning and expert . . . , a general understanding to judge of all matters whatsoeuer'," noting in particular that Lever uses the word *art* in Aristotle's "two senses": "It stands for technique, the means by which something is made[,] [b]ut it stands as well for true reason, *an understanding of the precepts by means of which something is made*" (17, italics mine). "Poetic language," therefore, "to the Elizabethans was *always a conscious language* and in origin and intent a rational one" (81, italics mine).

For Shakespeare not to have absorbed, consciously, these and many other lessons, all conducing to the development of an extraordinary artistic consciousness, seems at this point an extravagant claim.

Reading Shakespeare criticism with an ear newly sharpened for its rhetorical nuances, the pattern of criticism's reluctance to confront directly the question of Shakespeare's mind, becomes a very significant one. Even when admitting that there is either a Shakespearean or an Elizabethan mind with which one might engage, the understanding seems implicit almost across the board among the commentators that the subject is to be avoided. Identifying Shakespeare with "nature" is one way of avoiding it, and behind that identification may lie the awareness that alternatives are perilous, in the sense that the range and depth of Shakespeare's mind are manifestly such as to dwarf the capacities of the most comprehensive, equally with the most foolhardy, scholarly challengers—the physics of black holes or the biology of genes are puzzles of perhaps comparable magnitude in the scientific field; if his critics shrink from tackling such a daunting subject straight on it is hardly to be wondered at. That Shakespeare could actually have known what he was doing in all its

richness seems a fantastic proposition, too fantastic to be enter-
tained; on the other hand, that he nonetheless did those things,
deliberately or not, is incontrovertible. The simplest way of resolving this dilemma is to pass it by, which the vast majority of
critics do. Those who do not, like Mable Bruland again, court disaster. This is not to disdain Bruland's work, which contains
many things of interest. And one must also recognize that the
question of Shakespeare's consciousness is one that she could
hardly avoid entirely: as a fundamental structural element in
his dramas, his method of handling time relates directly to the
question of his overall structural control, in which consciousness
becomes a central issue. But by raising the question and then, by
her quick dismissal of it, immediately showing her fear of it
("perhaps the term 'juggler' implies too strongly that Shakespeare was fully conscious of his sleight-of-hand," etc.—) Bruland creates a tension, a dimension of irresolution, in her book
that in the end reduces her other conclusions to little more than
historico-technical trivia. Her thesis is finally mechanical—a
demonstration of the fact that others besides Shakespeare
among his contemporaries also use the "double-time" scheme in
their plays, leading to the egregiously lame conclusion that "neglect of precision in general" in their art is characteristic of "the
spirit of the Elizabethan age."

Bruland's conclusion may be instructively compared with
that of another writer on the same subject, S. C. Sen Gupta, in
his *The Whirligig of Time*. In contrast to Bruland, Sen Gupta
finds in Shakespeare's handling of time an exact parallel with
the use of perspective in Renaissance painting, showing the
same methodological precision and the same calculated awareness of how the method works. "The greatest art is superior to
nature," he says: "There are impossibilities [in Shakespeare's
plays], but they look probable . . .[;] the characters, too, are credible not only 'for the moment' but for all time."[26] Typically, Sen
Gupta does not mention a Shakespearean "consciousness" in his
book, but even in the subject's absence the implication cannot be
blinked that his theory requires an intelligence behind the plays
that to call extraordinary is to fall almost as far short of the
mark as Bruland's unfortunate "neglect of precision" does.

Even though the context of this study is sixteenth-century
conceptions of language, with quaint-sounding antitheses like
"art" vs. "nature" being as deep into the psychology of composi-

tion as the theory of the day goes, when the subject is Shakespeare's "consciousness," failure at least to acknowledge the existence of modern theoretical views on the question of consciousness might be interpreted as willful or the product of fear. It might be noted, incidentally, that neither the word *conscious* nor the antithetical *unconscious* appears in Shakespeare; *unconscious* does not occur at all in English until 1712, according to the *OED,* while its corollary *conscious*, in the general sense of being self-aware, has its first use around the same time as well. If this study shuns involvement with Freud and his followers, however, this is not because their theories would weaken its premises. Rather, it is that modern psychoanalytic theories of the mind as a conscious /unconscious hierarchy are in fact irrelevant to Shakespeare—either because (arguable but unlikely) the unconscious in the Freudian sense did not exist in the sixteenth century, or (more likely) his extraordinary mind simply transcends the Freudian system altogether, overpowering the conscious/unconscious division on which that system depends. *Hamlet* may be a textbook example of the Oedipus complex at work, but *Hamlet* is Shakespeare's creation just as much as the Oedipus complex is Freud's—the same degree of analytic consciousness may be plausibly inferred for either author. It should be remembered too that there are competing theories of consciousness to the Freudian psychoanalytic one even in this century, some of which entail dismissing the whole concept of the "unconscious" as fiction. If Freud's theory of the unconscious would have struck Shakespeare as fantastic, Sartre's comment on that theory might have been Shakespeare's own: "existential[ism]," Sartre says, "rejects the postulate of the unconscious" as a form of lying or *"mauvaise foi."*[27] And if existentialist criticism offers a challenge to Freud, he is an equally tempting target to Derridean deconstructionists. Derrida does his best "to do justice to Freud" as he has titled a recent article, but no concept better lends itself to the deconstructionist method of revealing gaps and inversions in the binary oppositions of western thought than Freud's conscious/unconscious division of the psyche does. The feminist critics have done perhaps the most effective work in deconstructing Freud in the last twenty years, but *"aporia* [sic] or impasses of meaning,"[28] as Terry Eagleton puts it, along the "margins" of Freud's writings invite a similar approach at many different points.

A more compatible entry into modern attempts, few and frag-
mentary as they are, to deal directly with Shakespeare's mind in
criticism, may be the sort of modified Freudianism employed by
commentators such as Leonard Unger and Murray Krieger. The
two have closely related theories, Krieger's actually being ex-
trapolated from Unger's, applying psychoanalytic principles that
Unger finds operative in some of Shakespeare's *characters* to
Shakespeare himself. Unger, writing in the romantic tradition,
treating Shakespeare's characters as "real" people, analyzes the
behavior of the two Henrys, Bolingbroke and his son Hal, in
their respective maneuvering for the crown, demonstrating that
in both cases the line between sincerity and hypocrisy is an impossible one to draw. Unger borrows from Freud's theory of "wit-
work" vs. "dream-work" for his thesis, suggesting that the
apparent hypocrisy in both Henry's and his son's behavior—
Henry's pious claim that he did not actually covet the crown (*2
Henry IV,* 3.1.70–73), and Hal's equally self-justifying rational-
ization of his own loose behavior (the famous "I know you all"
speech of *1 Henry IV* and others)—falls precisely on that border-
line between truth and lies. Both are "artless," or sincere in their
protestations—this is the conscious, avowed, "wit-work" side of
their personalities; but both are at the same time unconsciously
the opposite—that is, rhetoricians and manipulators: Henry's
pose of innocence in his quest for the throne was pure political
strategy; Hal's real but hidden ambition is as cold-eyed and
single-minded as his father's was.[29] Thus Unger demonstrates,
on the basis of Freudian theory, that it is possible to be both
truthful and a liar at the same time. What Krieger does, then,
using the example of Shakespeare's sonnets as the closest thing
to a direct authorial voice the canon offers, is to postulate that a
similar split in Shakespeare himself informs his style in that
work. The sonnets have been admired as "artless," "natural," in
their beauty, but like Hal's or Henry's "sincerity," that apparent
artlessness is in fact the product of a deeper, unconscious art:
"The 'innocen[ce],' is apparent only: on the face of it there is no
guile in the words as they marshal themselves into syntax[;] . . .
what artfulness there is, is artless, though its subtlety demands
our endless search—and admiration. For as the word 'wit' [in
Krieger's title, "The Innocent Insinuations of Wit,"] assures us,
everything has been under a shrewd aesthetic control all
along."[30] The proximity of this description to the similar formulae

of the Renaissance theorists of style like Castiglione and Gracián is striking—down even to the use of the word "wit" in a sense identical to Gracián's—indeed the only significant difference between the two, and it is a very significant one, is Krieger's implication of an "unconscious" element in Shakespeare's creativity, an anachronistic, but more importantly, an unwarranted expedient on Krieger's part, made necessary only by his fear, like Mable Bruland's, of a Shakespeare whose conscious art is of an order altogether beyond his capacity to believe.

Two final examples of astute commentators whose theses hint at the existence of a Shakespearean conscious mind of unparalleled acuity, but whose nerves fail them at the moment of confrontation, may be cited. Norman Rabkin begins his *Shakespeare and the Common Understanding* most promisingly, from my point of view, with the statement, prefacing an extended thematic analysis of *Hamlet*, that "what is problematic in *Hamlet* is not accidental but rather lies at the center of its intention. The confusions in which the play involves us, that is to say, are under Shakespeare's control"[31]—an invocation which suggests that what follows is going to deal directly with Shakespeare rather than by proxy in the usual way through discussion of his Hamlet, Horatio, or Claudius. But, again, like all his peers "[t]hat keep the word of promise to our ear, / And break it to our hope," Rabkin too disappoints, tying his analyses almost wholly to the "personalities" of the characters, Hamlet in particular, and once again foiling our expectations of finally coming to grips with the only real personality to be found anywhere in Shakespeare, that of the author himself. "What is Hamlet's problem?" Rabkin asks. "Not simply to determine the . . . ethical status of revenge, but rather to question his own nature and therefore ours"—woefully anticlimatic stuff indeed to follow from a thesis that seemed to promise more, and that throughout a long book continues to drop hints of a deeper perspective on Shakespeare that never quite reaches the surface of the text. Rabkin is capable, for example, of this penetrating insight into the weakness of both the Ben Jonson and the Mable Bruland critical positions: "However we choose to explain the playwright's unconcern with neoclassical principle, we cannot blame it on ignorance. The more one thinks about the problem, in fact, the clearer it becomes that Shakespeare's violation of the unity of time is a conscious decision" (239). Much of Rabkin's analysis is of the "meta-

dramatic" type, a critical approach that brings one closer in
many ways to the source of the illusion, Shakespeare himself,
than more traditional critical perspectives do. Metadrama to
exist *must* be conscious on the author's part; this is an underlying premise of all such criticism; Rabkin's observations on *Cymbeline*, for example, imply this clearly:

> Shakespeare's game is to engage us in the naive artifice of the
> piece, to make us believe in its reality, and then to make us recog-
> nize the game he is playing. If everything comes out happily, we
> must be aware in the end that it does so because the playwright
> has made it do so by tricks which he has made us acknowledge as
> tricks even while we believe in them. . . . The imaginative delight
> which had ever been a given of Shakespeare's art now becomes
> its *conscious focus*. (210, italics mine)

And the final critical voice I wish to discuss briefly, whose
work approaches but again fails to reach, full awareness of the
personality of Shakespeare himself at work within the plays, is
Jonathan Dollimore and his book *Radical Tragedy: Religion,
Ideology and Power in the Drama of Shakespeare and his Contemporaries*. This recent work is representative of a school of
criticism, which, like the metatheatrical of a few years back, has
given fresh impetus to Shakespeare studies, and in a direction
that is both new and old. The term "ideology" in his title marks
Dollimore as an adherent of the Lacanian-Althusserian-Marx-
ist-psychoanalytic school, while the thesis of his study, that the
theater of Shakespeare and his contemporaries is more politically subversive than it has usually been considered to be,
closely parallels the view of Shakespeare that this study pro-
motes. I call Dollimore's perspective both new and old, because
while the principles on which it is based are clearly of modern
origin—the concept of ideology in the Marxist sense in which he
uses it did not exist before the nineteenth century—he demonstrates at the same time that essentially the same ideological
awareness that Marx postulated for his (and our) day, though
with different terminology, underlay the Renaissance intellectual milieu as well, and is responsible for the shape of Jacobean
tragedy. Dollimore's thesis does not have the rhetorical slant of
the present study, but it supports it in focusing on the fact that
Shakespeare's drama is essentially political, though because of
Dollimore's Marxist orientation he cannot give the "conscious-

ness" question the emphasis nor approach it from the same standpoint as I am doing here. In fact, like the Freudianism of Krieger and Unger, Marxism as a philosophical perspective actually gets the critic off the hook on the question of artistic consciousness, in ways that may satisfy the dialectical materialists among his readers, but that leave the traditional humanist up in the air. The issue is too complex to explore in detail here, but it is a question basically for the Marxist whether full consciousness is possible even among the practitioners of a subversive art, on the theory that since thought is itself a product of socioeconomic forces, it cannot get outside the framework that has shaped it in order to question the premises on which that framework stands. The most it can express in its art is therefore an *unconscious* sense of its own "decentering," to use the fashionable term, its sense of being alienated from the institutions of society, from the "god" that sanctions and supposedly created the social order, and ultimately even from itself. From a plain commonsense standpoint this formulation is distinctly unsatisfying—on the one hand a Marlowe or a Montaigne is capable of *perceiving* that the dominant ideology is a hollow sham, as Dollimore says (quoting Marlowe's Machiavelli in *The Jew of Malta* to the effect that "'religion [is] but a childish toy'" and that "'Might,' not divine right, 'first made kings'"), but as a product of that ideology himself he is incapable (?) of transcending it or thinking outside its terms. If this sounds confusing it is, and quite neatly begs the question once again of the extent to which consciousness is even possible, in a Shakespeare or indeed anyone else. Dollimore is not going to fight "a new round in the old controversy over authorial intentions," as he says, and continues with studied vagueness that while "the author is never the autonomous source of meaning, . . . the articulation of historical process . . . in the author's text might well be intentional. . . . On the other hand, aspects of that historical process may be unconsciously pulled into focus, because, irrespective of intention, it is already there in the language forms, conventions, genres being used."[32] It is perhaps significant that the two sixteenth-century writers in particular that Dollimore singles out as articulating his "subversive" attitude most clearly, are just the two authors usually considered to have influenced Shakespeare intellectually the most: Marlowe, and probably even more importantly, Montaigne.

Reflecting briefly on the spectrum of critical viewpoints on Shakespeare covered by just the last few titles and authors cited, a list that could easily be augmented tenfold, an approach to the question of the Shakespearean consciousness suggests itself that may, as a conclusion to this section of the study, offer a fruitful alternative to all of them. A common element among almost all the schools, it seems, is the tendency to focus on Shakespeare's *characters*, and to speak of them as people in their own right. It goes without saying that this is a perfectly natural approach for commentary on Shakespeare to take, and, from a purely theatrical standpoint at least, in terms of how a character is to be "created" in performance, a perfectly valid one. Literary criticism has long been aware, of course, of the risks of this approach: L. C. Knights's essay on Lady Macbeth's children, mocking the pseudo-biographical school (Bradley's "Let us . . . ask ourselves what we can gather . . . concerning Hamlet as he was just before his father's death") has shamed all its practitioners. But even though modern criticism in general avoids the worst excesses of the neo-Coleridgeans in its discussions of character, it seems impossible for it to avoid that angle altogether, or even to reduce it to something less than the dominant critical focus. So while Dollimore's Marxism prohibits him from theorizing about *Shakespeare's* motives, it does not constrain him apparently in any way from talking about those of his characters: "Antony's conception of his own omnipotence . . . centres on the sexual anxiety . . . which has characterized his relationship with both Cleopatra and Caesar from the outset."[33] My alternative to all of this, then, which is to avoid on principle all talk of the characters as "people," has a theoretical foundation too, and one that brings us back again to our original concern, namely, the art of rhetoric and its special place in the Elizabethan world.

The Elizabethan theater is both shaped and inspired by the art of rhetoric. The practice of declamation as a recognized if marginal branch of the art gives a general sanction for the creation of rhetorical fictions, while the creation of "characters" is a direct extension of a number of specific rhetorical devices, the central one of which is probably the device of *prosopopeia* or personification. The rhetoricans' various definitions of these devices delineate quite precisely what can be done with them in the theatrical medium, a direct connection between the two arts which would surely have been understood by the theater's early practitioners. Peacham, for example, defines the figure *Sermocinatio* as "a forme of speech by which the Orator faineth a person and maketh him speake much or litle according to comelinesse[.] . . . [w]hen the person who the Orator faineth, speaketh all himselfe, then is it *Prosopopeia*, but when the Orator answereth now and then to the question, which the fained person obiecteth to him, it is called *Sermocinatio*.[34]

Connected as it is fundamentally to rhetoric, theater thus shares rhetoric's principles, which means that its practitioners also have, as their first objective, to *persuade*, to convince in words. As an oratorical aid, Quintilian tells us, *prosopopeia* or personification produces "effects of extraordinary sublimity,"[35] a statement which perhaps explains Peacham's Caution, that "the use of it ought to be very rare, then chiefly when the Orator having spent the principall strength of his arguments, is as it were constrained to call for helpe and aide elsewhere."[36] My point in quoting these further observations is to confirm again the Elizabethan dramatist's awareness, and in Shakespeare's case his conscious awareness, of the power of these devices, and also of how that power is liberated by the theatrical medium, while remaining constrained in everyday usage by the old Aristotelean "truth bias" that attaches to the practice of rhetoric outside the theater. If the end of rhetoric is to persuade, the personifications, or "characters," the dramatist creates are the most effective means to that end that the faculty of speech affords, a means that enables the *actual* speaker, Shakespeare himself, to disappear, while his words acquire a life of their own, insinuating themselves into the ears and minds of his audience.

The ideal of rhetoric may be expressed in terms of two related objectives, both of which Shakespearean drama realizes to a degree that has never been superseded. The first is the creation of a "reality" in the auditor's mind that is so convincing in its own right that the auditor actually forgets whose reality it is— namely Shakespeare's; the second and perhaps even more important goal is that for the first illusion to work, the auditor must not see that he is being worked on, a condition that places an even greater demand on the skill of the dramatist, and one that Shakespeare is again more than adequate to. The "reality" of his characters to both theater audiences and critics is testimony to his success in meeting both objectives. It almost comes as a shock then when we read something in criticism like James L. Calderwood's comment on *Romeo and Juliet* to the effect that "free will, necessity, and other crucial matters of belief about reality are from the standpoint of poetics merely so much grist for the dramatist's mill"[37]—we had forgotten that neither chance nor determinism have any role to play in Shakespeare's theatrical world, a world over which he has absolute and permanent control. To explore the rhetorical aspects of that world is the task of this study, and seeing the characters as people instead of the rhetorical devices that they actually are, is perhaps the greatest obstacle that we have to overcome in doing so. It should be remembered in this connection that the word *character* did not acquire its novelistic meaning of "fictional personage" until Fielding used it in that sense in the 1740s. In Shakespeare's day, and as he uses it in his plays, the term was associated exclusively with the practice of writing, and it had a variety of applications. It meant letters first, and also handwriting ("Here is the hand . . . of the Duke: You know the character"), but the suggestion of an individual style in the writer, and the germ as well of the word's later association with the concept of an individual personality were present in some of its uses as well—the Sonnets' connection of the words *mind* and *character* is a significant one, even though the primary reference is to *printing*:

> O that record could with a backward look,
> Even of five hundred courses of the sun,
> Show me your image in some antique book,
> Since mind at first in character was done.

The "character," a "sketch . . . of a person illustrating concretely the essential characteristics of [an] abstraction,"[38] was a popular literary exercise in the schools of the Renaissance, W. G. Crane reminds us, derived presumably from the rhetorical figure *charactirismus*, "the efficion or pycture of the body or mynde," in the words of Richard Sherry. The "ideas" of Hermogenes, with *decorum* at their head, we remember, were also sometimes called "characters," Annabel Paterson informs us, an usage that again reinforces the link between the rhetorical and the mimetic principles,[39] showing them as basically a single art.

4

"Invisible" Rhetoric and the
Shakespearean Allegory

If I have succeeded to this point in at least intriguing, if hardly expecting to convince the reader with my central thesis, that Shakespeare is a conscious artist, it remains to me both to validate that thesis in his writing and to connect it to his artistic aims. I have suggested that there is a paradox in the practice of rhetoric in the sixteenth century, in its carryover from the academy to the court—talked about in terms of the "art" vs. "nature" question in both its literary and social applications. Another way in which the paradox may be formulated, to relate it more closely to the subject of this study, is to say that rhetoric has two antithetical goals for its Elizabethan practitioners, the goals of rendering simultaneously *visible* and *invisible* the rhetorical skill of the user, courtier or poet. In the academic context, first, where the aim is to teach the principles of rhetoric, and where the discipline is conceived as a highly complex and structured system— comparable, say, to grammar in its complexity—all its uses are geared to visibility. In exercises that range from simple repetition of the instructor's dogmatic assertions, to the complex declamatory expositions that advanced students were expected to produce, the student demonstrates his mastery of rhetorical technique. In this manner, or in this special context, attention is drawn deliberately both to the rhetoric itself and to its creator. This is the public or "epideictic" art of rhetoric, by which distinguished practitioners had gained renown from the time of Cicero himself to that of his sixteenth-century peers like Vives and Ascham, whose fame in his office of "Public Orator" at Cambridge led directly to his appointment as Princess Elizabeth's tutor. It is not difficult to see, then, that the focus of the discpline must shift radically when the aspiring orator leaves the academy and takes his newly certified skills into the social, and particularly the political arena. Precisely at this point does the political thrust of the study, in the Aristotelean sense of the term ($\pi o \lambda \iota \tau \iota \kappa \eta$),[1] come to bear, *persuasive results* now becoming the test of the orator's skill, rather than the elaborateness, felicity, and originality of his language as expressed in images and figures.

Much has been written in the last thirty years about what George Williamson first called the "Anti-Ciceronian Movement"[2] in sixteenth-century rhetoric. Both Williamson and his followers give primarily an academic focus to their discussions, as indeed the sixteenth century itself did—it was Cicero vs. Seneca for dominance as a stylistic model—but Williamson is quite aware that the movement had a political dimension as well. I suggest, in fact, that in terms of the perspective on sixteenth-century life this study is developing, the real issue in the debate *is* political— that like much of the literary and political activity of the period this debate too is essentially a theatrical spectacle—the roles are played out in a pseudo-classical setting, but the conflict at the core of the drama itself is strictly contemporary. The real issue is the one we are dealing with here, the fact that ornate diction, because of its very ornateness, may be rhetorically less effective than a supposedly simpler style that calls less attention to the speaker and more to his argument. The origins of the debate are academic, as Williamson says, tracing it back to the publication of Erasmus's *Ciceronianus* in 1528, but even in that theoretical work it is significant that a part-time, though hardly amateur, literary personality like Thomas More cannot be passed over for discussion. No academic, he, "immersed in the floods of royal and state business[,]" and certainly no Ciceronian, with "hardly . . . a glance to spare for the cultivation of eloquence," nonetheless "in sophisticated polish [More] is no whit inferior to Cicero,"[3] says Erasmus. A key later figure in the movement, as Williamson also points out, who had similarly to be aware of the political limitations of the Ciceronian style, was Francis Bacon, whose words in *The Advancement of Learning* spoken against "*Copia* [copiousness] of speech" used "to . . . an excess" are among the most memorable in the period. Effective argument languished in the previous generation, Bacon points out, for men began to hunt more after words than matter; more after the choiceness of phrase, and the round and plain composition of the sentence, and the sweet falling of the clauses, and the varying and illustration of their works with tropes and figures, than after the weight of matter, . . . soundness of argument, . . . or depth of judgment. Then grew the flowing and watery vein of Osorius, the Portugal bishop, to be in price. Then did Sturmius spend such infinite and curious pains upon Cicero the Orator, and Hermogenes the Rhetorician . . . [.] Then did . . . Ascham . . . almost deify Cicero and Demosthenes . . . . In sum, the whole inclination and bent of those times was rather towards *copia* than weight.[4]

The paradoxical requirement of simultaneous visibility and invisibility in the practice of rhetoric in the sixteenth century suggests an interpretive approach to Elizabethan literature, and specifically to Shakespeare, that brings both sides of the paradox into focus. The literature of the period operates, in other words, on two levels—one, the academic or visible level, in which the author displays his mastery of rhetorical technique for the reader to see and appreciate, and in which "rhetoric" is taken as consisting essentially in textbook learning; and two, the political or persuasive level, in which the analysis focuses not on technique but on results—no academic exercise now, the work becomes instead a practical lesson in persuasion, with a whole set of new and more subtle criteria entering into its interpretation. Theater is on this level the ideal literary medium, offering scope for the creative use of persuasive rhetoric beyond that available in any other context.

A number of rather complex theoretical considerations come into play with this last statement. Shakespeare wrote both for the stage and for private reading, and could hardly have been unaware of major differences in an author's relations with his audience in moving from the one to the other form. *Publication*, as an option open to an author in either form, is also a complicating factor in the world of literature, the rhetorical implications of which could not have been lost on an aspiring literary professional of Shakespeare's generation. Scholarship has no evidence and can therefore offer only tentative opinions on the question of whether the publication of any of his plays during his lifetime was sought or authorized by Shakespeare himself. Alexander, for example, while observing sensibly that in general publication was not considered advantageous since it "might

affect adversely . . . takings at the theater," opines that "Shakespeare and his company . . . were not unwilling to print plays
that had become well known through frequent performance."[5]
Chambers similarly has "no reason to suppose" that most of the
so-called "good" quartos "were not issued with the assent of the
company."[6] I, on the other hand, will make a preliminary but considered statement of the contrary opinion here, that Shakespeare himself would probably not have wanted his plays to be
published at all while he was alive. Chambers can find "no
reason" to think he would have opposed such publication, but he
supplies at the same time no reason to think he would have supported it. I can give him reasons why Shakespeare would not
want publication. Some of the practical economic reasons Alexander has already touched on, but the rhetorical reasons have
never before to my knowledge been considered. But they are
clear enough: that his success rhetorically (in deception) depends
to a very significant extent on his audience *not* having the opportunity to read and reflect at their leisure on what they have
seen and heard in the theater. This is a general principle that
applies to all of Shakespeare's plays, and one that simple common sense suggests that he could not have been unaware of.[7]

It is difficult four hundred years after the event to reenter the
mind of that period and recover the view that his contemporaries had of Shakespeare, but it should be remembered that to
the vast majority of his contemporaries, including quite possibly
even a majority of the literary community, knowledge of Shakespeare was confined to seeing him in the theater, through the
performance of his plays. Just about exactly half (eighteen) of
the Folio plays were never published in his lifetime, and of the
nineteen that were, four or possibly five[8] exist only in "bad" quartos. Today, on the other hand, with our complete Shakespeares
always to hand, with access to scholarly editions by the score of
the individual plays, and with the innumerable structural analyses and probings of every scene Shakespeare ever concocted
that now fill the literature, everything implausible or thought to
be patched together in his writings is not only visible but has
been argued over for decades. Can we return to a view of Shakespeare where none of this was possible, and where the sheer
rhetorical virtuosity of a live performance literally overwhelmed
any possibility of the auditor leaving the theater with anything
at all on his mind but the memory of brilliance? Shakespeare

knew perfectly well that to print a script was potentially to open a play's secrets to intelligent analysts, and to make texts available for this kind of work would hardly be the way to maintain a reputation for theatrical wizardry and power.

A modern analogy for the concerns reflected here can be found in the efforts that Fred Astaire made in his last years to keep video tapes of his famous dance movies off the market, tapes which made possible for the first time the minute dissection of his work, turning it, at least potentially, into a mechanical process, and stripping his magic of its power. While it cannot be said that books like Bruland's or Sen Gupta's, for example, on the techniques of time manipulation in Shakespeare's plays, exactly "strip his magic of its power," still the security of knowing that such analyses could not be done in his own day could hardly have been other than satisfying to him. The mention of such books may in fact serve as a reminder again that perhaps the worry about exposure that I impute to Shakespeare was either not there, or I exaggerate its importance to him. I said that his concern was with what an "intelligent analyst" might be able to do in the way of dissection of his work. When he saw what actually was done, or as little of it as ever saw print at any rate, confined to things like Meres's tired platitudes and Jonson's knee-jerk neo-classicism, he need have felt no fear about his secrets not remaining safe. Indeed we may come full circle on this point, finally, and conclude that because his art turned out apparently to be proof against the "astonishingly primitive"[9] critical weapons that could be mustered in his day, that Chambers's suggestion that he did not oppose publication and may have even collaborated in it is perhaps as reasonable as the alternative. Perhaps the last word on the subject should be left, however, to his literary executors Heminges and Condell, who appear to have included *all* previously published versions of his plays in their blanket reference to the "diverse stolne, and surreptitious copies, maimed, and deformed by the fraudes and stealthes of iniurious impostors[.]"

I have suggested that sixteenth-century rhetoric in general, and Shakespearean in particular, operates on two levels, the academic, in which the measure of rhetorical accomplishment is visibility of the writer's technique, and the political or persuasive, having the opposite aim. It can also be seen that in some ways, again paradoxically, mastery of the first objective may aid in the achievement of the second. The display of a formidable technique may become, from the academic perspective, an end in itself, like a textbook illustration or a case study, inviting analysis as a technical exercise and effectively insulating the writer himself from either questioning or even interest. Alvin Kernan refers to Shakespeare's "quietly *ostentatious* use of nearly every known rhetorical figure" in his plays[10] (italics mine). And when, on top of this, the speech, a stylistic *tour de force* bristling with rhetorical flourishes, comes from one of the writer's "characters," then his deeper manipulative purpose is yet further concealed. Technique on one level, "character" on another, both become parts of the writer's deliberate disguise. There is, however, a third level in this process as well, one which in a sense combines the other two, and which I will now designate the allegorical or philosophical. Or it may also be called the *stylistic*, and in this last term is its connection to the first two levels perhaps most clearly conveyed. All three terms require clarification. I can begin that clarification by going back first to the sixteenth century itself, and the allegorical interpretive tradition still very much alive as a carryover from the rich heritage of medieval scholarship. An assumption of multiple levels in a literary work—"senses" is the word Sir John Harington used in his *Briefe Apology for Poetry* of 1591—was part of the literary experience of every educated reader in the sixteenth century. Harington's "senses" in fact quite closely parallel the three levels of rhetoric that I have outlined here:

> The ancient Poets haue indeed wrapped as it were in their writings diuers and sundry meanings, which they call the senses or mysteries thereof. First of all for the litterall sence (as it were the vtmost barke or ryne) they set downe in manner of an historie the acts and notable exploits of some persons worthy memorie: then in the same fiction, as a second rine and somewhat more fine, as it were nearer to the pith and marrow, they place the Morall sence profitable for the actiue life of man, approuing vertuous actions and condemning the contrarie. Manie times also vnder the selfesame words they comprehend some true vnderstanding of naturall Philosophie, or sometimes of politike gouernement, and now and then of diuinitie: and these same sences that comprehend so excellent knowledge we call the Allegorie, which Plutarch defineth to be when one thing is told, and by that another is vnderstood.[11]

Comparable formulations to these of Harington's come up frequently in Elizabethan criticism. Richard Stanyhurst's 1582 translation of Virgil, to which he says Ascham's *Schoolmaster* inspired him, is prefaced with the observation that Virgil, for full understanding, must be read on more than one level:

> What deepe and rare poynctes of hydden secrets Virgil hath sealde vp in his twelue bookes of *Eneis* may easelye appeere too such reaching wyts as bend theyre endewours too thee vnfolding thereof, not onlye by gnibling vpon thee outward ryne of a supposed historie, but also by groaping thee pyth that is shrind vp wythin thee barck and bodye of so exquisit and singular a discourse.... [T]hee shallow reader may bee delighted wyth a smooth tale, and thee diuing searcher may bee aduantaged by sowning a pretiouse treatise.[12]

Quintilian's definition of allegory would certainly have been well known in Shakespeare's day, and is probably as clear a definition of "conventional" allegory as has ever been given. As Carolynn Van Dyke notes, it is the definition that almost all discussions of the subject still begin by quoting. Allegory, says Quintilian, "'presents either one thing in words and another in meaning, or even something quite opposed'."[13] The principle of allegory applied to Shakespeare, then, is as simple as this definition—that it does apply to him in any way is quite another matter, of course, and a proposition that would be hotly debated, indeed, probably roundly rejected, by most scholars today. Assuming for the moment, however, that it may apply, its application would mean that in addition to the literal, narrative, and even dramatic levels of his works, to which Harington and Stanyhurst both refer, the plays contain a deeper or philosophical level of meaning that is at the same time also part of the author's intention. Quintilian's definition implies that the allegory may even contradict the narrative level of the work, functioning, in effect, as a commentary on that narrative level, and showing up the "truths" that are articulated on that level as something that the author wishes deliberately to undermine. It is important also, I suggest, that Quintilian's definition does not limit allegory to any specific philosophical function—the inculcation of a particular moral or theological view, for example, which has often been taken as the basis of allegory. Rather, an allegory may relate to any subject whatsoever, any aspect of life about which an author wishes to make a forceful, *and partially concealed*, statement—"to insinuate and glance at . . . matters . . . such as per chance had not been safe to have been disclosed in any other sort," as Puttenham,[14] with typical politic delicacy, puts it—indeed calling "*Allegoria*," one suspects for perhaps this very reason, "the chief ringleader and captaine of all other figures, either in the Poeticall or oratorie science."[15]

I stress this question of allegory's open-endedness for two reasons: first, because the focus of this study is exclusively on *rhetoric*, as the sixteenth century understood that term; and therefore any allegorical interpretation of Shakespeare that may be proposed here will pertain to that subject alone. And second, rhetoric is itself intimately related in that period to most of the other more familiar applications of allegory, in areas like politics, morality, and philosophy. Here, the moral or philosophic issue is a rhetorical one—where issues of truth, manipulation, and power are examined, and the allegorical key relates to the role of language in all of these basic areas of human life. The first principle of allegory is the existence of a "message" on the allegorical level, which puts the work into a larger philosophical frame of some kind. William Empson, in his *The Structure of Complex Words*, extends this principle into what he describes as a "correspondence" between two levels of meaning: "Part of the function of an allegory is to make you feel that two levels of being correspond to one another in detail, and indeed that there is some underlying reality, something in the nature of things, which makes this happen. Either level may illuminate the other."[16] Empson's definition reinforces the point made earlier about Shakespeare's allegory, that both the "visibility" (academic) and "invisibility" (political) levels may be incorporated into the "message" of the third. The message itself would be about how rhetoric works, and the deliberate use of disguise, both in terms of style and in the creation of "characters" (personifications), is the key to its interpretation. The message here has a subtle and paradoxical twist, however, in that it is, in part at least, *about* invisibility. This is the point that has made it difficult to interpret, indeed that for almost four hundred years has blocked awareness even of its existence, but that opens up our author to light immediately when the principle is grasped. I have said that on its first two rhetorical levels Shakespeare's art involves two things: visibility—where rhetorical technique, including the poetic, is viewed as an end in itself, and flourished deliberately before the hearer as such, to dazzle him with wonder, and cause him to put off any search for an author behind the brilliant display; and secondly, we have in a sense the opposite quality to this, invisibility—where the persuasion becomes such a compelling force, so convincing and so real, that it overwhelms any possibility of doubt in the auditor's mind, while the author himself fades from sight, as his creation magically assumes the mantle of nature. Taken together, these two qualities in Shakespeare's art form a combination of irresistible potency, and one that seeks deliberately *to undermine its own third-level allegorical message*, the message of invisibility, the implication that the whole "great game of rhetoric"[17] is political, played for power, and that the poet, and preeminently *this* poet, plays it best. It is only by distancing ourselves from the power of that rhetoric by a deliberate act of will that we can find the "lost" personality of Shakespeare himself, read his message, and understand his aim.

Allegory is the resort of an author who has a deep truth to convey but who is aware of either the limitations or the risks in too direct a statement of that truth. If his truth is religious he risks profaning its sacred mystery by presenting it baldly; if political he may be risking his neck; if artistic, the ornament of allegory is calculated to enhance his vision's power. George Gascoigne spoke in 1575 of the paramount necessity of avoiding the *"trita et obvia"* in art; one should heighten one's vision, of love, say, "by the example of some history, . . . discover[ing one's] *disquiet in shadows per Allegorium"*[18] (italics mine), words that Shakespeare would have understood as well as he understood both More's attempt in *Utopia* and Spenser's in *The Fairie Queene* respectively to conceal and to reveal their moral and political agendas under an allegorical covering. The late Elizabethan writer would have the preeminent example of Spenser before him, of course, either as a model to be emulated, or, as Shakespeare seems to have viewed the author of *The Fairie Queene*, an anachronism, practitioner of an allegorical method as old-fashioned as the politico/religious vision it tries to revive. Understanding the structure of his own society fully, especially in terms of its theatricalization of power, Shakespeare also understands that an authentic allegorical representation of that society must proceed in a manner opposite to Spenser's, and paradoxical: revelation *through concealment*—for his allegorical truth to be seen the author himself must not be; only by his own total silence may his speech be heard. No expression of the essential aim of Shakespeare's rhetorical allegory is more simultaneously accurate and concise than Marshall McLuhan's famous aphorism from the 1960s, "the medium is the message." In Shakespeare, the medium is the stage, and the message is that rhetoric (=eloquence=poetry=artifice=style=theater) not only defines but actually creates what we call "reality" or the world. The process works two ways as well, as Empson says: in the play rhetoric is applied imaginatively (i.e., poetically), with deliberate art creating a world that is an imitation of reality; in the real world rhetoric is applied politically, with artifice equally deliberate (if arguably less conscious in some instances) creating a world that is an imitation of the stage.[19]

In terms of Empson's "correspondence" idea, there is a whole other side of Shakespeare's allegorical message in addition—its "visibility" component, where, after first "disappearing" behind his mastery of rhetorical technique and the personifications he creates to employ it, the author once again emerges visibly as himself. The two processes take place simultaneously and are directly connected; indeed, so simply does the author's "reappearance" occur that it requires considerable concentration even to see it happening. I have remarked previously in this study that some of its central premises are grounded on what amount to truisms about Shakespeare, observations that have been made for centuries, but which we will be approaching here from a new and radical perspective. The deceptive simplicity of what I call Shakespeare's "reappearance" in his plays, then, achieved at the very moment when he is using all of his rhetorical resources to do the opposite, is an instance of such an elementary yet radical principle at work. I used the word *stylistic* earlier in speaking of the Shakespearean allegory, and it is in this context that that term's relevance becomes clear. Behind all of his characters, in other words, as behind the mastery of rhetorical technique that enables him to do literally whatever he wishes with the language, lies the inescapable fact of a personal style, the unique imprint of the man himself.

An important work on the subject of Renaissance allegory, and one that complements the view of allegory I am developing here, that a personal revelation of the artist himself can be a major allegorical theme in that period, is Michael Murrin's 1969

The Veil of Allegory. While much of Murrin's argument is traditional—he points out, for instance, that allegory always has two
audiences, the masses who understand only its narrative level,
and the adepts who are tuned to the deeper meaning[20]—his main
point is that while traditional allegory remained popular in the
Renaissance, new poetic criteria were in the process of supplant-
ing its principles even as Spenser was creating the monumental
work that represents its historical culmination. Murrin holds
that traditionally, allegory was identified with the revelation of a
"divine truth" (169) of some kind, a moral and theological vision
that is independent of the poet himself, whose role is that merely
of agent or conduit through which the divine voice speaks. While
this was the view that Spenser and Lodge held of the poet's function, writers representative of the age's more modern, neo-classi-
cal, intellectual wing, Sidney, Webbe, and Jonson, believed
instead with Horace that the "truth" the poet revealed was not
God's, but rather the poet's own. The poet's inspiration to create
may be a divine gift, but if there was revelation in poetry itself it
was human and individual, not theological:

> Jonson and Webbe saw this divinity in Horatian terms. The poet's
> ability to make came from heaven more than any truth he might
> try to express. For them divine inspiration . . . could be repre-
> sented by the old phrase: *"Orator fit, poeta nascitur."* The poet,
> "raunging within the Zodiack of his owne wit," astonished his au-
> dience and revealed his personal genius. (170)

To Murrin this change from a theological to a personal revelation as the new mission of poetry represents "the end of allegory," as he terms it, and he attempts to demonstrate that
Sidney and Jonson took a generally disparaging view of allegory
because of their unconscious perception of this shift. One way
they betrayed this attitude, Murrin thinks, is in their dislike of
Spenser's pseudo-archaic diction in *The Fairie Queene.* The new
"oratorical," as opposed to the older stylized "allegorical" poetry,
is geared to satisfying its audience's expectations directly, rather
than indirectly, through "the veil of allegory," which requires
elaborate interpretation of the poet's aim (178–89). While again
there are implications here that square with my own—the implication of a direct expression of meaning rather than one that
requires a gloss or key, for example—Murrin's thesis is still
faulty, I believe, chiefly because, like many others', its definition

of allegory is restrictive, limiting the message of allegory to "divine truth" rather than seeing it, as Quintilian and even Spenser actually did, as including any aspect of human experience whatsoever, large or small, within its scope. In fact, both Sidney and Jonson are allegorists themselves. Sidney, for example, makes explicit identification, in both the *Astrophel* and the *Defense*, of various classical mythological characters with the ideal virtues to which men may aspire; and Jonson in a sense communicates the opposite allegorical message in a number of his plays, naming and creating his "characters" intentionally as embodiments of the vices of excess to which humans are also subject.[21] The modern poet whose work actually influenced *The Fairie Queene* most directly is the Italian Tasso, who is praised in the famous letter to Raleigh that prefaced that poem not merely as an allegorist, but specifically for his vision of "Ethice," or the "virtues of a *private man*" (italics mine).[22] Tasso himself defined allegory in a heroic poem in similar terms to these, as "none other than the Glass and Figure of Humane Life"; the *mimesis* aspect of a poem gives us the exciting externals of the hero's character, while the allegory opens up the inner man: "Allegory respecteth the Passions, the Opinions and Customs, not only as they do appear, but principally in their being hidden and inward; and more obscurely doth express them with Notes . . . mystical, such as only the Understanders of the Nature of things can fully comprehend."[23]

The combination of all these views, then, capped by Tasso's, gives us a conception of allegory for the later Elizabethan period that conforms almost exactly with what I have suggested Shakespeare is doing allegorically in his dramas. In fact the "message" of that allegory is the thesis of this study, namely, of the hidden abstract principle of *persuasion* itself, as both the soul of the culture and the motive for its obsession with rhetoric. It is a message both universal and personal, speaking as much of Shakespeare himself as of his society. It transcends the plays' subject matter entirely, concerning itself exclusively with the "how" rather than the "what" of Shakespeare's writings; while all three rhetorical levels of which we have spoken make important contributions to its meaning.

The relevance of the term *stylistic*, as a key to Shakespeare's allegory, and thus a means of entry into his mind, should also be clear at this point. Indeed, even in broaching this particular subject we once again enter the realm of the obvious—of the literary truism, one of the most venerable of which is the maxim probably best known to us now in the version framed by the seventeenth-century French man of letters Buffon, in his *Discours Sur Le Style,* "*le style c'est l'homme meme*"—"the style is the man himself." It was probably in the sixteenth century, when the philosophy of individualism exploded so spectacularly in the political and social arenas in England, that this idea became established in the public, and particularly the literary mind. F. W. Bateson, in his 1934 book *English Poetry and the English Language,* suggests that criticism and poetry awakened simultaneously in the 1580s to the revolutionary awareness that "vitality," or "life," as they termed it, was the highest poetic quality, reflecting the organic nature of language, and that the achievement of this quality was linked directly to a poet's stylistic individuality: "[t]he test of the style's vitality is that it shall reflect the idiosyncrasies of its author."[24] Bateson quotes several contemporary commentators as backing for the view that Shakespeare's generation was closely attuned to Buffon's principle, among them Nash, Puttenham, and Jonson. Of all of Shakespeare's contemporaries it is once again Puttenham who proves to be the most discerning in his observations, expressing the possibility of a personal revelation through style in terms that could scarcely be made clearer:

> Stile is a constant & continuall phrase or tenour of speaking and writing, extending to the whole tale or processe of the poeme or historie, and not properly to any peece or member of a tale: but is of words speeches and sentences together, a certaine contriued forme and qualitie, many times naturall to the writer, many times his peculier by election and arte, and such as either he keepeth by skill, or holdeth on by ignorance, and will not or peraduenture cannot easily alter into any other.... And because this continuall course and manner of writing or speech sheweth the/matter and disposition of the writers minde, more than one or few words or sentences can shew, therefore there be that haue called stile, the image of man [*mentis character*] for man is but his minde, and as his minde is tempered and qualified, so are his speeches and language at large, and his inward conceits be the mettall of his minde, and his manner of vtterance the very warp & woofe of his conceits.[25]

It may have been Shakespeare's generation who had the most refined grasp of this idea—Murrin too believes that it was; he points to Jonson's remark in his *Discoveries*, to the effect that "a poet's style images his mind,"[26] but had Shakespeare lived fifty years earlier and had Vives for his tutor he would have received a similar lesson from him, or had he lived to read Robert Burton eighty years after Vives yet another restatement of the same precept would have greeted him there.[27] Indeed our modern criticism has by no means allowed the idea to languish, despite the efforts of Eliot and the New Critics to depersonalize the poetic art. Wallace Stevens, for example, has theorized about the inseparable link between poetry and personality in a manner that compliments my thesis in an almost prophetic way. He defines poetry, first, as "a process in the personality of the poet"[28] and adds that "this is the element, the force, that keeps poetry a living thing (45). The process of poetry, however, is not one that "involves the poet as subject" (45) directly; Aristotle rightly holds that a poet "should say very little *in propria persona*," a formula that "precludes direct egotism. On the other hand, without indirect egotism there can be no poetry. There can be no poetry without the personality of the poet" (46). As usual, of course, when one attributes or, perhaps better to say, when one desires to attribute similar views to the elusive "Shakespearean consciousness" one can find little directly to support the claim. If, however, it is self-evident that "our style bewrays us," as Burton said, and as it apparently was to discerning contemporaries of Shakespeare, there is little reason to suppose that the same was not equally so to the bard himself. In another of his critical essays, Stevens speaks of what he strikingly terms "the pressure of reality"—the world of hard fact within which the poet, like the rest of us, lives. I might borrow that phrase to suggest the way in which the truisms of his age would be forced upon Shakespeare's knowledge. Indeed, we recall Shakespeare's own similar use of the word *pressure* in the famous passage from *Hamlet* cited earlier. And there is further direct evidence in at least one place, sonnet 76, that he was familiar with this stylistic adage, a circumstance that makes it hard to argue that he did not see his own art in the same terms:

> Why is my verse so barren of new pride?
> So far from variation or quick change?
> Why, with the time, do I not glance aside
> To new-found methods and to compounds strange?
> Why write I still all one, ever the same,

> And keep invention in a noted weed,
> That every word doth almost tell my name,
> Showing their birth, and where they did proceed?

It is an interesting speculation also, in this context, to consider how Shakespeare may have viewed the artistic goals, and their links to style, of the only other Renaissance writer whose popularity, attunement to the deepest currents of his age, and intellectual authority approached his own at the end of the 1590s, Michel de Montaigne. Absolute stylistic opposites that they are, with Montaigne's rhetorical strategy focusing on the creation of that carefully crafted speaking voice that generations have taken for Montaigne's own, and with Shakespeare attempting something even more audacious, utilizing all the resources of rhetoric for the specific purpose of avoiding detection by his audience altogether, can one dare to suggest that the Shakespearean anonymity may actually have its origins in a deliberate decision to do the opposite stylistically from what his great contemporary had achieved? Without pursuing this speculation any further, one observation relevant to the present subject may nevertheless be made based on it, and this is that the real Montaigne is probably as far from the rhetorical image of him we meet in the essays, as the real Shakespeare is close to the "non-image" of himself he has created for the plays; and that both are fully conscious of the rhetorical strategies their respective approaches entail. What this paradoxical-sounding pronouncement is meant to demonstrate, with what I hope might be some rhetorical force, is that the man William Shakespeare himself, his personal quirks and biases all hanging out, is actually front and center all the time in his plays, every bit as much as Montaigne is present personally in *his* writings; and this notwithstanding the apparently much more direct revelation of Montaigne's own character that greets us there. "I have no more made my booke than my booke hath made me. A book consubstantiall to his author," said Montaigne,[29] but Shakespeare would have understood his meaning and how it could apply to himself with equal force, looking at his own very substantial "book" of plays. That Shakespeare himself is not seen in his plays means only that his rhetorical trickery has worked for nearly four hundred years, just as he must have known it would—and known as well, of course, that the rhetorical sleight-of-hand by which he achieves his "invisibility" must ultimately be recognized as such and seen through—"since all alike my songs and praises be."

The force that links all three levels of Shakespeare's rhetoric together, completing the circle of his allegory, and revealing what I will call his philosophy, as opposed to his mere use, of rhetoric, is the concept of style. "The meaning of life is style" in the Renaissance, as we have noted before, hitherto, however, focusing only on the political side of the stylistic equation, and forgetting that it has another, personal side, one whose authentic revelation must, to speak figuratively, peel away the deceptions of the equation's other side as fast as they are put in place. The revelation of which I speak is simultaneously of the man himself and of the age—half Adlerian nightmare of power lust and egotism, half palace of beauty, shimmering in all the imaginative richness of a Platonic dream—in either or both of these aspects it has one source, style, in its many manifestations, as rhetoric, as poetry, as theater. That Shakespeare's allegory be grasped, then, it is necessary to see him doing both things at once, creating the illusion of life, through the combination of language and performance that is so absorbing as to make it well-nigh impossible for its hearers to see beyond it, but at the same time distancing himself deliberately from that illusion, so that its actual basis in the man himself and in the arts that he uniquely commands may also be seen by the truly discerning in his audience. The element of paradox in this interpretation of his rhetorical aims cannot be missed, but I would insist again that Shakespeare is perfectly aware of what that paradox involves and remains totally in control on both levels. That the first half of his artistic endeavor succeed, thus, the second half must be missed by (most of) his audience; he must prove his ability to do anything he wishes with language; and he *has* proved it, as the history of Shakespeare criticism for the past four hundred years attests, focusing as it does, exclusively, on the illusory aspects of his achievement, in the characters and themes of the plays themselves. But at the same time, the deeper personal level of meaning is there all the time too in his plays, and not merely "there," but "there" front and center. In his rhetoric's second, persuasive, level Shakespeare disappears, and disappears successfully, yet the actual significance of that "disappearance" can be neither appreciated nor fully understood without making the leap to the third, allegorical level, the level of his reappearance. The medium is the message, that aphorism capturing the essence of Shakespeare's allegory: as the *medium takes us in*, lulling us into accepting something as both substantial and believable which in fact is not, the message is that we *can be fooled*, that we can build a perfectly satisfactory reality on thin air, and never think to question. To make the leap to the allegorical level of Shakespeare's rhetoric, we must learn to look at him rhetorically in a way that I do not believe he has been looked at before. When the subject of rhetoric is raised at all in discussions of Shakespeare, it is almost invariably looked at solely from the academic standpoint, analyzing the language in his plays in terms of the use he makes, usually ostentatiously, of the tropes, schemes, and figures that are the discipline's principal apparent *raison d'être* in the sixteenth century. It may be understood that these devices have persuasion as their ultimate aim, but a focus on that aspect of their use is rare, to say the least, in criticism, notwithstanding its manifest importance, as the plays themselves attest, as much technically as philosophically, to Shakespeare. To name the rhetorical figures Shakespeare uses in his plays is to operate, rather mechanically I might add, on the first level only of their rhetorical structure; to talk about how and why he uses the figures, as his "characters" try their rhetorical wiles on each other, is to move to the second level of that structure, the one that I say is rarely broached, but that has material in it to be the subject of virtually any number of book-length rhetorical studies of almost any of the plays. When we move to the third rhetorical level, however, we move totally out of the world of the play; there is only one rhetorician in the picture at this point, Shakespeare himself, and likewise only one persuasive target, his audience. And the rhetoric that is employed on this level, it may almost go without saying, is of an order of persuasiveness far beyond that of either of the other two; it is here that the "illusion of nature," the greatest of Shakespeare's artistic secrets, really comes into its own.

One of the other paradoxes of rhetoric as a discipline is that when it is subject to analysis its effectiveness as rhetoric must diminish, because it is susceptible of being viewed ironically, or with a skeptical eye. On the first two rhetorical levels of his plays, Shakespeare operates deliberately in this manner. Both the textbook examples of figures and tropes with which the plays are loaded, and the extraordinary persuasive permutations performed by the characters using these techniques invite admiration and analysis for their own sake. This is the perfect means of diverting attention from the puppet-master Shakespeare, the real rhetorician, controlling us, his audience, with the same ease and an even subtler skill than those exhibited by the master rhetoricians among his characters, many of whom manipulate their various audiences with devices and shifts of staggering dexterity, approaching rhetorical perfection, and effectively irresistible in their own right. Lost in admiration of the rhetorico/poetic wonders that everywhere surround us on the first two levels alone of Shakespeare's plays, we can do nothing but wander the mazes he has built for us, totally losing sight of the even higher levels of rhetorical finesse of which Shakespeare remains master. On these levels character, plot, and rhetorical flourishes themselves become tools of his manipulative trade, distractions to divert and mislead, supplying the final push into limbo of the image of the creator, and breaking the last thread that connects us to him, the supreme controlling power who no longer exists in his own work.

The "illusion of nature" he achieves in his language is a particularly important conception in terms of the relations between Shakespeare the man and his live audience, whether in the theater or in the study. There are two elements to this success, at least as far as our modern inability to see through Shakespeare's rhetorical illusions is concerned. The first, relating directly to our modern understanding of rhetoric, is the fact that, generally speaking, rhetorical awareness is not deeply planted in our twentieth-century consciousness; technical rhetoric is little taught today. As both Aristotle and his sixteenth-century followers knew, however, rhetoric is actually *used* by everyone all the time; in many ways it is synonymous with speech itself; but it is possible to use rhetoric either consciously or simply instinctively: the norm in our own day is largely instinctive use. I. A. Richards observes in his *Philosophy of Rhetoric* that rhetoric is a subject which "we all in a sense know extremely well already; . . . something so simple that it is hard to think of,"[30] catching in that observation one of our principal present-day difficulties in picking up Shakespeare's rhetorical cues. Modern linguistic philosophy also recognizes the universality of the persuasive principle in speech, but gives it a more instinctive, far less technical emphasis than the sixteenth century did. Charles L. Stevenson, quondam student and professed philosophical disciple of I. A. Richards, could have been speaking as much of Shakespeare's day as of our own when he said in his *Ethics and Language* (1944) that "to choose a definition is to plead a cause";[31] and that "words are prizes which each man seeks to bestow on the qualities of his own choice,"[32] though the linguistic norms of the two cultures nevertheless remain sharply distinctive.[33]

In the sixteenth century the culture was much further along the continuum toward the conscious use of rhetoric than is our own. In today's linguistic climate, because we do not ourselves study rhetoric systematically, as Shakespeare's contemporaries did, it is particularly difficult to see that even apparently casual speech can be as consciously rhetorical as the most elaborate Ciceronian diction. This consideration brings us to the second element in Shakespeare's rhetorical strategy, which probably worked as well for him in his own day as it continues to do in ours. It is based on the fact that when we hear the term "rhetoric" we instinctively think of an elaborate and cultivated style of some kind—Ciceronian or Senecan, as the case may be; myriad examples of either style, or any combination of the two, could be cited from Shakespeare's plays. When we think "rhetoric," in other words, we do not ordinarily think of a style that is neither Ciceronian nor Senecan, a style needing no tropes or figures to set it off, but as far beyond the jargon of the educationalists as it is beyond the rigidity of their methodologies. The schemes and figures of rhetoric may be used in the plays by the characters—they are visible in this form and designed to be seen—but Shakespeare's own rhetoric has no figures or schemes because it is beyond mechanical rhetorical principles altogether. Shakespeare's style is simple; it is precisely this quality that makes it so elusive; but its simplicity is based on a mastery of rhetorical principles that goes deeper than any mere Cicero's or Aristotle's. Harbage uses the oxymoron "complex simplicity"[34] to characterize it. There are no rhetorical strategies of which Shakespeare is not master. As Hardin Craig has truthfully observed, in him "rhetoric is so naturally employed as almost to escape notice. There is no . . . creaking of the machine."[35] Eloquence, studied or apparently casual, is but one *type* of rhetoric; roughness, or the affectation of coarseness, are equally rhetorical, and under the right circumstances will succeed where eloquence might fail. Aristotle defined rhetoric, it will be remembered, as the "faculty of considering all the possible means of persuasion on every subject," though it is doubtful that any writer has ever as fully taken to heart the actual scope of the expression "*all* the *possible* means" as Shakespeare. Again, the power of rhetoric lies in three things for Aristotle, of which the mechanics of rhetoric, its classification of tropes and schemes, is pointedly not one. The three things are, first, "in the thing itself which is said," which he calls *logos* or truth: "by reason of its proving or appearing to prove the point;" second, what he calls *ethos* or character, "when the speech shall have been spoken in such a way as to render the speaker worthy confidence;" and finally, *pathos*, or the sympathy of the hearers, "when they shall have been brought to a state of excitement under the influence of the speech."[36] It is particularly significant to Shakespeare, I suggest, that the latter two criteria are based exclusively on feelings, precisely the human faculties to which poetry most directly appeals, and to which *logos* (truth and reason) is at best only marginally related.

While style is a key in the allegorical interpretation of Shakespeare, other elements of his art suggest a deliberate intention on his part to communicate with his audience on the subject of rhetoric. Murrin's *The Veil of Allegory* raises another issue relevant here. It was a generally accepted view in the sixteenth century, Murrin states, that when incongruities, affronts to logic, and obscurities of well-nigh any kind are found in a work of literature, that these are deliberate, put there by the author to force his reader to go below the surface in order to find the work's true meaning. Murrin calls this the "absurdity principle" of allegorical criticism, "the principle of which distorted imagery forms a part, and it provided the means by which the poet could force his audience to go from the lower to the higher levels of allegory."[37] Murrin's discussion focuses mainly on sixteenth-century examples of the operation of this "absurdity principle," particularly in the work of Spenser, but he notes that it was understood in classical times as well, and is referred to by a number of classical authorities, especially in connection with the interpretation of myth. He quotes the fourth-century Roman Emperor Julian, for example, commenting on it in very specific terms: "'whenever myths or sacred subjects are incongruous in thought, by that very fact they cry aloud, as it were, and summon us not to believe them literally but to study and track down their hidden meaning. And in such myths the incongruous element is even more valuable than the serious and straightforward'" (147)—more valuable, Murrin adds, because "the absurd exposes the fiction as fiction and does not allow an audience to rest content with it. . . . The story must remain incomplete or absurd, if the poet wants to let truth shine through his pictured veil" (147). Other Renaissance intellectual historians also pick up on this principle as an important element of Renaissance allegorical thought. Edgar Wind, in his *Pagan Mysteries in the Renaissance* speaks of what he calls "constructive absurdity" as a basic principle of "persuasive allegory": "Allegory, . . . a sophistic device, . . . releases a counterplay of imagination and thought by which each becomes an irritant to the other, and both may grow through the irksome contact. . . . If the process seems absurd, it may be the more, not the less useful for that; for we remember the absurd more easily than the normal, and the monster often precedes the god."[38] The reference here to "remember[ing] the absurd more easily than the normal," Wind points out, has its origin in the *Rhetorica ad Herrennium* (3, 12), long attributed to Cicero, one of the most popular of Renaissance rhetorical texts, and largely the source of the period's elaborate *ars memorativa*.[39]

This absurdity principle, I am prepared to argue, is critical in the interpretation of Shakespeare, particularly as it relates to the question of an allegorical message in his writings. It is another truism of Shakespearean criticism that logical absurdities dot his writings from beginning to end. These range from the Plautine mistakes-of-identity silliness of many of the comedies, particularly the early ones, through the "most puzzling of Shakespeare's works,"[40] the impenetrably obscure sonnets, to the "radically schizophrenic"[41] problem plays again, and culminating perhaps with the "absurdity" that is the "core" of *King Lear*, according to Wilson Knight.[42] Clearly, a pattern of absurdity does exist in Shakespeare; whether that pattern has any special significance, of course, is very much a different question. Near unanimous critical opinion, certainly, would attribute no significance to it whatsoever, either in most individual instances or as a characteristic of his work as a whole. Where it exists—where it is noticed—it was either simply taken up with his sources or else it is a product of his own slapdash methods, the critics say; he may not have had time to worry about insignificant inconsistencies that his audience would not have noticed or cared about anyway. J. W. Mackail's comments, written in 1933 and still in print after seventy years, are typical critical views even today of Shakespeare as a craftsman. Haste governed virtually his every creative move, Mackail says. For the fact that certain expressions and thematic patterns appear both early and late in his writings, for example, Mackail says, "no reason need be sought beyond his desire to save himself trouble, his choice at any juncture of the easiest way. His plays were written at high speed, and produced before they had time to cool.[43] . . . Nor can we say of any single one of the plays that we possess it in a definite form approved by himself as, if not perfect, at least final. He did not take the trouble, it seems clear that he did not think it worth his while, to do anything of the kind (17). . . . Shakespeare took no pains to fasten up loose ends. He was concerned with dramatic effectiveness, not with finished artifice of construction" (23).

Thus go most of the explanations of Shakespeare's supposed carelessness with structure or motivation in the plays, when these are found. It is perhaps needless to say that such cavalier dismissals of Shakespeare's craftsmanship are antithetical to the view of him that I am advancing here, and antithetical as well to Murrin's "absurdity principle" discussed above. It is quite correct that in many cases absurdities were part of the package he inherited with his sources, but rather than his being unconcerned with such trivial matters, it is quite as legitimate to infer that these absurdities may even have influenced his selection of these particular plots for dramatic treatment. In many cases the most flagrant absurdities in the plays are the product of *changes* Shakespeare introduced into his sources, many having to do, for example, with time—compressing events into such a limited time frame that rational intepretation of the characters' actions becomes impossible; on examination they appear unmotivated or in other ways an offense to logic. The pattern of such deliberate manipulations will be looked at in specific instances later, but for the moment I wish only to make the obvious point that carelessness on the author's part is simply not a possible explanation in cases of this kind. Or the "problems," again, in the so-called problem plays are in most cases of Shakespeare's, not his sources', making. The archetypal instance here might be the case of the Angelo character in *Measure for Measure*, the epitome of hypocrisy and villainy. In George Whetstone's *Promos and Cassandra*, the source of the play's plot, the Promos character is duly punished for his crimes, a "more rational" treatment of the theme, in the words of Quiller-Couch,[44] than Shakespeare's incongruous comic resolution. And similarly, the deliberate exaggerations he introduces into his version of the *All's Well that Ends Well* story, as compared to his source, are clearly such as to *make* his resolution unacceptable to reason.[45]

Mysteries comparable to these abound in the plays, which we may now move to consider in both a more general and a more specific way in the remainder of the study.

5

Rhetoric and the Plays:
An Overview

As the reader will be more than sufficiently impressed with by now, the subject not only of rhetoric generally in the sixteenth century is a gargantuan one, but even with respect to Shakespeare specifically its dimensions may seem to be almost comparable. I have advanced the hypothesis first of three levels on which the subject may be approached in Shakespeare, the academic or visible, the political or invisible, and the allegorical, comprehending in an almost spiritual manner, in keeping with Elizabethan notions of allegory, the other two. It perhaps goes without saying that there is no real separation of the "levels," even hypothetically; their implications obviously shadow each other at every point. At the same time, however, it is also true that it *is* possible to discuss them separately; indeed, to the extent that they have been discussed at all hitherto in criticism, and this is not inconsiderable now, it has been separately; level one in particular has been the subject of several landmark treatises, and level two, touching the rhetorical deviousness/persuasiveness on display in various of the characters, has become a significant focus of critical attention in the last thirty years as well. The "first level" treatises of which I speak would be those that are directly inspired by the revival of scholarly interest in Renaissance academic rhetoric that shows up in the 1930s: T. W. Baldwin's massive study of how Shakespeare's education in the arts of language shows up in his plays, *Shakespere's Small Latine and Lesse Greeke* (1944) is a classic example, along with Sr. Miriam Joseph's *Shakespeare's Use of the Arts of Language* (1947); and perhaps the archetypal study in this kind, Milton G.

Kennedy's 1942 *The Oration in Shakespeare*, an analysis of some eighty-one different speeches from the plays as academic orations—demonstrations to the world of Shakespeare's mastery of the oratorical art and his absorption of the whole classical background. Approaches to Shakespeare on the second level, looking at the rhetorical sparring among the characters, the styles and skills that make them either effective or ineffective "politicians," are no longer exactly rare in criticism in recent years either, though it is clearly still no exaggeration to say that this remains largely unexplored territory.[1]

Though material for any number of studies of both first- and second-level rhetoric abounds in the plays, and, particularly as regards the second level, remains unexploited, this study must avoid any lengthy discussion of either topic. Not to suggest that this kind of work is easy to do or not worth doing; quite the contrary; on the first level it requires scholarly knowledge that is the commitment of a lifetime, and on the second critical acumen in the analysis of language and character that might pose a challenge to a Coleridge. The simple reason is that to do justice to these aspects of the subject *and* to hope to unmask the elusive Proteus, this study's goal, at once, is more than any single treatise could possibly encompass. Of his knowledge of first-level, academic rhetoric, suffice to say here merely that Shakespeare was both versed in the theory and imbued in the practice. He learned early and continuously flourished and polished the deliberate use of what he calls in *The Taming of the Shrew* his "rope-tricks": "he will rail in his rope-tricks," says Grumio, "throw a figure in her face [Katherine's], and so disfigure with it that she will have no more eyes to see withal than a cat" (1.2.111–13). It is perhaps in the comic domain in particular that the academic aspects of rhetoric are most clearly on display throughout the Shakespeare corpus, where the unsophisticated (or the congenitally incapable) in the arts of speech become the figures of fun and the butts of sophisticated "wits." Of this form very clearly, for example, is the constabular comedy of Dogberry and Verges in *Much Ado*, of Elbow in *Measure for Measure*, and of Costard and Dull in *Love's Labour's Lost*. Similarly, the principle of linguistic ineptness (indicating lack of mental agility) is largely the comic motive in the cases of the "foolish lout" Launce and his dog Crab of *Two Gentlemen*, of the clowns in *All's Well*, *Antony and Cleopatra*, and *The Winter's Tale*, and of the low-life

play-acting characters of *A Midsummer-Night's Dream*: we remember Quince's famous "Prologue," characterized by Theseus
as "speech . . . like a tangled chain; nothing impaired, but all dis-
ordered" (5.1.123–24).

Rhetorical comedy among the so-called educated is possible
on the technical level too, of course, and is widely exploited. One
may possess the paraphernalia of wit—the outfit, as it were, of a
rhetorician—and lack the wit to use it; so that it sits there in
one's brain as a jumble of incongruous and unintegrated verbal
claptrap, the effort to employ which results in mere hyperbolical
confusion and elevated absurdity—like Don Adriano de Armado's description of "L'envoy" in *Love's Labour's Lost*: "an epi-
logue or discourse to make plain / Some obscure precedence that
hath tofore been sain" (3.1.76–77). Sir Andrew of *Twelfth Night*
would be thus a soul brother to Armado, but in a contrary sense,
as one whose courtly education and wit are no burden to him at
all, since nothing has been retained of them except the need. Or
another variation on this same theme is found in Orlando of *As
You Like It*: "train'd . . . like a peasant," denied the "good education" his motivelessly malignant brother was charged by their
father to provide, "yet he's gentle; never school'd and yet learned"
(1.1.149), exemplifying the possibility of an innate capacity for
courtierly charm that may be the endowment of the fortunate
and ideal few. Ancient Pistol as a character, again, also probably
developed directly from the Armado of *Love's Labour's Lost*, and
is an advance in comic technique over the original comparable to
Sir Andrew, though in an opposite direction, as far as his use of
flowery eloquence is concerned. Sir Hugh Evans of *Merry Wives*
and Holofernes of *Love's Labour's Lost* would be then the schoolmasterly elite of this particular comic breed:—this is not to say
that they are major comic characters, but simply that they epitomize, Holofernes particularly, boring rhetorical pedantry in the
highest degree—carried to the point of utter exasperation (on
the part of the hearer) and beyond. To Holofernes, thus, speech
art consists, not as it does to the mature Shakespeare, in making
one word say as many things as possible, but just the opposite to
this, in finding and using as many words to say one thing as language can be milked to provide—Erasmus's *Copia* gone mad, as
it were:

> a kind of insinuation, as it were, in via, in way, of explication;
> facere, as it were, replication, or rather, ostentare, to show, as it

were, his inclination, after his undressed, unpolished, uneducated, unpruned, untrained, or rather unlettered, or ratherest unconfirmed fashion, to insert again my haud credo for a deer. (4.2.12–17)

The abuse of rhetorical art in characters like Holofernes implies, of course, its proper use in others, and we have in *Love's Labour's Lost* (among other plays) instances by the score of what would have been considered by Shakespeare's contemporaries exemplary language skill; as the reluctant aristocratic lovers and wits display their oratorical wares at every opportunity. As Rosaline says of her Berowne:

> His eye begets occasion for his wit,
> For every object that the one doth catch
> The other turns to a mirth-moving jest,
> Which his fair tongue, conceit's expositor,
> Delivers in such apt and gracious words
> That aged ears play truant at his tales,
> And younger hearings are quite ravished;
> So sweet and voluble is his discourse.
>
> (2.1.69–76)

It is interesting too in this connection, and more than incidental in the theme of this study, that at the same time as he indulges in this early play the passion for decorative eloquence that is the hallmark of the high Elizabethan style, Shakespeare betrays his impatience with mere decoration as any very fundamental attribute of genuine poetry, demonstrating his awareness at the same time of more powerful poetic effects potential in language that decoration may very well tend more to subvert than to bring out. *Love's Labour's Lost* is probably contemporary with the earliest of the Sonnets, and in both works the same need is expressed, to break through the conventions and into the pure essence of poetry:

> O, never will I trust to speeches penn'd,
> Nor to the motion of a school-boy's tongue,
>
> . . . .
>
> Taffeta phrases, silken terms precise,
> Three-piled hyperboles, spruce affectation,
> Figures pedantical—these summer flies
> Have blown me full of maggot ostentation.
> I do forswear them.
>
> (5.2.402–10)

It is when he has broken through convention utterly and come out on the other side, that he finds the character who is probably the greatest rhetorican, in the formal sense, and certainly the greatest wit of all his characters, Falstaff.

The final point I would make just here as regards rhetoric in its purely academic aspect, is that the plays show that Shakespeare had mastered everything that the schools could teach of rhetoric before he put pen to paper as a playwright, before he created a single "character" for the stage. This is perhaps the one component of Shakespeare's art that does not show growth throughout his career. And the reason it does not is plain—that it *cannot grow* past the stage that it has already reached in the earliest of his plays. His skills at *parodying* it develop, yes; if Holofernes is a bad joke as a school rhetorician, Polonius, for example, must be considered a very good one. It is significant, however, that of the eighty-one orations Kennedy analyzes, no less than thirty-seven are taken from what Alexander calls Shakespeare's "first period," ending with *Love's Labour's Lost* in 1594. This list includes ten plays of thirty-seven; and the fact that thirty-seven of Kennedy's orations,[2] a disproportionate number, are taken from this group suggests a number of things that relate both to the growth of Shakespeare's art and the allegorical theme of this study. As was discussed in chapter 4, there is an important allegorical principle, first, in the theatrical medium itself, as a context for the exercise of the rhetorical art. When the "art" is visible, and the characters flaunting the art likewise, the first elementary stage of the *writer's* message of *invisibility* comes into play. The noticeable change in style that comes after this period, then, marks Shakespeare's realization, and a corresponding shift in the thrust of the allegory, that "ostentation" in these matters is never ultimately as powerful rhetorically as subtlety, that hiding oneself behind the mask of a "character" is only the first elementary stage of a process of rhetorical refinement that he comes to realize *has no limits* in how far it may be taken. The expression "skill infinite" (*All's Well* 2.1.183) is no casual hyperbole at that point, but a simple fact: "What impossibility would slay / In common sense, sense saves another way" (2.1.176–77).

As my single illustration of Shakespeare's total mastery of technical rhetoric, I will cite one figure that he favors and uses in a special way in the plays, that both conceals and at the same time flaunts his skill. This is the device that has the technical designation *meiosis*, "the disabler or figure of extenuation," as Puttenham calls it,[3] in which the speaker deliberately deprecates himself, affecting modesty or lack of ability, for purposes of gaining credibility for the cause he advocates. *Meiosis* may well be the most devious of all rhetorical tricks, having the effect simultaneously of disarming the hearer and of subtly flattering the speaker; and as Shakespeare uses it particularly it has an effect of special challenge, for his favorite ploy is to have the character affect modesty in *verbal skill* itself—an affectation which is blatantly contradicted by the skills the speaker displays in its very utterance! Examples of the technique leap off his pages; Richard of Gloucester will of course be one of the first thought of:

> Cannot a plain man live and think no harm
> But thus his simple truth must be abused
> With silken, sly, insinuating Jacks?
>
> (1.3.51–53)

Prince Hal and Hotspur, master rhetoricians both, exhibit subtle skills in the use of *meiosis* that "honest" Iago himself might envy:

> *Ver.* No, by my soul, I never in my life
> Did hear a challenge urg'd more modestly,
> Unless a brother should a brother dare
> To gentle exercise and proof of arms.
> He gave you all the duties of a man;
> Trimm'd up your praises with a princely tongue;
> Spoke your deservings like a chronicle;
> Making you ever better than his praise,
> By still dispraising praise valued with you;
> *And, which became him like a prince indeed,*
> *He made a blushing cital of himself,*
> *And chid his truant youth with such a grace*
> *As if he mast'red there a double spirit,*
> *Of teaching and of learning instantly.*
> There did he pause; but let me tell the world—
> If he outlive the envy of this day,
> England did never owe so sweet a hope,
> So much miscontrued in his wantonness.

Hot.   Cousin, I think thou art enamoured
On his follies. Never did I hear
Of any prince so wild a liberty.
But be he as he will, yet once ere night
I will embrace him with a soldier's arm,
That he shall shrink under my courtesy.
Arm, arm with speed! and, fellows, soldiers, friends,
Better consider what you have to do
Than I, that have not well the gift of tongue,
Can lift your blood up with persuasion.
                    (*1 Henry IV*, 5.1.53–79, italics mine)

The great funeral oration of Marc Antony cannot be forgotten in this context, and the *meiosis* to end *meioses* with which it ends, as the plebeians scream around him for the blood of the conspirators:

I am no orator, as Brutus is,
But, as you know me all, a plain blunt man,
. . . .
For I have neither wit, nor words, nor worth,
Action, nor utterance, nor the power of speech,
to stir men's hearts; I only speak right on.
                    (3.2.217–18, 221–23)

To bring my "levels" one and three together, leading into fuller discussion of the rhetorical allegory the plays are directly geared to putting across, I can expand briefly here on one specific element of the academic background that makes a central contribution to Shakespeare's conception of the rhetorical art, and that his plays, as they reflect it structurally, simultaneously comment on it allegorically. While again nothing definite is known of Shakespeare's actual education, the plays provide ample evidence that it included much that we know was standard fare for middle- and upper-class youth of his generation, as T. W. Baldwin's meticulous analyses have clearly demonstrated. The thesis of this study, as regards Shakespeare's unique application of rhetorical principles in his work, has been that he transcends everything in the field that can be embraced under the rubric of *technical*, though that term has particularly wide-ranging reference when we are speaking of the special field of sixteenth-century rhetoric. Thus while his training, like that of his peers, would have been "severely technical," as M. L. Clarke[4] characterizes Cicero's popular text, the *De Inventione*, he at some point, and probably very early, grasped the deeper lesson of Cicero as well, that the teaching of oratory is "not the imparting of tricks . . . but the gradual bringing to bear of the whole man."[5]

A name mentioned previously here as one of the most illustrious in Renaissance rhetoric, but whose contribution may have been to some extent slighted in modern reconstructions of the educational curriculum of that era, is that of the later Greek authority, Hermogenes of Tarsus. While acknowledging Hermogenes's importance as a source, "the most read and the most influential Greek rhetorician . . . [d]uring . . . the Renaissance," George Kennedy calls him,[6] the pattern of references to him in modern educational histories of the Elizabethan era, and this includes T. W. Baldwin, tends to be to his name only, with no attempt to discuss any unique features that might distinguish his approach from that of other popular authorities. Did Shakespeare study Hermogenes? To this or any other question regarding Shakespeare's education, no answer is possible; but the general evidence of the period suggests a high probability that he would have. Already noted as authoritative voices in educational matters in the Tudor era are such names as those of Elyot, Vives, and Sturm, all of whom place Hermogenes specifically among the luminaries of the art, along with Aristotle, Cicero, and Quintilian.[7] Baldwin further speculates on a possible direct link of Hermogenes to Shakespeare through Thomas Jenkins, Shakespeare's "principal schoolmaster," an alumnus of St. John's College under its founding principal Sir Thomas White, in whose educational program "the rhetoric of Hermogenes" held a prominent place.[8]

Detailed discussion of Hermogenes is beyond the scope of this study; my comments will be restricted to those aspects of his work that may be be related to the dramatic practice of Shakespeare. Hermogenes, first, is a different *kind* of rhetorician; George Kennedy suggests something of that difference, striking to a modern reader, by saying "he is no Quintilian, and does not express himself in such a direct or pedagogic way."[9] Kennedy's specific reference here is to the first of Hermogenes's three major "technical works,"[10] *On Staseis*, but its implications are equally, if not more, pertinent applied to his "longest, . . . most polished, and . . . most interesting" (678) piece, *Peri Ideon*, "the most influential treatise on style [in] the Renaissance" in the words of its

modern translator Wooten.[11] As regards these differences between Hermogenes and the "traditional Latin authorities," John
Monfasini notes that "two are fundamental," his " 'method of division' " by "dichotomies," as a means of organizing "all possible
categories of issues and all possible arguments," and his *stylis-
tics*, "quite unlike the standard . . . division of style into grand,
middle, and plain,"[12] elaborating style into a complex system of
twenty-one stylistic categories, each further broken down into
eight component parts. While this description may sound like
something that, if different from the Latin, is equally rule-bound
and complex, in fact its greatest difference, and the basis of its
appeal to a modern reader, is that when one reads Hermogenes,
rules and categories are the farthest thing from one's mind. His
focus is on one thing only—rhetorical effectiveness; "severely
technical" he most definitely is not. In terms of my three Shakespearean rhetorical "levels," then, integrating the Hermogenean
system with that structure, it would precisely mark the transition from level one to level two, from the academic or technical to
the political. The word *ideon*, in Hermogenes's title, goes directly
into English in the word *ideas*, the word Patterson used in her
commentary on Hermogenes, it will be remembered, and which
Wooten renders as *types*, both Patterson and Wooten adding the
words *Of Style* as a further nuance. The addition of the word
style to the title is significant, because it reinforces what I have
said is the real aim of Hermogenes's rhetoric; that is, to teach the
method of rhetorical effectiveness; what his stylistic categories—
clarity, vigor, beauty, speed, simplicity, and the others—attempt
to do is *analyze persuasive techniques*, discussing exactly how a
particular "style," or combination of styles, is employed to maximum effect. It may seem like a stretch, but I believe it is a legitimate one, to relate Hermogenes's focus on style and method to
the main theme of this study, the thesis that *method*, calculated
and clear, is at the centre of Shakespeare's achievement, and
that central *to* that method is a philosophic grasp of how *style*
(persuasive rhetoric) translates to power.

　　It is worth noting also before leaving this point that the emphasis on method in Hermogenes's writings has drawn the attention of several recent commentators, whose observations
again implicitly reinforce the possibility of influence from Hermogenean rhetoric to Shakespearean thinking. All four of Kennedy, Patterson, Monfasini, and Walter Ong, note that the su-

preme stylistic virtue for Hermogenes is the final one of his major categories of style, *deinotês* in the original Greek, which involves the combining of the virtues of all of the other categories, and conveys the notion of absolute stylistic adaptability. It may not be without significance also, apropos Shakespeare, that several different translations of the word *deinotês* have been given over the centuries, suggesting the range of its connotations. To Sturm, in the Renaissance, it was *eloquentia*; Wooten and Kennedy render it *force*; Patterson calls it *gravity*, while Monfasini gives it in one place as "awesomeness" and in another "*terribilita*," the word that in the Renaissance he says was applied to Michelangelo, "to describe [the] overpowering impact and the greatness of his art."[13] Hermogenes actually speaks in *On Types of Style* of another treatise he intends to write specifically on *deinotês*; the treatise exists, though how much of it is Hermogenes's original is now in dispute (though it was not in the Renaissance); but it is the title in particular of that treatise that hints intriguingly at a possible unity of ideas between Hermogenes and Shakespeare. The title in Greek is περί μεθόδου δεινότητος, on which Ong makes the following highly suggestive comments:

> One is tempted to read this "On the method of securing rhetorical effectiveness." But any current sense of the term "method" in English fails to convey the signification of the original Greek cognate here, which means something more like mode of rhetorical organization or thought structure . . . , so that the title more properly might be rendered, *On the Pattern underlying Rhetorical Irresistibility*. The more philosophical . . . notion of μεθόδος as a systematic investigation—a meaning which the term conveys commonly in Aristotle—is hardly present in Hermogenes. For his whole work is dominated by the policy of leaving all explanation to the "philosophers" and erecting what von Christ calls a "wall of separation" (*Scheidewand*) between philosophy and his own field, rhetoric. The significance of Hermogenes as a major source of interest in methodology at the dawn of the modern world lies . . . in the fact that he shows that this interest arises in an area . . . clearly rhetorical and a-logical.[14]

That Hermogenes's rhetoric is different from that of the traditional Latin authors has been noted; one of its important differences, as a school text, is that it begins, from an Elizabethan perspective at least, at an advanced level. Kennedy puts it accu-

rately in saying that Hermogenes "assumes at the outset . . .
much of traditional . . . rhetorical theory"[15]—meaning that he
can, as he does, skip tiresome recapitulation of it—to which
Ong's observation that "his whole work is dominated by the
policy of leaving all explanation to the 'philosophers'" is a complement. His work is concentrated; *On Types of Style* runs to a
mere 159 pages in modern translation, and contains the names,
ignoring definitions, of, by my count, no more than twelve of the
traditional figures of speech. Concentrating exclusively on questions of style, which still keeps him in the academic mainstream,
he manages neatly at the same time to leave things like Aristotle's "truth bias" subtly in abeyance; *ethos*, thus, is discussed, but
as a stylistic trick, in effect, which its sub-categories of "simplicity," "modesty," and "sweetness" help to bring off. It can be seen
that there are a number of unique benefits that taking Hermogenes as one's rhetorical guide might offer to the Renaissance
student and teacher. As a near contemporary of Cicero and Quintilian, first, his classical pedigree is impeccable; whatever he
says *must* be gospel; coupling this, then, with his dropping of
most of the huge load of moral, and especially technical, baggage
the others carry, there is a freedom and lightness to what remains that must be powerfully appealing to the spirit of the age,
if only on a subconscious level.

The "specific element of the academic background" from Hermogenes that I see as strikingly applicable to Shakespeare's dramatic practice is the fourth of his seven principal divisions of
style, that he calls *gorgotês*, variously translated as *brevity* (Kennedy), *rapidity* (Wooten), or, my personal preference for an English equivalent, *speed* (Patterson). I have two reasons for suggesting a possible Hermogenes/Shakespeare connection through
the "idea" of speed; first, that "speed," as an element of Shakespeare's philosophy of rhetoric, is arguably more fundamental
than any other single attribute of his work, stylistic or structural; and, second, that as far as I am aware, Hermogenes is the
only prominent rhetorical theorist, classical or Elizabethan, to
make speed a major component of his program.

"Speed" in Hermogenes touches everything in oratory that
conduces to movement. While there are traditional figures of
speech associated with the rapid flow of ideas, figures such as
asyndeton and *brachylogia*, Hermogenes, "assuming" all of this,
as Kennedy says, goes beyond it to comprehend not just the tech-

nique but the *idea*. The one purely technical reference that comes up in his discussion of speed, as it happens, is one that Shakespeare employs everywhere and might have remembered—that speech that incorporates rhythm (Hermogenes does not say *verse* explicitly, though it is perhaps implied) is particularly suited to imparting the effect of speed to one's declamation. Hermogenes notes further that speed is the only one of his ideas of style that bears no relation to content; it is intrinsic in all oratory, and is simply the idea of *keeping things moving*. These are the limited senses, then, in which Hermogenes employs the concept; its significance to him is perhaps summed up best in the prescription of Sturm, his "single most important proponent . . . in the sixteenth century,"[16] that speed, as a stylistic principle, is "designed . . . to avoid boredom."[17] If Shakespeare was exposed to Hermogenes, and got nothing else from the experience, he surely absorbed *that* lesson at least, in the deepest possible way.[18]

I can prepare the ground for the somewhat more detailed analyses to follow by taking a brief look first at the several ways in which the concept of speed operates in the plays, and of how the rhetorical, and particularly the Hermogenean background may inform Shakespeare's awareness of its theatrical application. The obvious place to start for me is with an observation that came up earlier, in the discussion concerning the difference between reading a play as opposed to seeing it in performance, and of how these considerations might have affected Shakespeare's views on publication. I take it as a given that Shakespeare is not just aware of, but hyper-attuned, in everything he does, to the difference between the study and the stage as potential alternative sites for the presentation of his work to the world. A critical factor in that difference, which springs directly from the rhetorical background, then, is speed—another illustration, I would maintain, of how theater is the ultimate rhetoric. It does not take profound reflection to recognize that the concept of speed is intimately related to theatrical presentation; this, needless to say, was categorically the case in the sixteenth century; largely because of it, things can be made to work rhetorically on stage that would never pass on the street or in the court. For Hermogenes only a stylistic device, speed for Shakespeare is also, and much more importantly, a dramatic device: understanding, as he does, that the theatrical scene always *goes by quickly* and that there are no replays, he understands also, precisely because of this, how this enhances his power, that by its means all of rhetoric's infinite manipulative potential lies, like Prospero's magic staff, within his grasp.

While there may be little to add to this as far as "speed" per se is concerned in its dramatic application, speed also relates to time, and from this first elementary realization of his power in this area, there opens out for Shakespeare the whole vast panoramic field of time manipulation, over which he also learns to extend his rhetorical net. The subject is vast, and I can only, in this overview, touch on some of its basic principles and their structural implications for Shakespeare, offering only a very few specific illustrations for support. What I would claim about "time" in Shakespearean drama is that, unobtrusive to the point of invisibility as it is in the theater, and even in criticism largely ignored, its apparent minor role in the plays is a ruse, a product of method as exacting as Jonson's adherence to the unities, and bearing centrally for that very reason upon the allegorical message of the plays. It has long been a truism in criticism that time is, or appears to be, treated cavalierly by Shakespeare, as if whim were the sole governing factor in his either noting or ignoring it in structuring his dramas. Thus, for example, historical fact is the merest springboard for his creativity in the history plays, clearly; the actual time span from which events are selected to be presented in a single play may be a year (*1 Henry IV*) or it may be thirty years (*1 Henry VI*), with, typically, no specific time references in the plays themselves to give any indication of either. Time in the comedies and tragedies tends to be similarly vague, although references that are either important in the story (the sixteen-year interval between acts 3 and 4 in *The Winter's Tale*) or serve to connect certain scenes and events (*Romeo and Juliet*'s "Tomorrow night look that thou lie alone") are not infrequently employed. There are instances as well where the time sequence is both precise throughout and clear; indeed, from the point of view of this study there is an almost symbolic appropriateness in the fact that the two examples that fall most perfectly into this last category may mark exactly the end points of Shakespeare's playwriting career—*The Comedy of Errors*, whose adherence to the traditional Aristolelean "single revolution of the sun" unity-of-time rule is more explicit even than in its classical source,[19] and *The Tempest,* in which Shakespeare experiments daringly with an *absolute* unity of time, "play" and "real" time being made to coincide.[20] The "symbolic appropriateness," as I call it, of the structural exactness of these two plays with respect to time is that it demonstrates unequivocally that where time is concerned in the plays Shakespeare is *fully in control*, equally early in his career and late, cognizant both of classical tradition in relation to time and of the possibility of radical innovation. This being so, it follows, logically, that the same control is exercised throughout his career—that the absence of time references in one play, or their precise placing in another, are in both cases deliberate, and with the allegorical implications of the rhetorical concept of "speed" never far in the background.

If the above postulate is indeed accurate, that the myriad variations played on the issue of time in the plays are in all cases deliberate, the product not of carelessness but of method, this might suggest, as a theoretical basis for such manipulations, that dramatic action per se for Shakespeare is conceived as *beyond time*. That is to say, the very existence of time on the stage is under the dramatist's control; literally *any* temporal hoax can be passed off; the "time" of a play can be the actual three hours of its performance, and carefully noted as such; it can be thirty years historically; or it can be anything in between; in the absence of specific time references in a play it can consume no time at all, as time is measured in our "real" world. The point, again, about speed in all of this is that colorful display, fast-moving action, and the intrigues of character and plot, all supported on a rhetorico/poetic foundation of irresistible flash and brilliance, serve to disguise the hoax. The mesmerizing force of the illusion is such that the spectator is its helpless dupe; brazen affronts to reason in the temporal domain can be served up with impunity, waved literally, indeed with chuckling glee, in front of the spectator's unseeing gaze; and, climaxing it all, from an allegorical standpoint, by making or not making explicit time references, Shakespeare is *showing* us how we are being manipulated. If there is one lesson taught (and, by Shakespeare, learned [?]) by his first history play, *1 Henry VI*, it is surely that his power on the stage is absolute, not only over time but over reality itself; as Boswell-Stone puts it, "chronology and facts are utterly scorned."[21] He can bring "fiends" on stage to companion Joan Pucelle; he can give her twenty years of imaginary extra "life" so that she can be present at the death of Talbot; Rouen can be "lost and recovered in a day"—indeed, that "day" can be itself telescopically compressed into fifteen minutes of brisk stage action, when the superhero Talbot enters the fray.

Manipulations of time identical in kind, though differing in degree, fill the early comedies as well, accompanied in many of these cases by allegorical motifs exceeding in blatancy (the privilege of fiction, perhaps?) anything put forward in the histories. Giving a character in *Two Gentlemen* the name "Speed," for example, and then having that character continually dawdle, bantering, and land in trouble for doing so, sends an obvious allegorical message. In *The Taming of the Shrew*, of course, speed is the essential element in Petruchio's (*and* Shakespeare's; this is the point) situational control: comments like Petruchio's "my business asketh haste," (2.1.113) and his reply to Baptista's "How *speed* you with my daughter?" with "It were impossible I should *speed* amiss" (2.1.274ff, italics mine) are direct reminders of the method both use to accomplish their ends. Indeed, if "chronology and facts are utterly scorned" in *1 Henry VI*, the whole allegorical meaning of *Shrew* is that you can scorn these things and get away with doing so ("It shall be what o'clock I say it is" [4.3.191], says Petruchio) if you are, as in this case Shakespeare/Petruchio is, aggressive, outrageous, and open enough ("look you, sir, he tells you flatly what his mind is" [1.2.74]) in the rhetorical assault on sense you are prepared to carry through. With no likely antecedent source, this play may be Shakespeare's imaginative extrapolation from certain powerfully suggestive rhetorical concepts he retained from his schooling—figures with names like *abusio, dementiens, audacia*—terms all relating to the rhetorical use and effectiveness of deliberate untruths.[22] "Speed" ("was ever match clapp'd up so suddenly?" [2.1.317]) is but one facet of the rhetorical assault mounted in *Shrew*, clearly, but its central importance on all three of the rhetorical levels with which this study is concerned can hardly be exaggerated. And if *Shrew* is the first blatant example of speed as an allegorical motif, at least in the early plays, it continues to perform a central, if, in most cases, less obvious function in most of the plays that succeed it.

We have touched previously on its role in the plots of *Othello* and *Macbeth*, for example; and both Hamlet's procrastination and his mother's "o'er hasty" (2.2.57) marriage flaunt the same device. In the case of *Macbeth* we have an actual analogue, in certain ways, of the rhetorical method of *Shrew*. In *Shrew* flagrant abuses of reason pass because the verbal assault, the "bethump[ing] with words" (*King John*, 2.1.466), is unremitting; giving no one *time* to think, piling outrage instantaneously on outrage, a brainwashing in effect is accomplished, and we in the theater, like Katherine in the play, like rats in a maze, "with no more eyes to see, withal, than a cat," succumb under the assault, hallucinate, and accept the impossible. In a deeper way, then, *Macbeth* shows us that "the time you may [al]so hoodwink" (4.2.72). The implications of the issue are complex, but in *Shrew*, basically, the outrage committed is against all the canons of common sense, and is treated comically; in *Macbeth* the canons are the deeper, more spiritual ones of humanity, honor, and the moral sense, and the treatment tragic. "Speed," however, functions similarly in both: meeting the witches "in the day of success" (1.5.1)," and having the first of their predictions instantly confirmed, acts like a spell on Macbeth—"horrible imaginings" that "the speed of him" (1.5.32), the unyieldingness of his wife, and the continuity of events all combine to hold in place until all the prophecies are fulfilled. Hesitation, as it were, is impossible, first, because it would doom the enterprise: "The flighty purpose never is o'ertook / Unless the deed go with it" (4.1.145–46), as Macbeth has brought home to him to his ultimate cost when his nemesis Macduff escapes to England—a lesson, incidentally, that his modern-day counterpart Hitler could have used again at Dunkirk. Perhaps more important, however, are the moral overtones of hesitation—that it would break the spell; that direct continuity between the "thought . . . fantastical" of Duncan's murder and its completion in act is the only thing that makes the murder possible: "If it were done when 'tis done, then 'twere well / It were done quickly."

The final example of a motif relating to speed that I will cite in this introduction is one that is displayed throughout the canon, and that has been the source of puzzlement to many, as indicating not just carelessness, but even ineptness on Shakespeare's part. This is the device of instantaneous transformation, an abrupt attitudinal shift in a character, perfunctorily justified at best, which either sets a plot in motion or winds it up, but which, most importantly, offers a clear affront to logic. The most common of these transformations are those relating to love; these, I suppose, can scarcely be considered controversial, given that the convention of love at first sight was universal in the literary culture of the period. A similar justification might be made of the less conventional, but no less comprehensible at any time, instances where lust, rather than love is the instantaneous transforming force, and there are a number of these as well. Excluding these two categories, however, there are numerous examples where these reversals, as I call them, unrelated to the "love/lust at first sight" convention, come so fast that any explanation other than carelessness or haste has seemed unlikely. As with the theme of time, variations on the "instant reversal" formula are played; there are degrees of perfunctoriness, one might say, by which these shifts are explained in different cases. There is a significant difference between Leontes's explosion of jealousy at the beginning of *The Winter's Tale*, for example, and the seeming utter incongruousness of Valentine's forgiveness of and gifting of Silvia to the perfidious (indeed, the would-be rapist) Proteus at the end of the *The Two Gentlemen of Verona*, even though, based purely on the criterion of "speed," they are essentially identical. From an interpretive standpoint the common thread between these and the many other similar reversals that dot the plays—Bertram's declared "love" of Helena at the end of *All's Well*, Claudio's instantaneous acceptance of a substitute for Hero in *Much Ado*, the strange behavior of both Duke Vincentio and the "sainted" Isabella in *Measure for Measure*, even Malcolm's "testing" of Macduff in *Macbeth*—is that the logic of "character," or indeed any other logic, fails in the end to give satisfactory account of them; their speed is just too great. As to whether any of these are the lapses they are often considered to be, my verdict, as no doubt expected, is a resounding no.

A number of considerations come into this judgment. Murrin's "absurdity" principle as an index of a work's allegorical intention would be certainly be one; but there is a particular allegorical thread connecting these instantaneous reversals that can be related directly back again to Shakespeare's education in rhetoric. My reference here to his "education in rhetoric" is deliberate, because while Hermogenes may be a specific rhetorical influence on Shakespeare where the category of speed is concerned, there is a broad understanding as well in the period of its usefulness in persuasion, although this may itself be a product originally of Hermogenean influence. Caxton, the earliest English-language commentator on rhetoric, makes the point, for example, that "the pryncypall poynt of eloquens reityth [resteth] ever in the quyck sentence. And therfor the lest poynt belongyng to Rethorike is to

take hede that the tale be quycke."[23] The extent of this acceptance may be further judged by the frequent association of the
art of rhetoric, in the Renaissance, though its origins are classical, with the god Mercury, the figure, of all the classical pan-
theon, most immediately identified with speed—with speed, but
also, as Jewel was quick to add in his antirhetorical diatribe,
"frauds, deceptions, robberies, ... lies, [and] perjuries."[24]

To attempt an overview of second-level, political rhetoric in
Shakespeare, as part of this introduction, is at once both less and
more of a challenge than what I have been trying to do on the
technical level. It is less of a challenge, because one does not
have to be steeped in the theory of either classical or Renaissance rhetoric to appreciate the extraordinary power that is at
work on this level on virtually every page of Shakespeare; and it
is more of a challenge, paradoxically, for a closely related reason,
that there is an overabundance of material—too many too perfect examples of irresistible rhetorico/poetic force, presented in a
range of characters and styles that run the gamut, it would
almost seem, of possibility. The general principle that is involved
here can be represented succinctly in a final citation from Hermogenes. My use of the word *force*, above, while obviously appropriate in a Shakespearean context in its own right, is another
reminder of how closely associated all of these questions remain
to Hermogenes's rhetorical principles, *force* being Wooten's English equivalent of Hermogenes's *deinotês*, "synonymous with oratorical perfection,"[25] in Monfasini's phrase. Hermogenes speaks
in precisely these terms of Demosthenes, his example of the perfect orator, and they are terms that accurately describe Shakespeare's mastery of political rhetoric in the plays:

> That same man is forceful in every passage that he wrote, using
> the same unifying skill and the same talent in them all and em-
> ploying each type of style appropriately. Since he adapts his style
> to the subject and the occasions and the personages involved, ...
> what he says is always appropriate [.] ... If at one time he ap-
> pears to be forceful and another he does not, this itself is exactly
> what is forceful about his speeches. It is typical of real force to be
> knowledgeable enough to project any impression the situation de-
> mands.[26]

Finding a focus for my overview of technical rhetoric in the
plays in the specific stylistic category of "speed" from Hermo-

genes, I propose that a comparable focus for a brief consideration
of how political rhetoric operates in the plays may be found in
the concept of "honor." The ramifications of this concept are very
broad, carrying into areas such as kingship and the class structure, but all rooted in the principles and practices of rhetoric. I
have cited Puttenham's *The Arte of English Poesie* as an important background text for reading Shakespeare, whose subtle directions to Elizabethan courtiers and poets are a virtual commentary on the Shakespearean rhetorical method, a method
that has seemed beyond penetration, such that, according to the
bias of the critic, his work may equally be read as an endorse-
ment of the Elizabethan political and social status quo, or as a
revolutionary challenge to it. The clear sense one gets in reading
Puttenham on *decorum*, or, to use his more equivocal alternative
term, *discretion*,[27] is of a social structure actually fragile in the
extreme, founded ultimately on the single criterion of power, but
in which a facade of civilization, legitimacy, and stability is
maintained by means of style, with rhetorical style the key component in the mix. And, among the attributes of style, the one
that perhaps contributes the most to maintaining society intact,
simultaneously justifying and underpinning the class structure,
and confirming those who are allowed to claim its privileges in
their place in the hierarchy of power, is the one that in Shakespeare goes under the label of "honor."

   That honor, first, is a term of some importance in Shakespeare
is demonstrable on the basis of frequency of use alone—a concordance check reveals no fewer than 681 uses in the thirty-seven
plays, doubling or tripling (and more, with cognates *honor'd, honorable*, and so on) the frequency of use of many other terms that
it might be considered should be comparable in their social significance—words like *law, justice, right*, and even *power*. No precise definition of the concept is given in Shakespeare, possibly
because none is needed; its meaning in an Elizabethan politico/
social context is quite clear, then and now—that it is a privilege
of nobility, a form of status, an aura, even, that sets the class of
aristocracy apart from the people, and that in its claimants'
minds is associated first, in most cases, with their feudal rights
of land tenure, but with many vestiges of the age of chivalry
clinging to it as well.[28] While precise definition of the concept
may present certain difficulties, the critical point concerning it in
the context of this study is that it presents no difficulty of *recog-*

nition in the plays. That is to say, there is a stylistic form that comes into play in Shakespeare in association with "honor" that marks it unmistakably. The language of "honor" is always in verse (Brutus's speech on the death of Caesar the single exception, proving the rule[?]), the diction elevated, the tone dignified, lending what can only be called an aristocratic air of gravity (Hermogenes' *deinotês* again) to every speech and gesture performed by any member of the exalted fraternity of the "honorable." The effect of this stylistic association—I do not hesitate to call it a trick on Shakespeare's part—is to make it impossible for an audience not to attend with seriousness the weighty pronouncements, the grand ambitions and rivalries, captured in words of such impressive dignity. From the standpoint of this study, the key term in the above sentence is the word "trick," the implication being that we are made to take honor seriously purely by rhetorical art—persuasiveness—*manner* creating the illusion of *matter*, with full awareness, as always, on Shakespeare's part, of exactly what he is doing. And from this it follows, as was shown to be true of "speed" on the technical level, that an allegorical dimension in the concept of "honor" opens up on the political level as well, carrying the message that "honor" is, as Falstaff said, a rhetorical illusion, "a mere scutcheon" of no ultimate relevance or meaning.

Substantiation of the claim made in the last paragraph is not difficult. If nothing quite so sweeping has been claimed of Shakespeare before, it is again, I submit, that his rhetoric has beguiled us; so noble-sounding, stirring, and persuasive, with "honor" as its motive is it, that it has seemed impossible to get past it to the hand of the puppet-master himself, "cunning past man's thought," indeed as he is, pulling the strings of "character" and controlling our responses with disdainful ease. The key to this interpretation, then, must be found in the consideration not of character, nor even of language (in the sense of content), but in the manifest discrepancy, *in every instance*, between the "noble" style and what actually lies behind it—precisely that "Adlerian nightmare" of which we have spoken before: egotism at the very least, invariably, but generally much worse, a predatory ruthlessness that mocks all principle and makes of "honor" the hollowest of shams. There is a particularly significant allegorical point in the fact that individual "character" has no bearing on the issue under consideration here. "Honor," as Shakespeare presents it, is characterless; this is his point; it is rooted in style, and when honor is in any way the theme the language has the same vocabulary, the same cadences, the same lofty tone, and, most importantly, the same persuasive eloquence *no matter who* is speaking. As noted, honor has different aspects; the aspect to which these observations would apply most directly, the one closest to the Elizabethan political scene, would be that which marks the verse style of the English history plays, and it is to these plays that I must confine myself to keep this discussion within bounds. The aspect of aristocratic honor in the Roman plays (and *Troilus and Cressida*) does not differ greatly from this—the "honor" in Brutus and Antony's orations on the death of Caesar is equal—while the very large general field where "honor" encounters "love" must regrettably be left entirely to another place.

The take on "honor" that I am suggesting is Shakespeare's is only decipherable from the perspective of the whole set of history plays, not from that of either any individual play, or, even less so, of any individual character. Most of what pertains to "honor" in the plays is not presented directly; uses of the term by the characters imply, or, on occasion, even state, certain values as part of "their" conception or code, but it is precisely this rhetoric that we must get behind in order to reach the higher, Shakespearean perspective. From the "character" standpoint, and this of course has been subject to minute analysis innumerable times in the past, the question is one of seeing behind the character's *profession* to "his" truth. It is necessary to look at the whole set of history plays to read the allegory for a number of reasons: setting aside *King John* and *Henry VIII* for the moment, the two tetralogies of the "greater Henriad" (as I will for convenience sake christen it)[29] cover eighty-seven years of British history, of which the single theme, politically, is power—international power, in the rivalry between France and England, but in which the stakes are actually personal, in the egos and ambitions of their kings and nobles; and national, in the ferocious rivalries among noble houses and royal aspirants within England itself. It is significant too that while there may be a gap of as much as five busy years for Shakespeare between the end of the composition of the first tetralogy and the beginning of the composition of the second, and while in sophistication of style and depth of characterization the gap may seem even greater, that the allegory of "honor" is identical in both. It is idle to speculate as to why Shakespeare decided to extend his survey of the country's past back to the origins of the Wars of the Roses after having years previously left things tidily and on an upbeat note at the beginning of the Tudor era, but clearly something about the whole history of "civil butchery" in the country held a special fascination for him. The popularity of the first tetralogy (its first and last plays are known to have been very successful) was an obvious stimulus, but a desire to develop further the Machiavellian, even megalomaniacal implications in the historical process, cloaked in the language of "honor," seems undeniable as a motive as well. I suggest, in fact, that it is revealing of a larger, allegorical design that *Richard II opens* with the most reverberant passages on the subject of knightly honor in all of Shakespeare, in the quarrel between Bolingbroke and Mowbray, couched equally *on both sides* in epic poetic language that fairly bursts with the ideals, pride, and traditions of feudalism and chivalry. As with most of his material, Shakespeare has a source for these scenes, in Holinshed, but again, as is so frequently the case, it is his genius, in recasting the originals, to find symbolism that his sources know nothing of. The contrast between not only the virtuoso style of these scenes, but their content, with ringing reaffirmations on all sides of the oaths and obligations of knighthood; and the immediate subsequent *actions* of all the parties to these events, almost shouts its allegorical message. In particular, placing fulsome declarations of fealty to Richard in Bolingbroke's mouth as many as four times in the opening scene, words such as

> Many years of happy days befall
> My gracious sovereign, my most loving liege!

and

> In the devotion of a subject's love,
> Tend'ring the precious safety of my prince
> And free from other misbegotten hate,
> Come I appelant to this princely presence
> (1.1.20–21, 31–34)

opens an ironic gap that Shakespeare surely knows, for all the lofty rhetoric still to come, can never be closed.

While Shakespeare's art reaches a level of poetic power and general sophistication in the second tetralogy scarcely hinted at in the first, and there is a correspondingly greater subtlety in his handling of the "honor" theme in *1 Henry IV*, say, as compared to anything attempted previously, his fundamental view of honor as rhetoric was clearly established in the earlier work and does not change. *Titus Andronicus* has been regarded almost universally by the critics as inferior writing for, among other things, the exaggerated horrors of its plot; "honor," in this instance (and the topic is foregrounded throughout the play), is carried to the point of absurdity and beyond in terms of the things that are done in its name—Titus's cutting off of his own hand, his murder of his only daughter and almost the last of his surviving sons are but three of the more ordinary examples, all justified in similar terms to the following:

> Nor thou nor he are any sons of mine;
> My sons would never so dishonor me.
>
> (1.1.294–95)

The advance in dramatic characterization as between a Titus and a Hotspur, for example, may seem almost infinite, but it cannot obscure the same ultimate emptiness, not to say absurdity, of that "honor" in the pursuit of which the latter so eagerly seeks out death, while dooming his cause at the same time as a bonus, of course.

The key to aristocratic "honor" as empty rhetoric, then, is set in the style of the earliest historical plays, whose "spacious lofty pitch" of speech, carrying all, character and audience, before it, mocks itself in the unrelieved barbarism of the actions it excuses. That there is a conscious allegorical intent behind these depictions is shown throughout the canon of historical plays by the fact that there is nothing to choose between the rhetoric of either side in any of these quarrels, as there is likewise nothing to choose between their actions. This assertion might be challenged in the two cases of *1 Henry VI* and *Henry V*, both of which appear to cater strongly to British chauvinism in the characterization of their heroes (the latter an advance over the former, comparable to that of Hotspur over Titus), and both of which have been accepted as straightforward nationalistic paeans by generations of critics. Placed in the context of the "greater" Henriad as a whole, however, nothing in either the characterization of the heroes of these two plays or the apparent fervor of their nationalism can be taken as straightforward. Again speculation on such a subject is idle (although by the same token probably inevitable, given the circumstances), but it is at least interesting to note that Shakespeare both opens and closes his Henriad with plays that pull out all the rhetorical stops in lofty praise of England, praise which is in fact at best a celebration of English *power*, but which cleverly invites misreading as vindication instead of her *honor*, and thus expressive of entire satisfaction with her present political arrangements and position in the world. But what the larger context brings subtly to bear on even these plays is that however momentarily successful international adventurism may at various times in the past have been for the country, the "honor" it has bought is at best meaningless, at worst indescribable in its horror when measured against the cost in blood that it has entailed. Here as throughout the Henriad the gap between the rhetoric of honor and the reality of megalomaniac ambition, if time is wrested for thoughtful consideration, is unmistakable. My point is that this is exactly what is missed in taking anything these "characters" say at face value, by letting their rhetoric sway one. There is poetic symmetry, indeed, in that it was precisely Henry's "triumph" in the last play of the Henriad that prepared the ground for England's tragic loss in the first, the reality of Talbot, in that play, actually being "the scapegoat for the sins of the royal house,"[30] glossed over in a torrent of heroic speech:

> More than three hours the fight continued;
> Where valiant Talbot above human thought
> Enacted wonders with his sword and lance.
> Hundreds he sent to hell, and none durst stand him;
> Here, there, and everywhere, enraged he slew.
> The French exclaimed, the devil was in arms;
> All the whole army stood agazed on him,
> His soldiers spying his undaunted spirit,
> A Talbot! a Talbot! cried out amain,
> And rushed into the bowels of the battle.
>
> (1.1.120–29)

There is even an almost exact counterpart, on the domestic side, to Talbot as sacrificial lamb on the international side in the first tetralogy, in the figure of "that virtuous prince, the good Duke Humphrey" (*2 Henry VI*, 2.174), whose naive attempts to make

of "honor" *more* than just a word are similarly futile and costly to
himself. And while the glossing of these horrors in *Henry V* and
the rest of the second tetralogy exhibits a stylistic mastery infinitely in excess of that achieved in the first, the allegorical implication is the same. It is because of "Henry's" rhetorical flair
alone—

> that when he speaks,
> The air, a chartered libertine, is still,
> And the mute wonder lurketh in men's ears
> To steal his sweet and honey'd sentences
>
> (1.1.46–50)

[—] that "honor's thought/Reigns solely in the breast of every
man" (2.prologue. 3–4), and ruthless ambition is magically transformed into glory:

> But I will rise there with so full a glory
> That I will dazzle all the eyes of France,
> Yea, strike the Dauphin blind to look on us.
> And tell the pleasant Prince this mock of his
> Hath turned his balls to gun-stones; and his soul
> Shall stand sore chargéd for the wasteful vengeance
> That shall fly with them: for many a thousand widows
> Shall this his mock mock out of their dear husbands;
> Mock mothers from their sons, mock castles down;
> And some are yet ungotten and unborn
> That shall have cause to curse the Dauphin's scorn.
>
> (1.2.278–88)

Passing over the justifying of these adventures, with the connivance of a venal and self-interested clergy, on the trumped-up
grounds of "salic law," the authentic reality and chilling force of
this passage is in its arrogant dismissal of the particular element
in the equation of "honor" doomed in this declaration to pay the
full cost in blood of these undertakings, the "many a thousand"
unregarded commons of both nations. The commons have a
prominent role in both tetralogies, more subtle, perhaps, in the
second. In the first, for politic reasons, as rebels they can hardly
be shown overt sympathy; Jack Cade's rabid anti-intellectualism
and blatant megalomania ensure the audience's contempt for
him (unnoticed, of course, that his farcical self-aggrandizing is
actually only a mirror image of the aristocracy's own); in the

second, the more usual passive role of the common people, as pawns in the affairs of state, "food for powder" in the conflicts of the great, is what is shown. While Falstaff's comic characterization is what will remain longest in an audience's mind, the rhetoric of honor in relation to the role of the commons comes in deftly in the same play in such things as King Henry's earlier reference, complementary to his son's just quoted to the "[T]en thousand bold Scots, two and twenty knights / Balk'd in their own blood" at Holmedon—no disproportion noted between the "ten thousand" and the "two and twenty," just equivalence. These are the same commons, of course, whom Henry had earlier "stole[n] all courtesy from heaven, / And dress'd [him]self in such humility" to court, to win their allegiance in his own bid for the crown.

These are some of the implications, then, that lie behind the exalted rhetoric of "honor" in the history plays. Whether the political scene is England alone or includes France, the same tone, the same style, supports the rivalries and machinations of all sides. Though examples crowd the stage in every play, two short quotes from each of two plays must stand for now as sole support of this thesis; I deliberately take one domestic and one English-French example. The speeches of the new King Edward, erstwhile Duke of York, and ex-queen Margaret before the battle of Tewksbury in *3 Henry VI* make the allegorical point clearly, that skill with words can seem not only to justify, but actually glorify any proceeding, however barbarous; that, for the space of utterance, something out of nothing can indeed be made. York:

> And we are graced with wreaths of victory.
> But, in the midst of this bright-shining day,
> I spy a black, suspicious, threat'ning cloud,
> That will encounter with our glorious sun,
> Ere he attain his easeful western bed:
> I mean, my lords, those powers that the Queen
> Hath raised in Gallia have arrived our coast,
> And, as we hear, march on to fight with us.
>   (*3 Henry VI* 5.3.1–9)

. . . .

> Brave followers, yonder stands the thorny wood
> Which, by the heavens' assistance and your strength,
> Must by the roots be hewn up yet ere night.

I need not add more fuel to your fire,
For well I wot ye blaze to burn them out.
Give signal to the fight, and to it, lords.

(5.4.67–72)

Margaret: Lords, knights, and gentlemen, what I should say
     My tears gainsay; for every word I speak,
     Ye see, I drink the water of my eye.
     Therefore, no more but this: Henry, your sovereign,
     Is prisoner to the foe; his state usurped,
     His realm a slaughterhouse, his subjects slain,
     His statutes cancelled, and his treasure spent;
     And yonder is the wolf that makes this spoil.
     You fight in justice: then, in God's name, lords,
     Be valiant, and give signal to the fight.

(*3 Henry VI* 5.4.73–82)

For my second example, *King John*, whether earlier or later than the first tetralogy of the Henriad, comes closer to a direct broaching of the political allegorical motif than almost anything else in the canon. The speeches, first, of both the Kings and their heralds to the citizens of Angiers, political antitheses as they are, nevertheless make identical cases, with identical force, employing identical rhetorical flourishes:

[Here after excursions, enter the Herald of France, with trumpets, to the gates.]

Fr. Her. You men of Angiers, open wide your gates,
     And let young Arthur, Duke of Bretagne, in,
     Who by the hand of France this day hath made
     Much work for tears in many an English mother
     Whose sons lie scattered on the bleeding ground.
     Many a widow's husband grovelling lies,
     Coldly embracing the discolored earth;
     And victory, with little loss, doth play
     Upon the dancing banners of the French,
     Who are at hand, triumphantly displayed,
     To enter conquerors, and to proclaim
     Arthur of Bretagne England's King and yours.
               [Enter English Herald, with trmpet.]

E. Her. Rejoice, you men of Angiers, ring your bells!
     King John, your King and England's, doth approach,
     Commander of this hot malicious day.
     Their armours, that march'd hence so silver-bright,

> Hither return all gilt with Frenchmen's blood.
> There stuck no plume in any English crest
> That is removéd by a staff of France.
> Our colors do return in those same hands
> That did display them when we first march'd forth;
> And, like a jolly troop of huntsmsen, come
> Our lusty English, all with purpled hands,
> Dy'd in the dying slaughter of their foes.
> Open your gates and give the victors way.
>
> (2.1.300–323)

"Honor" in *King John* is actually explored in some depth in the character of the Bastard, designed deliberately, it might be argued, to raise our consciousness of the issue. The character's particular problem with "honor" is not precisely the audience's, but gives us a sidelight on the issue that is nonetheless illuminating: when he is acknowledged Richard Coeur-de-lion's son rather than mere Sir Robert Faulconbridge's, he reflects in an almost Falstaffian manner that he has both gained and lost by the change, that while he is "a foot of honor better than [he] was," he is "many a foot of land the worse" (1.1.181–82). The implication is that being Richard's son is a hollow "honor" indeed without either the real estate or the economic wherewithal to back it up, to which his famous later speech on "commodity" is a complement. If "honor" is nothing without possessions, it is little more *with* them and will quickly go by the boards when they, or indeed self-interest in any form, are threatened:

> Commodity, the bias of the world—
> . . . .
> This bawd, this broker, this all-changing word,
> Clapped on the outward eye of fickle France,
> Hath drawn him from his own determined aid,
> From a resolved and honorable war,
> To a most base and vile-concluded peace.
> And why rail I on this Commodity?
> But for because he hath not wooed me yet,
> Not that I have the power to clutch my hand,
> When his fair angels would salute my palm;
> . . . .
> Since kings break faith upon Commodity,
> Gain, be my lord, for I will worship thee.
>
> (2.1.574, 582–90, 597–98)

I cannot leave this discussion of "honor" without noting that it has made no reference to the two plays in which the topic in all its complexity, including its relationship to love, and particularly to women, is explored most directly—*Troilus and Cressida* and *Antony and Cleopatra*. I have two reasons for this omission: one, precisely because the treatment is more direct in these plays it is less in need of analysis; and, two, because the subject is so prominent in these plays, it is impossible to discuss it at all without doing so at length, in a study that has other objectives. One observation only about these plays I would make at this time is that, in the light of what I suggest is Shakespeare's real view of aristocratic "honor," Ulysses's famous speech on "degree" in *Troilus and Cressida* must be read ironically, not as the defense of social hierarchy that it is usually taken to be, but a realist's recognition that *however* human affairs are organized, ultimately "everything includes itself in power" (1.3.119). Placing beside this the later enigmatic reference that comes up in the context of Ulysses's other famous speech on time and honor, to the "mystery . . . in the soul of state, . . . with whom relation durst never meddle" (3.3.201–2), it becomes clear who, of "Ulysses" or Shakespeare, is actually speaking to us.

Having covered at least certain aspects of first- and second-level rhetoric as they operate in the plays, I will conclude this overview with a few general observations on one aspect of the third. Since the whole thrust of the allegory in the plays is the paradoxical idea of simultaneous concealment and exposure, Shakespeare is meticulous in almost never stepping out of the role of invisible man to offer direct evidence of what he is doing. Occasional references to the art of writing are probably the closest we ever come to actual contact with the allegorical motif itself. Instances of what *within the play* are mere figurative language are thus in allegorical terms direct references by Shakespeare to his art—if we can see them as such. King John's striking figure in reference to himself just before his death is an outstanding example:

> I am a scribbled form drawn with a pen
> Upon a parchment, and against this fire
> Do I shrink up.
>
> (5.7.32–34)

Lady Capulet's figure describing the County Paris to Juliet is comparable:

> Read o'er the volume of young Paris's face,
> And find delight writ there with beauty's pen;
>
> (1.3.82–83)

as is Othello's characterization of Desdemona late in that play:

> Was this fair paper, this most goodly book,
> Made to write "whore" upon?
>
> (4.2.72–73)

Indirect references to composition as done by various of the characters, either for persuasive or other special purposes, are of course legion in the plays, almost as common indeed as references to the art of acting. They range from the very nearly direct—Dogberry's "O that he were here to write me down an ass!" (*Much Ado*, 4.2.70–71), Malvolio's "Good fool, some ink, paper, and light" (*Twelfth Night*, 4.2.105–6), Romeo's "get me ink and paper" (5.1.25), or Albany's "know'st thou this paper?" (*Lear*, 5.3. 161)—to the much more indirect, as in Hamlet's various writings, or the unsuccessful therapeutic unburdening through writing attempted by Lady Macbeth (5.1.6–8). Speech likewise, as the other main aspect of rhetoric, has innumerable direct allegorical associations in the plays as well. We have seen something of this in the earlier discussion of "first" level rhetoric, but any number of further examples might be pointed out. There are clear allegorical implications, for example, in his "corrupter[s] of words," Feste in *Twelfth Night* and Parolles in *All's Well*, "proving" respectively, that mourning is foolish (1.5.53–67) and that virginity ("woman's "honor") is "the most inhibited sin in the canon" (1.1.138)—exercises of impeccable, if perverse, logic that might have been taken directly from Munday's *Defense of Contraries*. Perverse in a different way but equally interesting are a number of what might be called negative examples, where the allegorical key is in the character's *loss* of speech.

The case of the ravished and mutilated Lavinia in *Titus Andronicus* is such an instance: able neither to speak nor write her shame, she is in the worst imaginable state of hellish deprivation to the Elizabethan. This motif is employed in subtle ways in the plays: Macduff's stunned silence ("Why are you silent?" [4.3.137]) in the face of the rhetorical impossibilities Malcolm has just assaulted him with in *Macbeth* is such an instance, as is Edgar's famous line in *Lear*, "The worst is not, as long as we can *say* 'this is the worst'" (4.1. 28, italics mine). In *Pericles*, again, the hell of apathy into which Pericles (Shakespeare's own choice of name, by the way, and obviously known to him as the name of Athens's greatest orator) is sunk near the end of the play is symbolized by his condition of speechlessness, a state from which he is roused with only the greatest effort by the ministrations of his devoted daughter. It is probable also that Cordelia's failure to *speak* in *King Lear*, after her sisters have bilked their doting father shamelessly with exaggerated rhetorical persuasions, is intended by Shakespeare as a deliberate commentary on the same questions. The question of speech or language as a purely abstract consideration, for whatever significance the faculty per se of speech may have, is also cleverly worked in to various of the plays and has an allegorical significance. The nonsense language of *All's Well*—"oscorbidulchos volivorco"—is an instance of this, where Parolles ("words," of course) is for once rendered totally helpless by his inability to use his gift for words to weasel out of the corner in which he finds himself: "I shall lose my life," he says, "for want of language" (4.1.66). And similarly, one of the things that the monster Caliban in *The Tempest* stands for is the infernal uses to which language can always be put. "I pitied thee," says Miranda, "took pains to make thee speak,"

> When thou didst not, savage,
> Know thine own meaning, but wouldst gabble like
> A thing most brutish, I endow'd thy purposes
> With words that made them known.
>
> (1.2.355–58)

Unfortunately, the sequel to Caliban's learning speech was simply his using the gift for the furtherance of evil ends, his nature "being capable of all ill, and one which any print of goodness will not take." The "word," again, can also be the law in Shakespeare for both good or evil ends, depending upon the motive of the user. As Hamlet says to Horatio of his conversation with the gravedigger, "we must speak by the card, or equivocation will undo us"; so it transpires in *The Merchant of Venice*, where Shylock's downfall is hung upon the thread of a missing word. And again, in

2 Henry IV, the preservation of a throne is directly linked to the overly nice interpretation of a single word by Prince John, used to justify the unchivalrous arrest of the unarmed and unprepared rebel leaders (4.1.59ff). The "word" motif in this treacherous transaction, incidentally, is also Shakespeare's own, and is not found in Holinshed.

Just two significant larger examples of rhetorical allegory in Shakespeare I will call the reader's attention to before looking in detail at some individual plays. *The Taming of the Shrew*, again, first, as a Pygmalionesque transformation story, achieves its happy consummation by means almost exclusively of language. The line previously quoted from that play, concerning Petruchio's rhetorical skill, his "rope-tricks," could stand as a motto for the central theme of the play as a whole; for in transforming Katherine from shrew to model wife, Petruchio's method emphasizes, above all, a special form of rhetoric. He postulates unceasingly a *new version* of Katherine in his rhetoric, a Katherine who is not "rough, and coy, and sullen," but "pleasant, gamesome, passing courteous, . . . soft and affable"; (2.1.236, 238, 244) and he allows Katherine not an instant's respite nor an instant's return to reality and truth until she has shaped herself to fit that formula. And not only must she fit the pattern for her character that he designs, but other elements outlandish and extreme to the point of apparent (and highly comic) madness in Petruchio's vision must be accommodated to her mind as well, before she is her fully transformed self. The defeat of her own self-image thus is total in the play, and her "reality" in the end is dependent for its very existence on Petruchio's voice. So that when Petruchio declares "How bright and goodly shines the moon!" at high noon, it is with love and sincerity that Katherine finally learns to reply, that

> be it moon, or sun, or what you please;
> And if you please to call it a rush-candle,
> Henceforth I vow it shall be so for me.
>
> (4.5.13–15)

Katherine's transformation and the distortions of reality it involves, I submit, is a direct allegorical statement on Shakespeare's part of what rhetoric can accomplish, and drama quintessentially exemplifies, in the lives of men.

And *Twelfth Night*, finally, I propose as a further representative example of certain themes relating to rhetoric and drama that are prominent in many of Shakespeare's plays. The play is plotted, first, on the old *Comedy of Errors* principle of misunderstanding, and it contains several levels of illusion, many of which are deliberately rhetorical in character. The whole Malvolio subplot, for example, turns on the subjective misreading of an alphabetical riddle by a man comically disposed to interpret reality as favorable to himself. One of the implications here is that though we may think the playwright/entertainer/rhetorician "gagg'd" if we refuse to laugh or otherwise "minister occasion to him," Shakespeare knows we are wrong, that we will be "hoist with [our] own petar" in due course. More profoundly, the play as a whole is acted out in a fantasy/reality limbo-land that erases confusingly the line between stage and audience. This is one of several plays where women characters masquerade as men, a device with an obvious practical basis in Shakespeare's day, of course, to make the acting of women's parts by boys easier. But it is a device that is seriously disturbing at the same time to an audience's expectations and to their view of the play, because it brings into focus the myriad ambiguities in the relations between dramatic illusion and reality that are part and parcel of Shakespeare's philosophy of art. When Viola/Cesario attempts to woo Olivia with a "conned" speech of flowery language and conventional amatory design, a speech which he/she then proceeds to jump in and out of in confusing sequence, inevitably the question is raised in the audience's mind of what such a dramatic illusion "really" amounts to, and indeed how it is to be distinguished from "reality" itself. Thus, on the one hand, in dramatic terms "Viola's" adopting boy's "outside" (2.2.16) adds an additional dimension of illusion to the play—boy plays girl playing boy—but on the other hand, in "real" terms, it removes illusion altogether, as the boy actor again becomes the boy he really is. The question of how reality and illusion precisely divide in this characterization is pursued at some length in the play, and there are two statements in particular concerning it which are worth quoting. Questioned initially by Olivia as to whether he is "a comedian" (actor, playwright), Viola/Caesario replies "I am not that I play" (1.5.173–74), a valid enough statement in the context simply of the drama; but when the same point is pursued again later in the play the answer slides over into a classic expression of what I might call categorical ambiguity—an expression which Shakespeare did not forget, and repeated more than once in other plays, most notably in *Othello*—the expression "I am not what I am" (3.1.138).

This situation of categorical ambiguity in *Twelfth Night* is the archetype of innumerable instances in Shakespeare where audience and play are by skillful design made one—the play becoming, as he calls it again in *Twelfth Night*, "a natural perspective, that is and is not" (5.1.209). These range, for just a few outstanding examples in several of the plays, from the fake "deaths" of Juliet, of Falstaff, of Hermoine, and of Imogen;[31] to the proud claims of histrionic ability made by Bottom in *A Midsummer Night's Dream* (1.2.20–34), or by Hamlet in the closet scene, with his mother now alone for audience. That this is Shakespeare addressing the *theater audience* ("You that look pale and tremble at this chance, / That are but mutes and audience to this act") directly on the subject of dramatic poetry rhetoric cannot be doubted:

> Peace; sit you down,
> And let me wring your heart; for so I shall,
> If it be made of penetrable stuff;
> If damned custom have not braz'd it so
> That it be proof and bulwark against sense.
>
> (3.4.34–38)

6

"None are for me that look into me with considerate eyes": *Richard III* and Rhetoric

I t will come as no surprise to Shakespeareans that in a study of his work focusing on rhetoric *Richard III* should be selected as primary datum. The culmination of the first tetralogy and among the most popular of all Shakespeare's plays during his lifetime,[1] *Richard III* was and is instantly recognized as having engaged his creative energies arguably more powerfully than anything that precedes it in the theatrical canon. While it is the *tour de force* character of Richard that, as it dominates the play, also dominates discussions of it, it has not entirely escaped criticism's notice over the centuries either that a principal basis of Shakespeare's fascination with the character is that it offered him an opportunity to flaunt certain aspects of his art associated with rhetoric. The component of the hero's character that opens out into the general field of rhetoric as persuasion is the defining trait of that character, namely the protean histrionic ability that is his pride, and the triumphant manipulative use to which that skill is put. Thomas van Laan's description from 1952, for example, is both accurate and typical of modern views of Richard, that his "primary activity" does not only "consist of role-playing" but that he "thereby attains [his] identity."[2] Nor will it be difficult at this point for the reader to see that such a character and such a theme could have particular relevance in a study whose thesis is that Shakespeare's works have the persuasive powers of rhetoric/poetry as a primary subject.

In stating this last, the by now familiar caveat must again be entered that its implications are deeper than they might, in the context perhaps of this play in particular, at first appear to be. "Character," that is to say, and indeed the play's second or "political" level altogether, are not the concern of this interpretation. Where conventional readings also treat rhetoric as a major theme in the play, even the most resolutely contemporary of these still stop with the characters and their interactions as the sole vehicles of Shakespeare's meaning: "Whereas Rivers earnestly looks past the signifier to the signified, Richard knowingly capers on the swift surface of language," Russ McDonald,[3] for example, gives us in perfect postmodern style. The objective here, however, as always, is not the deciphering of Shakespeare's meaning *with* the characters but his meaning *without* them, the characters themselves being seen as part of the allegory, rhetorical strategies that conceal, but simultaneously subtly reveal, the only real rhetorician in the case, Shakespeare himself.

Perhaps the first consideration that any discussion of *Richard III* pretending to thoroughness must take into account, but one that the mesmerizing force of Richard's character and stylistic flair causes many if not most to overlook, is its intimate connection to the *Henry VI* trilogy; as between *Richard III* and the immediately preceding *3 Henry VI*, for example, were the two plays staged consecutively (as may well have been done), neither temporal nor thematic discontinuity would in any way be observable. It is taken for granted, of course, that some knowledge of the earlier plays must inform our experience of this one; only minimal information is provided in the play itself—we learn that Queen Elizabeth's family was elevated in rank by her marriage to the king, that Anne is the widow of the Lancastrian Prince of Wales murdered by Richard—but the information the play itself provides is shadowy, sometimes confusing (Queen Margaret's position?), and, most importantly, can be misleading taken out of the context of the tetralogy as a whole. This in particular is a test of critical awareness, a test devised by Shakespeare, in deliberately making Richard the whole tetralogy's irresistible cynosure, to use Frye's term again. It is a test that criticism generally fails, in giving only perfunctory acknowledgment at best of characters other than Richard for their roles earlier in the sequence.

A. P. Rossiter's stance is typical in his claiming that the play's "cumulative effect . . . is there even if we know only a few bare essentials of what has gone before."[4] In fact Rossiter is wrong; the

deeper rhetorical significance of *Richard III* cannot be grasped
without the reader/audience's full recollection that others in the
cast of characters besides Richard stand convicted of self-interest, opportunism, and general Machiavellianism fully as ruthless, however less conscious (which, as we shall see in a moment,
is important), as Richard's own. The discussion of "honor" in the
last chapter, as it relates to the *Henry VI* plays, would be an obvious complement to this observation. The major difference allegorically between *Richard III* and the other plays in the sequence is that the character of Richard, *conscious* of what "he" is
doing rhetorically, foregrounds Shakespeare's allegory in a new
and deliberate way. This foregrounding, it should be noted, is not
simplifying, however. Indeed, one of its subtler effects is that it
carefully fudges the common-sense distinction we naturally
make between Richard III as character and *Richard III* as play;
allegorically, that distinction disappears. But the critical point to
be established here is that there is nothing in either Richard's
motives or his actions in *Richard III* that exceeds in malevolence
acts either committed previously by many of the other characters
or, had history permitted, that they would not have been prepared to commit. Richard's treatment of Hastings, for example,
in terms both of its necessity to him politically and the cover of
"legality" in which it is cloaked, had been exactly foreshadowed
in the treatment of another "protector" named Gloucester in *2
Henry VI*, with on that occasion Queen Margaret, supported by
the ever-ready Buckingham as prime instigator, and with
Gloucester's own uncle (shades again of Richard and the young
princes) as spokesman:

> That he should die is worthy policy;
> But yet we want a color for his death.
> 'Tis meet he be condemned by course of law.
>
> (3.1.235–37)

Similarly, the notorious courtship scene with Anne repeats,
albeit with rhetorical flash of an altogether different order, a pattern that had already been established in the courtship scene between King Edward and the widow Elizabeth Woodeville Lady
Grey in *3 Henry VI*. Indeed, a lingering effect of the latter scene
in the memory of the thoughtful reader, and quite possibly accessible even to the thoughtful playgoer, could be to throw a
problematic light on the role of *Anne* in the former. Edward, not,

like Richard, the actual killer of the lady's husband, though re-sponsible for his death, is the ostensible wooer, but is smoothly outflanked by a superior Machiavellian wit, taking advantage of his passionate haste, and using her "honor" as trump card. And it should be noted also in this connection that if *Richard III*, taken by itself, might give the impression that the women are mere passive victims, their moral like their physical nature less given somehow to acts of war and violence, the towering example of Margaret, "she-wolf of France" in the trilogy, is there to ex-plode any such illusions—climactically so in *3 Henry VI*, in her cold mockery, preceding her brutal murder, of the abject and cap-tive York.

The rhetorical consciousness "Richard" so flamboyantly dis-plays and so effectively employs is the single outstanding feature that distinguishes this character from every other in the tetral-ogy, having the effect in that play, as suggested, of foregrounding Shakespeare's allegory. At the level simply of characterization, first, as is typical of Shakespeare, while he takes the broad and even many of the subtler features of the character directly from his sources, the final product is a transformation of that sketchy legacy that would have been unimaginable to its creators. The el-ement of his physical deformity, prominent in the sources, as the motive for his malignity and the spur to his ambitions, is the principal focus of his first two and most famous soliloquies, the longer introductory one from *3 Henry VI* (3.3.124–96), and its ex-tension in the "winter of our discontent" speech that opens *Richard III*, recapping and updating the progress of his plots. It is Shakespeare's genius to posit a direct link between the ugli-ness and the ambition in the historical Richard, to reveal this link in the character's first speeches, and then to add in, as a climax, the chameleonic rhetorico/theatrical ability (based again on specific hints from the sources as well as their general drift—More, for example, "He was close and secret, a deep dissembler"[5]) that will enable the character to turn what one would normally expect should be obstacles into advantages.[6]

The second-level rhetorical implications of all of this are straightforward; it is obvious that Shakespeare created his Rich-ard at least partly as an icon of the power of rhetorical skill as a manipulative tool. The famous courtship of Anne, being placed in the second scene, immediately following a brief warm-up exer-cise, figuratively speaking, for Richard, flexing his rhetorical

muscles in easy manipulations of Clarence and Hastings, is a virtuoso triumph of persuasion that Shakespeare clearly exults in
displaying. Minute dissection of the scene is not necessary to
have a secure sense of this *jeu d'esprit* exultation in its creator.
Since the scene is purely fanciful, though the known historical
circumstances make the courtship itself plausible to imagine,
Shakespeare is free to create it in any form he wishes. Doing so
in the particular way he does, however, ostentatiously defying
both historical and seemingly even rhetorical possibility at every
turn—having the freshly slaughtered (by Richard, of course)
corpse of Henry VI as central prop throughout, recapitulating
and justifying at length the abhorrence Anne must feel for
Richard, having Richard himself first brazenly lie about and
then with equal brazenness admit all the crimes of which he
stands accused—and still making an irresistibly convincing
show of the whole impossible mélange allows of no other interpretation but that Shakespeare is showing off his rhetorical wizardry and enjoying the exercise immensely.

While these last observations would appear to shade over
somewhat from the political to the allegorical level of interpretation, as in fact they do, I would remind the reader again of something said a moment ago about Shakespeare's deliberate foregrounding of his allegory in this play—that foregrounding is not
simplifying. Indeed, in terms of the basic allegorical principle operative throughout the canon, as I interpret it, precisely to the
degree to which rhetorical issues *are* openly flaunted in the
plays do they correspondingly conceal their deeper meaning.
And, as none would dispute, a most uncharacteristic openness in
the displaying of a rhetorical theme is indeed a unique feature
and the hallmark of this play. Nowhere else in Shakespeare, for
example, does he intrude actual pauses in the dramatic action to
speak directly of the rhetorico/theatrical maneuverings that are
being employed. There are several such intrusions, some possibly inspired again by hints taken from the sources. Buckingham
exulting in his ability to "counterfeit the deep tragedian," in 3.5,
as he and Richard prepare their faces to meet with and convince
the mayor of Hastings's treachery would be one such; and, similarly, the next act of the Hastings mock tragedy would fit this
pattern as well. Here the "scrivener" of the Hastings indictment
points out the discrepancy, in terms of the time involved, between the preparation of the indictment and the crimes it de-

scribes—that the indictment, so intricate and carefully in-
scribed, had to have been prepared *before* the "crimes" took
place! The key allegorical implication in the scrivener's speech,
however, is in its last lines. These are entirely Shakespeare's
gratuitous contribution; and they are spoken, it should also be
noted, with the scrivener alone on stage, with none but the theater audience to hear him—Shakespeare tweaking his audience's nose, as it were, to awaken them to their own involvement
with the same issues:

> Here's a good world the while! Who is so gross,
> That cannot see this palpable device?
> Yet who's so bold, but says he sees it not?
> Bad is the world; and all will come to nought,
> When such ill dealing must be seen in thought.
> (3.6.10–14)

It is not mere coincidence either in this speech that the words
"all will come to nought" echo a line, the climactic line, from the
first and the most flagrant of these pauses for rhetorical reflection in the play, Richard's triumphant soliloquy that ends the
courtship of Anne again:

> Was ever woman in this humour woo'd?
> Was ever woman in this humour won?
> . . . .
> What! I, that killed her husband and his father—
> To take her in her heart's extremest hate,
> With curses in her mouth, tears in her eyes,
> The bleeding witness of my hatred by;
> Having God, her conscience, and these bars against me,
> . . . .
> And yet to win her, *all the world to nothing*!
> (2.2.227–28, 230–34, 237, italics mine)

Placed where they are in this scene, and their radical potential
later reinforced by the scrivener's near repetition, it is difficult to
see these words as anything else than a direct statement by
Shakespeare of his conviction that the arts of language hold a
persuasive power that, in his hands at least, is literally infinite.

The scene with the scrivener can serve as a convenient entrance point into consideration of the deeper rhetorical allegory
of *Richard III* as well. It has been suggested that the issue of

rhetorical consciousness is central in the allegorical reading of this play, and it is an issue to which this scene in particular has a subtle but significant connection. It will be noted that when the words "rhetorical consciousness" have been used before here, it has been in reference to Shakespeare's characterization specifically of his hero, as the central feature of his character. That they are not so used in this instance is intended to signal a broader frame of reference for the concept than the level merely of characterization—that it has a relation to the play as a whole, and, most importantly, from an allegorical standpoint, that it has a relation to the play's audience. A couple of basic points about the issue of rhetorical consciousness in general should perhaps be established here before going any further. It is obvious enough, first, that it is meaningful to speak of *one* "rhetorical consciousness" only as directly operative in this play, that being, of course, Shakespeare's. "Richard" is a figment of Shakespeare's rhetorical imagination, from which the incontrovertible conclusion follows that "he" cannot possess any rhetorical consciousness that Shakespeare does not possess before him. A number of other significant and perhaps even surprising further conclusions follow from this first principle. If Shakespeare's endowment of a rhetorical consciousness to the character of Richard is done in full awareness, it follows that any *lack* of such consciousness in the other characters, Richard's dupes—Clarence, Anne, Edward, Hastings, Buckingham, et. al.—is equally a product of that same awareness. In a way, this is momentous: among other things it would appear to validate a speculation about Shakespeare that appeared earlier in this study, relating to the intellectual legacy of Freud. I suggested there the possibility that Shakespeare's "extraordinary mind simply transcends the Freudian system altogether, overpowering the conscious/unconscious division on which that system depends." If the conclusions above are logically sound, this becomes a statement no longer simply of possibility but of fact.

Shakespeare's "rhetorical consciousness" thus is absolute, his mind fully in control. Not just Richard as a character, but everything in the play is rhetorically aware in the same degree. Indeed it is precisely here that the play's allegory enters, signaled in subtle ways. With the allegorical message the dual one of simultaneous concealment *and* revelation, Richard and his dupes together carry both sides of this message. Richard being the towering presence and master manipulator that he is, absorbs the audience's attention fully; at the same time, however, by making Richard's *rhetorical* wizardry the primary focus of our attention, Shakespeare is craftily revealing to us our own besottedness as dupes of *his* greater rhetorical sleight-of-hand. "Richard's" schemes only succeed because his victims, Shakespeare's straw men, cooperate fully. "King Edward" can be (rhetorically) "true and just" (1.1.36), for the nonce, notwithstanding the remarkable record that is his of past and present injustices and falsehoods, including at that very moment the wholly unjust imprisonment of his only recently "ten times . . . beloved" (*3 Henry VI*, 5.1.103) brother Clarence, because it is necessary that he be so for "subtle, false and treacherous" (1.1.37) Richard to work his nefarious schemes. Clarence himself is handled in the same way, doubling the force of the allegorical message. "A quicksand of deceit" in Margaret's accurate characterization of him from *3 Henry VI,* he is now suddenly become "simple, plain Clarence," accepting imprisonment without a murmur, apparently no more capable than his brother Edward of seeing or imagining that there could be any ambiguity in the wizard's prophecy "that G / Of Edward's heirs the murderer shall be"—that there may be other individuals close at hand that the letter "G" could well designate besides himself.

While instances of Shakespeare's loading of the rhetorical dice similar to these, tricking and twitting his audience in one rhetorical flourish, could be multiplied, I will discuss briefly just one further rather special example which, similarly to the scene with the scrivener, broadens the context of the allegory to embrace certain key aspects of contemporary Elizabethan culture. All of the characters, thoughtfully considered, offer the same lesson, but the Buckingham character may make that lesson more explicit because of the somewhat different relationship he enjoys with Richard for much of the play. Hitching his wagon to Richard's star almost from the beginning of that meteoric (as the play presents it) rise, he appears to pick up something of Richard's rhetorical consciousness in the process, learning to "counterfeit the deep tragedian" as well, he believes, as his master. This is another case, it may be noted in passing, of Shakespeare extrapolating from hints in the sources to build his complex rhetorical and ethical structures. Later in More's account of Richard's rise and Buckingham's role in it comes an ex-

tended description, fairly dripping with irony, of their slick manipulation of the mayor and the citizens of London in Richard's
bid for the crown—Richard appearing before the people "with a
bishop on every hand of him,"[7] feigning the greatest reluctance,
even initially rebuking the citizens for their overzealous love of
him—many details which Shakespeare adopted directly to
create the irresistibly engaging theatrics of this pivotal historical moment.[8] On the level of allegory, however, Buckingham, I
suggest, occupies a "middle" position, rhetorically speaking, between Richard and those other characters who, from this perspective at least, are presented as merely his dupes. This
positioning of Buckingham raises several interesting interpretive issues that have implications well beyond the plot, or indeed
anything in the sources.

There is a hierarchy of rhetorical awareness, as it might be
termed, that while it starts in the play with the characters, extends beyond them, to the play's creator. At every "level" of that
hierarchy, from zero at one end to infinity at the other, the higher
levels control the ones beneath them. Within the *play*, then, at
least three levels are quite distinctly presented in major characters—hapless dupes like Hastings and Clarence at the "zero"
end, obviously; Buckingham, shown as understanding and utilizing *some* of the powers that style can put in our hands placed, as
I say, in the middle; and then Richard at the top. There are
grounds for interpreting levels somewhere between Richard and
Buckingham in the hierarchy as well. The allegorical structure
starts to get a little fuzzy here, perhaps, but there are characters
who, not flaunting any particular rhetorical awareness themselves, are presented as nevertheless possibly quicker to detect
the rhetorical sleights of a Richard than many of their peers,
Buckingham among them. This could certainly be interpreted as
the case with the Queen Elizabeth character, for example, in the
second courtship scene. While Shakespeare gives us a Richard
still operating at the top of his rhetorical bent, with the same
verve and flair, overcoming impossibility in an even greater
degree than he was faced with in courting Anne, and headed apparently for the same success, the sequel shows him as frus-
trated, outfoxed perhaps, by one whom unimaginably bitter
experience may at long last have rendered proof against his oratorical magic.[9] A similar and perhaps less ambivalent example is
found in the Stanley character, deftly, with exactly the right

degree of dutifulness in his demeanor throughout, balancing his own interests between those of both Richard *and* Richmond, successfully preserving both life and position while threading the hazardous political shoals of a dynastic transition.

The idea of a hierarchy of rhetorical awareness, which is also a hierarchy of power, however, remains clearest when considered in the bare-bones, three-level form that places mere dupes like Hastings at the bottom, Richard at the top, and a Buckingham somewhere in the middle. Where allegory intrudes into the equation is in the possibility this structure implies of a fourth and final level to complete it, the level of *ultimate* rhetorical awareness, this one outside the play, in the mind of its creator. This concept opens several potentially fruitful paths for critical exploration. That it is possible to look at the play allegorically in this manner, first, and that it is part of Shakespeare's intention to allow it to be seen this way, is supported by a suggestive symmetry in the operation of the play's rhetorical theme—a theme that represents Shakespeare's extrapolation from history, it must always be remembered. As we have seen, while Richard's rhetorical wizardry is dominant in the play, it is not absolute; in the end he fails. In the *matter* of this failure Shakespeare has no choice; the constraints of history tie his hands; in the *manner* of it, however, he does have choices, and the choices he makes are allegorically instructive. His representation does not misstate history in any way; as always he makes remarkably full and accurate use of his source materials in reconstructing dramatically the last acts of Richard's career, but he adds to it in ways that point clearly toward the area of rhetoric, with all that term connotes in an Elizabethan context, as instrumental in that failure. In pure historical terms, of course, that failure has no "cause," exactly; it simply happened; forces, events—jealousies, shifting allegiances, "the hazard of the die"—conspired to bring it about: such a simple thing as being left horseless on the battlefield at precisely the wrong moment, as Shakespeare knows, may have been the final determinant of Richard's fate. But as rhetorical factors conditioned his rise, so do they contribute to his downfall, as Shakespeare depicts it.

To explain this feature and its allegorical significance fully requires somewhat more elaborate development of the background, in relation specifically to this play, of what was termed above "the area of rhetoric." Everything this study has dealt with up to this point comes into that background, much of it entering also into *Richard III*, directly within the play itself, and indirectly, as it is pointed toward its Elizabethan audience. Coming immediately to essentials, a factor that involves both of these elements, the play itself and its audience, and is therefore central allegorically, is *speed*. The last chapter discussed some of the ways the concept of speed figures in the construction particularly of Shakespeare's history plays, so as to constitute, in effect, an allegorical statement. The general allegorical message suggested there is about the power of style, rhetorical style, with speed as one of its central components—that if style can be elevated sufficiently, made intense and absorbing *to the point of irresistibility*, the most flagrant impossibilities, perhaps temporal ones most frequently in the history plays, can be put past an audience without that audience twigging to the hoax. We might not as audience recognize these maneuvers as a joke played on us by the author, except that in many instances he advertises the fact, placing direct reminders in his text of the essential role speed plays in putting a convincing face on the illusions. *Richard III*, then, is the supreme early example of that method and that message in operation.

With at least three historical apprentice pieces, attempts to conquer time, behind him before *Richard III*, the stylistic miracle he has been seeking, of turning historical years into stage minutes without visible incongruity in the results, is both definitively accomplished and put on exhibition in that play. Among the weaknesses of the *Henry VI* plays as theatrical experiments was their general lack of a clear sense of structural unity. While their ostensible focus on the figure of Henry VI is at least vaguely suggestive of thematic unity, as little more than direct translations of chronicle excerpts from the page to the stage, they are plagued with an episodic jerkiness that even the occasional emergence of powerful subthemes and characters—the Joan Pucelle, Duke Humphrey, or Queen Margaret stories—fails to overcome completely. In *Richard III*, with its unwavering intense focus on the rise and fall of its hero, thematic coherence and structural unity are achieved at once. Central to that achievement, then, and to the cultural allegorical implications that I am suggesting flow from it, is speed. What as spectators we do not notice in this play, that we could not help but notice to some extent in its predecessors, are gaps, temporal or episodic, that stand out in any sense as interruptions of the dramatic flow. As the word *temporal* here suggests, the quantum leap *Richard III* makes over the *Henry VI* trilogy is in its solving of the problem of time in a history play. In the *Henry VI* plays, he dealt with the problem of time by ignoring it, trusting that his rhetoric was powerful enough to occupy the audience fully, so that its absence should not be noticed. In *Richard III* time is not so much ignored as annihilated, history as always impossibly compressed, but with from scene to scene such perfect dramatic continuity that fourteen years (from the death of Henry VI to the death of Richard III) is *believably* (*actually?*) reduced to three hours, the hoax succeeding without a murmur of dissent. The allegorical dimension opens up here for Shakespeare in that, having reached the point in his development of method that any challenge can now be met without fear, he has in the process also discovered that he need no longer hide, but can flaunt, indeed play games, with both his methods and his powers, in full confidence of their remaining undetected.

This, then, is the contribution of speed to this play. In Richard's method Shakespeare reveals *his* method, doubling, in effect, the revelation that is already visible in the structure and style of the play. The play stands, indeed, as the perfect case study in what the term *rhetoric* connotes in an Elizabethan cultural context—not, again, as the *public* may understand it, but as Shakespeare does, to include its actual, largely unconscious practice. This statement should need no further elaboration at this point; suffice to say that the Richard we meet at the beginning of the play and throughout his rise to power embodies precisely the qualities that constitute rhetorical perfection. The combination of superior wit and superior command of language, with *quickness* the hallmark of both, is of course primary; and no less so is a full Machiavellian self-awareness: the power to fool others can only be effective in inverse proportion to the extent to which one is prepared to fool oneself.

The point that the Richard these terms describe is Richard in his ascent is allegorically important because, as noted earlier, the coin has another side. By suggesting a direct analogy between rhetorical power and political (or, in symbolic terms, absolute) power in Richard, and then showing that rhetorical factors contribute as well to his downfall, as we shall examine in a moment, Shakespeare is at that point distinguishing allegorically between Richard and himself, leaving Richard, as he must, to his historical fate, while shifting the crown of rhetorical perfection from character to creator.

To separate the threads of allegorical significance delegated to Richard from those retained by Shakespeare is an analytic problem of some subtlety. In one sense separation is clearly impossible; Richard is an avatar of Shakespeare, representing directly in his characterization many of the rhetorical ideas that inspire the whole Shakespearean *ouevre*. Allowing Richard to demonstrate to the audience, in front of the footlights, the techniques Shakespeare himself continues to employ only indirectly and behind them, however, may be the wedge we need to drive between creator and character to separate their contributions. Richard is a walking textbook of rhetorical styles, but the feature of his general technique immediately pertinent to the discussion here is the one it particularly, and I suggest for allegorical reasons, flaunts, namely speed. From the standpoint both of his long-term goal, the crown, which does not of course take him "long" to achieve, and the immediate scene-by-scene histrionic maneuvers flourished before the audience that move him single-mindedly along that track, his method is geared to the mastery of time—always to be one jump ahead, never allowing time to his opponents to catch up to his tricks. He is aided mightily in this endeavour by Shakespeare; it is Richard's method, but it is his good fortune as well, to get Clarence safely "pack'd with post-horse up to heaven" before Edward has time to relent, but also before he too cooperates with Richard's schemes by himself conveniently dying: Thus, in 1.1, we are informed that Clarence "hath not another day to live"; news of his death is then first imparted to his children in 2.2; when lo, *their* lamentations are abruptly checked by news of the ultimate calamity of Edward's death as well! Things do indeed, with Shakespeare's aid, move fast for Richard in the accomplishment of his designs.

While examples like this still operate largely "behind the scenes" to insinuate the idea of speed into the texture of the play, more again from a Shakespearean than precisely a Ricardian perspective, the number of similar examples of Richard himself alluding to speed, as well as both moving and thinking fast, ensure the audience ample opportunity to make itself aware of its centrality in his method. The crowning, and indeed seemingly miraculous, instance of the last would probably have to be the courtship scene with Anne, again, although essentially all of Richard's verbal manipulations in the period of his meteoric rise exhibit the same facility and enjoy the same success. That success, as Shakespeare's structuring of the death of Clarence demonstrates, is due not solely to Richard's control of events by the combination of quick wits and quick action; it is also aided by events themselves. Things beyond his control, but not beyond Shakespeare's, are also shown as moving with (incredible?) speed, in consequence playing directly into Richard's hands, he alone being totally "in sync," as the pop term has it, with events, possessing the wit both to anticipate and move with them. Edward's death, for example, is no more than announced in the scene just alluded to when the *immediate* crowning of his successor is suddenly seen to be necessary, with both Rivers and Buckingham, each for his own reasons, urging it—"send straight for him; / Let him be crown'd" (2.2.97–98); Richard, meanwhile, a jump ahead as always, has his plans already in place, leading Buckingham even as he strokes his ego by flattering Buckingham that *he* has the leading role: "My oracle, my prophet, . . . / I, as a child, will go by they direction." (2.2.151–52).

Events moving faster than any but Richard can keep up with them is again the scenario, as it was in the Clarence episode, in the theatrics surrounding the death of Hastings. The "wing'd Mercury" who bore the order for Clarence's death, while the countermand was entrusted to a "tardy cripple," is paralleled in the Hastings case by the "friends" whose "loving haste[;] . . . something against our meanings," carried out the execution before "we [had yet] determin'd he should die" (3.5.52–55).

Two final examples of Richard's making direct allusion to the role of speed in his method should be cited here as obviously important in their own right, but as also providing a transition to the consideration of what I have called the other side of the rhetorical "coin" in the play, Richard's ultimate failure. Buckingham's desire for "some little breath, some pause" before he "positively speak[s]" (4.2.24–25) in the matter of the disposal of the young princes, is the occasion for the first of these, the most prominent of Richard's direct acknowledgments that as speed of movement brought him success, it alone can sustain him: when "High-reaching Buckingham grows circumspect" his end is very near, for "none are for me / That look into me with considerate eyes" (4.2.29–31). The other reference follows close upon this,

when, with the princes safely out of the way, Richard registers
his triumphant confidence in what he thinks at this point is the
continued predestined success of his method:

> Come, I have learn'd that fearful commenting
> Is leaden servitor to dull delay;
> Delay leads impotent and snail-pac'd beggary.
> Then fiery expedition be my wing,
> Jove's Mercury, and herald for a king!
>
> (5.3.50–55)

The emphasis on speed is to continue in the process of
Richard's downfall as contrived by Shakespeare, but whereas
speed worked *for* him in his rise, it will work against him now.
The hints are subtle that point in this direction in the remainder
of the play, but whatever the interpretation that is put on Richard's behavior, problems with speed are an inescapable factor in
his decline. It is a symbolic moment, for example, when Richard,
in the very next scene, though "in haste" (4.4.161) as always, still
gripped with the necessity to "be brief when traitors brave the
field" (4.3.57), pauses, allowing his mother to "intercept [his] . . .
expedition" (4.4.136) to curse and dress him down. It is the first
sign in the play of irresolution in Richard, and while an unlikely
attack of conscience is casually thrown out as a possible cause
("strike alarums, drums! / Let not the heavens hear these tell-
tale women / Rail on the Lord's anointed" [4.4.148–50]), both the
moment and the language fit too well into the rhetorical context
of the play as a whole for it not to be Shakespeare's intention to
relate it to that aspect of Richard's character as well. If there
could be any doubt on this point it is removed before the end of
the scene when it is made absolutely clear that something is
indeed happening to Richard's mind. After quickly recovering
himself and concentrating his wits for one more irresistible virtuoso rhetorical assault on, and seeming victory over, Queen
Elizabeth, his control first wavers again, as in his haste he gives
conflicting orders to Catesby and Ratcliffe, and finally almost
collapses in confusion, when after a rapid series of bad news
messages arrives, his frustration drives him to assault the third
messenger ("There, take thou that, till thou bring better news"
[4.4.510]).

It is clearly by design that speed is made a cause of Richard's
breakdown here, his only such complete loss of control in the

play. Because the indications of what is actually happening to Richard here are themselves curt and pass quickly, it is easy, and again I suggest by design on Shakespeare's part, to see them as unimportant, and thereby miss their considerable allegorical significance. What seems to be happening is that the anticipation of, and synchronicity with, rapidly unfolding events that has previously given Richard complete control in every situation is slipping away from him. The pointed message of these brief lapses is that synchronicity is somehow gone; it is a case either of Richard moving ahead of events or vice versa, his failing to keep up with them. The care taken by Shakespeare to convey this idea is too striking to allow for the possibility of it not being important to him. The actual exchange with Catesby and Ratcliffe makes its point more concisely than any attempt to paraphrase it could:

K. Rich. Some light-foot friend post to the Duke of Norfolk.
Ratcliff, thyself—or Catesby; where is he?
Cate. Here, my good lord.
K. Rich Catesby, fly to the Duke.
Cate. I will, my lord, with all convenient haste.
K. Rich. Ratcliff, come hither. Post to Salisbury;
When thou com'st thither—[*To Catesby*]
Dull, unmindful villain,
Why stay'st thou here, and go'st not to the Duke?
Cate. First, mighty liege, tell me your Highness' pleasure,
What from your Grace I shall deliver to him.
K. Rich. O, true, good Catesby. Bid him levy straight
The greatest strength and power that he can make
And meet me suddenly at Salisbury.[*Exit.*
Rat. What, may it please you, shall I do at Salisbury?
K. Rich. Why, what wouldst thou do there before I go?
Rat. Your Highness told me I should post before.
K. Rich. My mind is chang'd.

(4.4.440–56)

The interlude with the messengers a few lines further on is particularly direct in putting across the idea that Richard's problem at this point is one of too much speed. They appear in rapid succession, without any opportunity for comment between, and when the third bursts out as soon as he appears, with "My lord, the army of great Buckingham—" Richard strikes him, assuming that *his* message too is going to be bad news. Of course it turns out to be the opposite; Buckingham's army has been destroyed; but the allegorical message of Richard's loss of his previous perfect synchronicity is one that cannot be missed.

I earlier called Shakespeare's Richard a textbook of rhetorical styles, with his preternaturally quick wit as the attribute in particular that, certainly until these last instances at any rate, ensures his supremacy in all verbal encounters. In connecting Richard's decline to what looks like the overdevelopment of that faculty of speed that has always been his strength, Shakespeare may be remembering a tradition relating to quick wits that can also be found in the school texts of his day. Ascham's strictures are typical of Elizabethan educational theory on the subject, theories that Shakespeare's schooling is likely to have exposed him to, whether or not it served him consciously as a model for Richard here, or no:

> Quick wits also be, in most part of all their doings, overquick, hasty, rash, heady, and brainsick. These two last words, *heady* and *brainsick*, be fit and proper words, rising naturally of the matter and termed aptly by the condition of overmuch quickness of wit.[10]

Showing Richard betrayed by the very power that carried him to supremacy in the first place, however, and again it should be remembered that this is pure Shakespeare, unconnected with sources, is, from an allegorical standpoint, highly suggestive. It has the effect of deflecting our attention from Richard, as the perfect rhetorician that one was, to the authentically perfect rhetorician that still is, his creator. Richard's loss of control over his art reinforces Shakespeare's retention of control over his: the avatar disappears; the god remains. Having been shown, if we can detach ourselves from the illusion long enough to be able to notice, the importance of speed as a component of "Richard's" rhetorical wizardry, we are now invited, at an even deeper level of allegorical subtlety, to consider its importance as a component of Shakespeare's. The basic principles of its operation in the history plays were suggested in the last chapter; in *Richard III* those principles are brought to their fullest development. It is also the case that speed operates in essentially the same manner for both Richard in his heyday and Shakespeare; by being always a stage ahead of his opponents and events—the opponents, for Shakespeare, being us, the audience, and "events" the historical facts—and by his quickness leading us, as well as keeping everything off balance, he achieves his goal of transforming a patent impossibility into a convincing reality. It goes without saying, of course, that every other rhetorical trick in the book in addition to speed is also employed in these maneuvers, but to analyze and classify these would be material for virtually a book-length study in itself; it is for this reason alone that I single out speed as the focus of this discussion.

The patent impossibility that speed is instrumental in overcoming for Shakespeare in *Richard III*, then, is the representing of fourteen years of history, from the death of King Henry in 1471 to that of Richard in 1485, in three hours. Speed as a structural principle in the drama must be seen as actually functioning in two somewhat different though related senses, one historical and one purely dramatic. In the dramatic sense, success of the illusion depends on keeping the action on the boil, as it were—ensuring the audience's rapt attention by piling climactic event upon climactic event as the scenes pass rapidly before us—from regal sibling rivalry, to an amazingly audacious wooing, to vicious courtly intrigue, to murder leavened by remorse and guilt in the first four scenes, with the whole sustained in an unbroken rhetorico/poetic matrix of, as Shakespeare knows, irresistible power. And with this kind of dramatic power in his hands he also knows, to bring the second sense into play, that any kind of historical outrage can be committed with impunity, speeding up history if he wishes to the point not merely of impossibility but of manifest absurdity. We looked at one example of such absurdity earlier, Richard announcing in the first scene that while both of his brothers are shortly to die, it is critical to his plans that Clarence go first, a sequence that he *barely* manages to hold to. The historical facts here, for information, are that Clarence languished in the Tower for the best part of a year, and that Edward's death came a full five years later.[11] The compressions of act 4 are even more outrageous, realistically evaluated, insult added to injury in this case by the blatancy with which Shakespeare displays his maneuvers. Careful reading reveals that there can be *no time breaks* of significant length from the beginning of scene 2 to the end of scene 4 of act 4; all the action of these scenes is presented as having transpired in a single day. It is a long "day" indeed, because it takes in the rupture between Richard and Buckingham over the issue of the princes, the planting of the rumor of Anne's terminal illness, Richard's sending Catesby off to find "some mean, poor gentlemen" to whom he can marry Clarence's daughter, the murder and interment of the princes, the death of Anne and the marriage of Clarence's daughter, the proxy wooing and winning of the hand of his niece, and the mounting *and* capsizing, with the capture of the principal, of Buckingham's rebellion.[12]

Observations like these, seldom made, make clear that when Shakespeare put the words "none are for me that look into me with considerate eyes" into Richard's mouth, he was giving us, pointedly, the opportunity to apply the same maxim to himself, fully aware that he too can only succeed if those on whom he is working his magic can be kept from any pausing for breath before he releases them from the theater. And the allegorical point again is that while Richard in the end is not successful, Shakespeare in the end is. This not to say that we do not "know," in a certain sense, if we stop to think about it, what Shakespeare is doing in these scenes, compressing history into a time-span of presentation that in objective terms is utterly absurd. We may even draw satisfaction from this "knowledge" and think we have caught Shakespeare out. The deeper truth and certainly one of the deeper allegorical lessons of the play, however, is that we are wrong in thinking this, and Shakespeare knows it. Rather than what he is doing being unreal, it is our "knowledge" of its impossibility that is in fact chimerical. His point is that our "objectivity" is a phantom; only rhetoric is real. We *say* you cannot compress two years (from the princes' death to Richard's) into one "day," and that "day" in turn into an hour's stage time; but yet it is done and it succeeds; the "facts" are refuted. There is no test of this principle that vindicates it more triumphantly than the courtship of Anne, again, a scene created, I submit, principally for that very reason, to challenge and to vanquish "objectivity" in one virtuoso display. And we may be fortunate as well that a distinguished scholar has recently taken up that challenge, whose efforts may be taken as a gauge of its prospects for success. Inga-Stina Ewbank, without knowing it, springs a logical trap on herself when she remarks of *Richard III*, with this shorter of the two great courtship scenes obviously in mind, that the play is "full of examples" of Shakespeare's bowing to the "necess[ity], in the concentrated time-span of a play, to foreshorten acts of persuasion."[13] The logical trap lies in the fact that the statement is meaningless in the context of this or for that matter any other scene in the play. What it ignores, and in doing so defeats itself, is the *actual persuasiveness* of the language used; her word "foreshorten" implies some kind of falsification or cheat, the suggestion being that not even a Richard (or a Shakespeare) could "really" pull off such a trick in "real" life. But the scene itself gives Shakespeare's reply to that objection: what, then, *is* "real" life? Those are real people speaking real words on the stage; where is the "foreshortening" of anything if what happens on that stage is convincing, as every spectator to this scene, even Ewbank, must agree it triumphantly is? Robert Y. Turner surely speaks for all of us in observing that the courtship has a "mimetic verisimilitude" that "most readers would find credible."[14]

In a similar cavil from the nineteenth century another distinguished scholar of the day, James Russell Lowell, in an intended dismissal of *Richard III* as lesser Shakespeare, has the purport of his remarks backfire as well, when considered from the allegorical perspective developed here. He attacks the play for its stylistic exaggerations:

> Whoever has seen it upon the stage knows that the actor of Richard is sure to offend against every canon of taste laid down by Hamlet in his advice to the players. He is sure to tear his passion to rags and tatters; he is sure to split the ears of the groundlings; and he is sure to overstep the modesty of nature with every one of his stage strides.[15]

While the words themselves may be accurate, the assumption that lies behind them—that the play is therefore flawed in conception—is not; rather, it is the other way around. As Richard's deformity, not to mention his known and admitted exaggeratedly ruthless character and past history, prove no obstacle to his rise when rhetorical wizardry transforms them, so Shakespeare is showing us that blatant melodramatic exaggeration is no obstacle to an audience's being completely won over by *his* mastery of the same skill. The comic self-mockery he puts into the mouth of the character in several places, no hint of which appears in the sources ("Upon my life, she finds, although I cannot, / Myself to be a marvellous proper man. / I'll be at charges for a looking-glass, / And entertain a score or two of tailors [1.2.253–56]) is mockery as well of an audience whose susceptibility to rhetorical persuasion is as limitless apparently as that of Edward's court.

I come back with this observation to the fundamental allegorical issue of the play, in its relation to its Elizabethan audience, the issue of rhetorical consciousness. As we have seen, there is an analogy between Richard the character and Shakespeare the creator in their manipulations of their respective dupes, Richard's in the play and Shakespeare's in the theater. This is not to say that Shakespeare sees his theater audience as exactly analogous to his cast of historical characters, distinguished one and all for their self-serving ambition and ruthlessness, but that they are at any rate suspect in similar ways where questions of rhetorical awareness are concerned—rhetorical awareness, which he sees as tantamount in many ways, I am going to suggest, to self-awareness. Taken by itself, as we observed earlier, *Richard III* may give a somewhat different impression of many of the important characters of the tetralogy from that they brought with them from the earlier plays—Edward now "true and just," Elizabeth mother of innocents made an innocent victim herself, Margaret divine retribution and doom incarnate. In fact, however, the most significant distinction between Richard and those who may appear, in many cases at least, the undeserving targets of his malignity, is that his career moves are more successful only because more consciously pursued. As a moment's reflection on this statement will suggest, its implications are radical, in particular as the actions and attitudes of the aristocratic movers and shakers of Richard's world may be intended as a commentary on the same elements in Shakespeare's. It challenges conventional interpretations on both levels, that of the play itself and as it is directed to an Elizabethan audience, finding no innocence, with the possible exception of children, in either. In terms of my thesis about the power of rhetoric it is double-edged in the same manner: as it is not "innocence" or virtue in Richard's opponents that makes them such easy targets for his rhetoric, but rather their lack of self-awareness—largely the self-delusions of the aristocratic ego—so the same principle is operative in Shakespeare's manipulations of his audience.

We see clearly the rhetorical game Richard is playing in his affectations of religious piety, for example ("by God's holy Mother, / She hath had too much wrong; and I repent / My part thereof that I have done to her. [1.3.306–8]), a very entertaining game for us, of course, enjoying the adroitness with which he dons his pious mask whenever the slightest possibility of advantage to himself in so doing is discerned. What we do not perceive so readily in this, however, is that if piety is a mask in one instance it may be in others as well. The ploy works for Richard not because his dupes on the whole are any less hypocritical in their religious professions than he is, but because he alone is fully conscious of the hypocrisy this particular game involves and thus has an advantage in playing it. I referred earlier to the secondary characters in this play as "straw men," in a way, manipulated deliberately by Shakespeare (another form of melodramatic exaggeration) to illustrate certain things about the power of rhetoric. As exaggeratedly easy prey for Richard as they are made to appear, however, this does not prevent them from standing, in a rhetorical maneuver as brazen as anything in the canon, as audience prototypes, models for the equally easy Shakespearean victimization of us. The point is important in the context of the question of religious piety as a rhetorico/political game, because it implies the possibility—I am going to say the likelihood—that Shakespeare is actually playing the same game. Catering to a partisan Elizabethan public, and with the biased reconstructions of Tudor chroniclers, based on More, his only sources, Shakespeare's version of the Richard story must inevitably, on its surface at least, meet that public's expectation; it must come across as a morality play, with divine retribution visited upon evil, and concluding with the restoration of divinely sanctioned order. The success with which *Richard III* meets this expectation is unquestioned; from Shakespeare's day to ours no commentary I have seen suggests any possibility that the pieties with which key speeches of Richard's victims and opponents are so liberally laced can be taken otherwise than at face value. Over and above the fact that Richard, Shakespeare's avatar, uses religious piety ostentatiously as a rhetorical ploy, however, there are hints from various other quarters in the play as well that all may not be as it appears on the surface as regards this motif.

Some of these hints depend in part for their force on the larger context of the tetralogy as a whole, again, and the image of certain of the characters brought in from that, but probably the strongest of them need nothing from outside the play itself to justify this interpretation. The wholly fictitious use of the Queen

Margaret character, the strength of the Lancastrian throne and
its only real warrior in the trilogy, as the prophetic voice of
divine "justice" in *Richard III* would be an example of the former.
The name of God placed constantly in the mouth of one whose
own record of past ruthlessness easily matches anything that
could be claimed against her enemies must indeed echo with
heavily ironic overtones in the ears, Shakespeare must hope, of
some at least in his audience:

> O God that seest it, do not suffer it;
> . . . .
> If heaven have any grievous plague in store
> Exceeding those that I can wish upon thee,
> O let them keep it till thy sins be ripe,
> And then hurl down their indignation on thee,
> the troubler of the poor world's peace!
>
> (1.3.271–72, 217–21)

The most fulsome pieties in the whole play, of course, are
those either associated with or given to utter to Richmond, the
Tudor savior of the country. Richmond, emerging out of a historical background that has been little more than a catalogue of
horrors—a shifting slate of clashing egos, bloodthirstiness, trea-
sons and betrayals—and then having all virtue attributed to
him, might in itself arouse suspicion of Shakespeare's sincerity
in the portrayal, but in fact the play itself as well as its background contain evidence that there is less to the concluding
pieties with which this *deus ex machina*, thematically speaking,
is surrounded than meets the eye. The interpretation here is
subtle, but the element of melodramatic exaggeration is again a
significant factor. Starting with the dream sequence in which the
ghosts all curse Richard and call down blessings on Richmond
("Virtuous and holy, be thou conqueror"), and building to the climactic "God say Amen" that concludes his victory speech, the
whole inflated process belies the plain historical truth, a truth
that not even the chronicles can obscure entirely, that Richmond's role in history differs not a whit from that of any of the
five "usurper" kings that preceded him. He is as tainted with ambition, as much an opportunist careless of the cost in blood his
adventurism brings with it, as his nemesis Richard. It could be
argued indeed that he is more in the main line of his predecessors than Richard ever was, whose quest for the crown, while it

did involve deaths, they were few, and only of his rivals, while the cost to the country Richmond is prepared to contemplate is unlimited. There is a potent irony in the fact that Richard's last argument in his wooing of Elizabeth was a humanitarian one, that only by his marriage to her daughter can "death, desolation, ruin, and decay" for "thee / Herself, the land, and many a Christian soul" (4.4.467–69) be avoided, an argument that weighs as heavily with her as with the rival suitor to whom that daughter is shortly to be bartered. The historical motif of monarchal claims and aristocratic alliances cemented through marriage runs throughout the two tetralogies, of course, another reminder that Richmond's motives, however disguised by lofty-sounding rhetoric, must operate on the same political plane as that of his predecessors, pointedly including Richard. And it is perhaps the final ironic touch that in the closing speech Shakespeare gives Richmond to celebrate his triumph specific reference is made to "Richmond and Elizabeth" as "[t]he true succeeders of each royal house"—a direct acknowledgment by Shakespeare of the genealogical *equality* of the Yorkist and Lancastrian claims, and thus tacit recognition that nothing but rival personal ambitions have sustained a hundred years of civil butchery.

These are the sober realities on the basis of which I conclude that the excessive pieties associated with the Richmond character, and indeed all the references to divine oversight of any kind in the play, are Shakespearean rhetorical sleights exactly analogous to those so flamboyantly employed by his creature Richard. There is other evidence as well that "divine oversight" is at best a questionable matter in the world of *Richard III*. We have seen the pot/kettle irony in a Margaret calling on God as *she* castigates Richard as a "troubler of the poor world's peace," and the confusion surrounding "God's" role in any of these events becomes even murkier subsequently, going so far, indeed, in the matter of Richard's role in the deaths of his brothers and nephews as to make him the *hero* of Margaret's morality tale!

> O upright, just, and true-disposing God,
> How I do thank thee that this carnal cur
> Preys on the issue of his mother's body[.]
>
> (4.4.55–57)[16]

This passage is in fact a prototype of the motif of "divine retribution," if that is what it is, in the play, focusing its problematic implications. If we are going to believe in divine retribution, as in the play they profess to do, Shakespeare apparently catering in this way to his audience's expectations at the same time, we must somehow square that belief with the contradictory corollary that its primary *agent* is precisely the "fiend . . . hell govern'd," who holds the whole notion in contempt, over whom "nor law of God nor man" (1.2.34, 67, 70) holds sway, Richard. Richard's countering in this scene of Anne's pious description of King Henry in life as "gentle, mild, and virtuous," with "[t]he better for the King of Heaven, that hath him" (104–5), comes directly out of the tradition of declamatory paradox *a la* Anthony Munday's *Defence of Contraries*.

I spoke earlier of "pauses in the dramatic action" intruded deliberately by Shakespeare and hinting at the play's rhetorical allegory; with only slightly less directness the same hint comes through with this motif as well. As the end nears for each of Richard's victims, Clarence, Hastings, Grey, and Buckingham, he lets them pause to reflect on the extent of their deserving and the "justice" of God's punishment:

> *Buckingham:*   That high All-Seer which I dallied with
> Hath turn'd my feigned prayer on my head,
> And given in earnest what I begg'd in jest.
> Thus doth He force the swords of wicked men.
> To turn their own points in their masters' bosoms.
> (5.1.20–24)

The focus here on "God's" rather than Richard's agency in these dire outcomes is not, I submit, without significance, less a measure of the character's self-delusion than it is of Shakespeare's playing up, with a deliberate rhetorical irony, to the similar self-delusions in his audience. It is Richard's pious pose, a highly effective rhetorical ruse for him, appropriated by Shakespeare and transferred to the larger context of Elizabethan society.

A similar implication is carried, finally, in the larger motif of "rhetorical awareness," as I have called it, generally, in the play and in the world. I have spoken of *degrees* of rhetorical awareness in the various characters—Hastings with little or none, Buckingham with some, Richard in the period of his rise with full awareness. While in the context of the plot itself this "ranking" of the characters will appear somewhat mechanical, albeit not without some basis, it is in the allegorical context that its full significance emerges. The two contexts are never entirely separate, of course; earlier I used the phrase "the self-delusions of the aristocratic ego" as being the key to the susceptibility of many of the characters to rhetorical manipulation by such as a Richard, who does not share in these delusions. It is not difficult to see, purely on the level of plot, how the fate of Hastings, for example, could be interpreted as directly traceable to that very flaw. All the ideas about "honor" and its associations with aristocratic thinking as developed in the last chapter can be seen to have a bearing here as well. Granted that the Hastings character is set up as something of a straw man, again, the degree of his obtuseness obviously offering a severe test to plausibility (Hastings on Richard, for example: "I think there's never a man in Christendom / Can lesser hide his love or hate than he . . . [etc.]"), it is nevertheless Hastings's quite unconscious sense of his own supreme worth, of being insulated in his "nobility" from the follies of lesser mortals, that is his shocked undoing. It requires no great imaginative reach, then, to see in this situation a possible satirical reflection on an Elizabethan world whose uniquely fluid social conditions make it class-sensitive to an extent probably never in history exceeded.

The specifically rhetorical implications of this satire, however, tying it directly to Shakespeare's allegory, come through perhaps most forcefully in his characterization of Buckingham. He in particular is a contemporary archetype for Shakespeare, representative of a world hyper-attuned to the use of rhetorical stylistic tricks to gull the unwary in the game of politics, yet itself paradoxically susceptible, and apparently in an equal degree, of falling victim to those very tricks. The basis of this susceptibility for Buckingham, as it was for Hastings, and as it is, Shakespeare hints, for the whole class of aristocratic and would-be aristocratic Elizabethans, then, is ego, perennially the chink in the armor of aspiring spirits since before the dawn of time. However attuned one is to the tricks of style, including the judicious use of flattery such as Buckingham brings skillfully to bear in leading Hastings into Richard's trap ("Lord Hastings, you and he are near in love"), if vanity infects one's self-image the transformation from "deep-revolving [and] witty" to "dull-brained" can be very nearly instantaneous.

There is another very significant allegorical point the Buckingham character and the Buckingham/Richard relationship bring out. Buckingham has a special allegorical function in the play in being the *most* rhetorically aware, and therefore the most self-aware, of all the secondary characters. As such he reveals subtly certain artificialities in their, and, by extension, the Elizabethan world, that Shakespeare is concerned to point out. The earlier quoted passage from Buckingham's speech as he is led to execution contains a contradiction that I suggest gives evidence of Shakespeare's real views on the role of consciousness and conscience in human affairs. The theme of Buckingham's greater self-awareness than the other secondary characters, first, is maintained in his confession in that passage that his "prayer" in the reconciliation scene (2.2) was "feigned;" unlike the other participants in that scene, Richard always excepted, he not only knew he was lying when he swore "all duteous love" (2.2.33) to the queen and her kin, he knew also and was playing the same rhetorical game of false piety so effectively played by Richard. The contradiction, however, and it is one that I believe Shakespeare is fully aware of, is in his having the character consciously mock God as he did in this earlier moment of triumph and then acknowledge "Him" now, when facing death. It is of course profoundly human to behave in this way, to grasp at belief in our extremity, but it surely requires no small amount of mental prestidigitational skill, to which Shakespeare knows his audience will always be equal, to draw from this the conclusion that such a "belief" is in any way real. And the point is made stronger, then, when the other characters' behavior in the reconciliation scene, and subsequently, is looked at alongside Buckingham's. Where he, like Richard, lies consciously they lie *unconsciously*, both in terms of the newly found "love" they swear for each other and the "God" in whose name they swear it; the degree of consciousness is the only difference between them. The conclusion from this that Shakespeare sees the whole notion of the "unconscious" as just another rhetorical game, but this one a game we play with ourselves, is difficult to avoid.

A similar conclusion follows, finally, from consideration of another motif prominent in the play, and also linked to the conventional interpretation of it as a morality play, the motif of conscience. The speech in particular that seems to confirm all the traditional Christian notions of God's spirit still living within the breast of even the most depraved of sinners is Richard's tormented tirade upon awakening the morning of the battle in act 5. That this speech too, however, powerful and straightforward though it seems in its presentation of the case of conscience as an authentic force in man, cannot be taken at face value is implied in a number of ways. There was an earlier debate on the subject of conscience that actually set the stage for a possibly more skeptical audience reaction to *this* emotional outburst than it would appear on its face to demand. This was the exchange between the two murderers of Clarence, whose comic overtones ("it was wont to hold me but while one tells twenty") have already rather undermined any assumption of real authorial seriousness where the subject of conscience is concerned. It is partly with this background in mind that certain elements of Richard's speech take on a more questionable aspect in terms of the authenticity of their sentiments. It has been noted before, first, that the only time "conscience" is ever a problem for Richard is in his "timorous dreams"; Anne spoke of this, and it is brought home with particular force here, when as soon as Richard shakes off the effects of sleep all of his normal conscienceless determination quickly reappears. It is of course totally out of character from the start that "conscience" could be a significant factor in Richard's life, so its prominent presence here, taken again from a hint in Holinshed,[17] bespeaks the same game of rhetorical false piety, Shakespeare catering tongue-in-cheek to audience expectations, that we have seen practiced in most of its other ostensibly Christian references. The most powerful hint of the real significance of the motif of conscience to Shakespeare, however, is that it appears not in Richard's waking life but in his dreams, confirmation of, in Marjorie Garber's words, "the very equivalence of *dream* with . . . 'conscience',"[18] suggesting that it belongs with other rhetorical games of the imagination—"objectivity," "the unconscious"—games that can be exploited advantageously in the manipulation of others, but that pose risks when the victim of the manipulation is oneself.

7

"Much like to Madness":
Measure for Measure and Rhetoric

I select *Measure for Measure* as my second example of a rhetorical allegory in a play by Shakespeare for the specific reason
that it is not a play that has traditionally been considered to
have rhetoric as a central concern thematically, in the way that
a *Love's Labour's Lost,* say, or a *Richard III* obviously have. It
has a dozen other themes on which analyses typically focus,
issues of human psychology and sexuality, of ethical and moral
philosophy, of Christian theology, and of practical governance—
matters of power, law, justice, mercy, and civil order. All of these
issues are presented, interestingly, with a black-and-white
starkness in this particular play that is unique in the Shakespeare canon, clearly a deliberate maneuver on Shakespeare's
part, and one as clearly demanding of explanation and discussion on the critic's. The foregrounding of these very profound humanistic and social questions has the effect of forcing stylistic
issues somewhat into the background. That there is a "general
concern with argument and rhetorical skill,"[1] or with "persuasion and manipulation"[2] in the play may be noted; but the other
issues the play raises are so immediate and seem so deep that it
requires extraordinary concentration even in the study to give
more than passing attention to the rhetorical.

A hypothetical consensus of views on *Measure for Measure*
might be called up here that relates the play to the rhetorical
tradition of the sixteenth century more directly, however, than
the authors themselves of many of those views may be aware of.
If there is a common element in the myriad interpretations that
have been offered of *Measure for Measure* over the centuries,

with all of their varying emphases on different aspects of the play, from the legal to the religious, it is dissatisfaction—"uneasiness" is L. C. Knights's term[3]—the feeling that there is in the end, in the words of a recent commentator, "[no] satisfying resolution to . . . the play's complex themes."[4] Almost every interpretation of the play, from the earliest, and this principle could apply to its theatrical interpretation as well,[5] will feature a comment similar to the above: Johnson puzzled over the play's "peculiarities"; it "baffled" both Coleridge and Swinburne; and the words "contradictions," "inconsistencies," and "incongruities"[6] continue to appear regularly in criticism to the present time. And a related though less consistent thread in the commentaries is one that concerns the question of what might be termed the play's "ranking" in the canon; does it "work" in the theater and is it a "good" play? These questions are prompted in their turn by the further consideration of whether its inconsistencies are calculated, a product of design, or represent a "flaw in the [play's] structure,"[7] reflected in the makeshift nature of its ending, hastily cobbled together by a Shakespeare scrambling to find any kind of an exit from the impossible dramatic situation he had just created. Here critical opinion is rather more divided; few have the temerity of a Tillyard to suggest that in departing as he did from his sources Shakespeare "could only ruin the play," and that he "threw in his hand"[8] halfway through. Hedging on the question is more common, as in Leech's "it was the immediate situation that primarily engaged [his] attention" in explanation of the play's "inconsistencies"[9] or Campbell's puzzled reflection that the "critical contradictions" he finds in the literature "must reflect contradictions in the play."[10] On the other hand defenders of the play's "structural peculiarities[,] that they are what they are by intention,"[11] are by no means lacking either, theater people in particular now frequently recognizing it as "a strong piece . . . brimming with life," albeit containing roles "as difficult as ever an actor can have been called upon to play."[12]

A critical perspective on the play that recasts if it does not resolve its difficulties is to see them first as the product of a deliberate rhetorical strategy. Its starkly contradictory themes and styles can be unified by understanding the conflicts between them as rhetorical in nature. Many things about the play generally considered puzzling become immediately less so when viewed in this light. Many have remarked, for example, the abrupt stylistic shift from the main plot's exquisitely accomplished poetic blank verse in the first half of the play to a predominance of not especially distinguished prose in the second —"the play breaks in two here," Northrop Frye says.[13] If the play is looked at as *in part* a rhetorical exercise, this shift becomes a simple demonstration that rhetorical effectiveness (power) is equally accommodated to a prose as to a poetic form of expression. As well as taking an about-face in style at this point, something also happens to the plot, it is often noted, that where "the most rigid realism"[14] had hitherto been the note, now "artificial devices"[15] "hard to reconcile with the naturalness of [the] characters"[16] take over and continue to the end. Here again, considered from a rhetorical standpoint, there is an interesting paradox, and one suggestive of deliberation on the part of the author, that prosaic, "realistic" language is now made the vehicle of an "artificial" plot, where poetic, idealistic language had previously been the medium of a "real" one.

A number of other features, some notable, come into clearer focus when rhetoric is seen as a key element thematically in the play's conception. The first hard issue the plot engages, for example, the "absolutist" spirit of which is to become a leading motif for the rest of the play, is very much a linguistic if not quite a rhetorical issue in the strictest sense. It is the same issue on which the plot of the earlier *Merchant of Venice* also turned, an issue of principle, the principle of "the letter of the law," as it might be termed. In *Merchant's* case Shakespeare shows how the precise wording of a legal contract may have surprising unintended practical results when literally applied, while in *Measure for Measure* the even more extreme situation is presented where *words* are granted absolute power, having the potential to become the excuse, under certain circumstances, for the abdication by men of both reason and responsibility. This is the initial Angelo/Claudio plot situation, where Claudio is scheduled to be beheaded for what scholars familiar with Renaissance marriage law are unanimous in agreeing is a legal technicality hung on the most tenuous of verbal threads.[17] This theme, very much a linguistic one, is a major focus throughout, touching all of the play's marriages, proposals of marriage, and other liaisons, and bearing as well on the broader social questions of law and legal force generally. More specifically *rhetorical* implications come into certain of the play's situations that are directly pertinent to many of the things with which this study is concerned. The close relationship of rhetoric and power has been a major topic here, with the emphasis on rhetoric's application, for good or ill, as an instrument of power. A facet of that relationship not previously discussed comes out in *Measure for Measure* in circumstances that are as unmistakable in meaning as they are unique in all of Shakespeare.

Two situations in the play make a similar point, though in opposite ways, as it were, that place the relationship of rhetoric and power in a different light from that in which it has previously been seen. The question of rhetoric as persuasion is prominent in both the early encounter of Angelo and Isabella, when she goes to him to plead for Claudio's life, and the later one of Barnardine and the Duke, when the task of persuasion is to achieve precisely the opposite. Notoriously in both cases, and notwithstanding both pointed references to and brilliant examples of the skills of the persuaders, the persuasion is utterly ineffective. It is difficult not to see a quite blunt lesson about a new and problematic aspect of the relations between rhetoric and power in the similar outcomes of these contrasting situations. The basic contrast is in the location of the "power" in the two situations: that is, with Angelo, the "persuadee," in the first, and with the Duke, the *persuader*, in the second; and the lesson of the persuasion's failure in both cases would be that when either *power* or *powerlessness* is absolute, when no possibility of either benefit or loss to himself in attending to the arguments of the petitioner is at stake for the one being petitioned, rhetoric is futile and words effectively meaningless. This lesson is driven home, as noted above, by both the references to and demonstrations of the rhetorical resources at the command of our two persuaders, Isabella and the Duke. Thus, Claudio first takes heart when Lucio suggests that Isabella go to Angelo to plead on his behalf, because "she hath prosperous art / When she will play with reason and discourse, / And well she can persuade" (1.2.177–79) That Claudio knows whereof he speaks in this is then demonstrated in the powerful, indeed by any human standard unanswerable, however futile in the event, rational *and* emotional force she is finally (coached comically by Lucio) able to bring in the urging of her case. While we get no comparable scene between the Duke and Barnardine, the Duke's confident assumption, again misplaced in the event, that he has the skills to "persuade this rude wretch willingly to die (4.3.77) is

grounded, apparently reasonably enough, on his having performed, with Socratic finesse, precisely that amazing feat with
Claudio just a few short scenes before.

A further broad hint of a thematic significance for language
and rhetoric in the play is found again in the particular form
Elbow the Constable's sparklingly inventive malapropism is
given to take. Comically effective in the highest degree to begin
with, it has also, in its style of *reversing* intended meanings—
benefactor for *malefactor*, *detest* for *attest*, *respected* for *suspected*
—a clear symbolic connection to the "letter of the law" motif.
Elbow is an instrument of the law, and his linguistic ineptitude
is again suggestive of both the ambiguities and the potential
dangers in too absolute a reliance on that principle. We have
touched before as well on how, among other ways, Shakespeare
hints of a rhetorical allegory in comments certain of his characters are occasionally given to make, that can be seen to speak
tantalizingly of precisely this possibility of meaning, if one can
detach oneself from plot and character long enough to reflect,
Richard's "none are for me that look into me with considerate
eyes" being a classic case in point. As there is perhaps no other
play in the canon that so "impresses while it puzzles"[18] or whose
"enigmas" have for so long "excited, fascinated, [and] perplexed,"[19]
so it is not surprising that lines and speeches hinting at this
"dual awareness"[20] on the part of the author are notably frequent
in this play. Certain lines spoken of and by the Duke in particular lend themselves to speculative interpretation along these
lines. The message as well as the method of the Shakespearean
rhetorical allegory, again, is that of *revelation* by *concealment,*
Shakespeare revealing himself through the theme of deception
and manipulation in the plays, sometimes with a central character, as a Richard or a Prospero, functioning indirectly as a
Shakespearean avatar, a role that many assign to the Duke in
this play. Francis Fergusson is typical in seeing in the "Duke's
role . . . an analogue of that of Shakespeare," and the character
"the center of the play, and the clue to its intention."[21] It is in this
spirit that various pronouncements on and by the Duke take on
a resonance that lifts them above the plot and into the allegorical realm. Almost anything in the play might be found suggestive when considered in this light, but certain lines and images
in particular stand out in their potential to express the "dual
awareness" in which we are interested.

Initially, the Duke's disguise, retained for virtually the whole of the play, places the role in our familiar Shakespearean play-within-a-play limbo, where the line between theater and reality blurs and double meanings blossom. And this effect is further reinforced in this instance by the obtrusive "stage director"[22] function he performs in bringing the play to its comic conclusion, in which "the artful technique of the dramatist"[23] is visibly on display. It is in this context that the Duke's reference to "my hidden power" (5.1.390), which, to Angelo, is "like pow'r divine" (5.1.367), in its capacity to decree life or death on the strength of a word, takes on obvious allegorical overtones. If something appears "obvious" in Shakespeare, of course, that is in itself a pretty good clue to our having been duped, so it perhaps goes without saying that considerably greater subtlety is in demand in order to be able to see many other tantalizingly suggestive remarks in the play as having allegorical intent. Shakespeare's skill in misleading is at this point in his career so advanced that I take it as a given that when we *think* we see what he is up to we are wrong, that he is certain to be one or two jumps ahead of us still. The very fact that *Measure for Measure* has been interpreted and reinterpreted a thousand times, to a universal chorus of dissatisfaction, is testimony to its having been shaped by intent to precisely that end. By creating, with rhetorical artifice whose level of mastery approaches infinity, the *appearance* of rationality in what is actually totally irrational (this play, that is), Shakespeare tempts us into the false belief that with reason its mystery can be solved and its "meaning" determined, himself knowing all the time that no such solution is possible, and laughing up his sleeve at our efforts. It is from this far more tenuous allegorical standpoint that certain other lines and references, clearly forceful in many instances, but frustratingly enigmatic in appearance, take on real symbolic energy—Lucio's, of the Duke, "His givings-out were of an infinite distance / From his true-meant design" (1.4.54–55), Escalus's description of him as "one that, above all other strifes, contended especially to know himself" (3.2.218–19) or the Duke's own "all difficulties are but easy when they are known" (4.2.196–97).

The whole long scene that is act 5, in which the brazenly theatrical maneuvers to tie up all the disparate threads in a quick comic conclusion are most blatantly on display, is, when looked at from this perspective, virtually an unbroken string of hints of the *actual* impossibility of what is *seemingly* being brought off in the scene. It is part of the Duke's/Shakespeare's rhetorical strategy in the scene, indeed, to build up outrageously the supposed "tragic" elements of the situation initially—insisting to Isabella that Claudio did actually die, thereby making certain that there can be no mitigation of the heinousness of Angelo's actions—*before* letting everyone blithely off the hook with forgiveness and happiness all around. The most egregious insult to reason in the whole situation prior to its abrupt reversal at the conclusion may be the Duke's ingenuous (and unnecessary) further admission to Isabella that Claudio's "execution" was actually *his* fault; he intended to intervene, and would have, but it *slipped his mind*, apparently:

> It was the swift celerity of his death,
> Which I did think with slower foot came on,
> That brain'd my purpose—[!]
>
> (5.1.392–94)

The parallel with Edward and Clarence in *Richard III* on the "speed" issue is patent here, but a dimension of absurdity in the sequel is added in *Measure for Measure* in the notable absence of any expression of regret or remorse on the Duke's part for what happened, together with the bland acceptance by the passionate Isabella of the mere preacherly saw he proffers instead:

> That life is better life past fearing death,
> Than that which lives to fear. Make it your comfort,
> So happy is your brother.
> *Isab.* I do, my lord.
>
> (5.1.395–97)

It is in the light of considerations such as these that the many references, particularly in the play's latter stages, to things being "strange and strange" (5.1.42), "madly spoken" (5.1.89), and "against all sense" (5.1.431), become allegorically significant. Indeed, the question, explicit or implicit, is prominent throughout as to whether what we are seeing on stage is or is not rationally coherent at all. The Duke's "actions show much like to madness" (4.4.3); while Isabella's "madness hath the oddest frame of sense" (5.1.61). The thrust of these remarks, along with the outcome of the play, comes down, or appears to, on the side of

reason, suggesting that madness in appearance is not necessarily madness in fact:

> *Isab.* O Prince! I conjure thee, . . .
>
> . . . .
>
> That thou neglect me not with that opinion
> That I am touch'd with madness. Make not impossible
> That which but seems unlike.
>
> (5.1.48, 50–52)

What these words do not state, but what is implicit, and from an
allegorical standpoint most significant in them, is the hypothetical possibility of their sense being inverted. If it is a mistake,
that is to say, as the passage states, to assume casually or hastily
that the unlikely is the impossible, it may be equally a mistake
to allow oneself to be *taken in*, casually or hastily again, by an
art that can make the impossible seem the likely.

In terms of the Renaissance rhetorical tradition that I contend is the primary shaping influence in Elizabethan drama
and Shakespeare's art, the inspiration for *Measure for Measure*
comes not from Whetstone or Cinthio, whose works provide
Shakespeare with merely a bare-bones plot, but from a much
older and more illustrious source than either, one, like Hermogenes' *Types of Style*, whose influence had been with him from
his earliest rhetorical studies, the *Controversiae* of the elder
Seneca. The Senecan texts, exercises in forensic oratory used in
the training of lawyers, in which spirited arguments and
sparkling epigrams are marshaled in defense of *both sides* of
particularly knotty points of Roman law, have been mentioned
before as important texts in Renaissance education, considered
the epitome of the Roman art of declamation. They were probably studied most widely by those preparing for a legal career in
the Renaissance as well,[24] but as educational texts they exhibit
certain unique features that it is possible to see as rather strikingly reflected in the "ten times strange" (5.1.42) effusion that is
Measure for Measure. To say this is not to equate their accomplishments in any way; the language, the range and depth of the
issues the play engages leave Seneca far behind in the comparison. It is the problematic way, primarily, that the issues are developed in the play that hints of a possible Senecan connection.
The mere fact that *Measure for Measure* has a particular law, the

law on marriage and fornication in Shakespeare's "Vienna," as a central plot device is in itself a faint evocation of Seneca, for example.

I have also mentioned before the thing that is perhaps most disturbing to a modern reader of Seneca, and may even have appeared the same to an Elizabethan community steeped in Christian rhetoric, namely the pure legalism of his approach. Motives of filial feeling or charity may sometimes appear in the orations of his pleaders to justify their or their clients' actions, but this is irrelevant to the point at issue, which is solely the question of whose position can make the better claim to have the sanction of the law. Most of Seneca's cases are hypothetical, specifically designed to show off the ingenuity of the pleaders in interpreting the law to their advantage; a few are historical, based on actual famous cases from the past; but all have the same flavor of essential inhumanity, where the one issue certain never to be raised in the discussion is the pain of the participants. Each case begins with a bald statement of the legal point at issue, in which the characteristic "flavour" of inhumanity is succinctly caught: a typical hypothetical case is that of the man who "trained his two sons as pancratiasts [a martial art combining boxing and wrestling] . . . to compete at the Olympic Games. They were paired off to fight each other. The father went to the combatants and said he would disinherit the one who lost. The youths were both killed together[.] . . . The father is accused of maltreatment by his wife."[25] And from the historical side we have the notorious case of Flaminius, who "when proconsul, was once asked a favor by a whore while dining. She said she had never seen a man's head cut off. He had a condemned criminal killed. He is accused of *lèse-majesté*."[26]

I am suggesting that the problematic moral atmosphere of *Measure for Measure*, unique in Shakespeare, is in certain of its aspects not dissimilar to, and could have been inspired by, that revealed in these specimens from Seneca. While far from the whole story in the play, the style and tone of the arguments from principle that are the initial focus of the main plot—Claudio is to be a sacrificial victim first of a legal and subsequently of a religious principle—are, from a humanistic standpoint, disturbing in a manner essentially identical to the Senecan. Indeed, in another of the plot's principal devices, the Mariana/Isabella bedtrick, Shakespeare comes suggestively close to actually duplicating one of Seneca's hypothetical cases. The *Controversiae* play many variations on the theme of the legal rights of rape victims, one of which is the following:

THE MAN WHO RAPED TWO GIRLS
A girl who has been raped may choose either
marriage to her ravisher without a dowry
[shades of Mariana and her lost dowry!] or his death.

On a single night a man raped two girls.
One demands his death, the other marriage.[27]

While the controversial mode and the heartless attitudes shown, particularly in the first half of *Measure for Measure*, are strikingly reminiscent of Seneca, these constitute but one facet of the play's complexity, and where it departs from Seneca is at least as important as where it resembles him. However much the Renaissance is still in thrall to Rome, its civilization has had 1,500 years of the softening influences of Christianity to give it a moral sensibility, or at least a notion of one, utterly foreign to Senecan thinking, a qualification nowhere more prominently reflected than in Shakespeare's *Measure for Measure*. If there is one feature of Senecan thinking striking to a modern reader, it is the seeming total unawareness of compassion as a possible human emotion or of mercy as a legal consideration. Shakespeare effects a radical transformation of the neo-Senecan legalism of *Measure for Measure* by bringing this Christian motif, the same one he had explored earlier in *The Merchant of Venice*, boldly into the mix. Indeed its presence is for many thematically dominant, giving rise to interpretations of the play as a parable or otherwise exemplary of Christian values.[28] To take the play as a one-sided defense of Christianity is certainly a mistake, however; Shakespeare undoubtedly expands the Senecan intellectual legacy by introducing Christian considerations into the argument of *Measure for Measure*, but this does not mean the abandonment of its central declamatory principle. That principle is a modification of the ancient principle of oratorical debate, where declaimers are assigned to defend opposite sides of a controversial proposition, with a winner declared at the end. The modification of this format made by the *Controversiae*, and important to Shakespeare to the extent that *Measure for Measure* is influenced by Seneca, is that while Seneca presents the arguments on both sides of the proposition, he himself remains neutral; there is no "winner" declared. What emerges as end product of this method is something that, from a logical standpoint, is rather strange: two arguments, both persuasive, upholding contradictory points of view on a human issue. This is the classic form of what is defined in logic as a "dilemma": "an argument in which a choice of . . . alternatives, each being conclusive and fatal, is presented."[29] I should note that I take this particular nontechnical definition of the term *dilemma* for the serendipity of its use of the word *fatal*, when Roman law happens to be the context of discussion!

Elizabethan students of rhetoric must recognize, and the Shakespeares among them fully consciously, the territory this method takes us into as the dangerous one where the foundations of rhetoric as a bulwark of the culture begin to tremble. It is not merely that the alliance of rhetoric with truth is exposed in these exercises as questionable, the even more threatening possibility of "truth" itself being a fraud is potentially open to view. Anthony Munday's *The Defence of Contraries*, it will be remembered, is in some ways an Elizabethan counterpart to Seneca, perhaps even more blatant however, in its anarchic implications. Seneca merely gives us contradictory versions of "truth"; Munday's "paradoxes against common opinion," on the other hand, while at first glance they may appear merely absurd, can be seen on reflection to be less absurd in *themselves* than in what they hint of the greater, existential absurdity of believing that "truth" or even "meaning" are anything more than words.

The strangeness of what Shakespeare is doing in *Measure for Measure* is to some extent clarified, I suggest, by these considerations. The play's contradictions are basically Senecan, with what is "right" being shown as having two different, mutually exclusive but equally binding faces. Its complexity is infinitely greater than Seneca, because its range of reference is not limited to, although it incorporates, questions of law; in fact it ranges over a spectrum of humanistic concerns that, considering its short compass, is almost staggering in breadth, while carrying the same principle of antithesis into every topic touched on. One of the most outstanding of these antitheses, for example, and a particularly good illustration of what I call Shakespeare's expanding of Seneca, is his introduction of the value system of

Christianity into the world of *Measure for Measure*. Perhaps the most difficult to resolve of all the play's antithetical perspectives on what is right—what terms like "justice" and "love" are to be taken to mean—arise from the clash Shakespeare sets up in the play between heavenly and earthly imperatives. The basis of the dissatisfaction that critics invariably find with this play, amply illustrated in this particular conflict, is that while it is possible to uphold and argue convincingly for two antithetical value systems in a single oratorical exercise, it remains impossible, all the fancy rhetorical manipulations and sleights in the world notwithstanding, that they should ever actually be accommodated.

The play thus becomes exactly such an exercise, having overtones of both Seneca and Munday, but pushing into territory that only the hyper-attunement of a Shakespeare both to rhetoric generally and to the deeper philosophical implications of declamation in particular would be capable of conceiving. Absolute confidence in his own mastery of these arts is part of the mix as well, as he sets out to demonstrate, as a challenge to himself and a joke on his audiences, exactly how far and to what degree of actual absurdity one can go in an exercise of this kind *without being detected*. The really monumental challenge, in addition, is to do this in a dramatic format: the play, that is to say, must *work*. Simply setting opposed unassailable arguments side by side, like Seneca, or, like Munday, hinting slyly and probably unconsciously at the gaps in conventional thinking, is not going to be enough. The contradictions, the explorations of the absurd, must all be there, visible and plain, impossible either to accommodate or make sense of; but the greater rhetorical task is at the same time to suppress the absurd, make things appear to cohere, create the illusion that antitheses can be integrated and merged.

In all the wide range of humanistic questions the play addresses, there is a common feature—contradiction. I contend that the play is deliberately structured so as to bring out clearly the impossibility of any resolution of its contradictions, but at the same time to conceal this harsh reality under the cloak of a comic resolution that appears to do the opposite. The contradictions among the humanistic issues the play raises are numerous and form the substance of most of the criticism of it that has accumulated over the centuries. The social form of these issues is

202 PROTEUS UNMASKED

an extension of their individual form, and both are explored; conflicts within the individual between reason, conscience, love,
desire, self-control, and self-indulgence translate into the same
difficulties for society at large. The play's apparent concentration
on humanistic questions, however, which has successfully drawn
critical attention heavily into these topics is, I contend, a device
—I almost said a ruse—contrived by Shakespeare to draw attention away from the questions that really are primary in the play,
namely the rhetorical. It is accurate to say that the play's humanistic questions are *rhetorical* questions, in the full sense of
that term—questions posed not to elicit an answer, but strictly
for effect, the "answer" itself being part of the rhetorical strategy,
prepared in advance and ready for delivery by the *questioner* to
achieve maximum persuasive impact, in the form, in this case, of
the play's "happy" ending.

In another of the ways that this play is unique in the canon,
Shakespeare departs daringly from his usual practice of making
character his prime manipulative tool, to divert audience attention, by making *issues*. One of the most disquieting difficulties
critics find with the play is that its most important characters—
Angelo, Isabella, and the Duke in particular—have been conceived to such an extent as the tools of the narrow principles
they represent, and have to be so blatantly manipulated for
things to work out in the end, that plausibility is for many deliberately sacrificed. "Unmistakably," Angelo Caputi informs us,
"character was not his primary concern,"[30] which Kenneth Muir
roundly endorses by observing that in the second half of the play,
"the characters become puppets."[31] It is one of the most interesting of the play's contradictory effects, however, that for every
Muir or Caputi there is also a Webster to insist that however
"difficult" these characters are, the possibility of bringing them
to life on stage is never entirely beyond reach; Shakespeare's
artistry for them remains supreme. Indeed, finding the *issues*,
however dominant thematically they appear to be, difficult to resolve, critics are commonly drawn back to character, *faute de
mieux*, as the hoped-for key to an integrative perspective on the
play and to a meaning otherwise elusive. And it is perhaps needless to say that this desperation strategy tends to give results
as unsatisfactory as the original project of seeking meaning
through resolution of the issues. As critics on both sides of the
endless "character" disputes delight in pointing out to their op-

ponents, the Duke or Isabella can only be made heroic *or* vice versa by ignoring aspects of their behavior of manifestly an opposite character.

From a philosophical standpoint, the reason the contradictions in the play cannot be resolved in the end, however much its rhetoric creates the illusion of that possibility, is that each of its oppositions, as Shakespeare knows and again makes clear, is categorical. This principle is operative whether analysis of the play approaches it from a character perspective or an issues perspective; categorical oppositions within individual characters make integration impossible, categorical oppositions between issues of principle make accommodation impossible. And the whole thing is rhetorical in the sense that both the problem *and* its apparent "solution" are linked inseparably to the power of language. The play does two opposite things at once, rhetorically: it shows us that while its categorical oppositions are linguistic in origin—they begin, that is, as mere words: *fornication, marriage;* the sex act itself is *one*, its legal standing two, and diametrically opposed—they are nonetheless real. This established, however, the deception is then perpetrated that if language can *create* such contradictions, it ought also to be able to resolve them.

The "letter of the law" motif, broached almost at the beginning of the play, establishes the broad linguistic basis of its plot, but the theme is reinforced by many subtle early hints that play on the idea of language as an instrument of power, in both positive and negative senses. The Duke's opening speech, for example, contains a number of such thoroughly ambiguous hints, difficult to interpret as its critical history attests, but unmistakably linked to our theme. It would be "to affect speech and discourse" in him "of government the properties to unfold," to an Escalus whose "science" already "exceeds" his own. The *words*, "the organs / Of our ... power," (1.1.21–22) that will become law in his absence are thus, at great risk, to be left unspoken, "mortality and mercy" (45) entrusted absolutely to "live in th[e] tongue and heart" (46) of Angelo. The play on the word *sound* between Lucio and "a gentleman" early in the second scene (52–54) continues the ambiguous rhetorico/linguistic emphasis. *Sound* may mean "healthy and solid," but sound may ring "hollow" as well. The several references Claudio makes immediately on his appearance to his situation and the character of his offense carry the same implications, significantly in the context, very nearly into the realm of direct speech. He is being prosecuted "for a name" (162) only, he says, whose "character . . . is writ on Juliet" (148). Being prosecuted "for a name," of course, is not just Claudio's problem in "dark corners" Vienna; it is Pompey's too: bawdry might well be "a lawful trade," "if the law would allow it" (1.2.214–45). Both are caught equally in a Job-like situation: "by weight / The words of heaven" (1.2.115–16) have fallen, arbitrarily, as it seems, on them, "yet still 'tis just" (117). The climactic moment early in the play where the cumulative effect of all these "letter of the law" implications hits home with full force is in the first Angelo/Isabella scene, in the repeated references, on Isabella's side to the voice of authority as a *living* power—"I that do speak a word / May call it back again" (2.2.57–58)—on Angelo's the opposite, to the word of the law as absolute—"He's sentenc'd, 'tis too late" (55); and "It is the law, not I condemn your brother" (80).

I have said that whether interpretation approaches the play from an "issues" or a "character" perspective, the contradictions are equally irresolvable and the results equally unsatisfactory—more illuminating, as a rule, as regards the rhetorical sleights employed by the critic in his analysis of the play, than of Shakespeare in his writing of it. As a "problem" play, *Measure for Measure*'s greatest problem, for the critic, is the problem of finding or creating a meaningful distinction between the characters and the principles they represent anyway; certainly as regards the main characters, Angelo, Isabella, and the Duke, this is absolutely the situation. They are probably the outstanding examples in all of Shakespeare of the actual illusory nature of "character" in his plays; indeed, I would go so far as to say they are created in part for that very purpose, as embodiments of the idea of "character" *as* pure rhetoric. Because they cannot be separated from the categorical principles for which they speak, and because the incompatibilities among those principles are impossible to resolve, they cannot in the end be spoken or thought of in any meaningful way as "people"; they are quite literally in the final analysis nothing more than the words they are given to speak. The approach to the play that at least recognizes this fact, as "the only possible way to get meaning out of the play,"[32] is the one that blends characters with issues, the allegorical. The play has been interpreted as a dynastic historical allegory, with the Duke representing King James; the many Christian interpretations are all basically allegorical as well, at least one of them following the trail as far back as St. Bonaventure's original use of the term,[33] but inevitably psychoanalytic, Marxist, and now even Foucauldian interpretations have joined the allegorical parade.[34] From my perspective, of course, the allegorical is indeed the only approach that can make sense of what Shakespeare is doing in this play; not, however, with any hope of resolving its contradictions, but simply of coming to grips with its purely rhetorical nature and aim. Each of the three main characters is conceived on the basis of the same formula, given a name and assigned a role in the plot so as to look on the surface like a "real" character, but to belie that appearance in the impossible combination of absolutely contradictory qualities and principles each is made to comprehend.

The Duke, as the ultimate controlling power in Vienna, is the central character, his role often likened to Prospero's, Shakespeare's, and even God's, in his capacity to manipulate outcomes with the sublime arbitrariness of divinity. His specialized function in this, however, is of less immediate allegorical significance than his embodiment of contradictions identical in degree if not precisely in kind, partly because of these additional symbolic resonances, to those expressed in the characters of Angelo and Isabella. The godlike, supra-scenaric dimensions of the Duke's character are indeed one of the principal irresolvable contradictions "he" embodies; he functions both as a character in the play—fallible, credulous, human—and as its absolute controlling genius, its "writer," as it were—"like power divine" infallible, all-wise, perfect.

The first clear opportunity we are given to make ourselves aware of the many irresolvable contradictions in the Duke's character is in his explanation to Friar Thomas in 1.3 for his decision to retire from his role as "absolute power" (13) in Vienna. The explanation he gives is well known and does need repeating, but what does need to be said about it is that it does not hang together, and blatantly so, though it has apparently *seemed* plausible for four hundred years. He says that "bits and curbs" (21) on libertine behavior in the people are "needful" (22), and that the state has "strict statutes" that could be enforced to achieve this end. Since he, however, has ignored the statutes, giving "evil deeds . . . their permissive pass" (32) for fourteen years, and it would be "tyranny" (35) in him at this point to change, he has

"imposed the office" (41) of enforcement on Angelo, who, by reputation at least, "is precise" (51), and can therefore, he hopes, be
trusted to hew to the letter of the law. Several logical problems
exist with this explanation. If we remember that the Duke is absolute ruler and has been in office for the fourteen years in
which he has "give[n] the people scope" (36) to flout the law, what
he says has in fact no logical meaning: that his principle of rule
is to be both strict *and* slack at the same time. As well, while the
plot has already found its principal focus in one particular area
of "lawless" behavior in Vienna before this scene—extramarital
sex—it is important to note that the reference to "evil deeds" and
to "justice" (29) generally as being flouted, envision the enforcement of a higher moral standard for society in all areas. The
catch in all this, however, is that if "justice" and the idea of a
higher moral standard for society are considered to be in any
way related to truth-telling, the Duke's going into disguise and
having it "strewed in the common ear" that he is "travell'd to
Poland" (14), is again in contradiction to his professed aim.

These examples by no means exhaust the list of logical impossibilities his "explanation" contains. There are at least two more
flagrant absurdities in the things he now says regarding
Angelo's commission. After reinforcing, as we have just seen, the
point made first in 1.1 that Angelo is to be "at full ourself" (44)
during the Duke's "remove," he concludes his explanation with a
flat contradiction of this. In fact there is to be no remove; he will
remain in Vienna and thus *in control* all the time, the commission now becoming nothing more apparently than his private
test of Angelo's "seeming" moral absoluteness, to "see / If power
change purpose, what our seemers be" (55). We have here several
things that one does not have to be a genius of Shakespeare's
caliber to see simply do not add up: he has empowered Angelo,
and he has not; he trusts him, and he does not; he wants the
laws enforced, and yet here again he does not—this based not
only on the Duke's past slackness but on his returning at the end
to flout their enforcement totally in several clear instances. The
best is saved for the last, however, in the stand of moral superiority Shakespeare has him affect over hypocrites—"seemers"—
with which the explanation and the scene conclude. The scene
break may give us time to reflect that such a sentiment, coming
from one whose own "seemings" must leave one wondering if
anything at all lies at the bottom of them, surely mocks itself—a

consideration that it may well cross one's mind could have a certain application to play and playwright as well.

Perhaps the most glaring of the impossible contradictions embodied in the Duke is his function both as a character within and as the controlling force "outside," at least in a sense, of the play world. The suggestion of an analogy with Shakespeare in this second function is apt: Vienna, as the Duke "leaves" it at the beginning, with events free to transpire as they will, would be analogous to Shakespeare's inherited plot from Cinthio; the shifts and sleights the Duke then intervenes to employ to bring about the neat conclusion he desires, are exactly analogous to Shakespeare's radical reworking of that plot. The godlike dimensions of the characterization are implicit in this analogy to some extent as well, but, interestingly, and I suggest daringly on Shakespeare's part, these contradictory aspects are brought out more directly *within* the play, in the character's actual words and behavior there, than in his Shakespearean interventions from "outside," as it were. Using the term "godlike" to describe the Duke's behavior, and this would apply primarily to his active participation in the plot after 3.1.151, is not, it should be noted, tantamount to calling it "Christlike," or even exactly benign, just in case the obvious Christian implications prominent in both the Isabella role and the "divinely" comic resolution may at first glance seem to lean in that direction. Indeed in its "godlike" activities the role of the Duke is clearly and deliberately contradictory. There *is* a strong Christian element in the last-minute reversals of the very end, where mercy is allowed to overcome strict justice in the Duke's dispositions, and, in Barnardine's case, without even the normal Christian requirement of repentance as a preliminary to the granting of "salvation."[35] Of equal significance, and certainly of equal prominence, however, in the Duke's behavior in the scene is what precedes these final benevolent outcomes, which is precisely their antitheses. That certain of the Duke's "actions show much like to madness" is noted within the play; the example cited earlier of such madness in this scene was in his seemingly unaccountable treatment of Isabella regarding the "death" of Claudio. In fact the only way *to* account for that, and the identical treatment accorded Mariana, Angelo, and Lucio in the same scene—"Let him be whipped and hanged" was his sentence on Lucio a mere twenty-seven lines before the play ends!—is in terms of a "godlike" function opposite in character to Christlike. This is the God of the Old Testament exercising his absolute power over man with the sublime indifference shown for the fate of Sodom and Gomorrah or the sufferings of Job. The rhetorical associations of this exercise of power cannot be passed over either in assessing the Duke's godlike role; his *word* in Vienna—"mortality [or] mercy"—like God's in the world, is the final arbiter of his people's destiny. The *word* motif in the scene, moreover, is handled in the perfect form in a Senecan philosophical dilemma, where after first mercilessly "killing" the helpless offender spiritually by *sentencing* him to death, he then arbitrarily pardons him. The antitheses, in effect, cancel each other out, with "meaning" lost somewhere in the middle. A hypothetical real-world analogy to this situation might be the case of an infant born with some horrible physical affliction, who, after a lifetime of torture dies and goes to heaven. Is the bliss of heaven an adequate compensation for the hell on earth that was decreed by the creator in the first place?

From the dilemma of contradiction the "godlike" functioning alone of the Duke's character gives rise to, we can come back to the further dilemma his simultaneous possession of a "human" dimension in his character also poses. This is where the Duke's role is linked closely to that of the other characters and to the central humanistic issues of the play. Two impressions, in effect, of who or what the Duke is, run side-by-side throughout the play. Two characters, in addition to any function in the plot and intrinsic interest they may have as dramatic personalities, are linked to the Duke in delineating, rather specifically, these alternative versions of his character, with the Duke himself, in the reflected light of their comments, also contributing to the contradictory impression of him Shakespeare makes us form. The two characters are Escalus and Lucio; Escalus giving us a Duke, who, if not absolutely godlike, at least strives to rule with wisdom; Lucio countering this impression with his consistent digs at the Duke as after all but a human being, by no means above the foibles of other mortals. The litmus test for mere humanity in the play, as opposed to the ideal of perfection that is its symbolic opposite, to which in our higher moments we sometimes think we might aspire, is the issue already mentioned as the key area of "lawless" behavior in Vienna, sex. The index of a higher wisdom, leading potentially to an improved society, is epitomized in this impulse, in the understanding of it and the channeling of it in the approved, implicitly Christian direction. This is the wisdom that the Duke and Escalus between them manage to give the impression the Duke has achieved, and which the happy ending, with marriages all around, foresees the extension of to the state in his rule. It is important to note that it has two components: first, self-knowledge, which, coupled with the second, Christian understanding, leads to self-control. It is the accommodating of the godlike to the human, in a sense; and one of the two conflicting impressions we receive of the Duke's character, then, suggests that he has managed this. He himself creates part of this impression, which Escalus, aged and a counselor, like Polonius, though his antithesis for wisdom, gives strong support to. We received our initial clear impression of the Duke wishing to be seen as above fleshly concerns in 1.3 in his explanation for his supposed remove from Vienna. It might be typically Viennese to assume, as Friar Thomas apparently does, that the sexual plague in Vienna infects everyone equally, but the opening lines of the scene give the Duke's assurance that this is not the case with him, and that indeed, as he reveals subsequently, it is to effect a cure of that plague that is his primary goal in perpetrating his ruse:

> No, holy father; throw away that thought;
> Believe not that the dribbling dart of love
> Can pierce a complete bosom. Why I desire thee
> To give me secret harbor hath a purpose
> More grave and wrinkled than the aims and ends
> Of burning youth.
>
> (1.3.1–6)

It is this version of the Duke, as under a wise personal governance and therefore committed to the same standard in his rule, to which both Escalus, and again the Duke himself, later give strong reinforcement. When queried of the Duke's "disposition" (3.2.217) Escalus is brief, speaking only two sentences, but they are consequential: that he was "[a] gentleman of all temperance" (223), and "[o]ne that above all other strifes contended especially to know himself" (219). There is a suggestion of irony in the fact that it was the Duke in his Friar's disguise that put this query to Escalus, looking to confirm, as it were, the image he has cultivated and has just had to defend against the ostensibly comic slanders of Lucio earlier in the same scene. I call these slan-

ders—that the Duke "would be drunk" (119), that he "knew the
service [i.e. the trade of sex]" (111), and that he was "[a] very superficial, ignorant, unweighing fellow" (130)—*ostensibly* comic,
because while they are plainly calculated to arouse laughter in
an audience at the Duke's discomfiting, their purport, from the
standpoint of what I maintain is Shakespeare's Senecan rhetorical allegory, is actually much deeper. They suggest a Duke the
exact opposite of what the Duke claims his public image, "his
own bringings forth" (135), show him as—"a scholar, a states-
man, and a soldier" (136), and that "for women[,] he was not in-
clin'd that way" (114). Their special significance, for my purposes, however, is in their implications in one particular area,
where the godlike and the human both meet and part, the area,
and in the play the philosophical paradox, of knowledge. This is
certainly one of the central philosophical issues the play engages, touching not only the Duke's, but the comparably symbol-
ically significant characters of Angelo and Isabella as well.

The issue as it relates to just the Duke at the moment, however, is that it shows up the actual impossibility of the combination of the godlike and the human his character supposedly
embraces, that the combination has to be a rhetorical hoax. In
the Duke's and Escalus's depiction the Duke is one who both
knows himself *and* is above the needs of the flesh, specifically
the sexual needs. The Lucio character then gives the lie, the
Shakespearean lie, to this possibility. Not to be sexual is not to
be human, as Lucio points out; for Angelo, for example, to be as
pure as his reputation has him, then he is "motion generative"
(104), a puppet, and "was not made by man and woman after this
downright way of creation" (96–97). Where knowledge comes
into the question from the Lucian/Shakespearean philosophical
perspective is that human knowledge *means* carnal knowledge;
to believe oneself to be above or beyond such needs is precisely
not to have knowledge of oneself as a human being. If the Duke
in his godlike role sees himself as such, then he must indeed be a
"very superficial, ignorant, unweighing fellow." But the other
side of the coin of the Duke for Lucio at the same time is that he
is not this, not godlike; he does not, like Angelo, demand absolute
purity; rather he *is* a human being, imperfect, and therefore possessed of human sympathy; a Claudio could not have become a
sacrifice to the law under him, because "he had some feeling for
the sport . . . and that instructed him to mercy" (111–12). Ulti-

mately, since the Duke demonstrates mercy in the end, he must
have knowledge, and Lucio be right; but on the other hand, his
actions *prior to* the last-minute reversals again suggest the opposite, a godlike inhumanity as great as Angelo's appeared to be
at the beginning. While the kind of "knowledge" such inhumanity on the part of the Duke implies may be compatible with God's
definition of the word *knowledge*, it is incompatible with man's.
Through Lucio we are allowed to see the dilemma of contradiction the Duke's character involves. From the human standpoint,
that is, of the animal in man, the "godlike," or even perhaps the
Christian at all, is at best a pose, at worst a lie. In effect, Lucio
"knows" the Duke better than the Duke appears to know himself; as he says, the Duke "would eat mutton on Fridays" (170),
meaning that while we may follow and even affect to believe in
these religious prohibitions, we do not know ourselves if we
think our bodies care.

Besides Lucio's direct comic advertings to the Duke's necessary humanity beyond the godlike pose, other subtle clues support the same interpretation in the very face of the Duke's
contradictory assertions that he "lives not" in Lucio's "reports"
(4.3.155). As God, as we imagine Him, may understand man's
carnal need without being touched by it Himself, so the Duke in
his very desire to reform his society betrays his carnal knowledge. The paradox of the "divine" vs. the "human" in his character is focused perfectly in the lines quoted earlier that open 1.3;
in his very denial that the sexual "aims and ends / Of burning
youth" are a motive to him, he confesses his full knowledge of
these forces, while, like God, remaining himself above them. The
testing of Angelo's "seeming" that is the contradictory alternative purpose of his going into disguise also contains the same
paradox. To imagine for a second that a human being *can* be
pure is, from a human standpoint, naive, though from a divine
perspective?—who knows, the Duke may be right. On the other
hand, however, the Duke *as a human being* has already tested
Angelo for purity and knows that he has failed, that he has long
since proved his "well-seeming" (3.1.217) to be a fraud in the
"unjust unkindness" (227), not to mention the taint of carnality,
"pretending in her discoveries of dishonor" (221), shown in his
treatment of Mariana. No matter how approached, the combination of a godlike perspective on man, and a human perspective
on God, cannot be accommodated. If the hope of man's reforma-

tion is a divine illusion, an illusion never lost by the naive Duke in his godlike function, however often Angelo and Barnardine demonstrate its futility to him, the same exactly must be said of man's hopes in God, that they too are futile, with this side of the issue exemplified typically again by the Duke's (as God) callous treatment of Claudio, going out of his way—taking his "good leisure"—to "discredit" to him the "many deceiving promises of life" (3.2.230) on which he has relied.

The same categorical opposed principles that are made to appear fused in the Duke's character appear again, and in magnified form, in the characterizations of, and the results of the encounters between, Angelo and Isabella. Here the "clash between heavenly and earthly imperatives," slickly evaded by Shakespeare in his characterizing of the Duke as "a gentleman of all temperance," though potential at every point, is given stark expression. Any "temperance" whatsoever, either in his absoluteness for both the word and the moral principle of the law initially, or in the corresponding absoluteness of his capitulation to the demands of the Freudian id subsequently, is exactly what Angelo lacks. The issue of heavenly versus earthly absoluteness wears a different though equally problematic face in the Isabella character—eager, like a good Christian as she tries to be, to sacrifice principle and temper justice with mercy until the principle to be sacrificed happens to be the one that *she* regards as absolute. What we have in both cases is essentially the same thing as we had in the Duke, a demonstration of the actual incompatibility of the human with the divine—that, as in a Senecan debate, the mere fact that the criterion of truth may equally be met by both arguments does not in itself constitute any resolution of their differences. To put the issue this way, of course, is to oversimplify greatly the moral confrontations Shakespeare builds into the situation through both his characterizations and the arguments of the adversaries, which present a daunting appearance and demand careful analysis. Behind this appearance, however, these remain the basic principles on which the debate is grounded. Indeed it is in the encounter between Angelo and Isabella that the play comes most closely to resemble the declamatory exercise that I maintain is Shakespeare's hidden allegorical conception of it, albeit in its ingenuity, verbal felicity, and the depth of its engagement with basic human issues a conception triumphantly without an equal elsewhere in rhetorical literature.

The first interview between Angelo and Isabella in particular is contrived by Shakespeare to evoke the atmosphere of a Senecan debate. The whole point in the art of declamation is that the declaimer should be prepared to defend *any* position whatsoever that she is given to defend. It is traditional practice in school debating that both the proposition to be debated and the sides to be taken on it are assigned arbitrarily, on the principle that forensics and personal feelings operate in completely different spheres. It can hardly be accidental, I suggest, that Shakespeare parallels this situation in the first Angelo-Isabella encounter, having Isabella state explicitly as she goes into it that the position she must argue is one that she herself categorically opposes, "for which I would not plead but that I must" (2.2.31). In the labyrinth of contradictions Shakespeare has designed in *Measure for Measure*, one of his most ingenious is that while Angelo and Isabella are made to be opponents from start to finish, the personalities they are given are similar; both not only hold principles absolute, they actually hold most of the same principles. This is stressed in Isabella's beginning the interview by agreeing with Angelo that Claudio's vice "should meet the blow of justice" (30), and capitulating instantly, showing she agrees with him also on issues of power and authority in the state, when Angelo asserts the legal position:

> O just but severe law!
> I had a brother, then. Heaven keep your honor!
>
> (2.2.42–43)

The point, however, is that when she finally does mount an argument, and one that shines (inevitably, of course) with a uniquely Shakespearean brilliance, it is her declamatory skills, not her personal convictions, supposed in fact to be directly contrary to these, that are on display.

Thematically, the argument between them hinges on the familiar issue again of absolute or divine principle versus humanistic principle, and because their arguments fall on opposite sides of the dividing line between man's and what we think of as God's world, the force each has within its separate sphere exactly equals the other's. Human ourselves, we will inevitably be touched more deeply by Isabella, but he would be a bold advocate indeed who would hazard an opinion as to whose argument *God* would incline to, were He judging the debate:

Ang. The law hath not been dead, though it hath slept.
     Those many had not dar'd to do that evil
     If the first that did th' edict infringe
     Had answer'd for his deed.

                                                    (90–93)

It is thematically significant as well in this first debate that the Lucio character is again given a prominent role, not allowing Isabella simply to capitulate cravenly, using deference to authority as her excuse, but encouraging her to the fray, and to put at least the semblance of a human heart into her argument. The similarity here to the function Lucio performs in relation to the Duke is surely not accidental, as once again he becomes the representative of ordinary humanity against the cold absolutes of "divine" authority. The humanity he may be said to represent appears perhaps nobler when voiced by Isabella than it does when Lucio himself is spokesman, and the actual "ordinariness," without rhetorical embellishment, of his humanity is placed front and center. Without Lucio, nevertheless, and what he represents, the arguments from human feeling and motives of Christian forgiveness she mounts could not hit home with such power.

In pointing out the perfect Senecan dilemma that is presented by the equal cogency of Angelo's and Isabella's arguments, from the standpoints respectively of divine justice versus justice with a human face, it may be noted also that precisely the same pattern, with a couple of interesting twists, is followed again in the Duke's arguments as against Claudio's in 3.1 over the issue of Claudio's acceptance of the sentence of death for his "crime." There is a near parallel first, in the roles of Isabella and the Duke in the two situations, Isabella faced with the task of persuading Angelo to spare Claudio, the Duke with the task of persuading Claudio to accept death. Neither succeeds in the end, although momentarily the Duke seems to, until hope reappears to discredit his argument, but a neat rhetorical twist comes into the comparison when we reflect that where Isabella's plea is a perfect academic demonstration that it is possible to be persuasive without being sincere, the Duke's demonstrates equally well the exact opposite, that it is possible to be sincere without being persuasive. It is interesting also that where Isabella's argument appeals primarily to Christian humanist feeling and gets its persuasive force thereby, even while Isabella's own feelings are supposed not to be involved, the Duke's, like

Angelo's, appeals entirely to abstract reason and fails thereby—
not because the reasoning is faulty, but because reason alone
can never be finally persuasive without some evidence of the
heart's being engaged as well. The Duke's speech to Claudio is
justly famous and does not need to be quoted; I would note only
that its cold opening words are "be absolute for death," and that
the remainder—introduced with the grand rhetorical flourish
that Claudio should "[r]eason thus with life," (3.1.6)—is a straight
series of detached, however eloquent and profound, preacherly
maxims on the worthlessness of existence. Claudio can of course
say nothing at the time to refute the Duke, but it requires only
the leaven of hope that Isabella later reintroduces to inspire him
with the rhetoric to express the other, the human side of the
dilemma with equal power:

> The weariest and most loathed worldly life
> That age, ache, penury, and imprisonment,
> Can lay on nature is a paradise
> To what we fear of death.
>
> (3.1.130–33)

The engagement of the heart that was so conspicuously missing in the first meeting of Angelo and Isabella surges with re-
doubled force, proportional to its earlier repression, then, in their
second meeting and its sequent events. And while again no resolution of the dilemma of heavenly versus earthly imperatives is
possible, truth expressed with eloquence also once again proves
equal on both sides. The key to the engagement of the heart on
both sides in this instance is that the issue between them is now
no longer one primarily of principle, but one that involves the
deepest personal motives, to the extent at least that they are
imagined as capable of understanding them, of the debaters
themselves. The qualification "capable of understanding them" is
important here, suggesting, what is obvious enough in the debate though challenging on several levels as an interpretive
problem, that Shakespeare's understanding of the characters'
motives is different from and much deeper than the "characters'"
own, another of his typically devious rhetorical maneuvers. It is
on the basis of this greater Shakespearean depth that irresolvable issues of principle are retained centrally in the conception,
though from the characters' perspective it is passion more than
principle that now gives force to the debate. It is in the Angelo

character that this shift of focus is most obvious, partly because
it is carried to the greatest extreme in him, and while the theatrical effectiveness of the transformation is unquestioned, even
the rhetorical magic of a Shakespeare cannot render completely
invisible the same dilemma of impossible contradiction that we
saw hidden in the character of the Duke. Where he finessed the
contradiction in the Duke by styling him a "gentleman of all
temperance," he tries the even bolder move with Angelo of
making *him* a "gentleman of all *in*temperance," as it were, as absolute now in his capitulation to the demands of the id as he was
previously in his denial of its existence.

Character critics of Shakespeare have performed many interesting contortions over the years to explain this character reversal in Angelo as plausible, with the "unconscious" invariably
prominent in the analysis. "Angelo, indeed, does not know himself," says Wilson Knight; "no one receives so great a shock as
he himself when temptation overthrows his virtue."[36] But the
Shakespearean view of the question, I suggest, transcends all
such explanations. This is not to say that the transformation
does not have a realistic appearance; Margaret Webster, again,
astutely notes its closeness in feeling to the famous "lust in
action" sonnet 129.[37] Indeed, even in the context of the interpretation offered here, insisting on the incompatibility of "heavenly" with earthly values, there is a certain logic to the case. The
logic would be that when life is conceived as Angelo has supposedly conceived it, in terms of absolutes, and a "heavenly"
standard of behavior, with the power as well to enforce that
standard, is demanded of earthly beings, the words *good* and
evil no longer have meaning in earthly human terms. "Good"
itself *becomes* an "evil," because impossible of achievement and
therefore false, leaving the victim of the delusion, the enforcer,
with no way out of the dilemma, if he is to act at all, but to
pursue his "evil" humanity to its absolute opposite pole. The
theory of such behavior is logical; it is in the translation of that
theory into practical reality that impossibility, indeed absurdity,
rears its inescapable head. We do not have a scene in the play,
as we did for both Isabella and the Duke, that brings Angelo together with Lucio to, as it were, sharpen the heavenly/earthly
dialectic and clue us in directly to the contradictions the character's behavior betrays, but the nagging presence of the Lucio
character alone, along with comments he makes about Angelo,

give us most of what we need to see clearly where irresolvable problems lie.

We have already seen that the index of humanity for Lucio/Shakespeare, focused in the Duke, is carnal knowledge. Those who would try to square the Angelo of the play's beginning with Angelo after his fall will invariably quote Lucio's comment on him, that he is "one who never feels / The wanton stings and motions of the sense" (1.4.58–59); and indeed, for Angelo as he is up to the very moment of his fall to be in any manner credible as a character this would actually *have to be the case*. That this simply will not wash, however, is manifest in several ways. Not only does such a notion contradict the very basis of the play's, not to mention the Bible's, philosophy of man, that humanity and carnality are inseparably joined, but it is a test that Angelo has already failed, as shown in his earlier treatment of Mariana, among other ways. These "other ways" would again include the same dilemma we saw manifest in the behavior of the Duke, that one cannot abhor and proscribe as a crime the act of "fornication," and have it suggested at the same time that one is not perfectly familiar with what fornication is. The plain fact is that the "heavenly" standard of goodness that Shakespeare gives the affectation of to Angelo at the beginning of the play is as impossible in a real human being as the equally absolute "badness" to which he has him later sink; it is by verbal trickery alone, deliberately exploited, that either or both are made to *seem* plausible. Among the many tantalizing clues to his trickery Shakespeare seeds the play with is one that gives particular insight into the deception he is perpetrating in Angelo. In proposing the bed-trick to Isabella, the Duke excuses the deception Isabella must enter into by assuring her that "the doubleness of the benefit defends the deceit from reproof" (3.1.248–49). Of Angelo it may be said that the brazen doubleness of impossibility in the character is Shakespeare's defense, from which he incidentally benefits, not so much against reproof as against exposure.

It is in the Isabella character, finally, however, that the contradictions inherent in attempting to accommodate the human to the divine, whether in terms of standards of behavior, of meanings, or of needs, are most openly flaunted. She plays basically just another variation on the theme of contradiction we have already seen played in the Duke and Angelo, but with the

overtones of absurdity even more visible in her situation than
in theirs. The feat of characterization performed with Isabella
in the second interview scene with Angelo has been much admired, particularly in the way it blends human emotion with religious fervor to give a portrait that, while it is difficult not to
see it as distorted in some of its aspects, nevertheless rings with
a sincerity that is immensely persuasive. No words Shakespeare ever wrote ring any truer than Angelo's reluctant tribute
to the "cunning enemy that, to catch a saint, / With saints dost
bait thy hook" (2.2.180–81), capturing exactly in those words
the irresistible attraction Isabella's blend of sexual and religious passion go on to exert not only over him, but over us as
audience as well. Analysis of Isabella's behavior in this scene
and with Claudio subsequently, up to the point of the Duke's in-
tervention in the plot, must invoke the "unconscious" again to
account for its more extreme manifestations, but fortuitously in
this case with clearer warrant, or at least with less stretching of
the parameters of psychoanalytic theory than is required to
make the same case for Angelo. Indeed Shakespeare seems
almost to have anticipated his psychoanalytic critics in the care
with which he has insinuated an apparently unconscious but
unmistakably sexual energy into Isabella's passionate defense
of her purity and her devotion to Pauline Christian principle. It
would be difficult to conceive a scenario with greater potential
for theatrical fire than this confrontation between a lecher with
the power of life and death in this hands, and a would-be saint
whose bodily nakedness under the clothing of her convictions is
only too tantalizingly evident; and Shakespeare exploits that
potential fully in his construction of the scene. The sexual tension in the scene is present from the outset, but is allowed to
build slowly below the verbal surface, neither character touching the subject directly until Angelo, in Shakespearean mock
exasperation, finally makes the situation clear. His manner of
presentation again places front and center the problem of contradiction between human carnal needs and Christian spiritual
claims, a contradiction that only the cloak of the "unconscious"
covers:

> *Ang.* Nay, but hear me;
> Your sense pursues not mine, either you are ignorant
> Or seem so, craftily; and that's not good.
>
> (2.4.73–75)

The question of "ignorance" or "craft" in Isabella is left tantaliz-ingly unanswered, though the questionable implications of carnal "ignorance" must hang over her similarly to Angelo and the Duke. That her religious passion nevertheless *is* a form of sublimated sexuality could not, without a direct statement, be made clearer than it is made in her climactic declaration of how, were she, like her brother, under sentence of death, she would welcome martyrdom:

> were I under the terms of death,
> Th' impression of keen whips I'd wear as rubies,
> And strip myself to death as to a bed
> That longing have been sick for, ere I'd yield
> My body up to shame.
>
> (2.4.100–104)

The element in the situation that pushes the contradiction to the point of manifest absurdity, however, is in Isabella's remain-ing adamant, indeed passionately reaffirming to Claudio her al-legiance to "divine" principle when he questions her right, knowingly at the cost to Claudio not just of his life, but of the "lingering sufferance" (2.4.167)—i.e., torture—which Angelo has decreed must precede his execution if she refuses him. This is a variation on the theme of contradiction expressed as well in the Duke and Angelo, similar to the "godlike" Duke in its total disre-gard of Claudio's human failings and fears, and to the monster Angelo in the totality of its submission to the lust for domination that lives in the heart of the id.

While many other examples of words and actions in the play could be cited to further reinforce the picture of impossibility this play presents, the mélange of contradictory "truths" of which it consists, I will leave the reader with just one more to ponder, the debate on sin between Angelo and Isabella early in this scene. It precedes Angelo's explicit proposal to spare Claudio if Isabella will yield to him, and in this still hypothetical form has exactly the character of an academic debate. The subject is a per-fect one for rhetorical practice, because open endlessly to debate with no possibility of resolution:

> *Ang.* Answer to this:
>   I, now the voice of the recorded law,
>   Pronounce a sentence on your brother's life.
>   Might there not be a charity in sin
>   To save this brother's life?

> *Isab.* Please you to do't,
>   I'll take it as a peril to my soul,
>   It is no sin at all but charity.
> *Ang.*   Pleas'd you to do't, at peril to your soul,
>   Were equal poise of sin and charity.
>
> (2.4.60–68)

This passage may stand, I suggest, as an epitome of the play as a whole, catching something of Seneca in its subject matter and the irresolvability of the issue, something of Munday in the absurdity into which its paradoxes of heavenly versus earthly "truths" must dissolve.

8

Supersubtle Shakespeare:
Othello as a Rhetorical Allegory

Criticism has been aware for more than three centuries, since Rymer first raised the question in 1693, of a striking contradiction in *Othello* and in the character of its hero. E. E. Stoll, writing in 1915, sketched something of the critical history of this contradiction, noting that while the contradiction has sometimes been acknowledged by the critics, it has invariably been ignored in interpretations of the play. The contradiction has to do, of course, primarily with the incredible facility of Othello's fall at Iago's hands, leading directly and precipitately to the murder of his wife. Whether in terms of time, of method, of motivation, or of character, the whole process of Othello's conversion is manifestly incredible and absurd, it is suggested. Many approaches to the problem are possible, but, most succinctly, I can perhaps demonstrate the supposed absurdity of this transformation in terms of a fundamental character trait that his fall necessarily predicates. The particular trait has various labels, whether considered a commendable or a censurable trait, but its essence is trust—a trusting or credulous nature is, one way or another, Othello's downfall, we are told. To Coleridge it is "unsuspiciousness";[1] to Bradley "his trust, where he trusts, is absolute";[2] to Wilson Knight Othello is "a symbol of faith in human values of love, of war, of romance."[3] Now it is readily apparent in the case of all three of these descriptive expressions that something is wrong—wrong, that is, on the plain evidence of the play itself, in the murder of Desdemona. For each description involves the critic in what amounts (or at least very nearly) to a contradiction. Coleridge's *unsuspiciousness* can apply thus only in the case of Othello's relations with Iago—quite clearly its opposite obtains in his relations with Desdemona, of whom he is wildly, irrationally suspicious to the point of utter absurdity. And similarly with Bradley's criticism, if Othello's trust (of Iago) is "absolute," then plainly his *lack of trust* of Desdemona is equally absolute. Bradley further calls Othello Shakespeare's "greatest poet," a "character . . . so noble," whose "sufferings are so heart-rending, that he stirs . . . in most readers a . . . mingled love and pity which they feel for no other hero in Shakespeare."[4] Considering again the obvious contradictions in Othello's behavior, such criticism cannot be better tagged than Shakespeare himself tags it in some lines taken from the very play in which this paragon appears:

> It is a judgment maim'd and most imperfect
> That will confess perfection so could err
> Against all rules of nature, and must be driven
> To find out practices of cunning hell,
> Why this should be.
>
> (1.3.99–103)

As these lines I believe deliberately hint, there is more to the conception of *Othello* than Bradley's criticism (or any other that passes over the contradictions in the play) sees: it is this "symbol of faith in human . . . love" who smothers his new wife on their second nuptial night, we must remember. Even in Stoll, who discusses at length both the contradictions themselves and criticism's failure to resolve them, no real attempt is made to deal with the problems they raise. Thus Stoll cites only the "immemorial convention" of the "calumniator credited," as he calls it, as explanation, listing analogues in Shakespeare and other playwrights of the fall of a "blameless hero," and concluding that "[p]roof or probability is not required."[5] I do not believe that this is a sufficient answer to the problem, and suggest that the evidence is overwhelming both that Shakespeare was fully conscious and fully in control of his pen in *Othello*—in other words, that he knew the contradictions were there and put them there for a purpose—and that whatever else *Othello* may be, it is also, arguably even *primarily*, an implicit allegorical commentary on the functions and powers of rhetoric.

Besides its stark contradictions (laying aside for a moment the question of whether these are intentional) at least two other

qualities in *Othello* make it unique in the canon, further reinforcing the suggestion that it is a special conception for Shakespeare. The first of these qualities is the obvious one, its construction. Samuel Johnson called attention first to this quality,
and almost all other commentators have remarked on it. John
Munro's remarks are typical:

> Recognition of the play's masterly construction is well-nigh uni-
> versal. It is all of a piece, devoid of sub-plot and extraneous mat-
> ter, the whole of it turning on Act III, Scene iii, a scene unrivaled
> for dramatic power and development, to which all before in the
> action inevitably leads up, and from which the denouement inex-
> orably follows. Act I is a dramatic entity in which the unities are
> but little departed from: and in no other Shakespearean play is
> the unity of action so definitely observed throughout.[6]

Other critics have noticed a further uniqueness in *Othello's*
poetry. This is a trickier thing to prove, of course; as a product of
the great period of Shakespeare's drama, *Othello's* supreme
poetic accomplishment is perhaps taken for granted, but its
supremacy in poetry may be more than this: there is a concentration or brilliance of poetic effect in *Othello*, a sculptured quality, a peculiar romantic richness of vocabulary and image that
makes it unique. These qualities apply especially to the speeches
of Othello. Bradley noticed this, as we have seen, as did Ulrici,
who relates it to the masterful structuring of the play as a whole,
what he calls its "beauty of composition," its "harmony, clearness,
and design."[7] To Wilson Knight, again, *Othello's* poetry possesses
"a rich music all its own";[8] and to Helen Gardner *Othello* is
"supreme in one quality: beauty."[9] It is my contention that these
qualities too are a part of Shakespeare's allegorical design in
Othello, the design of rhetoric to a preconceived illusory end that
is one of the principal themes of the play.

As a final brief critical preliminary to the analysis of *Othello*,
let me cite a further few lines from that very important play in
developmental terms for Shakespeare, *Henry V:* In unmasking
the traitors Cambridge, Grey, and Scroop in 2.2, Henry has occasion to say the following:

> 'Tis so strange
> That, though the truth of it stands off as gross
> As black and white, my eye will scarcely see it.

(102–4)

And in the same speech but six lines further down,

> And whatsoever cunning fiend it was
> That wrought upon thee so preposterously
> Hath got the voice in hell for excellence.
>
> (111–13)

These lines, though written before *Othello*, constitute a retroactive criticism of that play, suggesting ideas which not only stayed in Shakespeare's mind when he wrote *Othello*, but which may well have helped determine his choice of subject in that work. *Henry V* is further unique among Shakespeare's plays in its choruses, as is well known. The choruses are addressed directly to the audience and ask its cooperation in adding imaginatively to the meagerness of the production, a request which must have met (especially in its great battle scenes) with success sufficient to inspire Shakespeare to further and more subtle manipulations of audience responses, thus leading directly, again, to *Othello*. And while on the subject of thematic analogues for *Othello*, I might point out also that the plays generally considered to have immediately preceded and succeeded it in composition, *Hamlet* and *King Lear*, likewise offer respectively retroactive and retrospective criticisms of *Othello*. Hamlet's notorious procrastination in avenging his father's murder—sworn to follow "as swift / As meditation or the thoughts of love," but with "the native hue of resolution" later to become "sicklied o'er with the pale cast of thought"—is implicitly countered not only in the plot of *Othello*, where revenge comes with *too* great haste, but in the theme, where, "proof" being seen, as Othello says, "away *at once* with love or jealousy." And similarly with Lear—as shamefully duped as Othello by the flattering words (the "glib and oily art") of Goneril and Regan, he casts off Cordelia as irrationally as Othello Desdemona, and is chided for doing so in terms that are a direct and explicit commentary on *Othello*:

> This is most strange,
> That she, whom even but now was your best object,
> The argument of your praise, balm of your age,
> The best, the dearest, should in this trice of time
> Commit a thing so monstrous to dismantle
> So many folds of favor.
>
> (1.1.213–18)

Coming, then, to *Othello* itself, let me direct the reader first to an episode in the first scene of the play. Iago, unseen, is informing Brabantio, at the top of his voice and in coarse, blunt terms, of his daughter's elopement with the Moor, and in the course of his tirade he throws out a particularly vivid and characteristically "Iagesque" image for their liaison—the image of "the beast with two backs" (1.1.118). The image is from Rabelais originally (bk. 1, ch. 3), and means of course fornication, but as well as its manifest drift in *Othello*, it is an organic poetic motive that has echoes throughout the play: indeed it might stand as an archetype of the really extraordinary linguistic care that Shakespeare has lavished on this play from beginning to end. Illustration: for a pattern of deliberately contrived imagery that this single motive evokes, consider first the name of the inn at which Desdemona and Othello lodge: the Sagittary—as it happens a literal "beast with two backs" in the figure of the centaur from classical mythology. The image of the centaur in turn then calls up further associations, of the mating of men with animals, for example—Iago's "you'll have your daughter cover'd with a Barbary horse," his offer to "change [his] humanity with a baboon," or Cassio's "to be now a sensible man, by and by a fool, and presently a beast!" And the "Barbary horse" image, finally, ties in directly with the "Barbary" name in Desdemona's willow song of act 4. Patterns of imagery like this are only discovered by careful and repeated readings of Shakespeare in the study; they are never observed in performance, but their existence illustrates both the degree of control over his material Shakespeare clearly has, and also that a play like *Othello* was obviously composed in the study with great care, and not in haste prior to a performance. Such patterns of imagery are particularly significant in this, however, that they illustrate strikingly the fact that *Othello* in the study and *Othello* on the stage are really quite different animals—that the play is a "beast with two backs," in this respect as well, in yet another application of this profoundly suggestive motive which may well have occurred to Shakespeare.

The most obvious image pattern in *Othello* is the pervasive black/white or light/dark opposition, a pattern which I believe is suggestively and consciously prefigured (as well as its complication) in the first quotation from *Henry V* above, and to which the "beast with two backs" also relates. This image pattern in *Othello* is probably the most prominent such pattern in all of Shakespeare; and it is a pattern not only of images, but of character, plot, theme, and even of staging, that touches every facet of the play. As the world of the play divides both literally and metaphorically into elements of light and dark—of "good" and "evil," if one wishes—the "beast with two backs" becomes a subtly generalized device to suggest this opposition. Thus, if the "beast with two backs" means (among other things) the act of love, then in the coming together of Othello and Desdemona we have precisely such a union of black and white; but the emotion and the act of love itself divides further in *Othello* into "black" and "white" components: on the one side love is mere animal coupling, with lust and brutality the keynotes—this is Iago's version to Roderigo (1.3.329–31), and the source and motive of most of the animal imagery in the play; and on the other side love is anitthetical to this—an idealizing sacrifice, angelic in its purity, of all that one has and is for another, the archetype of which sacrifice is made by Desdemona in her willing submission to and forgiveness of Othello, even to the point of condoning her own murder. There is almost no end of further ways in which the opposition of white and black can be seen as developed in the play: Iago's "black" heart is masked by his "white" ("honest") appearance (Othello's character the opposite, of course); or Desdemona's unblemished virtue is contrasted with Iago's unmitigated villainy. Othello's "occupation" (see 3.3.361) as a soldier has a white/black connotation: as in war the "cause" (5.2.1) is always white and black—enemies and friends are clearly distinguishable—so in peace the *clarity* of this white/black picture is obscured, and one cannot tell a "false, disloyal knave" indeed from one's own lieutenant without, as the joke has it, a program. There are calculated light/dark oppositions worked into the staging of the play as well: both the first and last scenes (among others) open in darkness, with "light," both literal and figurative, later to be dramatically introduced, extinguished, and "relumed" on stage.[10]

The primary black/white opposition in the play, however, from the point of view of this study, is in the writing. It is in rhetorical or compositional terms that the enigma of *Othello* is unlocked and the contradictions resolved, for *Othello* is first and foremost a play about words—about rhetoric and poetry—about what they are and what they do. Essentially, the *appearance* of plausibility in the plot and the action of the play is sustained by the extraordinary richness, care, and skill in the web of language ("There's magic in the web") Shakespeare weaves; while behind this appearance, and perfectly well known to Shakespeare at the same time, lies the *reality* of an absurd and incredible imposture. Both "backs" of the beast, as it were, are in equal balance, which is to say that the "real" imposture is no more the final answer to *Othello* than the "apparent" plausibility; and this in turn also means, surprisingly but unquestionably, that *all* interpretations of *Othello*, no matter (at least theoretically) how extreme, are probably correct—whether Rymer's, who called it "a bloody farce," and said that "it had need be a *supersubtle* Venetian that this Plot will pass upon"; or Macaulay's, who said that *Othello* is "perhaps, the greatest work in the world."[11]

There are two levels, again, on which rhetoric in *Othello* can be analyzed, and two basic avenues by which the play can be approached as a rhetorical allegory. The "levels" here are the "second" and "third" rhetorical levels with which we are familiar, and my two avenues of approach for convenience sake I will call at this time the *linguistic* and the *structural*. These elements are all closely interrelated, but for analysis they can be considered, initially at least, as separate problems. In "second" level rhetorical terms, then, the key at every point to the plot of the play is found in rhetoric or speech art. For the character of Iago, first, enough has been said in past criticism of his acting and rhetorical skill, verging on the supernatural, to require no further embellishment here. One particular descriptive term is perhaps used more often than any other to describe his machinations and deceptions—the word (and its cognates) "art." Johnson used the word, Coleridge and Swinburne as well, and Granville-Barker expanded the concept fully (104–12); and this is not even counting its use by their legions of critical followers of every stripe. It is a word that indeed says all as far as Iago's character is concerned: he is exactly the second-level counterpart of what Shakespeare knows himself to be in his own third-level rhetoric—the artist *par excellence*, putting across with compelling rhetorical force and invincible conviction that "transparent and unplausible imposture," to quote E. E. Stoll once again, that is Othello's downfall. There have been fewer commentators who have seen the rhetorician in the character of Othello comparable to Iago, but this is a critical viewpoint that has some important adherents in this century as well, notably T. S. Eliot and F. R. Leavis.[12]

Iago's developing plot apart, it seems to me that the climactic moment of the first stage of the tragedy is in the confrontation of Othello with the Venetian council 1.3, defending his marriage, and defending especially the manner of his courtship. It is his great opportunity to show his character as a man as well as to shine as an orator, and he triumphs on both counts, winning the hearts of his audience both on and off stage. His responses are shaped in such a manner, moreover, that the dramatic or oratorical basis of his character is unmistakable—indeed it is in the forefront of the audience's consciousness.

There are two principal ways by which this emphasis is brought about. First, Brabantio's strident accusations of witchcraft against Othello, assumed by Brabantio as conclusive and repeated several times early in the play, raise intriguing questions in the hearer's mind about the nature of this match and prepare him to listen with special interest to whatever account of his actions Othello might give. The contrast, then, between Brabantio's near hysteria and Othello's masterful calm and self-control, exemplified in the unhurried eloquence and spontaneous grace of his every spoken work, is winning to Othello's cause and persuasive to the auditor in the highest degree. And the climax of the interlude is in Othello's recounting of the actual courtship itself, in which we learn that, quite frankly and unblushingly, he won Desdemona's heart by *oratory*. The last lines of the statement in particular epitomize the oratorical basis of his courtship (as Othello conceives it), and set forth as well the rather strange conception of love as essentially nothing more than a romantic poem that Othello seems to hold:

> My story being done,
> She gave me for my pains a world of sighs;
> She swore, in faith, 'twas strange, 'twas passing strange;
> 'Twas pitiful, 'twas wondrous pitiful.
> She wish'd she had not heard it; yet she wish'd
> That heaven had made her such a man. She thank'd me;
> And bade me, if I had a friend that lov'd her,
> I should but teach him how to tell my story,
> And that would woo her. Upon this hint I spake;
> She lov'd me for the dangers I had pass'd;
> And I lov'd her that she did pity them.
> This only is the witchcraft I have us'd.

> (1.3.158–69)

There are several significant inferences that can be taken from these lines. First we may note that it was his *story* (at least in Othello's view) that won Desdemona's heart, and not the person of Othello himself: since "a friend," apparently who could tell such a story could have won her too—Desdemona, or indeed, in the Duke's awe-struck words, any other girl: as he says, "I think this tale would win my daughter too" (171). Second, and perhaps more significant in the light of later events, it appears almost to have been the same "story" again, that won Othello's heart to Desdemona, rather than the girl herself being his object. Loving Othello "for the dangers [he] had pass'd," Desdemona is loved in turn *because* of this, that "she did pity them." His love of Desdemona is thus really a love not of her, but of the romance of his own life seen reflected in her eyes. The third and most significant inference in the speech, however, has to do with the old question of witchcraft again. Oratory, as Othello says, is the "only" witchcraft he has used, but to say this is very pointedly not to deny that oratory is indeed a form of witchcraft—a witchcraft that can turn "a thing" like Othello—a middle-aged Ethiopian mercenary and outsider—into a desirable mate for a Desdemona, and that can turn disaster, flood, slaughter, cannibalism, appalling freaks of nature, and other "bragging and fantastical lies" into romance.

It is crucially important also to note that Iago alone among the characters sees through the rhetorician and poseur to the hollow man that Othello really is. That Othello is a liar indeed we ourselves know, or we should—his outrageous *meiosis* "Rude am I in my speech [81], . . . And therefore little shall I grace my cause / In speaking for myself" [88–89] is still ringing in our ears from five minutes before!—and likewise only in a poem, as we also know if we reflect, is slavery or the "occupation" of war ever the glorious adventure that Othello pictures it as being. Iago's insights here are Shakespeare's as well, as we remember again the famous "I am not what I am" paradox: the character of Iago in effect brings "second-" and "third-" level rhetorical implications together. And it is finally particularly interesting that in spite of Iago's straightforward and wholly accurate estimate of Othello, not to mention the plain evidence of the character and the speeches of the man himself, criticism until recently has not seen his hollow side, being taken in by the same mesmerizing spell of magnificent poetry that took in Desdemona and the

Duke, and missing Shakespeare's message—the message that to
fall under the spell of rhetoric is to lay oneself open to the most
flagrant abuses of reason; a message that is brought home with
the ultimate of compelling force in the preposterous and impossible plot that snares Othello—that becomes, indeed, "the net /
That shall enmesh them all" (2.3.350–51).

These are some of the second-level rhetorical implications in
the character of Othello, but there are additional third-level,
Shakespeare-to-the-audience implications that further support
the picture of the character as a poseur and rhetorician, and of
the play *Othello* as a farce on the theme of rhetoric. I have suggested that the "linguistic approach" to the question of allegory
and the problem of meaning for Shakespeare is a fruitful one. By
this term I mean the critical study of words, their contexts and
special meanings in individual plays, as indices to possible
deeper revelations of Shakespeare's thought in those plays. Such
analyses are matter exclusively for the study, and never for the
theater; and their primary tool accordingly is the pedant's delight, the Concordance.[13] The reservation is always there, moreover, in advancing conclusions from linguistics, that these can
never be more than merely suggestions, "ocular proof" in such
matters being in the nature of things impossible. Linguistic hints
and leads can be fascinating for their own sake notwithstanding,
however, and at times they can be highly suggestive and strongly
inferential.

There are, then, for example, several generically rhetorical
words that have either their most frequent or very nearly their
most frequent use in *Othello* of all the plays, a fact which suggests a special and conscious rhetorical purpose in this play. The
word *speech*, for instance, has more uses in *Othello* than in any
other play except *Hamlet*; and similarly with the words *speak,
say,* and *act.*[14] Frequency of use of such words, of course, while
perhaps suggestive, is not conclusive in itself without support
from a special manner in their use as well, such that deliberate
hints of double (second- and third-level) meanings may be conveyed. With eye and ear cocked for nuances, however, we can
indeed spot such hints in various of these words as they are used
in the play, and especially as they are associated with other
words of similar theatrical and rhetorical purport. A classic instance of precisely this kind of doubleness occurs early in the
play in one of Othello's speeches. This particular line, as it hap-

pens, does not use any of the words listed above, but as a response to an accusation of being "a practiser / Of arts inhibited and out of warrant," it has a closely associated meaning: "Were it my cue to fight," says Othello, "I should have known it/Without a prompter" (2.2.83–84). Such an allusion passes unnoticed in performance, but it has the effect of subtly putting Othello's whole performance into the context purely of theater, which is exactly what it is intended to do. This is the only use of the word *prompter* in the whole Shakespeare canon, incidentally. Similar implications are with equal subtlety insinuated into the other words as well, as they are frequently used in *Othello*, viz. (italics mine on key words):

Bra.   Fathers, from hence trust not your daughters' minds
         By what you see them *act*.
                                              (1.1.171–72).

. . . .

Duke. [To Othello]   What, in your own *part*, can you *say* to this?
                                              (1.3.74)

. . . .

Cass.   Drunk! And *speak parrot*! And squabble, swagger, swear!
          And *discourse fustian* with one's own shadow!
                                              (2.3.270–71)

. . . .

Iago.   You shall observe him;
          And his own courses will denote him so
          That I may save my *speech*.
                                              (4.1.275–77)

. . . .

Des.   Upon my knees, what doth your *speech* import?
                                              (4.2.31)

. . . .

Oth.   I know *this act* shows horrible and grim.
                                              (5.2.206)

It is in the context of third-level rhetoric as well, that the enigmatic last words of Iago—"From this time forth I never will speak word"—are no longer an enigma; for such a statement simply recognizes in effect, that "Iago" is and will always be a puppet—mere words, a voice, an actor going through some motions—whose silence, when decreed by the puppeteer at his whim, is total and final.

The final example of rhetorical doubleness in a speech in this play that I will draw the reader's attention to, is to Othello's garbled speech just before his collapse in 4.1. It has been noted that this speech is a "travesty," probably an intentional parody, of the "rounded harmonies"[15] of the earlier Othello style, symbolizing his reversion at this point to total bestiality, from the lofty pinnacle of civilized humanitarianism that was his distinction and his greatness when we met him first. The speech is also often called "incoherent"—Stephen Cohen, for example, sees Othello "reduced to gibberish"[16] in it—and is usually passed over without comment; an easy enough omission, given the more facile images and actions that surround it in the rest of the scene, and it seems clear what Shakespeare (in performance again, of course) would have us do. To take the easy way out with this speech, however, is to fall into the old Shakespearean trap of inobservancy that is set for us on every page of this play. Though logically disconnected, the speech is not incoherent; quite the reverse in fact, it is an extraordinarily carefully constructed recapitulation of Iago's whole plot against Othello. This becomes a rather involved question of interpretation almost immediately when we get into it, but concentrating for the moment just on the speech itself, we note very clearly first that its primary subject is *words* and their ambiguities. It is worth quoting the last few lines that lead up to the speech as well:

Oth.   What hath he said?
Iago.   Faith, that he did—I know not what he did.
Oth.   What? What?[17]
Iago.   Lie—
Oth.   With her?
Iago.   With her, on her; what you will.
Oth.   Lie with her—lie on her? We say lie on her when they belie her. Lie with her. Zounds, that's fulsome. Handkerchief—confessions—handkerchief! To confess, and be hang'd for his labour—first, to be hang'd and then to confess. I tremble at it. Nature would not invest herself with such shadowing passion without some instruction. It is not words that shakes me thus—pish!—noses, ears, and lips. Is't possible? Confess! Handkerchief! O devil!

                                                            (4.1.31–44)

There is considerably more of penetrating meaning in this statement than at first glance appears. Considering (as we may in the study though we do not on the stage) that up to this point in the play Iago's plot is constructed wholly of words—in actual fact, of course, it never does have much more than words for backing, but up to 4.1 not even the scintilla of ocular proof that the handkerchief constitutes has yet been produced: there is simply nothing—it is perhaps surprising that Othello is obsessed, *here*, with precisely the question of the ambiguities and the imaginative effects of words, the very means by which he is being duped! Shakespeare, I suggest, is daring us to see what is going on. Can Othello, we must ask, come *this close* to his answer and still not see what is being done to him? The falsity, thus, the tissue of words, that is Iago's whole plot is explicitly laid out in the speech; it is clear, it is exposed, and it is Othello its victim who speaks it. He uses the word *lie* not once in this exchange but five times, noting its ambiguities: "We say lie on her when they belie her"—this statement asking, in effect, *is* someone belying her?—and this in turn raising the natural next question, who could such a someone be? One can really do little more with such absurd incongruities as these are seen on reflection to be than to throw back at them Desdemona's rhetorical question to the Clown in 3.4: "Can anything be made of this?" It is no accident either, I submit, that the subject of that earlier conversation as well happens to be the question of the ambiguous meanings of the word *lie* (see 3.4.1–12). And as if to bolster and confirm even further our awareness of his game, Shakespeare does not let the "words" question go at this point, but returns to and expands it in ll.41–43: "Nature would not invest herself in such shadowing passion without some instruction. It is not words that shakes me thus." These lines too are far from nonsense when carefully considered; though somewhat obscurely worded, their meaning is crystal clear, to wit: that Nature does not put on a passionate act like this without cause; there must be more to this than words![18] There is not, of course—not to Iago's plot (second- level rhetoric), and not to the play as a whole (third-level rhetoric); and at this point we can finally see Shakespeare's game, I believe, without illusions. The implications of this conclusion are complex, and I must back off the question briefly and approach it again in a somewhat more roundabout manner to present them fully. "'Tis here," as Iago says, "but yet confus'd."

I will start by observing that the tragedy of *Othello*, as any reader of even average alertness must note, hinges to an extraordinary extent on coincidence. Apart from considerations of character, whereby Othello is interpreted (and quite legitimately) as prone to this type of delusion and manipulation, the simple fact remains that if one small question had been asked by anyone, indeed if a single word were out of place from the beginning of 3.3 to the death of Desdemona, Iago's spell would be broken and his plot come to ground. The necessary question is never asked, of course, and the tragedy proceeds as inexorably as fate to its predestined end; and it is convincing and moving in the highest degree in accomplishing that end. It is only when one steps back a pace from the spell of the play's music and its passions, however, that these coincidences begin to be seen. And "stepping back," one quickly discovers, is itself a matter of degree: for the further one steps back—the more rationally and critically one looks at the play—the more incredible, absurd, and contradictory it becomes. Stepping back, we see indeed what Shakespeare meant when he said in *Richard III*, "none are for me / That look into me with considerate eyes." Viewed rationally, in fact, these contradictions and absurdities cannot be accidental. The speech of Othello before his collapse is a classic case in point. Realistically considered it is impossibly contradictory: on the one hand Othello "knows" (because he *says* it) that words are ambiguous, that "lie on" can mean "belie," and that it *could* be "words" that "shake" him; on the other hand he not only fails to act on that knowledge, he fails seemingly even to grasp it. One could say of this contradiction, of course, that it is just another example of Shakespeare's preternatural tragic sense—to bring his Othello thus within the veriest whisker of the truth, to tantalize him to the ultimate degree, and yet to deny him.[19] One could say this and in fact be right, in a *poetic* sense, but one cannot say it and be logical. That is to say, no real Othello could be so utterly blind; a play Othello on the other hand, whose *very being* is poetry, can be anything his creator wants him to be; and this is exactly Shakespeare's point. The play is a beast with two backs—in rhetorical or poetic terms a tragedy, in rational terms a farce. As soon as rational criteria are applied to the play it falls apart; but the magic of the play and the witchcraft of its words are such that rational criteria are not applied without the greatest difficulty. In performance they are impossible to apply, and even in the study the illusion of logic and sense[20] is so strong that only a conscious effort on the part of the reader to stay alert can withstand it. Without this effort, however—and this is virtually the history of *Othello* criticism for more than three hundred years—reason is led literally "tenderly by the nose as asses are," and we ourselves are the victims and the goats of Shakespeare's rhetoric, in exact parallel to Othello being the goat of Iago's rhetoric.

Criticism has often noticed the contradictions and coincidences in *Othello*, but it has never known quite what to make of them; it has never known why they are there. Bradley's remarks are typical:

> Again and again a chance word from Desdemona, a chance meeting of Othello and Cassio, a question which starts to our lips and which anyone but Othello would have asked, would have destroyed Iago's plot and ended his life.[21]

"A chance meeting, . . . a question . . . which anyone but Othello would have asked"—precisely: the meeting does not take place and the question is not asked because Shakespeare does not *let* them take place or be asked! There is no such thing as "chance" in this play! They are considerations such as these that give new depth and meaning to the questions which *are* asked in the play, however, like Iago's "Are you a man? Have you a soul or sense?" (3.3.378)—an innocuous enough question in dramatic terms perhaps, but in third-level rhetorical terms absolutely loaded. Its answer of course is *No!*—Othello is not a man; like Iago's plot and like Iago himself he is a creation wholly of Shakespeare's words, whose life, actions, and death obey the whims of his creator.

We have looked at a few of the ways in which Shakespeare's language betrays his allegorical purpose in *Othello*, but as indicated earlier the structure of the play betrays it too, and perhaps even more egregiously. I will consider this structural problem first briefly in the context of *time* in the play. This is an area of difficulty that has been noticed frequently by critics in the last century. Essentially the problem that has been pointed out is that the action of the play is so constructed that there is literally no time when the supposed adultery between Cassio and Desdemona could have taken place.[22] This fact, of course, is probably *the* fundamental absurdity of the whole play, sufficient in itself, without qualification or comment, to elevate Othello and his whole crew to the realm of farce. To counter this possibility, however, and to salvage the tragic reading of *Othello*, there is the additional device of "long" time in the play, whereby numerous references are made in the later scenes to longer periods of time than the 36 hours that the actual clock on Cyprus records. The discrepancies between the two "times" are not noticed in performance, all the critics concur in this; and they almost all concur likewise in the necessity for the two times. Kenneth Muir's explanation is typical:

> From Iago's point of view, every hour increases the danger of his exposure. Shakespeare was faced with an acute problem. The action has to be exceedingly swift or it becomes incredible; and yet considerable time has to elapse or the action becomes incredible in another way.[23]

I reiterate that these words present, in a very succinct form, the traditional justification for the double time in *Othello*: they are identical in principle to what Furness, Granville-Barker, or Ridley say at greater length about it. My emphasis on this point has a purpose; because the statement, when read carefully, contains a logical absurdity. Put into approximate syllogistic form, it says in effect that the action of the play is incredible if it does not move swiftly, and on the other hand that the action is incredible if it does move swiftly. The conclusion is that the action is incredible. This straightfaced affirmation of absurdity by Muir is a perfect illustration of the "nameless, mysterious power"[24] in *Othello* to warp the mind, such that even as one states clearly the logical absurdity of the play, like Othello in his speech before his collapse one does not *see* what one has stated. Furness, paraphrasing Professor Wilson, suggests that even the "'Artificer of Fraud'" himself was not totally conscious of his trickery in *Othello*; but to imagine such a thing is simply to fall victim again to Shakespeare's rhetorical wiles.

Shakespeare's indubitable exact knowledge of *Othello's* necessary absurdity, in terms of time, can be demonstrated in both simple and complex ways. Logically, first, disregarding the issue of credibility, it scarcely needs pointing out that the play can function on only one time scheme. It can be either "short" or "long" time but not both. If the two time schemes could in some supernatural manner be kept separate in the play, then possibly it could work, but, as Iago says, "thou know'st we work by wit, and not by witchcraft" (2.3.360); the only witchcraft Shakespeare has is in his words. It does not require much perception, then, to note that in terms of "short" time logic Iago's "I lay with Cassio lately" (3.3.418–36—going on with the recitation of Cassio's "dream") contains a calculated absurdity that we are taunted by Shakespeare to catch: "lay with Cassio?" logic answers, "Impossible! you only arrived on Cyprus yesterday, and you were up all night with that brawl! And you couldn't have slept with Cassio on shipboard because you came on different ships!" The point of such tauntings, in both second- and third-level rhetorical terms, is to demonstrate that, however logically untenable a claim may be, under the spell of a powerful rhetoric it can be made to seem plausible. This particular example is perhaps absurd in its obviousness, but there are many other instances in the play where the deliberate sleight-of-hand maneuverings with time are paradoxically so simultaneously blatant and deft that one can only shake one's head in wonder at their wizardry, when awareness finally dawns. "Do but encave yourself," urges Iago, telling Othello to mark Cassio's gesture as he tells "the tale anew" of

> *Where, how, how oft, how long ago,* and *when,*
> He *hath,* and is *again* to cope your wife.
> (4.1.85–86, italics mine)

Or equally absurd the confrontation of Desdemona and Othello in the boudoir (4.2), as she replies, with irrefutable "short time" logic, to his accusation of her being "false": "To whom, my Lord? With whom? How am I false?" (4.2.41)—which is reinforced later by Emilia's "who keeps her company? / What place, what time, what form, what likelihood" (138–39)? It is in these terms that a totally new dimension of the play opens up. Speech after speech takes on new meaning; like Iago's disquisition on reason and sense to Roderigo:

> If the balance of our lives had not one scale of reason to poise another of sensuality, the blood and baseness of our natures would conduct us to most preposterous conclusions. (1.3.327–29).

The "preposterous conclusions" here are not only those to which Othello's blindness to "short-time" reason conducts him in the play, but those as well to which criticism is similarly driven in attempting to rationalize its time scheme. The invariable conclusion is that it is a case either of Shakespeare "nodding" when things do not seem logical, or that "his handling of time [is] both careful and suggestive" when they do.[25] In the light of what we have observed above, the likelihood of Shakespeare ever "nodding" as regards time in *Othello*, when he can, for example, insert references as specific as Cassio's "watch[ing] the horologe a *double set*" (2.3.22, italics mine), seems infinitely remote.

And these are far from the most complex levels on which Shakespeare's manipulations of time are operating in *Othello*. "Double" time should not be the designation for his trickery, but rather *triple* time; or even more accurate, perhaps, would be Iago's striking term "dilatory" (2.3.361), suggesting an almost infinite capacity for time manipulation. It has been noticed before of Shakespeare that there is considerable foreshortening or telescoping of time in many of the plays. By this term is meant the phenomenon of accelerating time during the course of a single scene so that much more "time" elapses dramatically than the auditor's watch has recorded. Irwin Smith points out that it is common in Shakespeare to accelerate time as much as forty times and more over the actual—that is, where in terms of lines spoken (calculating an average of twenty lines to the minute) ten minutes can consume up to six "hours" and more of dramatic time. In *Othello* Smith instances only the accelerations of 2.1, where in the space of 180 lines (nine minutes) three ships appear on the horizon, dock, and discharge their passengers, all of this taking place during a raging storm. This particular instance is one of the easiest seen of *Othello's* telescopings of time; in fact one has almost the impression in this scene, with its repetition of the sightings and dockings, that one is being invited to actually observe and be aware of the manipulations that are taking place. There are numerous other scenes in the play, however, where more outrageous yet harder to detect accelerations are worked in, which, if seen, are absurd, but unseen are quite unexceptionable. Such is 2.3, the scene which begins at "not yet ten a clock" (l. 13) and ends 375 lines later (approximately nineteen minutes playing time) with "By the mass, 'tis morning," and includes the cashiering of Cassio as well as the supposed consummation of the marriage of Othello and Desdemona. I say "supposed" by design in this case, because with the accelerated consumption of time in the scene there is every possibility that the consummation does not take place because there was no time for it! We have a reminder of this at l. 171:

> Friends all but now, even now,
> In quarter, and in terms, *like bride and groom*
> *Divesting them for bed*; and then, but now,
> As if some planet had outwitted men,
> Swords out, and tilting one at other's breast
>   (2.3.171–75, italics mine)

—a reminder that in the approximately nine minutes since Othello and Desdemona left the stage they can hardly more than have "divested them" for bed, let alone have had a moment for "love's quick pants" before the brawl disturbs them. The special emphasis on the word *now* in this speech, moreover, is a clear reminder that Shakespeare's stealing of time in this scene is a hoax, for plainly *now* cannot refer to any time except "real" time—that is, the audience's—since it was "but now" in real terms that the brawl in fact took place. It was Othello's last opportunity for sleep this night, as well, it seems, since he concludes his disciplinary measures with an offer to be Montano's "surgeon" (l. 245) himself for the binding of his wounds. Desdemona's "Faith that's with watching" (3.3.289), as she places her handkerchief on Othello's aching head the next morning, would then be a direct reference to the fact that Othello had spent a sleepless night the previous night. It is speculation, but it is my opinion that Shakespeare has deliberately arranged this scene as an *"ex obliquo"* tip-off that no consummation of the wedding could have taken place; and therefore when Othello strangles Desdemona the following night—on her bed with its wedding sheets again in place (See 4.2.105–6), it is (irony of ironies) with her virginity still untried.[25, 26] This possibility is at least consistent with the mad logic that leads to her murder, since even an Othello could hardly have forgotten in the space of 18 hours or so the "lust-stain'd" (? 5.1.36) bed of his wedding night, if indeed it had "with lust's blood [been] spotted."

I called attention above to the reiterated *now* of the Iago speech in 2.3, and this is only one instance of a repetition that is thrown at the reader from one end of the play to the other; viz:

> *Iago.*   Even now, now, very now, an old black ram
>   Is tupping your white ewe.
>   (1.1.89–90)

. . . .

Cas.   To be now a sensible man, by and by a fool, and presently
a beast'.

(2.3.295–96)

. . . .

Des.   My advocation is not now in tune;

(3.4.124)

. . . .

Emil.   He went hence but now,
And certainly in strange unquietness

(3.4.133–34)

A *Concordance* check once again reveals that with two excep-
tions[27] *Othello* of all Shakespeare's plays uses the word *now* the
most times. And putting these together with other forms of "time"
reference in the play, there is no comparison with any other play
in the emphasis that time receives in *Othello*. References are particularly numerous to various words suggesting speed—"haste-
post-haste," "post-post-haste," "on the instant," "incontinent,"
"alacrity," "quicken," "there is no pause." This consistent emphasis on immediacy, again, tends to make the telescoping of time in
a sense illegitimate, since such words, as I said of *now* above, can
scarcely suggest any greater acceleration of time than that with
we already see things moving on stage even as we glance from
time to time at the clock in the theater. One particularly suggestive double-edged "time" reference in *Othello* is the oft-repeated
word *tonight*, which is used twenty-four times in the play, almost
double the number of its next most frequent use in another play
(*Romeo and Juliet*'s fifteen), and often enough that the consciousness of a single "to-night"—the audience's night in the theater—becomes subliminally almost a part of one's experience of
the play.

I must add, as well, that there are a good number of antithetical time references in the play, in which the emphasis is on the
excessive slowness with which time can pass—Othello's "I would
have him nine years a killing," (4.1.173) or Emilia's "may his per-
nicious soul / Rot half a grain a day!" (5.2.158–59).

Perhaps the most glaring incongruity, and for this reason the
most controversial instance of time acceleration in the play, is
the great scene of the temptation and fall of Othello in 3.3; considered in the context especially of the famous last utterance of
Othello that he is one "not easily jealous." Act 3 scene 3 is 483

lines in length, and in the course of its approximately twenty-five minutes playing time Othello is transformed from a doting newlywed husband to a raving maniac whose one aim and obsession is the immediate murder of his wife. Speaking of a later scene in the play F. R. Leavis used the expression "superb *coup de theater*"[28] to describe Shakespeare's handling of it. It is a phrase that must be applied to this scene as well, for there is nothing comparable in Shakespeare or any other dramatist to the concentration of rhetorical persuasiveness that is achieved in this scene. Every word is in place, everything is plausible, indeed overwhelmingly so, and yet by every rational canon or consideration the absurdity of the whole transaction is "gross in sense" to the highest possible degree. And notwithstanding the fact that as late as line 186 we have Othello confidently asserting that he will never become jealous over "exsufflicate and blown surmises," and that Iago as late as line 436 admits that "yet we see nothing done," the inevitability of Othello's fall is never once doubted. Perhaps most significant, and I suggest by deliberate design on Shakespeare's part, there are no direct chronological references to suggest telescoping of time, so there is no way of assuming that more than the approximately half an hour's stage time is elapsed. The one "timing" event that the scene contains is Desdemona's reference to "your dinner, and the generous islanders / By you invited," (l. 284–85) which locates the scene in the course of the day but gives no certainty as to duration.

The "handkerchief trick" in *Othello*, as the key by which "probation . . . without hinge nor loop / To hang a doubt on" is achieved, is as flagrant a bit of sleight-of-hand as the annals of literature afford. As the vaunted "ocular proof" of infidelity the sighting of the handkerchief is the culminating event in a series of "vision" references in the play that form as prominent a pattern as the "time" references.[29] From Iago's "I, of whom his eyes had seen the proof" (25) in 1.1; through the Duke's "I did not see you," (50) and Brabantio's "look to her, Moor, if thou hast eyes to see" (292) of 1.3; and ending with "the object poisons sight" (367) of 5.2, the "vision" motif is present everywhere in the play; and its clear implication is that *vision* is never absolute—what you *think* you see, whether you are Othello or Othello's audience, and what is actually before your eyes may be two different things. This implication relates to both second- and third-level rhetoric

in the play, where, like Othello, the audience is tricked into
thinking it sees a tragedy in spite of the truth that it is actually
involved in a farce. The handkerchief trick is the quintessential
visual manipulation in the play. The first appearance of the
handkerchief on stage is in Desdemona's hand in 3.3, when she
uses it to bind Othello's aching forehead, placing it *directly in
front of his eyes* (see 288–91) to do so, of course. It is but a few moments from this (437) that Iago drives Othello to the final degree
of murderous rage ("Now do I see 'tis true") in his story about
having seen the handkerchief in Cassio's hand, introducing the
story (absurdity to end absurdities) with the words "Have you
not sometimes seen a handkerchief / Spotted with strawberries
in your wife's hand?" This handkerchief—the last legacy of his
dying mother and Othello's first gift to his adored wife, *unseen in
her hand* though placed in front of his eyes[30]—constitutes, then,
ocular proof of her infidelity when seen at a distance in another's
hand but minutes(?) later, in the next scene. That such a preposterous display is not laughed off the stage at every performance
is a permanent tribute to the spellbinding, almost supernatural
power, that this *tour de force* of poetical persuasion puts forth.

There is much more indirect evidence than this of Shakespeare's allegorical intentions in *Othello*. In third-level rhetorical terms, the theme of the power of rhetoric and its potential for
deception is returned to over and over. Especially in the early
scenes of the play, as it were in anticipation of the great catas-
trophe to come, do these implications receive emphasis. Brabantio, for example, whom Iago characterizes with uncanny (yet
obviously conscious on Shakespeare's part) allegorical appropriateness as having "in his effect a voice potential / As double as
the Duke's" (1.2.13–14) pays unconscious tribute to Othello's
rhetorical skill in his words

> For nature so preposterously to err,
> Being not deficient, blind, or lame of sense,
> Sans witchcraft could not.
>
> (1.2.62–64)

And as well as reflecting on Othello's winning of Desdemona by
words, these lines also reflect both Iago's and Shakespeare's
greater skill at taking in their respective dupes in an even more
preposterous way. The Duke's reply to Branbantio's accusations
of witchcraft constitutes another instance of the same—saying,

in Othello's hearing, word which are directly prophetic of his own fall and the absurd folly of Iago's "proof" of infidelity:

> To vouch this is no proof—
> Without more wider and more overt test
> Than these thin habits and poor likelihoods
> Of modern seeming do prefer against him.
>
> (1.3.106–9)

Perhaps the most glaring "double-voiced" reference of the whole play is the Duke's earlier

> This cannot be,
> By no assay of reason. 'Tis a pageant
> To keep us in false gaze.
>
> (1.3.17–19)

Spoken of the Turkish ruse against Rhodes, the words reflect with stark allegorical clarity on the "pageant" that is *Othello*. They have a significance comparable to that of the final allegorical motif in *Othello* that I will give example of—the phrase "Is't possible?," which is repeated five times in the play,[31] with gathering emphasis, and crying out more loudly with every repetition for the answer *No!*

It is perhaps fitting that the last words here should be from Shakespeare, rather than from me, but I leave them with my readers, to whom they are not unfamiliar, that they may decide for themselves the extent to which they may or may not apply to the thesis (and the author) of this essay.

> I conjure thee, as thou believ'st
> There is another comfort than this world,
> That thou neglect me not with that opinion
> That I am touch'd with madness. Make not impossible
> That which but seems unlike.
>
> (*Measure for Measure*, 5.1.48–52)

9

"Nothing will come of nothing":
King Lear and Rhetoric

Looked at from a rhetorical allegorical standpoint, *King Lear* shares certain features with all three of the dramas previously discussed: it has the melodramatic exaggerations of *Richard III*, the absurdity of *Othello*, the impossibilities of *Measure for Measure*; with its rhetorical technique, also like them, at once boldly advertising and triumphantly concealing its maneuvers in all of these problematic areas. Shakespeare proceeds more daringly, indeed, in *Lear*, in placing his rhetorical agenda directly before the audience than perhaps anywhere else in the canon. Of the five plays to be considered here this is the only one on which there would be critical near-unanimity on two seemingly paradoxical, but for my purposes both important and closely related questions, that the play *is* seriously structurally flawed, and that it may be Shakespeare's greatest piece. If recent criticism of *Lear* does not emphasize these points particularly it is not that either of them is in dispute, but simply that they are now so much a part of the lore of the play as to be taken for granted and in no need of repetition. They will not be ignored here, needless to say; I have called them closely related, but I might better have characterized them as mutually dependent, with supreme tragic grandeur playing off against, overcoming but at the same time undermined by, the "absurdity" that to Wilson Knight is "the core of the play" (*Wheel* 168), a judgment, though admittedly in his case based on different criteria than mine, with which I am in full agreement.

The universally acknowledged particular problem area of the play is its opening scene, which Bradley long ago characterized as "absurdly improbable,"[1] echoing a judgment that goes back at least as far as Johnson; but far more vehement attacks on the scene have been commonplace in criticism, even while praise of the play's overall grandeur of conception invariably follows these denunciations. The well-known exception to the second part of the above statement is Tolstoy, whose preference for the old *Chronicle History of King Leir*, Shakespeare's main source, as "incomparably and in every respect superior to Shakespeare's adaptation"[2] is notorious. But where the opening scene itself is concerned, even as committed a Shakespearean as Allardyce Nicoll must recognize that the source play "at least provided [its] main characters with normal and appreciable motives, whereas Shakespeare has left us with something which simply cannot be tolerated . . . , for . . . Lear's decisions and demeanor in this first scene . . . are perfectly unintelligible."[3] I could no doubt find a balancing quote from Nicoll on the other side of the issue as well, on the overall grandeur of *Lear's* conception, but Dowden's voice may speak for him and indeed for all Shakespeareans in his praising of the play as "the greatest single achievement in poetry of the . . . Northern genius. By its largeness of conception and the variety of its details, by its revelation of a harmony . . . between the forces of nature and the passions of man, by its grotesqueness and its sublimity, it owns kinship with the great cathedrals of gothic architecture."[4]

The first principle of this study throughout has been that Shakespeare is fully conscious and fully in control. On that basis, the apparent "faults" of construction, epitomized in the logical gaps sophisticated and unsophisticated readers alike have difficulty with in the opening scene, are in no way either inevitable or inadvertent; rather, they are central to the play's meaning, the paradoxical other half of which meaning is then found in its also being, in Maeterlinck's words, "the mightiest, the vastest, the most stirring, the most intense dramatic poem that has ever been written."[5] As with *Othello* and *Measure for Measure*, there is a contradiction in *Lear*, its existence is deliberate—the logical absurdity of the play is as calculated as the transcendent artistry that seemingly overwhelms that absurdity—and its significance is related to the allegorical theme of this study, of rhetoric/poetry as an almost magical power, that in Shakespeare's hands can create illusions of reality out of wholly implausible materials that are an entirely satisfying substitute for the real thing. *Lear* is a greater achievement than *Measure for Measure* partly because it does a better job of masking its contradictions; indeed, a comparison of *Lear* with *Measure for Measure* in terms of the rhetorical theme leads to an appreciation of how much greater a work the former is in this respect as well. On the one hand the element of absurdity in the play's conception is considerably more immediate and direct in *Lear*, in the inescapable logical difficulties the first scene raises; on the other hand the vague "dissatisfaction" most critics confess to come away from *Measure to Measure* still feeling is almost never echoed in the feelings they express about *Lear*. About the closest even a modern critic will come to recognizing that the play's greatness cannot *entirely* overcome its absurdity is Jan Kott's describing the contemporary attitude to *Lear* as "ambiguous and somehow embarrassed," capturing in that phrase the unresolved dilemma of its being at once "recognized as a masterpiece, beside which even *Macbeth* and *Hamlet* seem tame and pedestrian,"[6] while dependent at the same time on an initial premise that no amount of sophistication in the attempt can in the end reduce to reason.

If the irrationalities of *Lear* are deliberate, a product of design—and it should be noted as well that they do not by any means end with the first scene—this raises problematic questions about the play, and how to interpret it, of several different kinds. I would observe, first, that few critics make a serious attempt to probe specific problem areas of the play in any real depth. That certain things in the play *are* irrational will as a rule be duly noted; Bradley, in a schoolmasterly near-parody of Shakespearean subtlety, after first ingenuously observing that *Lear's* "improbabilities . . . far surpass in number and grossness . . . those of the other great tragedies,"[7] goes so far as to give us an exact count of them (an unlucky thirteen!); but beyond noting those in the opening scene little more will usually be done by critics than to dismiss them as inconsequential—explained as various combinations of permissible dramatic license, intractable story elements inherent in the play's sources, and simple carelessness on Shakespeare's part—knowing as he must have that the rhetorical passions he was about to unleash in this "the most terrible work of human genius,"[8] as Swinburne characterized *Lear,* would instantly overpower any motivational loose ends or other structural anomalies.

Two quite straightforward explanations for why serious consideration of the play's irrationalities is rarely attempted suggest themselves. It is not difficult to understand, first, why there might be some reluctance to acknowledge the possibility that the absurdities of the plot could have been deliberately retained from its sources, or indeed augmented and even new ones introduced by the play's author. If he made it impossible to rationalize *some* of the characters' actions, the basis for attributing rational motives to other actions of those same characters is undermined. And at that point the very foundations for criticism of the play begin to tremble, as all interpretations that depend in any way *on* such motivations, as virtually all in one way or another do, seem directly challenged. Nor is the challenge to the conventional assumptions of criticism the only effect these considerations necessarily have; it goes without saying that questions about the author as well, his artistic and philosophic intentions in creating this strange hybrid are simultaneously raised— equally dangerous territory. The glossing over of the inconsistencies implied in blithely having it both ways where the issue of probability in the play is concerned makes at times for some uncomfortable if still apparently unconscious squirming on the part of some very respected names in criticism. The best Duthie and Wilson can do in their introduction to the New Cambridge *Lear*, for example, is to assure us that while the initial situation in "Shakespeare's version has more improbabilities . . . than . . . any of the older versions," they "doubt whether [this will] trouble any audience in the theater; for the might of Shakespeare's poetry [is such that] . . . we do not think *altogether* in terms of *commonplace* probability" (italics mine).[9]

The second consideration is that no explanation of these issues that can actually satisfy the reason is available anyway; the attempts that are occasionally made to justify the first scene, say, invariably terminate in logical cruxes that are as plainly evident as those in the scene that caused the problem in the first place. Kenneth Muir, not to be deterred by anything that may have troubled others about Shakespeare in the past, leaps heels up into the same logical trap in attempting to justify the plot of *Lear* that we saw him fall into in his "explanation" of the time-scheme in *Othello*. The implications of his explanation of *Lear* are particularly interesting in their unintentionally confirming another one of the principal tenets of this study, that Shakespeare in the study and Shakespeare on the stage are two very different propositions. And not only is Shakespeare fully cognizant of that difference, and plays on it in his allegory, his awareness is one that we too, if only subliminally for most of us, must share. Muir begins as usual by citing Bradley and his list of the play's "gross improbabilities," dismissing them, also in the usual manner, with a confident "most . . . would not be noticed in the theater, and they cannot therefore detract from the effectiveness of *King Lear* as a stage play."[10] The interesting twist and its logical trap, however, come in when he adds the corollary that in any case Bradley "seems to have had little experience of the play in the theater," and that "improbabilities . . . detected in the study can be explained away in the study," which he then proceeds to do. This is a remarkable conclusion: it is hardly indeed surprising that the play's logical inconsistencies "are unlikely to be noticed during a performance,"[11] if, when we go home and peruse the text at leisure in our study, we are unable to detect them there either!

That a degree of unconscious discomfort with *Lear*, in spite of the general consensus on its greatness among modern critics, still remains, is attested to again by the fact that Tolstoy's 1906 diatribe has stayed in the critical canon ever since Orwell resurrected it to psychoanalyze its author in 1947. Collections of essays and critical excerpts on *Lear* invariably now contain one or both of these essays, Tolstoy's as a rule printed without comment, to be sure, but the mere fact of its still being in the canon, like Rymer's comments on *Othello*, is significant, implying *some* merit at least in what it has to say.

One could extend examples of intelligent critics dancing around the *Lear* problem, while the play itself sits recalcitrant and untouched in the middle, indefinitely, but I will cite only one more here as an epitome of them all, Maynard Mack's "Actors and Redactors" lecture of 1965, reviewing the stage history of *Lear* with emphasis on its twentieth-century incarnations. Given his eminence as both a literary critic and a student of the theater, Mack's perspective would be broader than that of most commentators, who can claim expertise in one but rarely both of these areas. Two things are significant in the Mack assessment. He first of all concludes that the failure of most modern productions lies in their "determination to rationalize . . . according to a particular plan what is not . . . rational, . . . on that plan."[12] The implication of this statement is significant, that a "plan" of the play, Shakespeare's plan, one would assume, does exist—*must* exist, for so manifestly great a play—but it is not a plan that anyone, including Mack himself, since he proposes none, has so far discovered. The second point he makes is yet more parodoxical, and serves to confirm the suspicion that some of the other criticisms we have looked at may have raised, that "the siren rock on which efforts to [stage] *King Lear* (as well as . . . critical efforts to interpret it) oftenest split is the desire to motivate the bizarre actions that Shakespeare's play calls for in some 'reasonable' way."[13] This statement, somehow at once categorical and enigmatic, is particularly revealing when looked at from my perspective. If we put it together with what he also implies about the undiscovered Shakespearean "plan" of the play, it attributes the frequent failure of both closet *and* stage interpretations of *Lear* to the mistaken notion that a rational key to its structure must exist, but that in fact reason is no part of the Shakespearean plan, whatever that plan is.

What *Lear* does, then, allegorically, is what *Measure for Measure* does, but better, so integrate rational absurdity with "hypnotically" persuasive rhetoric/poetry that the contradiction between them, both categorical and clearly visible, slips by even the most alert and seasoned of observers. I said earlier that part of *Lear's* superiority over *Measure for Measure* is that by making its absurdities more immediate than those of *Measure for Measure* it must overcome an even greater challenge in successfully "getting away with" this, as it were, not to leave its audiences "dissatisfied," the critical consensus on *Measure for Measure*. Indeed, the achievement of *Lear* is even greater than this, because while *Measure for Measure* also deals in contradiction, the dilemma there is philosophical; a rational case can be made for both positions in the figurative "debate." There is an element of absurdity in such a situation, to be sure; but the case of *King Lear* is far more extreme, because here reason is the *issue* of the debate—not *my* reasoned argument facing *yours* on the other side, but reason per se facing unreason on the other side, a challenge to Shakespeare's rhetorical powers of an altogether different order.

That rhetoric and its powers are first of all to be a central motif in any retelling of the King Lear story was determined for Shakespeare before a word of his version was penned. That he chose to write this play is thus in itself testimony that he had the rhetorical theme centrally in mind at the outset. There are substantial differences in a number of elements in each of the four versions of the story available to Shakespeare, and suggestions in the play that all four were probably consulted in the process of its composition, but the fateful love-test, in a form roughly similar to Shakespeare's, contrasting extravagant and successful flattery on one side with a blunt refusal to flatter on the other, is the event that sets the action in motion in all four versions. It is surely significant as well to Shakespeare in this episode that few situations offer more powerful lessons about concerns that lie at the half-conscious, half-unconscious heart of Renaissance culture. These would be concerns about the actual tenuous nature of power in the Renaissance state, about the ambiguous function of rhetoric in the exercise and allocation of that power, and about "legitimacy," with all the Machiavellian connotations that concept carries in the period, the theme of Edmund's soliloquy that comes immediately after the love-test in Shakespeare's version. Perhaps the deepest symbolic appeal of the episode to Shakespeare, however, as a reflection of Renaissance culture and politics, judged from the prominence it is given in his version, is in its highly visible theatricality; it is staged formally; her command of hyperbolical adulatory rhetoric is to be the sole determiner of each daughter's share in the spoils of the kingdom. We cannot know how much such suggestive analogies between his art and his culture may have meant to Shakespeare, but it is difficult to conceive of him not intending that they should at least be noted in his decision to retell the Lear story.

While interpretations of *Lear* that focus on rhetorical and other linguistic issues raised in the first scene, and whose implications are then shown to extend to the play as a whole, have become frequent in recent years, the limitation noted of *Richard III*, that even postmodern readings still remain on the "character" level only, applies in the case of *Lear* as well. Typical is Daniel Cottom's reading in *Text and Culture: The Politics of Interpretation*, which is keyed to what Cottom calls "dramatically awakened language" in that scene, in *Lear's* unprecedented transfer of "authority" from its authentic extralinguistic historical roots to *words*: "As soon as he makes his authority appear subject to discourse he makes it . . . appear that [it] had never

really been his."[14] That these issues are thematically central to
the play as a whole is sealed for Cottom in the fact that the
play's closing lines return to the same theme, of the dangers of
loosening the ties between language and traditional authority, in
Edgar's "The weight of this sad time we must obey / *Speak what
we feel, not we ought to say*" (5.3.323–24, italics mine). Cottom's
view is that Shakespeare wants his audience to see this idea as
misguided.

Paolo Valesio's 1980 *Novantiqua: Rhetorics as a Contemporary Theory* also has a section on *Lear*, his interpretation taking
a more technical rhetorical slant than Cottom's. The oxymoronic
coining *novantiqua* in his title is intended to suggest the time-
lessness of the rhetorical art, as being both ancient and modern,
and indeed inseparable from language itself. In Valesio's words,
"rhetoric is coextensive with human discourse and it is no more
possible to speak without using rhetoric than it is to live without
breathing."[15] In keeping with this principle, Cordelia's attack on
the "glib and oily art" of her sisters is seen as entirely disingenuous, "a rhetoric of moralism, of pretended disgust for those very
weapons that she is handling with consummate skill" (58). It
must follow as well, given Valesio's premise, that critical interpretations that support Cordelia's "truth" are also disingenuous,
a radical-sounding position that nevertheless becomes plausible
in the context Valesio builds: the love-test is a game, and Lear
has set the rules; he has commanded a rhetorical performance
from his daughters, a display of their epideictic skills, nothing
more; by refusing to play, "by setting herself up against her
father, Cordelia is saying that she does not want a slice of the
kingdom—she is getting ready to take it all; at the end she will
embark at Dover with the French army" (58–59).[16]

It is a perhaps unique phenomenon of *Lear* criticism, which
these and myriads of others comparable to them admirably ex-
emplify, that as long as the interpretation stays within the parameters set by the play itself, as long, that is, as "real world"
standards of logic are not applied in its analysis, plausible-
sounding results in endless variety actually do come forth. The
rules by which the world of the play operates are set by the
dramatist; that they are bizarre is deliberate, a demonstration of
his power; the characters have no choice but to obey them, and
all do the best they can under the circumstances. The love-test,
the spring of the action in all versions of the story, is perceived as

an analogue of the dramatist's art. Its rhetorical associations and its irrationality are linked; together they demonstrate what the play as a whole also demonstrates, the power of rhetoric to control, indeed to *become* reality. Cottom would have it that the play illustrates the dangers of empowering language; when words become instruments of power in and of themselves, then is "all coherence gone . . . and all relation," in Donne's famous words: anything becomes possible. I rather see the play, however, as Shakespeare's demonstration that this was always the case; language *is* empowered, it *is* dangerous, and we are all—and particularly was this the case for Shakespeare's contemporaries—characters in a *Lear*-like play, reacting to a situation not of our making, but empowered to exploit its possibilities up to our capacities.

That Shakespeare wishes to suggest an analogy between the love-test and the rhetorico/theatrical principle, of creating a believable reality out of mere words and theatrical gestures, is shown again in one particular important addition he makes to the story as he received it, the emphasis on the word *nothing* in the exchange between Lear and Cordelia when she refuses to co-operate in his epideictic game.[17] After three repetitions of the single word "nothing," two from Cordelia, Lear's final "Nothing will come of nothing" rings solemnly as a declaration of absolute principle, the principle that in the *Lear* world, rhetoric and rhetoric alone empowers, is "something."

As the crucial moment for both the plot of the play and in pointing its allegorical message, while it is taken for granted that the opening scene contains improbabilities, even absurdities, the scene has never yet quite been seen, I suggest, for what it really is. That is to say, it is not the mere presence of absurdities in the scene that is important, but that they are *intruded calculatedly* by Shakespeare in such a way, first, that it is impossible that they not be noted by the audience; and second, that they be rationalized. No element of the scene, for example, poses more problematic challenges to reason than the question of whether and to what degree the outcome of the love-test is supposed to be premeditated. Agreement would be well-nigh universal among the rationalizers of the scene, first, that Lear has decided, and made known his decision, before the curtain rises, to resign his regal responsibilities, dividing them equally among his three daughters. Such a view has actually only one clear war-

rant in the scene itself, though admittedly an apparently substantial one, in the exchange between Kent and Gloucester at
the very beginning, in which the words "now, in the division of
the kingdom" are used, to be then followed immediately by the
ceremony of the division as staged by Lear. While this looks
straightforward, a number of discrepancies, first in the Kent/
Gloucester exchange itself and then in developments, as well as
in certain terms and expressions that come after it, reveal that
this is anything but the case. The first rather striking discrepancy in this scenario of a supposedly pre-planned three-way division of the kingdom is that Kent and Gloucester make no
mention of such a division, but rather, and it could certainly be
argued, in a definitive way, of a *two-way* division only, between
the dukes of Albany and Cornwall. If it is Shakespeare's intention to have it inferred that anything *but* a two-way division is
set to take place, it is strange to say the least that he would deliberately avoid, as he clearly does, any mention not only of a
third daughter's "moiety" having to be considered, but indeed of
his daughters having a significant place in his plans at all, in
this exchange.

The use of the world *moiety* in reference to the division is a
particularly suggestive touch at this point as well, suggestive because of a possibly deliberate ambiguity in its meaning. The
OED gives three sixteenth-century definitions of the word, one
primary, as meaning "a half, one of two equal parts," the others
given as: the first, that "occasionally" it may mean one of "more"
than two "not necessarily equal" parts; and, the second, that
"contextually" it may also mean "a small part." The first example
of the second usage cited is Hotspur's well-known reference to
his smaller "moiety" in Shakespeare's earlier division-of-the-
kingdom scene, 1.3, of *1 Henry IV*, but of the fifteen uses of the
term in Shakespeare, Hotspur's is the only instance where it has
that meaning, and in all others (*Lear* excepted) but one it either
probably, in two cases, or definitely, in eleven, carries the primary meaning of half.[18] Its use in the present instance is especially intriguing because it could mean either a half *or* a third.
Certainly in the way Shakespeare has Gloucester use the
word—"equalities are so weigh'd that curiosity in *neither* can
make choice of *either*'s moiety" (italics mine)—it appears quite
clearly to mean "half"; did this reference come at the end of
scene 1 rather than at the beginning no reader would dream of

suggesting that it could mean anything else. Appearing where it does, however, with what is to follow, the ambiguity of its meaning is impossible to resolve.

Several more interesting speculations as well may arise from these considerations. Leaving aside for the moment the question of the one half/one third ambiguity in the use of the word *moiety*, the careful reiteration of the exact equality of the two dukes, in terms of their standing in both the king's regard and in the portions of the kingdom they are to receive, turns out to be problematic as well, apparently conflicting with what Lear himself goes on to declare in the love-test, that to the daughter that "[we] shall . . . say doth love us most, . . . we our largest bounty may extend"—there will *not* necessarily be exact equality in the division. Conventional criticism might say of this discrepancy that, like many others, it means nothing in particular either; we can choose between Shakespeare's carelessness or Lear's simply having changed "his" mind in explanation; but if one holds to the maxim that there is no carelessness in Shakespeare, that he does nothing without conscious intent, such a dismissal is far too easy. Thoughtfully considered, the discrepancy between the two statements represents an irresolvable contradiction and a potentially very important one thematically. If what Kent and Gloucester say is taken to be true, then the division of the kingdom has been planned in detail and made known in advance, at least to them and the two dukes, but probably to the court as well. Lear's later reference in the ceremony to his "constant will" and his desire to "publish [his] daughters' several dowers" at "this hour" would also be in accordance with this interpretation. Contradicting it, however, is first the enigmatic reference to a "darker purpose," an expression which can logically only mean one to which no one is privy but himself, followed immediately by his revelation of that purpose, which is to hold his rhetorical love-auction, making his three daughters' legacies depend entirely on the words they can muster, at the moment of utterance, to declare how much they love him. Who is to receive what part of the kingdom, if indeed any part of it at all, is by these indications not known in advance—Cordelia at least has apparently not heard of it—but simply sprung in this outlandish contest form on the whole court, completely out of the blue.

It is worth noting that what Shakespeare does in this latter scenario is to extrapolate in an interesting way from the opening scenes of his primary source, the old *Chronicle History of King Leir*. There, as here, the love-test is conceived as "a sudden strategem,"[19] though imparted to a select few before it is put in play; the evil sisters then manage by treachery to learn of it in advance, leaving Cordelia the only one unprepared. The decision to abdicate and divide the kingdom is also a spur-of-the-moment product of Leir's anger at his third daughter in the source play. It can be argued, of course, that the discrepancies in Shakespeare's version of this pivotal scene are the result of carelessness, in his cobbling together of a single rapidly unfolding scene out of several in the source play and other versions of the story. Spenser, for example, has it "decreed" by Leyr, "mongst [his daughters] . . . his realm . . . equally . . . / To have divided" before the love-test (book 2, canto 10, stanza 27). There are several plausible reasons, however, for thinking otherwise of the contradictions inherent in Shakespeare's shaping of these events. Like the ambiguity in the opening exchange between Kent and Gloucester, nothing comparable to which appears in *any* of Shakespeare's sources, this situation too—was an exact division planned in advance or is the whole thing a spur-of-the-moment decision?—has the effect of keeping us carefully off balance,[20] in a state of logical indeterminacy. It is yet another case where the audience finds itself in an analogous situation to that of the characters, held captive by a "darker purpose" to which we are not privy, but which it is instinctive in us to try to turn to our advantage as best we may.

A further and final consideration may also come to bear in these speculations, in which the opening Kent/Gloucester exchange, in the light of subsequent events, has a special and unexpected purpose. I said earlier that if this exchange had come at the end rather than at the beginning of the scene, there would be no ambiguity in anyone's mind as to how the term *moiety* is used there—it would mean half the kingdom and nothing else. The startling possibility in this suggestion is that that may be exactly what Shakespeare intends—to foreshadow the division of the kingdom as it turns out in the end: "Beloved sons, . . . / This coronet part between you"—an illumination of the "darker purpose" of the scene that is wholly unexpected. If this proposal seems at first glance farfetched, I would say in its defense that it does at least resolve, rather than, as is usual, merely ignore, the ambiguities inherent in the difference between what is said at

the beginning of the scene and what transpires at the end; and it
does so with no stretching of what the words themselves allow,
something that cannot be said of every other attempt that has
been made over the years to find such a resolution. The possibilities of interpretation this suggestion opens up are somewhat
startling as well, even perhaps bizarre, although whether more
bizarre than the scene viewed objectively already was before
they came along is a point that could be argued. But they might
mean, for example, that Lear has divined or somehow learned in
advance of Cordelia's scheme, a la Valesio, to gain the whole
kingdom by a rhetorical strategy superior to her sisters', and has
determined to thwart it. More subtly, if it does not tell us that
"Lear" necessarily knows the outcome of the love-test before it
takes place, it at least tells us that someone, someone with a
rhetorical purpose darker even than his, very definitely does.

If these are some of the subtler incongruities in the scene that
most commentaries either fail to notice or consider not important enough to call attention to, the gross behavioral ones that
no one *can* miss, but that seem to defy explanation when found
in work of a late Shakespearean level of accomplishment, also
yield interesting results when considered as components of a
rhetorical allegory. From this standpoint, the first necessity in
justifying the claim that these incongruities have a specific
rhetorical purpose is to demonstrate that they are presented in
the play in such a way that their utter absurdity, not to say impossibility, is clearly manifest to the audience. I am speaking of
such obvious facts as, for example, that the idea of a love-test,
equally as an epideictic exercise prepared in advance *or* as a
"sudden strategem," as the sole criterion for disposing of a kingdom is incompatible with reason to begin with, and, when actually carried through, even more egregiously so. The context of
these inexplicable acts is crucial in our appreciation of the whole
situation's necessary absurdity. The focus is on Lear, eighty
years old, his kingdom's patriarch, "ever honor'd, . . . lov'd as [a]
father" by the noble Kent, and the majesty of whose character as
it emerges in the remainder of the play amply justifies both that
devotion and his own later description of himself as "every inch a
king." Albeit that his evil daughters hint broadly at the possible
onset of senility in their father's unaccountable actions, a borrowing again from one of the play's sources,[21] I would reiterate
what centuries of criticism universally supports, that the same

character's behavior elsewhere in the play is resoundingly incompatible with any such hypothesis. Indeed we do not even need the remainder of the play to grasp this point clearly. Shakespeare makes sure that his insults to reason in the love-test do not go unseen by his audience by including an explicit reference to them at the very moment of their taking place—when France, absent from the stage for the mere five minutes that the casting off of both Cordelia and Kent consumes, records his incredulity at "this . . . most strange" (shades again of *Measure for Measure*!) turn of events:

> That she, whom even but now was your best object,
> The argument of your praise, balm of your age,
> The best, the dearest, should in this trice of time
> Commit a thing so monstrous to dismantle
> So many folds of favor[,]

(214–18)

climaxing his statement by protesting that for him, and these are key words, "reason without miracle" could never accept such a thing as possible. There is no dramatic necessity at this point in the play for a speech with this focus; in thirty years of studying commentary on *Lear*, I have never seen this speech cited; the only explanation for it is therefore that Shakespeare, rather than wishing to conceal his strategy from the audience, wished on the contrary to challenge them by waving it in front of their eyes. The "trice of time" motif as an element in the absurdity of the situation we are familiar with from its similar use in *Richard III* and *Othello*, but in neither of those cases does he make its absurdist implications quite so explicit as he does here in these words of France.

If one such blatant maneuver were still not proof of his intentions, all our doubts must be definitively scotched when a virtually identical and equally impossible transformation is carefully arranged for the subplot in the scenes immediately following. Here Gloucester is instantly duped into hatred of his legitimate son Edgar by a few words read from a conspiratorial letter Edgar is said to have sent to his bastard brother Edmund. Edmund, illegitimate and thus possessed *on the face of it* with every motive for wishing to displace his brother in their father's affections, is instantly believed, Edgar never again to be spoken to, asked, or allowed to give an account of himself to his father—

the father that, to quote that father's own words, "so tenderly and entirely loves him." The ease with which Edmund is allowed to dupe both Edgar and Gloucester mocks reason in itself; but here again, as with France in the earlier speech, Shakespeare goes the further step of actually revealing his hand, having Edmund explain *Edgar's* supposed treachery by openly describing, to his father and victim, his own:

> When I . . .
>   . . . threaten'd to discover him[,] he replied,
> "Thou unpossessing bastard! dost thou think,
> If I would stand against thee, would . . .
>   . . . any trust, virtue, or worth in thee
> Make thy words faith'd?

[and the really key lines follow:]

>   No . . . .
>   . . . though thou didst produce
> My very character

[exactly what Edmund has just done!]

>   I'd turn it all
> To thy suggestion, plot, and damned practice:
> And thou must make a dullard of the world,
> If they not thought the profits of my death
> Were very pregnant and potential spirits
> To make thee seek it."
>
>   (2.1.63, 66–77)

Kenneth Muir, again typical of those critics who try to confront the believability issue in *Lear*, offers an explanation of this doubling of the insult to reason of Shakespeare's by citing what he calls "the artistic law . . . that two similar improbabilities are more credible than one,"[22] betraying in the very arithmetic of such a lame conclusion that he is floundering for an answer.

The egregiousness of Muir's own absurdity in trying to find a rationale he can somehow live with in these scenes, some way to hold them together as it were, is, though obviously not in the way he intends, highly instructive. There is, perhaps surprisingly, a rational other side to the coin of Muir's floundering here that the history of *Lear* criticism illustrates. This is that criticism of the play that ignores its irrationalities completely, pretending they do not exist, can not only be immensely fruitful, as the record obviously attests, but is, in fact, the only possible way the play can be approached critically at all. There is a revelation of Shakespeare's allegorical intentions in *Lear* in this paradoxical-sounding pronouncement. The play has what might be termed a split intellectual personality: it is at one and the same time absolutely irrational and absolutely convincing. On the irrational side, first, main plot and subplot both, because they take off from what (assuming their key characters possessed, as they subsequently show themselves to be, of normal intellectual capacities) are impossible premises, are irredeemably tainted with unreason throughout. Nor, it should be noted as well, is this taint allowed only to the plot's initial premises; as Bradley's careful follow-up analysis shows, it is reinforced again and again in other, perhaps less obtrusive, but equally anomalous behaviors.[23]

What must follow from this categorical picture in terms of the thesis just articulated, then, is that in spite of impossibility, of what rationally *cannot be*, the play nevertheless convinces absolutely, overcoming all resistance. From start to finish it has a compelling rhetorico/poetic force, even a compelling logic, that represents Shakespeare at the very top of his artistic game, an exhibition of mastery that critics are quite justified in crowning with all the superlatives in the language. Further superlatives here would be superfluous; more to the point would be at least brief consideration of how it is possible that such a coup could be made to succeed. The contribution of the rhetorical instrument itself scarcely needs comment; it is basic and succeeds by being simply the life. Every form of language employed, every combination of language and character, of which there are many and all extreme—of villainy and virtue, of loyalty and treachery, of kingly arrogance, kingly folly, and kingly grandeur—is made to fit perfectly in every situation. The real heart of the coup, however, lies in the play's having, in spite of impossibility, a compelling logic. It is a maneuver of unparalleled daring, in which Shakespeare again anticipates his critics by employing the exact strategy that he forces them to employ in their interpretations, namely, ignoring that which in reason cannot be ignored, making it his straightfaced premise that all the things that happen in the play *could* happen. If it were possible to *be* rational and behave as Lear, Gloucester, or Edgar do, tautological but true, how they behave is exactly how rational people of their particular character *must* behave in these situations. It is both understandable and plausible.[24]

The concepts of kingship and aristocracy come under critical scrutiny in the play, obviously, nor need I recapitulate the mountains of subtle commentary that surround every aspect of these subjects in the critical literature; it is worth noting, however, that much in Lear's and Gloucester's behavior has thematic affinities with certain topics touched on here before. In my discussion of *Richard III*, for example, the "self-delusions of the aristocratic ego" were noted as a factor in the susceptibility to rhetorical manipulation many of the characters demonstrated in that play, with the suggestion also of a possible satirical application to Elizabethan society. It is not difficult to see a similar implication with respect to the characters of Lear and Gloucester here, these considerations thus lending a degree of credibility to their actions. The scale is grander here, of course, monumentally so in the case of Lear, and, without the immediate historical associations that attach to the saga of Richard for Tudor audiences, more abstract and philosophical in its implications. The tribulations of Lear in his pilgrimage to self-knowledge entail primarily, nonetheless, his coming to an understanding of the limitations that nature imposes even on kings in their exercising of power, and most especially of power in the linguistic sphere. Indeed if there is a linking motif in the whole *Lear* tragedy it must be one that relates closely to the issue of the delusive power of language; the process of Lear's coming to *this* realization appears ironically to cost him as much pain as anything else in his life. Scene 6 of act 4, in which he laments the folly of his confusing words with things contains moments of poignancy comparable to any in the play:

> To say 'ay' and 'no' to everything that I said!
> 'Ay' and 'no' too was no good divinity.
> . . . .
> Go to, they are not men o' their words.[25]
>
> (4.6.99–100, 104)

Shakespeare does two contradictory things at once with this motif. He first satirizes the culture's buying into the Aristotelean myth of the alliance of rhetoric and truth by giving an exaggerated demonstration of its absurdity, making sure by the degree of its exaggeration that the lesson cannot be missed. Looked at from the allegorical standpoint, this is the basis of Lear's behavior in the first scene. As the archetypal kingly embodiment of that myth, he makes no distinction between flattery and truth, beguiled totally by the perfect rhetorical gilding in which that flattery is dressed by Goneril and Regan. The ambiguity surrounding the question of spontaneity in the epideictic speeches of Goneril and Regan may be part of the allegorical message here as well. It would appear from Lear's "darker purpose" lead-up in the scene that we are to see them as "spontaneous"; for such perfectly honed performances to have the extra perfection of spontaneity is thus the final touch to make them irresistible in the ears of their deluded victim. The absurdity of their exaggeration comes out, further, in the fact that Regan's speech, coming after Goneril's, actually builds on it, and successfully, though that itself would plainly *seem* impossible; did we not have the language in which it is actually done it would be difficult to imagine anything more exaggerated than Goneril's encomium already was:

> *Gon.* Sir, I love you more than word can wield the matter;
> Dearer than eyesight, space, and liberty;
> Beyond what can be valued, rich or rare;
> No less than life, with grace, health, beauty, honor;
> As much as child e'er lov'd, or father found;
> A love that makes breath poor and speech unable:
> Beyond all manner of so much I love you.
>
> (1.1.54–60)[26]

One of the points that Valesio's argument makes regarding Cordelia's rhetoric in this scene is that her sisters leave her absolutely no further space in the direction of flattering, or "upward-moving,"[27] hyperbole to expand in, so as to impress her father and thereby earn his approbation. If she hopes to surpass them in any way, to gain her "third more opulent," it can therefore only be by taking an entirely different, indeed an antithetical rhetorical approach from the one whose possibilities they have exhausted; hence her inspired, if futile, strategy.

The contradictory simultaneous triumph of rhetoric in the scene, then, with Shakespeare now the rhetorician, and the victim of the manipulation the audience, is in making these outrageous behaviors plausible, making Lears of us all, as it were, compelling us to identify with him and accept the transparently empty rhetoric of the scene as truth. That this is precisely what we do in the scene, as both readers and audience, is confirmed again by the critical history of the play; as audience we receive exactly the same admonitions regarding *Shakespeare's* nonsense as Lear receives regarding Goneril's and Regan's, admonitions that have exactly the same effect in both cases, which is to say none at all. However shockingly "unmannerly" in Kent, to the ears of a class-sensitive Jacobean audience, to call his king "mad," he is patently correct, and is acknowledged as such by that audience; what they do not see any more than Lear does, however, is that they, the educated among them at any rate, are being chided by Shakespeare in the very same words and in the very same vein. Taught from their earliest schooling to keep clear in their minds the distinction between words and things— "rerum et verborum" in Erasmus's Latin[28]—they hear that same elementary lesson again in France's "[l]ove's not love / When it is mingled with regards that stands / Aloof from th' entire point," but fail to heed it. And if its reiteration here were not sufficient to make the lesson sink in, opportunities of equal bluntness are offered at several other junctures as well, one notable example already seen in Edmund's reference to Edgar's supposed scoffings at the possibility of Edmund, as against Edgar, "mak[ing his] words" to their father "faith'd."

There is one direct reference only in the whole play to rhetorical style as such, and it is significant that the character to whom it is given to provoke the issue is one of the only two whose speech is distinguished, and marked for comment for being so, for its plainness. This is the Kent/Cornwall exchange before the walls of Gloucester's castle in 2.2, in which a key point as regards the Shakespearean rhetoric is made explicit, that a "plain accent" in the mouth of a "plain knave" can be as effectively deceptive as any other. Though Valesio does not cite this particular passage, he might well have done so to support his reading of Cordelia's rhetorical strategy in the opening scene. On the other hand, however, there may also be a reason why he does *not* cite it, for it can in the end serve no such purpose. There is in fact a clear absurdity, testified to subtly in the play, in any such notion, that one manner or style is inherently less or more deceptive than any other. This point is put beyond dispute early in the play, prior to what Kent has to say on the subject, by Lear's first having banished, of course Cordelia, but more importantly here Kent himself, known and supposedly trusted, for *speaking plainly* in the first scene, and then instantly welcoming "Caius," a complete stranger, into his service, apparently *for the same reason*, that, among several "honest" qualities he lays claim to, he "can . . . deliver a plain message bluntly" (1.4.32–33).

Two other episodes that have frequently been singled out for critical comment as particularly problematic may be shown to have a bearing on the thesis of this discussion as well. Students of *Lear* may already anticipate that the episodes to which I refer might be those of the storm scenes that open act 3 and the Gloucester/Edgar Dover scene of act 4. The rhetorical implications of the two episodes differ significantly from each other as well as from those of the opening scene, but they have in common all three that they demonstrate the power of rhetoric, "in despite of the teeth of all rhyme and reason," as Falstaff once said, to make language and reality, words and things, irresistibly merge. Both involve the rhetorical scheme called in Greek *hypotyposis*, rendered in English by Puttenham as "the counterfait representation": "to describe and set forth many things, in such sort as it should appear they were truly before our eyes though they were not present, which to do it requireth cunning: for nothing can be kindly counterfait or represented in his absence, but by great discretion in the doer."[29] It is a scheme, that, with its many subtypes—*prosopopeia*, "the Counterfait in personation" (239); *pragmatographia*, "the Counterfait action" (239); *chronographia*, "the Counterfait time[!]" (239); and others—Shakespeare employs virtually nonstop in his plays. There are few examples of its use elsewhere, however, that so strongly imply deliberation, that the audience should *notice* it, as these instances in *Lear*. By the variations of method employed, and by the daring implications they carry, both call attention to the device itself, while at the same time testing, as it seems, the limits of possibility in its use.

Its use in the storm scenes, for example, is cumulative, and clearly calculatedly so. It begins with anticipatory references near the end of scene 4 of act 2: first broached in Cornwall's "Let us withdraw; 'twill be a storm" (286), the menacing atmosphere is added to in Gloucester's "Alack, the night comes on, and the high winds / Do sorely ruffle" (299–300), with the storm itself then fully launched in the scene's closing lines, Cornwall's "Shut up your doors, my Lord, 'tis a wild night. / . . . Come out of the storm" (307, 308). The exact stage effects that should accompany these words are not precisely indicated: Q gives no stage directions, F "Storm and tempest" after 281; that this hardly seems quite appropriate in the context, however, as preceding Cornwall's initial reference to an *oncoming* storm has caused some editors to alter it. Duthie and Wilson, for example, adopt Capell's "Storm heard approaching," sensibly enough, I believe, as more suitable to the effect the play's language itself suggests. The Gentleman's extended description of Lear's "contending with the fretful elements" (4) that opens 3.1 builds powerfully, then, on the mere "weather report" sense we had of the storm to that point, raising the imaginative barometric pressure to exactly the level necessary to prepare us for Lear's own climatic appearance and the storm's unparalleled verbal assault in 3.2.

Lear's two tremendous "Blow winds, and crack your cheeks," and "Spit, fire; spout, rain" speeches that open scene 2 have drawn as much comment over the years as probably any others in the play, targeted for both scathing criticism and fulsome praise as stage material, and more recently recognized as having thematic implications of no little importance as well. Lamb famously considered the scene unplayable, as much from the stage manager's as from the actor's perspective:—"The contemptible machinery by which they mimic the storm . . . is not more inadequate to represent the horrors of the real elements, than any actor can be to represent Lear"[30]—sentiments that have been seconded many times since he uttered them. Webster, for example, very nearly echoes him, and Mack reserves perhaps his strongest criticism of modern *Lear* productions for their failure to meet the challenge of this scene.[31] The most cogent well-known directorial defense of the scene, on the other hand, is probably Granville-Barker's, who noticed something in Lear's speeches that those who lament the impossibility of creating a theatrical illusion correspondent to their violence overlook. Lamb's complaint is of inadequate stage machinery, while Webster's veers in a way to the opposite, of overadequate stage machinery; what Granville-Barker sensibly observes is that Lear's speeches are simply the ultimate expression of Puttenham's *hypotyposis*: "no mere description of a storm, but in music and imaginative suggestion a dramatic creating of the storm itself; and there is Lear—and here are we, if we yield ourselves—in the midst of it, almost a part of it."[32] That Shakespeare in fact created these speeches to do exactly what Granville-Barker says here is corroborated, I suggest, by the contradictory views of Lamb and Webster on the question of stage machinery: that the storm *is not in* the staging anyway; neither the primitive technology of the Elizabethan stage nor the sophisticated technology of the modern stage have any bearing on it. It is, rather, entirely in the language; in the language and the genius of a Burbage or a Gielgud to give that language life.

There is a significant tie-in as well with the thesis of this discussion in the thematic importance attributed to Lear's words leading up to and during this scene by a number of modern critics.[33] George Williams makes the point that Lear's nine-line opening speech in scene 2 "must be understood as direct orders to the winds, the waves, . . . and the lightning[,] . . . in the same vein [as] those given throughout the earlier part of the play." The speech represents the acme of "his proud, arrogant, stubborn authority," in the belief that his "commands"[34] can sway the elements themselves. It is thus pivotal in the humbling process of self-discovery set now to begin, which Williams finds epitomized in the later "When the rain came to wet me once, and the wind to make me chatter; when the thunder would not peace at my bidding; there I found 'em, there I smelt 'em out. . . . They told me I was everything; 'tis a lie—I am not ague-proof" (4.6.101–3, 105). It is the focus again on language at both ends of this process that links it to the Shakespearean rhetorical allegory in the play— the manifest absurdity of "Lear's" outrageous, impossible delusion that his "word" commands the elements, played off against Shakespeare's demonstrating in the language of the play his own power to do exactly that.

The culminating example of the rhetorically outrageous in the whole play, of course, is the rhetorical sleight "Edgar" puts over the audience simultaneously with his father in the Dover scene, the allegorical implication so direct in this instance as virtually to rule out any other explanation for the episode's inclusion. There is an analogy as well, in the comparison of this scene with the storm scenes, with some of the rhetorical implications of the opening scene. We observed earlier of Goneril's declaration of love for her father in that scene, that it would hardly have seemed possible that hyperbole could be stretched further than her declaration takes it, did we not have Regan's speech to prove

us wrong; in similar manner it would surely not have seemed
technically possible to make the device of *hypotyposis* do more
than it is made to do in Lear's two "storm" speeches, did we not
have the Dover scene with which to compare them. We are not
surprised, incidentally, when we find Tolstoy's passionate revul-
sion with the first scene—"[no] king, however old and stupid . . . ,
could believe the words of the vicious daughters . . . and not believe his favorite daughter, but curse and banish her"—dwindled
almost to deadpan comedy in viewing the culminating insult to
reason the Dover scene presents, as if having exhausted outrage
all he can still muster of contempt at this point is his sense of the
ridiculous, a sense that his style challenges the unbiased reader
not to share:

> Gloucester again appears with his still unrecognised son Edgar,
> who (now in the guise of a peasant) pretends to lead his father to
> the cliff: Gloucester is walking along on level land, but Edgar per-
> suades him that they are with difficulty ascending a steep hill.
> Gloucester believes this. Edgar tells his father that the noise of
> the sea is heard; Gloucester believes this also. Edgar stops on a
> level place, and persuades his father that he has ascended the cliff
> and that in front of him lies a dreadful abyss, . . . he leaps on the
> level ground and falls, imagining that he has jumped off the cliff.[35]

While Tolstoy would have us entertain no illusions about the persuasiveness of these absurd goings-on as far as he at least is concerned, that his skepticism is less than universal says something
about the susceptibility to rhetorical persuasion of twenty generations of readers and audiences who lack even Gloucester's
blindness to justify their acceptance. It must in fairness be pointed out, however, that that acceptance is facilitated by a descriptive technique of an order of visual realism—a "verbal *trompe
l'oeil*" is what John Greenwood calls it[36]—never attempted previously, and perhaps rarely seen since, in all of literature.
McLuhan notes that in Edgar's key speech, beginning "here's the
place. / Stand still" (4.6.10–24), "the illusion of the third dimension . . . is given its first verbal manifestation in . . . history":

> What Shakespeare does here is to place five flat panels of two di-
> mensions one behind the other . . . He is utterly aware that . . . [b]y
> giving these flat panels a diagonal twist they succeed each other,
> as it were, in a perspective from the "stand still" point. (15, 16, 17)[37]

They are considerations such as these that justify us in accepting this scene, that may indeed justify us also in conceding to
Shakespeare the same "clearest" powers that his "Edgar" as-
cribes to the "gods" themselves—"who make them honors / Of
men's impossibilities" (4.6.73–74).

Where it was suggested of *Measure for Measure* that the key
to Shakespeare's rhetorical allegory in that play lies in the ancient linguistic paradoxes of Seneca the Elder, I will offer, to conclude this discussion of *Lear*, the far more startling suggestion
(which I am even prepared to say is, however impossibly, almost
hinted at in the well-known line of the Fool's, "this prophecy
shall Merlin make, for I live before his time" [3.2.95]) that a comparable clue to its allegory may be found in certain analogies between that play and a doctrine that lay centuries in the future at
the time of its composition, the later linguistic philosophy of
Ludwig Wittgenstein, as developed in detail in his final major
work, the *Philosophical Investigations*. If the enigma of *Lear* is
not resolved, it is at least clarified by crediting Shakespeare with
insights into the power and use of language that have not been
duplicated until this century, that may even parallel those developed by Wittgenstein in his *Philosophical Investigations*.

Sketching the Wittgensteinian background briefly first, two
theses about language, both relating to the problem of meaning,
form the core of the argument of the *Philosophical Investigations*. The first is a thesis it shares with Wittgenstein's other
major work, the *Tractatus Logico-Philosophicus*, the second is
precisely the point on which the doctrines of these two works
part company. It is not a new observation that in some ways the
Philosophical Investigations is a direct lineal descendent of the
Tractatus, and in others a radical departure from it. I cannot get
into the *Tractatus* here other than to state that what the two
works share are the same resolute anti-metaphysical bias and
the linguistic corollary of that bias, the belief that language's
function, or better perhaps to say its meaning, is in its capacity to
provide information about the real world. In the *Tractatus* logic
is the link between language and the world, and the truth or
falsehood of every proposition is determined absolutely by
whether or not it accurately depicts reality in any of its aspects
(this last statement is a paraphrase of proposition 2.21 in the
Tractatus.)

Where the *Philosophical Investigations* parts company with the *Tractatus*, then, is that it reconsiders the nature of that link between language and the world, concluding that while there is a link it is not the absolute one the *Tractatus* postulates. Wittgenstein demonstrates this over and over in different and ingenious ways in the two hundred-plus pages of the *Philosophical Investigations*, but there is a common thread in all of them, that the idea of absolutes of any kind, and the belief in the capacity of language to say meaningful things about such absolutes, are "grammatical illusions,"[38] a product of languages's power to "bewitch" (sect. 109), to trick us into thinking that forms of expression that may be meaningful in one context can be meaningful in all—that a proposition, for example, such as "it is five o'clock here" (sect. 350) has the same relation to reality as the proposition "it's five o'clock on the sun"; or that the statements "how high Mont Blanc is" and "how a clarinet sounds" (sect. 78) have a meaningful equivalence. The extension of this perhaps esoteric-sounding principle into the real world is both direct and impeccably logical. His many examples come down to one simple idea, that meaning in language is contextual only: that is, meaning cannot be separated from use; to quote Wittgenstein, "meaning is not a process which accompanies a word" (sect. 218). Applying the principle in reality is again as simple as, for example, taking the idea of the thing we call a "leaf" or the color we call "green" and trying to envision these concepts as existing apart from actual examples of them (sect. 73, 74). And I would cite one final illustration of Wittgenstein's thesis before turning back to *Lear*, one that as it happens has a direct bearing on the *Lear* problem. This is his discussion in section 89 of St. Augustine's aphorism on the mysterious nature of time: "What is time? If no one asks me, I know; if I try to explain it, I do not know"—the implication being that the word *time* has only an applied meaning, as we use it without difficulty in everyday life; remove it from that context and it has none.

This particular point touches an issue central to the *King Lear* allegory. The issue has two components, one that I can relate directly to the concept of time, the other bearing on the more general theory of language and meaning and their relation to philosophy developed in the *Philosophical Investigations* as a whole. Considering the "time" aspect of the question first, if time has meaning only contextually, applied to *King Lear* this principle would state that the *King Lear* world must be considered as temporally self-contained. That is, it is meaningless to speak of time in the play as extending in *any sense* beyond the boundaries of the rise and fall of the curtain. To do so is to succumb to the "bewitchment of . . . intelligence by . . . language" which Wittgenstein warns us against and of which Shakespeare is clearly cognizant. The absurdities of the characters' behavior *if* placed in any other temporal context than the play's own are deliberately intruded by Shakespeare to apprise us of that fact. Taking the play as a self-contained world temporally, however, it may be said that there are no absurdities in Lear's or any other of the characters' behavior. If the ancient Lear, the equally ancient Gloucester, and the young Edgar, the three apparently most troublesome cases behaviorally in the play, are seen as *born literally* at the moment of their first appearance on stage, then the exhibitions of moral blindness, moral innocence, and infantile naivete they put on initially are in no way exceptionable or irrational but perfectly normal. And here we may return again to the analogy with Wittgenstein's philosophy in its concern with the real world: the simple and inescapable fact is that Lear is born elderly—a delightful paradox to Shakespeare, tweaking our noses at the "bewitching" power of language; as he no doubt derives similar enjoyment in waving around terms like Kent's "ever honor'd" and Regan's "yet he hath ever but slenderly known himself," understanding that the "ever" in these expressions can only cover the twenty minutes the scene takes to play. And the same may be said of Lear's otherwise incomprehensible "They flatter'd me like a dog, and told me I had white hairs in my beard ere the black ones were there" (4.6.97–99)—that this statement too becomes perfectly rational rather than insane when looked at in these terms. It is thus possible with Wittgenstein's help to resolve the dilemma of *Lear* without having to destroy the edifice of reason three hundred-plus years of criticism has erected around this work. The thing that keeps the critical edifice intact and its analyses coherent is precisely that by and large it avoids these problematic issues. As St. Augustine said, time is not a mystery until we examine it. Understanding its operation in the play may add another dimension to our appreciation of Shakespeare's art, but it does not invalidate those critical approaches in which it does not figure as an issue. That Lear's emotional development, from classic anal-retentive infant at the beginning, through all the stages of maturity, to final tragic greatness at the end is a mere three-hour process in no way diminishes its reality or its power to move.

From the consideration of time, then, we can move to the other component of the issue, in the general analogy between the grammar of the play and the linguistic principles explored in the *Philosophical Investigations*. One of Wittgenstein's principal aims in the *Philosophical Investigations* is to set philosophy on a new footing, to establish the fact that the limitations of language are necessarily philosophy's limitations as well. As meaning in language can never be absolute, but only contextual, tied to the real world, so too philosophy: "There must not be anything hypothetical in our considerations. [sect. 109] . . . Philosophy may in no way interfere with the actual use of language; it can in the end only describe it" (sect. 123). The manner in which this principle relates to *King Lear*, then, and it fits perfectly with its enigmatic form, is that by its terms the only meaningful approach there can be to the problem of the play is grammatical, descriptive—how the play is structured, not what it may ultimately mean. This is a fundamental point in itself, but the analogy goes much further. Probably the single issue on which the *Philosophical Investigations* expends the most intellectual energy and the most ink is the issue of the connection between language and thought; is there a basis in reason for considering language and thought separate processes or are they really one? The *Philosophical Investigations* was not Wittgenstein's first attempt to answer this question though it became his most elaborate. He made a preliminary reconnoitering of the problem and sketched his tentative answer in the lecture notes he dictated to his philosophy class in Cambridge in 1933, notes subsequently published under the title *The Blue Book*, which I cite here for their comparatively greater expressive simplicity in presenting the issue: "I have been trying in all this," he says, "to remove the temptation to think that there '*must* be' what is called a mental process of thinking, hoping, wishing, believing, etc., independent of the process of expressing a thought, a hope, a wish."[39] This statement might have been Shakespeare's own, had he wished to comment on the enigmatic form, as I have called it, of his play. The problem of *King Lear* was always the problem of rationalizing not primarily the actions, but the utterances, the actions' verbal cues, of certain of the characters—Lear in the critical first scene, Gloucester and Edgar in subsequent scenes. The mystery is always *motive*—*what* they say and do, we see; *why* is the question that cannot be answered. And I do not mean by this that we do not *know* the answer, I mean that Shakespeare proves his adherence to the principle of the inseparability of thought and utterance by making any separate answer impossible. Why does Lear instantly disown Cordelia when her testimony of love is less fulsome than her sisters'? Why?—because he does. The question raised earlier, of whether or not these utterances, Lear's *and* his daughters', are supposed to be *spontaneous* comes in here as well, the Wittgensteinian perspective reinforcing that question's ultimate unaswerability. The motive of disowning Cordelia, like the motive of asking for the testimony in the first place, has no meaning apart from the words and the act. And by the same token, Cordelia's later "No cause, no cause" also takes on a different, though perhaps no less heart-rending, meaning when considered from this perspective. We can say the same of Gloucester and Edgar: what are their motives in succumbing instantly to Edmund's machinations? They are in and only in their words, in which Shakespeare pointedly allows no mention to be made of possible ulterior motives on Edmund's part in the events he sets in motion. And I quote Wittgenstein again: "We must do away with all explanation, and description alone must take its place" (sect. 109). And "after I have exhausted [all] justifications I have reached bedrock, and . . . I . . . say: 'This is simply what I do'" (sect. 217).

I have about reached bedrock here myself, and probably exhausted all justification too, but I will close with one more brief suggestive illustration of a strong philosophic affinity between *King Lear* and the *Philosophical Investigations*, an affinity in the area of what I will borrow an expression from Wittgenstein and call "language games." No student of Shakespeare can be unaware of his skill in language games of every variety, and though Wittgenstein's concept in the *Philosophical Investigations* of "language games" is developed primarily theoretically, there is an interesting example of an actual language game played similarly in both texts. Wittgenstein, to illustrate his thesis that the meanings of words are necessarily contextual rather than absolute, takes the word *game* as an example, developing over several pages an elaborate demonstration that it is finally impossible to define the word in the abstract—that, in his words, "the concept 'game' is a concept with blurred edges" (sect. 71).

Shakespeare in *King Lear* performs a similar exercise with the word *nature*. Critics have long noted that the game played with this word is like no other in Shakespeare's writing.[40] The word and its cognates appear in the play with a frequency that approaches double the frequency of its use in any other play, and in contexts that range the gamut of the word's possible meanings, from Edmund's "lusty stealth of Nature" in his speech on bastardy to Lear's doctor's benign reference to "repose" as "foster nurse of nature." The special appositeness of this particular word as subject of a language game for Shakespeare, however, is not only in its wide range of possible meanings, but in its embodiment of antithetical meanings. As love between parents and children, say, is appropriately called "natural," so too, in a manner that is surely a delight to Freudians, is it considered equally "natural" for a child of any age, from eight to eighty, to be wholly self-centered and grasping. That perhaps the only concept in the language capable of expressing apparently absolute moral opposites in one term should be the word Shakespeare chooses to play a game with in this particular play, may illustrate the profundity of his awareness of the Wittgenstein law of the ultimate contextuality of meaning.

10

"Murd'ring Impossibility": *Coriolanus* and Rhetoric

The prominence of the rhetorico/linguistic motif in *Coriolanus* is such as to suggest that it could well have been Shakespeare's main consideration in choosing to dramatize the life of *this* noble Roman, rather than that of any of the twenty-five others in Plutarch he was content to ignore. It is a measure of Shakespeare's complete mastery of his art at this late stage in his career that this play, in which direct "verbal borrowing [from its sources] is perhaps at its greatest,"[1] is also one in which many of the topics that have been the concern of this study are explored as comprehensively as anywhere else in the canon. The same comprehensive grasp is further evident in the seamless blend the play achieves of classical history and contemporary culture, not only in its discerning of the centrality of rhetoric in the politics of both periods, but, "more impressively,"[2] down even to the timing of the play, on the basis of observed parallels between republican Roman popular discontents and similar outbreaks occurring in England early in the reign of King James.[3] Usefully as the concluding chapter of this study, indeed, *Coriolanus* can be read as a recapitulation of most if not all of the rhetorical issues discussed heretofore—of the education/art/nature issue; of the Erasmian words/things precept, again; of rhetoric as a form of witchcraft, as in *Othello*, or hyperbolically enhanced as in *Lear*, with power literally to make the impossible real; of the rhetoric of "honor" and its associations of hollowness; and finally of the ultimate realities of egotism and power-lust for which rhetoric serves as a cover.

Because *Coriolanus* is a play in which reliance on its primary source, Plutarch, is particularly close, any significant departure

from that source, and particularly where no obvious dramatic
necessity appears involved, would be rather strongly suggestive
of thematic intention on the author's part. To begin my analysis
of the play I propose to nominate one such departure as an example, in the special focus Shakespeare gives to the term *Coriolanus*, which hints strongly at why Shakespeare chose this
particular life from Plutarch to make a play, and which may
indeed epitomize the rhetorical philosophy of the piece, and perhaps even the canon, as a whole. One significant point rhetorically about the term *Coriolanus* is that it is the only instance in
Shakespeare where the hero is renamed in the course of the
play, and where the new name is assigned specifically to recognize the character of the nominee. One of the central rhetorical
issues of the play concerns Marcius's supposed contempt for
words as in any way adequate representations of deeds; and
with deeds themselves defined as "real," in his notion, only when
accomplished on the battlefield, in combat, with actual physical
mementos—wounds and scars—to testify to their authenticity.
This is Marcius's character as Plutarch creates it, intriguing
initially to Shakespeare perhaps partly as a particularly striking
illustration of the Erasmian *rerum et verborum* distinction mentioned briefly in the last chapter. The paradoxical use Shakespeare makes of the distinction here, however, is that the play
demonstrates precisely that it cannot, either in the play or the
real world, in the end hold, a conclusion epitomized for him in
the word *Coriolanus*. The issue is the focus of the drama and fascinating to Shakespeare because it touches a basic philosophical
conundrum, one he discerned clearly more than 350 years before
Derrida made it the centerpiece of his deconstructive critical enterprise, the "signified/signifier" semiotic pairing, with the first
term of the pair traditionally privileged (Marcius's position in
the play), but whose actual equality and mutual interdepen-
dence can be demonstrated logically.

While I have suggested that it is in his departures from
Plutarch that the deeper meanings to Shakespeare in this
naming are betrayed, the spring in his thought here may actually be tripped, a common feature in his use of sources, by something Plutarch provides. Both in the play and in Plutarch the
motive in Cominius, his commander's, bestowing of the name
"Coriolanus" on Marcius is because he refuses any *material* re-
wards as recognition of his feats of arms. It may be significant

that while Shakespeare does not in this instance use Plutarch's own words at this critical moment in the play, that these words may nevertheless have suggested to him the philosophical meaning the moment appears to have—when, in North's rendering, "the consul Cominius began to speak in this sort":

> We cannot compel Marcius to take these gifts we offer him, if he will not receive them: but we will give him such a reward for the noble service he hath done, as he cannot refuse. Therefore we do order and decree, that henceforth he be called Coriolanus, unless his valiant acts have won him that name before our nomination.[4]

One could scarcely ask for a more explicit posing of the words/ things rhetorico/linguistic paradox that is at the center of this play than this statement provides. Because the *reality* of his battlefield accomplishments, the pure basis in honor which they have, would be corrupted by his acceptance of any material compensation for them—"[a] bribe to pay my sword" (1.9.38)—their only appropriate acknowledgment must therefore be an intangible—a title, in fact a *word*—a precise reversal and confounding of what hitherto has been claimed as the central principle of his life, that authenticity is measured by deeds only, for which words can never be an adequate substitute. That Shakespeare has digested this implication is shown, then, in a number of departures he makes from Plutarch's account of subsequent events in the Coriolanus story.

The first of these departures follows immediately after the bestowal of the name itself, significant because the act of naming, with all that it connotes, is in the forefront of the audience's consciousness at this moment. As his first act after the naming, a sealing, as it were, of the nobility that is celebrated in the name, Coriolanus requests that Cominius pardon one of their defeated enemy, "a poor man" at whose house in Corioli he "once lay," and who "us'd [him] kindly" (1.10.83). Noble as it appears, the gesture is thwarted, however, in Shakespeare's version, when Coriolanus is unable to remember his benefactor's *name*. Adapting the interlude in this manner, when placed as it is so close to Coriolanus's own naming, clearly betrays intentionality on Shakespeare's part, reinforcing the point again that while signifiers and signifieds, names and the things named, are and must always remain separate entities, at the same time without a name to represent it a deed becomes as insubstantial, as much a mockery of itself, as the very words that Coriolanus claims fail so completely to represent it.

There is another modification Shakespeare makes of the original here as well that is suggestive in another but equally striking way. In Plutarch the benefactor was anything but the "poor man" Shakespeare makes him; but rather "an honest wealthy man,"[5] with his "great wealth," noted twice in as many lines. This is problematic because one of the Coriolanus character's distinctive personality traits, in both Plutarch's and Shakespeare's version, is his "constancy" (138), as North styles it, his determinacy and inability to adapt. There was no necessity for Shakespeare to make Coriolanus's benefactor here a "poor man"; that he does so tells us more about Shakespeare than it does about Coriolanus—the point being that Coriolanus's constancy throughout the play, except in this one conspicuous instance, is always *against* the poor, the plebeian mob for whom he maintains unmitigated and frequently expressed contempt. To reverse Plutarch, changing this component of his constancy into its exact opposite on this single occasion sends a message about who is really in control that cannot, I suggest, be otherwise intended than as a deliberate test of our awareness.

A second verbal addition to Plutarch that relates in a small but quite specific way to the words/things issue relating to the "naming" of Coriolanus, is Volumnia's reference to Cominuis's letter to the senate, after Corioli, giving Marcius "the whole name of the war" (2.1.128), an explicit reinforcement again of the point that the name of a thing and the thing itself form a binary pair in which any privileging of one term over the other is a meaningless exercise: the "war" itself paradoxically consists in, and is inseparable from, the act of its naming. And an even more powerful variation on the same theme is provided, finally, in another Shakespearean departure from Plutarch in the same context. When Marcius returns to Rome in act 5, now as its conqueror, and Cominius reports the failure of all his attempts at appeasement—"urg[ing] our old acquaintance and the drops / That we have bled together," significantly, "He would not seem to know me" (5.1.8), we are told:

> 'Coriolanus'
> He would not answer to; forbad all names;
> He was a kind of nothing, titleless,

Till he had forg'd himself a name i' th' fire
Of burning Rome.

(5.1.11–15)

While none of these "naming" references are found in Plutarch, then, something in Plutarch, similarly to the example cited earlier, may have inspired this passage as well, Volumnia in this instance providing the hint that Shakespeare adapts in this revealing way. When Valeria and the other ladies of Rome come to her requesting that she and Virgilia lead an embassage to Marcius to plead that Rome be spared, Volumnia knows how much her "grief exceedeth" theirs, because of the dishonor that Marcius's actions bring on the family: "to feel the loss of my son Marcius' former valiancy and glory, and to see his person environed now with our enemies in arms"[6]—implications to which Shakespeare gives powerful affirmation in linking these events to Marcius's repudiation of his heroic Roman name.

With North's Plutarch his only significant source, and that a very full one from which, as A. L. Rowse has it, "whole passages ... go straight into blank verse with little change,"[7] it is the more remarkable that in spite of this close adherence to the original, Shakespeare manages at the same time to give a rhetorical focus to his play Plutarch hardly hints at, there being scarcely a scene in the play in which issues relating to rhetorical persuasion are not foregrounded and essential to the action.

The political aspects of the play, first, to which rhetorical issues are of course closely linked, have been the focus of much of the critical commentary, going back at least as far as Hazlitt,[8] most of it concerned to show that in dramatizing the political tensions that infected republican Rome, Shakespeare was in some manner commenting at the same time on the very similar tensions prevalent in Jacobean England. The disturbances in the Midlands in 1607, which touched Warwickshire and which Rowse observes that Shakespeare, "now a landed gentleman, could not be indifferent to,"[9] have been mentioned as probably tied directly to the play's composition, but it was already an established literary tradition from long before, that stories from Roman history could illuminate contemporary political problems in England.[10] Thomas Heywood, popular contemporary of and occasional borrower from Shakespeare, for example, comments explicitly on this connection in his *Apology for Actors*, published in 1612, but probably composed in 1608, the likely date of *Coriolanus* as well:

If wee present a foreigne History, the subject is so intended, that
in the lives of *Romans*, *Grecians*, or others, either the vertues of
our Country-men are extolled, or their vices reproved.[11]

As far as specifically rhetorical culturo-political analogues of
Rome found in Renaissance England are concerned, this is a
narrower question but one on which considerable light can also
be shed by comparison between Shakespeare's source and his
play. The one clearly rhetorical concern Plutarch raises in his account of Coriolanus's life is the one that in the public mind in
Shakespeare's time is identified most closely with the principles
and application of the arts of rhetoric, namely the field of education. Plutarch opens his life of Coriolanus by observing that Marcius's personality problems, that he was "choleric, . . . churlish,
uncivil, and altogether unfit for any man's conversation,"
stemmed from his "lack of education," that he missed "the greatest benefit [of] learning: that it teacheth men that be rude and
rough of nature, by compass and rule of reason, to be civil and
courteous."[12] These are words that go straight to the heart of Renaissance educators, engaging as well most of the issues with
which this study is concerned; and it is perhaps significant again
that while Shakespeare does not use them directly, their implications nonetheless resonate throughout his play. Indeed they
may have provided hints that Shakespeare expanded fruitfully
in several directions, both in terms of the larger rhetorical allegory of the play and of the characterization of Coriolanus as its
chief focus. The reference to the curbs on "nature" placed by
"learning," for example, that it inculcates "civil and courteous"
behavior, would be recognized by any Renaissance reader as
standard fare; which Shakespeare then foregrounds in his hero's
characterization, making "what he cannot help in his nature"
(1.1.40) lead directly to his tragic end, and, most importantly, ensuring that the audience understand the issue as primarily a
rhetorical one: "Must I / With my base tongue give to my noble
heart / A lie that it must bear?" (3.2.99–101), Coriolanus says,
showing that while the essential conflict here *is* rhetorical—
whether one should with the "base tongue" use *art* to "dissemble
with [one's] nature" (3.2.62)—the challenge to interpretation the
characterization offers extends into areas not in themselves obviously rhetorical. In particular, psychoanalytic implications of
several kinds may come into the question. Marcius's Oedipal fixation, for example, bespeaks an undeveloped, essentially infan-

tile, surprisingly even Lear-like character, precisely the point of weakness discerned and played on by Aufidius, baiting him, for example, with the epithet "boy" in the closing scene, and betrayed in his instantaneous reaction to the word: "Measureless liar, thou has made my heart / Too great for what contains it. 'Boy'!" (5.6.103–4)—exactly what the conspirators counted on as an excuse for cutting him down.

Coriolanus offers a particularly good opportunity to demonstrate the methodology of this study as compared to those I have previously termed more "conventional" in their approach to rhetorical issues in Shakespeare. I spoke earlier of Shakespeare's departures from Plutarch, certain of which have been noted by scholars as bearing on the question of the relations between rhetoric and politics in the Renaissance. Many of these are concerned with Shakespeare's probable use of other sources in modifying the picture of republican Rome presented by Plutarch. The principal additional classical source he almost certainly used is Livy,[13] and many scholars consider it likely that he had seen Machiavelli's *Discourses*, commenting on Livy, as well. Considering Livy first, it is plausible that Livy's primarily historical interest in Coriolanus's career, in contrast to Plutarch's more biographical approach, would have influenced Shakespeare's reconstruction of the story as well. One thoughtful commentator on the subject, Anne Barton, noting that when Livy writes of Coriolanus's "arrogance . . . , [and] his stubborn refusal to countenance the tribunate," it is "with the Tarquin kings and their tyranny in mind, and also with full awareness of what (historically) was to come: an increase in the number of tribunes to ten, publication of the laws,"[14] and various other concessions designed to popularize the offices and obligations of state. She sees the specific influence of Livy's view in Shakespeare's version, then, when Plutarch's straightforward "in those days, valiantness was honored in Rome above all other virtues,"[15] is subtly qualified by Cominius's "*if* it be" in his formal oration in praise of Marcius after Corioli (2.2.83, italics mine), hinting that the warrior cult of Rome's earliest centuries is now passé, and Marcius a man born out of his time.

With regard to Machiavelli, Barton does not ascribe direct knowledge of the *Discourses* to Shakespeare, but she feels that their spirit, expounding the ideas implicit in Livy's history, has surely been imbibed by the author of *Coriolanus*. She sees Shake-

speare as reflecting the lesson Coriolanus's life offered to Machiavelli; that by refusing to concede anything to the plebeians he
threatens the state; in coming together to banish him, plebeians
and patricians recognize a mutual interest, a mark of Rome's
progress toward a truly republican polity. Her whole thesis on
Machiavelli, indeed, is that restrained public debate was Rome's
metaphoric steam valve, "precisely the equilibrium in which . . .
Livy had located the strength of the Roman republic," which she
sees epitomized in the heading of chapter 4 book I of the *Discourses*, that " 'the disagreement of the People and the Senate of
Rome made the Commonwealth both free and mighty'."[16] The one
specifically rhetorical reference that she does cite in this context
is Machiavelli's key observation on Coriolanus, that he breached
the unwritten understanding between patricians and plebeians,
that the language of debate must be kept within politic bounds—
that "in a republic, . . . the man who is proud and uses insulting
language, who openly displays his contempt for the commons, is
intolerable."[17] The subject will come up again later, but one observation on Shakespeare's concurrence with these Machiavellian
principles in his *Coriolanus* I would note here is that his Rome *is*
clearly conceived as symmetrical in its political structure, in
exact agreement with Machiavelli's prescription: plebeians and
patricians—their conflicting claims, rights, roles, and responsibilities balance each other; to the extent that "Rome" exists, it is
both, and they are equal. This basic structure is the starting
point of meaning only for Shakespeare's play, of course; the scope
for interpretation offered by the maneuverings, follies, and
machinations found on both sides of the political divide in the
play are vast, but the principle of an exact balance of power between them is never lost. Whatever might be said for or against
either group, something comparable to be said on the other side
is never far to seek.

    If the evidence of direct influence of the *Discourses* on *Cori-
olanus* is equivocal, a stronger case can be made for Machiavelli's last work, *The Art of War*, as a probable contributing
source. Arguably better known in Shakespeare's day than either
the *Discourses* or *The Prince*,[18] *The Art of War* is the most explicit
of the three in its linking of the arts of oratory and war. Weithoff's article on this subject cites book 4 as the section in which
Machiavelli "explain[s] his concept of the martial virtue of
rhetoric most carefully,"[19] quoting the same passage in illustra-

tion of this feature as was quoted earlier in this study from Gray. I have discussed several instances where Shakespeare's departures from Plutarch suggest a different, specifically rhetorical, thematic agenda in this play not present in Plutarch, an emphasis nicely congruent with that given in Machiavelli. Thus, while Plutarch merely notes Marcius "calling [his troops] . . . to fight with a loud voice" at the gates of Corioli, and again that he becomes "marvelous angry" when "spoil"[20] distracts the soldiers from the greater task of pursuing final victory, the fiery rhetoric in which these matters are couched in the play goes much further, clearly following the Machiavellian maxim that "[i]t is requisite for excellent Captaines to bee good orators":[21]

> If any such be here—
> As it were sin to doubt—that love this painting
> Wherein you see me smear'd; if any fear
> Lesser his person than an ill report;
> If any think brave death outweighs bad life
> And that his country's dearer than himself;
> Let him alone, or so many so minded,
> Wave thus to express his disposition,
> And follow Marcius.
>   [*They all shout and wave their swords, take him up
>   in their arms and cast up their caps.*
>   (1.6.67–75)

It is further suggestive of a possible *Art of War* influence in these scenes that reference is made several times in both stage directions and text to the martial instruments of war—"the sounde of the Trompet"[22] in Whitehorne's rendering—as a rallying point and means of command less problematic than a human voice may often be. It may be with this thinking in mind that Shakespeare gives his Coriolanus to declare the unequivocal voices of the instruments of war "profaned" by the "acclamations hyperbolical" heaped on him after Corioli by the far less reliable voices of men:

> [*A long flourish. They all cry* 'Marcius, Marcius!'
> *cast up their caps and lances. . . .*]
> May these same instruments which you profane
> Never sound more! When drums and trumpets shall
> I' the field prove flatterers, let courts and cities be
> Made of all false-fac'd soothing.
>   (1.9.41–43)

This quotation, touching the most prominent "second level" rhetorical issue of the play, Coriolanus's constantly proclaimed mistrust of "false fac'd soothing" language, when set beside the speech quoted just previous to it, is a convenient introduction to the allegorical level of the play as well. The key idea the first speech illustrates, when placed beside the second, is that it shows Coriolanus himself *doing* precisely what he affects in the latter to deplore, pulling out all the rhetorical stops in "acclamations hyperbolical" that have both the aim and the effect of persuading others to buy into the heroic picture his words create. This is one of almost innumerable examples, any of which would be equally convenient for the purpose, of the principle on which the play's rhetorical allegory is based, the principle which the reader may by now even anticipate my returning to, of *impossible contradiction*. There are parallels with both *Lear* and *Othello* in Shakespeare's construction of the allegory in *Coriolanus*, presented in *Coriolanus*, however, in an even more exaggerated manner than was the case with the other two. And it is perhaps interesting as well, for the same reason, that *Coriolanus*, of the five plays looked at, may be the one that shows Shakespeare directly engaging the intellectual issues that dominate criticism today, namely, the fields of language theory and deconstruction.

To dispose of the less challenging, though not less interesting, of the above assertions first, if my suggestion, that there are important rhetorical allegorical parallels in *Coriolanus* with both *Othello* and *Lear*, seems at first glance dubious, putting ourselves again briefly into the rhetorical mindset behind those plays should quickly demonstrate the contrary. In the case of *Othello* a clear parallel with *Coriolanus* lies in the profession of the two heroes and its relation to rhetoric, both being soldiers and thus both supposedly more men of action than of words. The "supposedly" is accurate here, because equally in both cases is the premise shown to be blatantly false. The manner in which that falseness is brought out differs in the two situations: Othello has no opportunity to use Coriolanus's Machiavellian rhetoric of war, but shows that he can perform as effectively in the council chamber or the boudoir as Coriolanus on the battlefield anyway; Coriolanus's ploy, on the other hand, is to affect a disdain for rhetoric altogether. The point, however, is that the element of falseness is present equally in both characters: we have noted Othello's statement that he is "rude" in his speech for the sly rhetorical maneuver that it is; in Coriolanus's case it is Menenius that makes the same plea on his behalf, that having "been bred i' the wars," he "is ill school'd / In bolted language" (3.2.320, 321–22), a claim that Aufidius for one, knowing his man, does not wish to see tested at the end, and Coriolanus given any opportunity "[t]o purge himself with words" (5.6.8) in the Volscian council.

When we come to *Lear*, the parallels with *Coriolanus* are at once more subtle and more revealing. As we saw in Valesio's interpretation of Cordelia's role in the opening scene in *Lear*, that silence can be as much a rhetorical tactic as eloquence, having the potential indeed even to outmaneuver it in certain situations, so the same may be said of Coriolanus's "rejection" of "flattery" (3.2.137). In his Lear Shakespeare gave us a character the apparent rhetorical opposite of a Coriolanus, to whom *only* hyperbolical flattery, absurdly enough, is "real," and whose tragedy has its origin in his deriving his sense of self entirely from the words of others. In *Coriolanus*, equally absurdly, his affected disdain for flattery actually carries self-flattery to hyperbolical heights *beyond* eloquence altogether. I will reserve further comment on this important subject for later, for the moment observing only that this whole device on Coriolanus's part can be read as another and perhaps the supreme example in Shakespeare of the effectiveness of *meiosis*, again, as a rhetorical device. As Cordelia's affectation of "truth" over rhetoric in *Lear* was her only hope of topping her sisters' hyperbole, so Coriolanus's rejection of Cominius's "acclamations hyperbolical" after Corioli—"too modest are you," says Cominius—has the effect of making him appear even *more* noble than the glorious picture Cominius has just painted of his battlefield accomplishments has already done—at the anticipated later retelling of which, like Desdemona hanging on the words of Othello, "ladies shall be frighted / And, gladly quak'd, hear more" (1.9.5–6).

If we seek a mantra expressing the allegorical essence of *Coriolanus*, the perfect one may be found, perhaps not merely fortuitously, in the title of one of Shakespeare's sources for Menenius's fable of the belly, William Averell's 1584 *Mervailous Combat of Contrarieties*. It hardly needs pointing out that the "violentest contrariety" (4.6.73) informs every aspect of this play, starting with the politics—internal, external, personal—that govern its plot; but what is truly "marvelous" in this is that while these contrarieties are clearly such that they *cannot* in reality hold together, the power of the play's language is such that they successfully defy all rational necessity and actually do retain their coherence. Simultaneously challenging and mocking us in virtually every speech, Shakespeare has created a rhetorical structure, a "reality," in *Coriolanus*, that is entirely self-contained: a set of signifiers that even as they correspond in every way to "normal"—grammatical, syntactical, lexical—usage, paradoxically at the same time proclaim their defiance of any attachment to "real-world" signifieds of any kind. I am aware of the tenuously theoretical sound of the above statements; pointing simultaneously to both the play's "second" and "third" rhetorical levels, a degree of abstraction is unavoidable in the initial presentation of such a thesis; fortunately, however, with specific textual application the abstract can become quickly concrete.

I will begin with the general observation that it is made apparent from the first in the play that verbalization/rhetoric—the "voices" of the plebeians to which aspirants to political power must appeal, the "absolute 'shall'" (3.1.90) of Sicinius that so infuriates Coriolanus—is not only the ruling principle of its world, but becomes a substitute for reality itself; while reality, mute, beyond verbalization, is successfully, even as it cannot be, set aside. A quick analysis of the first scene, for example, selected for discussion merely because it *is* the first scene, as almost any other segment of the play could be similarly broken down, can illustrate these principles in action. The opening exchange among the "*mutinous* Citizens," prior to the entry of Menenius at l. 50, the citizens armed with "staves, clubs, and other weapons," broaches the motif of impossible contradiction immediately. It is significant, first, that one voice only, that of "*1 Cit.,*" speaks for the citizens here and throughout the scene, significant because while Shakespeare obviously could have assigned different issues of complaint to different individuals, having what are essentially unrelated issues raised instead by the *same* voice effectively undermines the value, indeed the meaning in those complaints. If what Citizen 1 says initially, then, is "true," that the "commonality" in Rome are left to "famish" (l. 4) while the patricians hoard a "superfluity," an "abundance" of grain, then their situation is truly desperate and their rebellion amply justified. These words are not even uttered, however, before a second, tangential at best but, most importantly, *blatantly incommensurate* issue is also raised, that of Caius Marcius, "chief enemy to the people," who, while the citizens recognize the "services he has done for his country," is resented because he is "proud, . . . even to the altitude of his virtue" (1.1.39).

One logical conclusion only, and that a strange one, can arise from this collocation of grossly incommensurate complaints; this is that *neither can mean anything*: if the "hunger for bread" (l. 24) issue is real, then the issue of Marcius's pride cannot be, or at least cannot be significant; and, of course, vice versa must also be the case. Nor is the mere juxtaposing of the issues in this manner the only basis for concluding that all that has been uttered here is meaningless; the appearance of Menenius, also a patrician, but one who, it is said, "hath always lov'd the people" (l. 50), gives further strong reinforcement to the point. We now have two patricians singled out as individuals in the mind of the rebellious mob, one as their "chief enemy," the other as his complete antithesis. If the patricians can be seen as individuals in this way, ranging in their attitudes from antipathy to sympathy, then simultaneous reference to them also as an exploiting *class*—"[w]e are accounted poor citizens, the patricians good" (l. 14)—is logically negated. The element of impossible contradiction, contrasting reality with its rhetorico/linguistic substitute, comes into this picture front and center in the fact that while these things *cannot* in logic be, in the play they nonetheless effectively *are*—and not just rhetorically but apparently actually —as clearly confirmed, we might observe, in the four hundred years of both theatrical and closet experience of the play that has yet to find anything whatever logically exceptionable in its first fifty lines.

The debate between Menenius and Citizen 1 that follows the impossible problematics of the scene's opening continues the same pattern, but now, in confronting the patricians and the plebeians, presents it more boldly, in closer to black-and-white form, as it were, pointing that much more clearly, if still indirectly, to the Shakespearean magic itself. Two things stand out rhetorically in this exchange. The first is that both positions, patrician and plebeian, are stated categorically at the outset and are starkly irreconcilable. The tone is chilling on the patricians' side when Menenius observes that rebellion, should it come, will be ruthlessly crushed:

[T]he Roman state . . . will on,
. . . cracking ten thousand curbs
Of more strong link asunder than can ever
Appear in your impediment.

                                              (1.1.67–70)

Citizen 1 in response then reiterates with equal directness the
citizens' principal, life-and-death, complaint, that the patricians
"suffer us to famish, and their storehouses cramm'd with grain"
(77–78), adding to this a general condemnation of the rule of
those Menenius has called "the helms o' th' state." These statements represent the "truth" of the situation, as seen from both
sides. What happens next, however, when Menenius expresses
the desire to "tell . . . a pretty tale," and Citizen 1 allows, while
warning Menenius that he "must not think to fob our disgrace
with a tale," that he will "hear it," is that the "truth" somehow
fades away with the telling, the tale substituting it in effect, the
grounds of rebellion no longer urgent, the punishment for rebellion no longer needing to be urged. This strange turn is both an
example of, and another deliberate lesson in, the ability of
rhetoric to create an impossible reality, of importance in the context of this analysis in two ways. In the broader setting of the
study as a whole, first, it functions on two levels, our familiar
"second" and "third" rhetorical levels. In the play the lesson is political, in the conduct of the citizens, who willingly suspend their
knowledge of the *facts* in the face of a pretty tale presented by a
master; in the real world it functions on the allegorical level, in
the audience, us, who allow ourselves to be similarly deceived. It
is the second significance that is perhaps the more striking at
this point, however, because the key element of *impossibility*
again enters with it—that a "pretty tale," verbal sleight-of-hand,
whether on the political or the allegorical level, cannot, *even as it
does*, alter the facts.

Of Marcius's role in this scene, beginning at this point, while
again rhetorically central, I will comment only briefly, saving
most of what I will have to say about him for discussion of the
later consulship scenes, act 2, where the rhetorical implications
of his role are perhaps more pronounced. His "spontaneous" ha-
rangue against the plebeians, all-encompassing in its sweep,
masterful in verbally annihilating any scrap of worth or right
they might try to claim as Romans, works subtly two ways to
further reinforce the rhetorical lessons the scene provides. The

point, first, that they make themselves *willing* victims of rhetorical manipulation, is here made explicit as one of the main thrusts of the speech. Totally lacking will or spirit of their own, indeed, as Marcius pitilessly exposes them, they are *nothing but* the words that fill these gaps: speak the "good word" (l. 164) to them that they crave, and "every minute you do change a mind" (180). The ironic "they say," twice repeated in the speech, again reflects this hollowness, which is further bolstered by the open contempt for his hearers Menenius then displays in observing that his pretty tale has the rebels "almost fairly persuaded" (199). And the point is climaxed, finally, in Marcius's account of the "other troop" of rebels, who we see are similarly shaped and as easily disarmed by rhetoric. After having "vented their complainings" (207) in the "shreds" (206) of "proverbs—/ That hunger broke stone walls, that dogs must eat" (203–4), and "being answer'd, / And a petition [—tribunes, 'to defend their vulgar wisdoms' (214)—] granted them"

> they threw their caps
> As they would hang them on the horns o' th' moon,
> Shouting their emulation.
>
> (210–12)

With one troop thus instantly converted from rebels to supporters by rhetorical manipulation, and the other left to "steal away" (stage direction, l. 248) as the scene ends, willingly adapting their behavior to fit Marcius's scathing description, the picture of the plebeian half of "Rome" actually *being* as he describes it—that is, nonentity, a verbal construct—is set. The scene ends as well with a final rhetorical irony, with Sicinius and Brutus, the newly installed tribunes, alone on stage, bringing things full circle by reverting again to what it now appears is the rebels' only "real (?)" grievance in the first place—not food, but Marcius and his patrician pride, shown specifically in the rhetorically most galling possible form, "his taunts" (253). This would refer to his not merely refusing the plebeians Menenius's "good word," to allow them the harmless delusion that they are Romans too, but his going out of his way to do the contrary, using every rhetorical resource to denigrate, alienate, antagonize, and altogether consign them verbally to utter annihilation.

It may be further noted, finally, before leaving the scene, that the "contrariety" theme is displayed prominently in several

other ways than just Marcius's so eloquently expressed hatred
for the plebeians. His diatribe clearly implies "a tacit identification of himself with Rome," in Visnawathan's words,[23] a phrase I
would modify by placing the word *patrician* in front of "Rome," as
connoting something absolutely antithetical to plebeian Rome—
a Rome of deeds, not words, authentic in its values, and constant,
as opposed to inveterate plebeian inconstancy, in defending
those values. The other central element of "violentest contrariety" in the play also receives its first mention before the scene
concludes, the Rome/Volscia Marcius/Aufidius rivalry and conflict, later to spawn a confusion of further contrarieties both
verbal and real of such complexity as virtually to defy resolution.

In the consulship scenes, as I call them, covering the whole of
act 2, all of the rhetorical implications of the opening scene are
carried further, stretched indeed to the point that, comparably to
Othello, the case for this being deliberate, Shakespeare *daring
us not to see* exactly what he is doing, cannot, I submit, be seriously challenged. The test of our awareness may in this instance
be more daring than *Othello*, given the explicit focus on rhetoric
even at the level of plot in *Coriolanus*, an emphasis that commentary on the play significantly reflects, though still with one
common feature in every discussion, that the topic is approached on the technical or political levels only, never on the allegorical.

A suggestive feature of *Coriolanus* criticism that aligns it in
interesting ways with at least the latter three of the plays previously discussed is that its critical history is marked by strong divisions of opinion on both the play's merits and its meaning,
ranging, in well-known instances, from the "hope" Coleridge expresses that some day "becoming wiser, I shall discover some
profound excellence in what I now . . . detect . . . imperfection,"[24]
to T. S. Eliot's terse edict that the play is "Shakespeare's most assured artistic success."[25] To quote Traversi on the critical canon,
"the only point on which there seems to be agreement is that
Coriolanus is difficult and . . . its artistic quality . . . peculiar."[26]
That Traversi himself supports this judgment is further reflected in his use of terms like "grotesque" in reference to the
hero, and "puzzling and inconsistent" in referring to his antago-
nist—such qualities being "contradictions" in a play in which
"the mastery displayed in the verse . . . does not suggest declin-
ing powers or lack of interest."[27]

I will invoke Michael Murrin's "absurdity" principle once again to suggest that writings that are "peculiar," "puzzling," and contain "contradictions" invite allegorical interpretation, and that the history of "critical uneasiness"[28] with *Coriolanus* reflects both the need for and failure of criticism to find such a key. I have said that *Coriolanus's* allegory is based on the "principle" of impossible contradiction. If this concept still seems obscure, it can be clarified by an analogy with some of the things said about *Othello*, to which it bears, in allegorical terms, a close similarity. Comparing Rymer's notorious dismissal of the play as a "bloody farce" with Macauley's canonization of it as "the greatest work in the world," I said that neither opinion can be a "final answer on *Othello*" because the play is both—"in rhetorical or poetic terms a [sublime] tragedy, in rational terms a farce." The analogous impossible contradiction in *Coriolanus* would be that in rhetorical/poetic terms it is unexceptionable (i.e., plausible, believable, convincing—*historical!*), while in rational terms impossible.

As is the case with *Othello*, essentially all of the commentary on *Coriolanus* assumes that the first, plausibility, term of the above formula contains the whole of the play's meaning. While not everything that might be said about it from that perspective has yet been said, obviously, significant additions continuing to appear, I will entrust further development of that side of things to the competent hands of others, focusing my analysis instead on the other half, the rational impossibility that I suggest is the underlying source of the commentary's "critical uneasiness," and in which the allegorical essence of the play is located. One approach already suggested as potentially fruitful in this undertaking is by looking objectively at the extensive use of hyperbole in the play's rhetoric, particularly in references to the virtues of the hero, though it is by no means confined to that. That we as audience are intended by the author to *see* and reflect on the use of this device is implicit in the hero's outspoken strictures on the subject of rhetoric generally—that words are empty and deeds alone are real—and made explicit in his specific reference to "acclamations hyperbolical" as the worst form of flattery, and thus the epitome of the falsity of language. Pointed as these indications are in the text, however, they can have the paradoxical effect of actually lessening our alertness to the issue, by drawing our attention to what Marcius says *about* hyperbole, and diverting it from the hyperbole used in the play *about* which he says it.

For conventional criticism to have missed the really excessive prominence of hyperbole in the play as a whole suggests the possibility of this having happened.

Renaissance rhetorical texts, such as Puttenham and Peacham, make the point that hyperbole is an effective figure "when either we would greatly advance or greatly abase the reputation of anything or person," but one that, "for his immoderate excess," "must be vsed very discreetly, or els it will seem odious, for although a prayse . . . may be allowed beyŏd credit, it may not be beyŏd all measure."[29] In Peacham's "Caution" on the use of the figure he names two vices, "offending in contrary extremities," to which hyperbole is subject: "*Bomphiologia*, which giveth high titles to base persons, and great praises to small deserts"; and "*Tapinosis*, that is when the dignitie . . . of a high matter is much defaced by the basenesse of a word, as to call . . . an Oration a tale [!], or as if one should say to a king: may it please your mastership."[30] He notes also, significantly in the present context, the close relation of the latter vice to the figure *meiosis*, as representing its excess. Exquisitely diplomatically phrased in the manner of the period, these definitions nevertheless cannot entirely conceal certain deeper, potentially subversive, even anarchic, rhetorical implications they necessarily carry. The operative principle in both, clearly, is Puttenham's *decorum*; that we must ever be on guard against the dangers of rhetorical excess—unspoken recognition of the political, linguistic, moral, and philosophical abyss that threatens just beyond the limit of decorum's vision.

Shakespeare shows his conscious awareness, testing that of his audience/readers at the same time, of all the implications, spoken and unspoken, of the above, and much more in addition, in his exploration of the concept of hyperbole, its vices and excesses, in the consulship scenes. It should be noted first that there are two roads to excess in hyperbole and two associated dangers. The first is the one that Peacham speaks of, that hyperbole may be taken too far; if a man is called a God, for example, the risk is that embarrassment rather than awe may greet the person so described and contempt rather than admiration the speaker. The second form of excess, though closely related to the first, is rather theatrical than precisely political, or likely to be observed in the real world, namely overuse of the figure itself. For hyperbole to be effective at all it must be reserved for that very rare occasion that can legitimately be considered unparalleled, or almost so, something that we can refer to in these terms and be sincere in doing so. But when virtually every statement about, or reference to, a *person,* particularly, is hyperbolical, then the device itself becomes absurd—visible for what it actually is—empty verbal encomia that leave far behind any possible relation to the real human world.

Shakespeare goes overboard in both directions, in all directions, in fact, in *Coriolanus,* climaxed in the consulship scenes. I say *climaxed,* in these scenes, because the first examples in the play come earlier, Cominius's battlefield hyperbole, for example, being one. Similarly, Marcius's verbal annihilation of the plebeians in 1.1, using language that virtually screams its excess—that "stretcheth things to the uttermost length," in Peacham's phrase[31]—is surely, when applied to *one's fellow citizens* as calculated an example of *tapinosis* (also known by its Latin name, *humiliatio*[32]) as could be conceived:

> Would the nobility lay aside their ruth
> And let me use my sword, I'd make a quarry
> With thousands of these quarter'd slaves,
> As high as I could pick my lance.
>
> (1.1.195–98)

Also, as a lead-up to her rhapsodies on her son's transcendent soldiership in act 2, Volumnia's testaments to honor in act 1 already smack heavily of excess, putting us in mind again almost of the absurdities of *Titus Andronicus*; especially when placed as they are deliberately to contrast with her daughter-in-law's perfectly normal concern for her husband's safety above all. Even as one hears Volumnia "profess sincerely" (1.3.22) that "had he died in the [wars] . . . [t]hen his good report should have been [her] son," a nagging sense of hyperbole, impossibility, attending such sentiments, when war becomes an occasion for "mirth" (l. 105), in which Virgilia's "solemness" (108) is out of place, cannot but be subconsciously felt:

> The breasts of Hecuba,
> When she did suckle Hector, look'd not lovelier
> Than Hector's forehead when it spit forth blood
> At Grecian sword, contemning.
>
> (1.1.40–43)

This verbal inflationary process—"there's wondrous things spoke
of him" (2.1.130)—is climaxed in the consulship scenes, building
up from Volumnia's glee at Marcius's wounding—"O, he is
wounded, I thank the gods for't" (2.1.114). Of course he is not
just wounded, but wounded twenty-seven times (the number is
Shakespeare's gratuitous contribution), giving his mother even
greater joy, that she has "lived / To see inherited [the] very . . .
buildings of my fancy" (188–90). All of this and more is then triumphantly reaffirmed—indeed, added to, like Regan's building
on Goneril's hyperbole—in Cominius's recapitulation of Coriolanus's whole martial career: from when "at sixteen years . . .
with his Amazonian chin he drove the bristle'd lips before him"
(2.2.89); then "waxed like a sea, / And in the brunt of seventeen
battles since/ . . . lurch'd all swords of the garland" (97–99); and
culminating in Corioli, "where he did / Run reeking o'er the lives
of men, . . . and till we call'd / Both field and city ours he never
stood / To ease his breath with panting" (116–20). Nor does he
fail to mention, to cap (and further hyperbolize) his commendation, the supremely noble gesture of spurning any material
reward in recognition of his achievements—"[o]ur spoils he
kick'd at; . . . [h]e covets less than misery itself would give" (122,
125). And when these wonders are combined, finally, with his
dislike of hearing himself commended, refusing to stay to "hear
[his] nothings monster'd," (74) the apotheosis of Coriolanus into
a "warrior-hero [of] awesome, Olympian or Herculean dimensions,"[33] "as if that whatsoever god who leads him / Were slyly
crept into his human powers" (209–10), is complete. The "god"
Brutus / Shakespeare refers to here is of course rhetoric, language's capacity to put foundations under "the buildings of [our]
fancy," to bring into being that which in nature is not and cannot
be, with that impossibility all the while manifest both *in the
medium of language itself*—Coriolanus's continual, and amply
justified, devaluing of language—and, most conspicuously, in the
actions and attitudes displayed, here and subsequently, by all of
the actors in these events.

The allegorical element of impossible contradiction comes
into these considerations in several ways, both straightforward
and subtle. The combination of outrageous hyperbole, in building
up the image of Coriolanus, with his outspoken strictures
against that very thing, first, constitutes an almost direct allegorical statement from Shakespeare—telling us, in effect, that

Coriolanus is right; hyperbole *is* words only, and not to be believed. The same lesson is both broadened rhetorically and deepened allegorically in the remainder of the consulship scenes, where the game of rhetoric, understood as a game by all participants *even as they play it*, is the central question taken up. On Coriolanus's side the point is very straightforward and is the same one he was making regarding Cominius's extolling of his deeds, that rhetorical gilding "monsters"—shames and dishonors—the integrity of the deeds themselves. Despising the plebeians, he will go through the ritual asking for their "voices" in approval of his consulship bid because "custom" says he must, but perform it in such a way that his contempt for them and the process must be clearly understood by all:

> I will, sir, flatter my sworn brother the people to a earn a dearer estimation of them; 'tis a condition they account gentle; and since the wisdom of their choice is rather to have my hat than my heart, I will practice the insinuating nod and be off to them most counterfeitly. . . . Therefore, beseech you I may be consul. (2.3.93–98, 100)

On the plebeian side the charade is played out in a somewhat more indirect way, but their knowledge that it *is* a charade they are going through is as unmistakable as Coriolanus's. They note first that their power to reject Coriolanus as a candidate for the consulship is hypothetical only; tradition names it "power," but it has no connection to reality: "It is a power that we have no power to do; . . . if he tell us his noble deeds, we must also tell him our noble acceptance of them" (2.3.5, 10–11). The irony in the use of the word "noble" here is primarily Shakespeare's, but the follow-through in the play is predictable and according to script, confirming again that Coriolanus is right in his estimation of the plebeians as empty shells moved by whatever words are poured into them, as, sheeplike, they accept their role, approving his consulship without a dissenting voice. All it takes, of course, is one such voice, raised after Coriolanus has left the forum, one of the very voices that five minutes before approved him, now voicing *doubts about his sincerity* (about which there was never any doubt to begin with!), and, with the debate skillfully manipulated by the tribunes, instantaneously the whole process is inverted and relations between Coriolanus and the plebeians returned to the position we found them in at the beginning of the play.

Never forgetting the *contrariety* side of the question, however, a particularly subtle element comes into Shakespeare's allegorical equation here, in that even as he is warning us bluntly not to take hyperbole at face value, he is himself playing the hyperbolical game with his character. By making Coriolanus stand for *truth*, for reality, against the deceptions of rhetoric, he is in effect playing Cominius's rhetorical game himself, compounding (at what point does compounding become overloading?) the hyperbole by giving Coriolanus yet another great virtue, to add to those of supreme military achievement and glory, of which he can justifiably boast. Cominius's praise placed him on an Olympian pedestal as the living embodiment of Roman virtue, "if," as he says, "valour is the chiefest virtue" (2.2.82); but he may be seen as more than this, as the very word made flesh of Rome itself, of all the grandeur that the word *Rome* connotes in both its own and its Renaissance admirers' heroic imaginations. This is a view Coriolanus himself shares of what he represents, although with significant and allegorically important qualifications.[34]

There are two closely related components to these qualifications. The version of Roman virtue Cominius's encomium presents is essentially Plutarch's, with "valiantness" as its sole measure. Both Coriolanus's opening diatribe against the plebians and the consulship scenes, however, with their focus on rhetoric, go beyond this simple concept, adding the principles of constancy and truth as other essential "Roman" qualities. It may be suggested that Cominius's description of Coriolanus implies these values as well to some extent, but they are certainly not singled out, and with the latter particularly, at least as far as the language of the encomium is concerned, clearly nowhere in the picture. Is this a difference between Coriolanus's concept of Roman virtue and that of the rest of his patrician class? The question is significant, because the second qualifying component of Coriolanus's identification of himself with the spirit of Rome is that in his estimation, when he made his opening speech, the Rome he identifies with *is* patrician Rome, an entirely different Rome, indeed antithetical in its values to any "Rome" his plebeian nemesis could represent. Emphatically not plebeian Rome, then— not even including them, apparently, since "Romans . . . they are not/Though calved i' the porch o' th' Capitol" (3.1.239–40)—if his Rome is not quite patrician Rome either, as their later desertion of him confirms, the concept of "Rome" must begin to lose its moorings in reality, becoming essentially a verbal icon or free-floating signifier, available for shaping in any manner that the needs either of the individual or the moment dictate.

This is an important allegorical idea in the play, having ramifications in several directions. On the hyperbole question again, first, Coriolanus's embodiment of a nobler "Romanism" than his patrician peers can aspire to, shown in their capitulation to the tribunes and connivance in his banishment, a number of points might be taken up. Most importantly, perhaps, a strong case can be made that his characterization of them as "dastard nobles" (4.5.75) is totally justified. In the discussion of 1.1 earlier, the point was made that the only difference between Coriolanus and the rest of his class, represented there by Menenius, is that Coriolanus will not hide his contempt for the plebeians behind a veil of rhetoric, while Menenius will. Between the lines of Menenius's soothing rhetoric is that the "Roman state" is patrician: "Rome and her rats are at the point of battle" (160) closes his "pretty tale," making the point clearly that he is as contemptuous of the plebeians in fact as Coriolanus is—"multiplying spawn," as he also calls them, of which there are a "thousand to one good one" (2.2.76, 77). One significance of this fact is that it completes the aggrandization of Coriolanus as the only authentic patrician, and thus the only authentic Roman. As the one to whom "the nobles bended as to Job's statue" (2.1.255) after Corioli, he is only one whose utterances are more than rhetoric, and to whom the words *honor* and *honesty* in particular can never be completely detached in meaning. This is the first time "honor" has come up in this chapter, though not in this study, where the questionable authenticity of the concept has been touched on before; similar ambiguity shadows it here. In many ways the concept *Rome* or *Roman*, and the concept *honor* are synonymous in the thinking of the characters, so "honor" is never far in the background whenever Rome is the topic of discussion.

There are two significances to Shakespeare's apotheosizing of Coriolanus. I have said that the allegorical lesson of the play relates to the idea of impossible contradiction—two mutually exclusive realities, both of which are nevertheless magically sustained in one package through the power of Shakespeare's rhetoric. As one side of this contradictory package, then, the Marcius depicted in the play's words, from start to finish, is the perfection of all the achievements and virtues that the word *Rome* at its greatest would be seen as standing for. The phrase "from start to finish" is critical here because it is a key to the idea of impossible contradiction. Constancy, that he *does not change*, is a hallmark of Coriolanus's character insisted on throughout, and kept in our awareness by frequent reiteration. The source of this constancy, a companion motif that is brought up with comparable frequency, is *nature*, a motif that itself has a close connection to the rhetorical theme. The second citizen's reference to "what he cannot help in his nature" (1.1.39) in explanation of Coriolanus's conduct is there from the beginning, and it echoes back and forth with references to his constancy literally through to the end of the story. Thus his first words committing himself to the Volsce wars in 1.1 were "I am constant" (l. 237); his refusal to be "false to my nature" (l. 15) to appease the plebeians then led directly to his banishment in 3.2, which he goes into assuring his friends that whatever they hear from his exile will contain "never of me aught / But what is like me formerly" (4.1.52–53). Finally, the most surprising though still accurate reiterations would be those that come *after* his shift of allegiance, Aufidius complimenting his "constant temper" (5.2.90), the Volscian Watch's calling him "the rock, the oak, not to be wind-shaken" (5.2.105), and, finally, Aufidius's lying "pretext" to justify his charge of treason, that he "bow'd his nature / Never known before" (5.5.25).

The allegorical significance of this pattern is probably quite clear, hardly needing Sicinius and Brutus's "not possible" and "I know this cannot be" (4.6.57–58) to bring it home. It is that something has to be wrong: this arch-Roman, whose "country's dearer than himself" (1.6.72) cannot, logically, while all the time possessed of a "nature / Not to be other than one thing" (4.6.41), be the *anti-Roman*, "tearing / His country's bowels out" (5.3.102–3) that he nevertheless becomes in his Volscian phase. Two short quotes drawn from that phase contain the allegorical clue to how this impossibility is finessed by our author. "I do not know what witchcraft's in him" (4.7.2), Aufidius's lieutenant first observes of Coriolanus's power to draw allegiance from his Volscian troops; we, of course, do know what that witchcraft is, having seen its operation at Corioli, as well as throughout the Shakespeare canon, and know that it is oratory, rhetoric, with the use of the loaded word "witchcraft" pointing to its ultimate source, Shakespeare himself. Cominius's reference in the same context to Coriolanus being the Volsce's "god . . . like a thing / Made by some other deity than Nature" (4.6.91–92), has a similar implication, Shakespeare being the "other deity," "murd'ring impossibility [with his rhetoric], to make / What cannot be slight work" (5.3.61–62).

Both absolute contrariety and impossibility, in this and other structural elements of the play, have a bearing on the important allegorical question of "Rome" as free-floating signifier, as I have called it, as well. In history, in Plutarch's simple world of facts, "Rome" exists; it is tangible and real; in Shakespeare's world of rhetoric on the other hand the question is by no means so simple. I mentioned earlier the perfect symmetry in the political structure of republican Rome, that Machiavelli sees as the key to its strength, and that Shakespeare is careful exactly to reflect in *Coriolanus*. From a rhetorical standpoint, the fact that the state is divided into two parties, both of whom use the word *Rome* in reference to their particular interests and, as they consider them, rights, but with each regarding the other as an obstruction to the enjoyment of those rights, means that "Rome" cannot be one thing. The word cannot mean the same thing to either party, and in many ways indeed must have an opposite meaning to each. Probably not much more needs to be said on this paradox than this, which hangs as a irresolvable verbal conundrum just past the edge of consciousness, I suspect, for most of us, in our experience of the play. But Shakespeare does more than simply leave the matter a disturbing undertone in the play, rather prodding it into consciousness again and again with specific references that reinforce the point in all its impossible strangeness.

References abound in the mouths of all, plebeians and patricians, as groups and individuals, to "Rome" or to "country"—the terms are effectively interchangeable—that both point *to* and at the same time *away from* any factual reality assumed to be designated by the words. The paradox is raised as early as the first scene, in the Second Citizen's reference to the "services" Marcius "has done for his country" (28–29), which is balanced against the First Citizen's qualifying "soft-conscienced men can be content to *say* it was for his country" (36–37, italics mine). Marcius himself understandably takes the Second Citizen's position, with "As for my country I have shed my blood" (3.1.76ff.). His mother too concurs, lamenting the injustice of banishing one who has "struck more blows for Rome" (4.2.18) than his accusers have "spoken words"—his accusers the tribunes, who themselves have to concede that "he hath / Serv'd well for Rome" (3.3.84). Whatever "Rome/ country" signifies in such references as these, then, it cannot also signify in many others. There is an early reference to Marcius as "of Rome worse hated than of [Aufidius]" (1.2.13), for example; or, similarly the officers in 2.2 recognize Marcius as "deserv[ing] worthily of his country" (l. 23), while at the same time he "seeks [the people's] hate, . . . and leaves nothing undone that can fully discover him their opposite" (18, 19–21). The *contrariety* represented in the word "opposite" here is then climaxed in the fear Menenius later expresses of "parties [, which may] break out / And sack great Rome with Romans" (3.1.315–16).

The unavoidable if strange conclusion to which we are driven regarding the use of the word and concept "Rome" in these various contexts is that as a *word* it functions in absolute freedom, in *mental* frames of reference peculiar to the user and independent of any mere geographical or historical actuality. Nor need such frames of reference be the same at all times even for the users: "Rome" means patrician Rome and his notion of patrician values in Coriolanus's early references, but when his class breaks rank with him, the "country" *they* now represent becomes "canker'd" (4.4.90–91). And a similar flexibility is visible on the plebeian side as well, in the tribunes, condemning Coriolanus as an "enemy to the people and his country" (3.3.118), while themselves are as contemptuous of the "stinking breaths" (2.1.226) of their ostensible constituents, behind the screen of their manipulative rhetoric, as any patrician.

The trick of impossible contradiction Shakespeare pulls off in *Coriolanus* can perhaps be seen most clearly in the problematic concept once again of "honor" (interchangeable with "nobility" in this instance), closely associated with the idea of *Rome*, but lacking the concrete, physical basis of the latter to potentially cloud the issue in any way. The background already developed in this essay will have given some direction to the consideration of how this concept functions, but there are additional implications of the term's use in this play that bring out its essential rhetoricality with particular force. As far as the association of "Rome" and "honor," conceived as essentially a single concept, is concerned, the figure of Volumnia stands as the personification of that notion, having shaped her son in its image—ready to "die nobly for [his] country" (1.3.24–25)—and maintaining it consistently throughout the play. The first of many impossible contradictions inherent in the concept at the same time, however, has already shown up prior to these first hyperbolical effusions of Volumnia, in that same son's confession of "envying [the] nobility" (1.1.228) of his and Rome's archenemy Aufidius, testimony that nobility/honor may be conceived abstractly, as a personal attribute and ideal *not* necessarily linked to country in any way. Just as Othello's "love" for Desdemona, which, since its real basis was not in her but in his own inflated self-image, is easily abandoned, so too Coriolanus and his "love [of] his country" (3.1.305). Indeed, the situation is even more blatantly problematic in his case than in that of Othello, given the simultaneous emphasis on his "constant temper" throughout, as well ironically as the fact that the end of the adventure brings him effectively back to where he started, with personal "honor" sacrificed to the greater "honor" of country.

The idea of "honor" as an abstraction, particularly as it is associated with the figure of Coriolanus, clearly its central focus, introduces another impossible contradiction into the play that Shakespeare again ensures his audience, even if only subliminally, must register. The contradiction in this case is, for a number of reasons, more directly rhetorical in nature than that associated with *Rome*. There is an initial similarity in the two cases; as the word *Rome* detaches itself from the factual realm, taking on a definition "peculiar to the user," so in a sense the word *honor*, with the critical difference, however, that "honor" has none of the factual reality of Rome to detach from, but as a purely ideal concept has literally no existence except in the medium of language. The contradiction this fact entails in Coriolanus's case is obvious; thus while one of the pillars of his "honor" is the devaluation of language—that only deeds weigh, not words—there can be at the same time no "honor" *without* the words that describe, that indeed create it; rhetoric is inescapable. We have already seen that Coriolanus's refusal either to flatter or to accept "flattery" is itself a rhetorical device, like Cordelia's first speech in *Lear*, but a necessary corollary of that fact completely overlooked by all it may be but Shakespeare is that, protests notwithstanding, he does, as he *must*, derive his sense of self, to the extent at least that "honor" is a component of that sense of self, from exactly the stirring rhetoric and flattering

words that have surrounded him since infancy—the "praises" of
Volumnia that "made [him] first a soldier" (3.2.108). That this is
in fact the case, whether conscious or no on "his" part, is patent
both implicitly, in the monumental egotism with which his sense
of self, of honor, and of Rome are inextricably intertwined; and
explicitly as well, in things he himself says that betray the trans-
parency of his antirhetorical stance. The examples seen earlier of
his battlefield oratory loom large among these, and an even more
explicit example of the same would be his parting words to his
mother going into banishment, that "you were us'd to load me /
With precepts that would make invincible / The heart that conn'd
them" (4.1.9–11). The seal, finally, is put on this aspect of his
character in the pride he continues to take in the "surname"
(4.5.68) *Coriolanus*, an epithet of honor coined for the sole purpose of crowning the uniqueness of his achievements and gifts.

Another essential contradiction is also associated with
"honor" in the play, that further rhetoricizes it, isolating it in the
domain of language, separate absolutely from any real-world application or meaning. Detaching "honor" from love of country, as
we saw Marcius do in his first reference to Aufidius in 1.1, prob-
lematizes the concept from the beginning of the play, placing it
in a kind of limbo whereby all later references to it are called
into question. What *is* "honor" if at one time it is inseparable
from love of country, and at another, as happens when Coriolanus attacks his "canker'd country," is transformed into its opposite? There is but one answer to this question—that it is a
word, and nothing more. As well as its association with war,
where love of country is essential to its meaning, dictionary definitions of the term will cover personal applications, in such
things as honesty and uprightness of character, components that
Marcius is equally proud in the possession of. Yet here too in several ways Shakespeare makes it impossible in the course of the
play to link these traits to the characters, including Marcius, in
any meaningful way. The questionable integrity his antirhetorical stance involves hardly qualifies as entirely "honorable" in the
personal sense, but there are deeper implications in both his and
others' behavior in the area where personal and national honor
overlap.

Of particular relevance here is the role of what both claim as
"honor" in the relations between Marcius and Aufidius. The separation of personal from national honor in their rivalry is a prob-

lem in itself, but it is compounded by the later revelation, to us, though not to Marcius, that the "nobility" he "envies" in his rival is in fact nonexistent: "sham'd" (1.8.14) for the final time by Marcius when having to be rescued again by his "seconds" in the battle of Corioli, Aufidius's "emulation" of his rival, (1.10.12) that once "had . . . honor in't" (13), is no more:

> for where
> I thought to crush him in an equal force,
> True sword to sword, I'll potch at him some way,
> Or wrath or craft may get him.
>
> (1.10.13–16)

Marcius is not himself necessarily tainted directly in this repudiation of "honor" in his rival. To the extent that national honor is related to personal integrity, however, as being the same trait carried into a larger arena, he is marked by the failings that honor on the battlefield may itself be subject to, offering no argument to his mother, indeed accepting her slippery rhetoric in justification of "dissembling with [one's] nature":

> If it be honor in your wars to seem the same you are not, which for your best ends you adopt your policy, how is it less or worse that it shall hold companionship in peace with honor as in war? (4.2.46–50)

The rhetorical implications of "dissembling with [one's] nature" bring us back to what has been the central question in this essay and this book, and may provide a focal point again around which both can be brought to a conclusion. The distinguishing feature of Coriolanus's personality as bequeathed to Shakespeare from Plutarch was the combination of "rude and rough . . . nature" and the "lack of education" which together provided a recipe for tragedy. Through all the complexity of character and plot in *Coriolanus*, both personal and political, that Plutarchian essence is retained. We touched earlier on this as an "art vs. nature" issue, developed by Shakespeare into the central rhetorical issue the play engages. The "art" aspect covered, the "nature" component of the problem has important thematic implications yet to be considered.

At the beginning of act 2 there is a brief exchange between Menenius and the tribunes that hints subtly at some of the darker aspects of this side of things in the play:

Sic.   Nature teaches beasts to know their friends.
Men. Pray you, who does the wolf love?
Sic.   The lamb.
Men. Ay, to devour him, as the hungry plebeians would the noble
        Marcius.
Bru.   He's a lamb indeed, that baes like a bear.

                                                    (2.1.5–10)

The juxtapositioning of the words "nature," "beasts," "friends,"
and "love," in this exchange is rhetorically significant for its suggestion of an impossibly contradictory human essence—at once
"noble," capable of "friendship," and even "love," yet by "nature,"
whether plebeian or patrician, "beastly," driven by appetite and
poised to "devour" everything that stands in its path. The conventional function of the art of rhetoric, then, given this situation, is to cultivate the former qualities, restraining the latter;
while the subversive perspective on the same art is the opposite—that rhetoric is a *mask only* of civilization and benevolence,
no check, indeed, but an aid to devouring nature in pursuing its
relentless course. And while conventional interpretations of both
the historical Coriolanus and of Shakespeare's play would see
the former as its major theme, and fairly so, faithful to his
deeper rhetorical principle of impossible contradiction, Shakespeare is equally careful to provide data in his play for the latter
interpretation as well.

    Much of what has already been covered here can be seen as
offering indirect support for this interpretation, but references to
nature specifically, primarily in relation to the main character,
provide direct evidence for it. Particularly prominent here would
be Coriolanus's oedipal fixation again, indicative of a nature that
remains fundamentally infantile. In classic Freudian theory, of
course, to be infantile means to be self-centered, driven by the
animalistic id, a feature of Coriolanus's character that not only
his detractors are pleased to point out—counting on him to "fall
in a rage" when provoked, "as is his nature" (2.3.255)—but, more
importantly, that he himself is driven to admit at critical junctures in his career. The case is straightforward, the evidence
abundant, that *egotism* is the actual driving force, behind
"honor," behind "country," in everything that Coriolanus, and by
implication others as well, do. Aufidius and the tribunes serve
thus as foils to Coriolanus in this regard, reflecting back, as in a
mirror, the image he presents to them. The tribunes "blame Mar-

cius for being proud?" says Menenius; "infant-like," they are themselves "unmeriting, proud, violent . . . fools" (2.1.34, 39). And similarly with Aufidius, who behind his rhetoric of "honor" recognizes only one value, namely the satisfaction of his ego by the annihilation of his nemesis. These are the same features that come out—in aggrandized, tragic form—in Coriolanus's reply to the plebeians on his banishment:

> You common cry of curs, whose breath I hate,
> As reek o' th' rotten fens, whose loves I prize
> As the dead carcasses of unburied men
> That do corrupt my air—I banish you
>
> (3.3.122–25)—

or, similarly, in the monumental egotism of his wrath at being called by Aufidius "boy":

> False hound!
> If you have writ your annals true, 'tis there
> That, like an eagle in a dove-cote, I
> Fluttered your Volscians in Corioli
> Alone I did it, 'Boy'!
>
> (5.6.113–17)

The closest parallel to what Shakespeare does in *Coriolanus* is probably with *Lear*, in making the impossible magically not only believable but irresistible, indeed *true*, in the main characters in both plays. As there is authentic nobility in Coriolanus, so there is authentic kingliness in Lear, but at the same time childishness, egotism, moral confusion in both. Coriolanus's dilemma becomes our own:

> My soul aches
> To know, when two authorities are up,
> Neither supreme, how soon confusion
> May enter 'twixt the gap of both, and take
> The one by th' other."
>
> (3.1.108–12)

Notes

Chapter 1. Introduction:
The Culture Connection

1. Hanna H. Gray, "Renaissance Humanism: The Pursuit of Excellence," *Journal of the History of Ideas* 24 (1963): 503.

2. Quoted in Nancy S. Streuver, *The Language of History in the Renaissance* (Princeton: Princeton University Press, 1970), 115.

3. C. S. Lewis, *English Literature in the Sixteenth Century* (New York: Oxford University Press, 1954), 61.

4. J. W. H. Atkins, *English Literary Criticism: The Renaissance* (New York: Barnes & Noble, 1947), 68.

5. Elizabeth J. Sweeting, *Early Tudor Criticism, Linguistic and Literary* (New York: Russell, 1964), 114.

6. Samuel Daniel, *Poems and a Defence of Ryme*, ed. Arthur Colby Sprague (Chicago: University of Chicago Press, 1972), 96.

7. Thomas Wilson, *The Art of Rhetorique* (1553; reprint, Amsterdam: Da Capo, 1969), Fol. 86.

8. Leonard Cox, *The Arte of Crafte of Rhethoryke*, ed. Frederick Ives Carpenter (1530; reprint, New York: AMS, 1971), 41–42.

9. Quoted in T. W. Baldwin, *William Shakespere's Small Latine & Lesse Greeke,* 2 vols. (Urbana: University of Illinois Press, 1944), 2:45.

10. Sir Walter Raleigh, introduction to *The Book of the Courtier*, by Baldassare Castiglione (New York: AMS, 1967), lxii.

11. T. S. Eliot, *Selected Prose,* ed. John Hayward (Harmondsworth: Penguin, 1953), 102.

12. Quoted in Baldwin, *Shakespere's Small Latine,* 1:104.

13. Desiderius Erasmus, *Collected Works of Erasmus,* 86 vols. (Toronto: University of Toronto Press, 1974–93), 24:667.

14. Roger Ascham, *The Schoolmaster* (1570; reprint, Ithaca: Cornell University Press, 1967), 138.

15. Cf. the following from J. E. Spingarn, about developments in France:

With Du Bellay's *Defense et Illustration de la Langue francaise* (1549) modern literature and modern criticism in France may be said to begin. The *Defence* is a monument of the influence of Italian upon French literary and linguistic criticism. The purpose of the book, as its title implies, is to defend the French language, and to indicate the means by which it can approach more closely to dignity and perfection. The fundamental contention of Du Bellay is, first, that the French language is capable of attaining perfection; and, secondly, that it can only hope to by imitating Greek and Latin. (Spingarn, *A History of Literary Criticism in the Renaissance* [1924; reprint, Westport Conn.: Greenwood, 1976], 177–78)

16. Quoted in Richard Foster Jones, *The Triumph of the English Language: A Survey of Opinions Concerning the Vernacular from the Introduction of Printing to the Restoration* (Stanford: Stanford University Press, 1953), 12.

17. Sir Thomas Elyot, *The Boke Named the Gouernour,* ed. Henry Herbert Stephen Croft, 2 vols. (1531; reprint, New York: Burt Franklin, 1967), 1:123.

18. Seneca, *The Tenne Tragedies of Seneca,* (1581; reprint, New York: Burt Franklin, 1967), 162.

19. Daniel, *Poems,* 96.

20. George Puttenham, *The Arte of English Poesie,* ed. Gladys Doidge Willcock and Alice Walker (1589; reprint, Cambridge: Cambridge University Press, 1936), 5.

21. See Frederick Ives Carpenter, introduction to *The Arte or Crafte of Rhethoryke,* by Leonard Cox (1530; reprint, New York: AMS, 1971), 25–30.

22. William Harrison Woodward, *Desiderius Erasmus Concerning the Aim and Method of Education* (1904; reprint, New York: Burt Franklin, 1971), 167.

23. Ibid., 63.

24. Ascham, *Schoolmaster,* 150, 152.

25. *The Schoolmaster* as we have it breaks off just as its discussion of Cicero ("that example to follow") was apparently set to begin (Ascham, 162). Ascham also mentions in *The Schoolmaster* (141) that he is going to treat Cicero "more fully in fitter place," which may mean in his book *De Imitatione* that he intended to write, which would presumably have been his manual of style, based on Cicero. For discussion of Erasmus's less idolatrous approach to the whole question of Ciceronian imitation see "Erasmus and the Ciceronians," in Woodward, *Desiderius Erasmus,* 51–60.

26. Walter J. Ong, *Ramus, Method, and the Decay of Dialogue* (New York: Farrar, Straus & Giroux, 1979), 92.

27. Stephen Cohen, *The Language of Power, the Power of Language: The Effects of Ambiguity on Sociopolitical Structures as Illustrated in Shakespeare's Plays* (Cambridge: Harvard University Press, 1987), 2. For additional background on the struggle between Latin and the vernacular in the later sixteenth century in England see chap. 2, "The Expanding Vocabulary," of S. S. Hussey, *The Literary Language of Shakespeare* (London: Longmans, 1982), 10–33, and the chapter "Language Environment" of N. F. Blake, *Shakespeare's Language: An Introduction* (London: Macmillan, 1983), 15–27. A somewhat different view of the uneasy relations between classical and vernacular languages in this period is that taken by James S. Baumlin, who sees the vernacular as "borrowing" its historical legitimacy from the classical tongues:

For nationhood and a prince's claims to legitimacy of rule demand a myth of origins for the nation's language as well as its people, a cultural identity located within a heroic or "classical" linguistic past. The poet of

The Shepheardes Calendar ennobles—and in a sense enables, empowers—the vernacular by archaizing it, valorizing it vis-à-vis the dead and venerated classical languages; in a word, the shepherd poet classicizes English, elevating it to the status of a classical language by uncovering its quasi-mythic past and exhuming its ancient vocabulary. The "native strengths" and beauties of this "classical" English become a source of cultural pride and translate, ultimately, into self-legitimizing political power–ample compensation for the fact that the shepherd poet's language is as dead, as far from the living spoken vernacular, as the classical languages it emulates. (Baumlin, *John Donne and the Rhetorics of Renaissance Discourse* [Columbia: University of Missouri Press, 1991], 1)

And Paula Blank extrapolates from Mikhail Bakhtin to express a similar view to Baumlin's on this question. Bakhtin holds that the Renaissance cult of classical Latin was paradoxical in several ways. Medieval Latin as the *lingua franca* of Europe had grown more and more debased over the centuries; but the classical revival, rather than reinvigorating the language, actually spelled its doom: "Cicero's Latin, thr[owing] light upon the . . . ugliness and limitations . . . of medieval Latin . . . made it a dead language. The contemporary world . . . broke the bonds of Cicero's language and its pretense at being a living idiom . . . The vernacular invaded all the spheres of ideology and expelled Latin" (Bakhtin, *Rabelais and His World* [Bloomington: Indiana University Press, 1984], 466, 465). Agreeing with Bakhtin to this point, Blank then rejects his view of this change as marking the end of "linguistic dogmatism" (Bakhtin, *Rabelais,* 473) in Europe, holding instead that a new "elite dialect . . . repossessed . . . the domains . . . once held by Latin, [a] new modern myth of monoglossia . . . as powerful and totalizing as the last. Latin was dead—but long live the King's English" (Blank, *Broken English: Dialects and the Politics of Language in Renaissance Writings* [London: Routledge, 1996], 14).

28. Lee A. Sonnino, *A Handbook to Sixteenth-Century Rhetoric* (London: Routledge, 1968), 2.

29. See Lawrence V. Ryan, introduction to *The Schoolmaster,* by Roger Ascham (1570; reprint Ithaca: Cornell University Press), xix.

30. Lewis, *English Literature,* 61.

31. Brian Vickers, *The Artistry of Shakespeare's Prose* (London: Methuen), 30. V. K. Whitaker notes that because of the scarcity of books, "a high proportion of the grammar and rhetoric was memorized outright. So the contemporary theorists on education commanded" (Whitaker, *Shakespeare's Use of Learning* [San Marino, Calif.: Huntington, 1953]), 395). M. L. Clarke notes that in John Brinsley's school, "the evening was the time for memorizing and the morning for repetition," for "the statutes of Westminster lay down that at seven o'clock in the morning all the classes shall recite from memory the passages read the previous day" (Clarke, *Classical Education in Britain* [Cambridge: Cambridge University Press, 1959], 13–14).

32. Ascham, *Schoolmaster,* 14.

33. Quoted in T. W. Baldwin, *Shakespere's Small Latine,* 1:281.

34. That the term "sixteenth-century rhetoric" is assumed by twentieth-century scholars to mean *only* this system is demonstrable even in the most recent studies of the Shakespearean rhetoric, of which Whitney French Bolton's *Shakespeare's English: Language in the History Plays* (Oxford: Basil Blackwell,

1992), Gert Ronberg's "The Art of the Matter," in *A Way With Words: The Language of English Renaissance Literature* (London: Edward Arnold, 1992), 128–90; and Christy Desmet's *Reading Shakespeare's Characters: Rhetoric, Ethics, and Identity* (Amherst: University of Massachusetts Press, 1992), may be cited as examples.

35. Donald Lemen Clark concisely covers the moral biases of classical rhetoric in his *Rhetoric and Poetry in the English Renaissance* (New York: Columbia University Press, 1922), 23–26. He notes Quintilian, for example, "defining rhetoric as the *ars bene dicendi*, or good public speech (II, xv, 38). Here the *bene* implies not only effectiveness, but moral worth; for in Quintilian's conception the orator is a good man skilled in public speech." He further notes the *Ad Herennium* "defin[ing] the subject matter of rhetoric . . . as 'whatever in customs or laws is to the public benefit'" (25).

36. Wilson, "The Preface," in *Arte of Rhetorique;* Henry Peacham, *The Garden of Eloquence* (1593; reprint, Delmar, N.Y.: Scholars' Facsimiles, 1977), "The Epistle Dedicatorie" (A.B.ij.iij); Francis Bacon, *The Advancement of Learning*, 5th ed., ed. William Aldis Wright (Oxford: Clarendon Press, 1963), 178–79.

37. Bacon, *Advancement*, 178.

38. William Fulwood, *The Enemy of Idlenesse. Teaching How to Indite Epistles* (London: Henrie Middleton, 1582), 9.

39. His translation of Ortensio Lando's *Paradossi*. See Celeste Turner Wright, "'Lazarus Pyott' and Other Inventions of Anthony Munday," *Philological Quarterly* 42 (1963).

40. Baldassare Castiglione, *The Book of the Courtier*, trans. Sir Thomas Hoby (1561; reprint, New York: AMS, 1967), 301–2.

41. See Sonnino, *Handbook,* 221, 198.

42. Niccolò Machiavelli, *The Prince*, trans. Robert M. Adams (New York: Norton, 1977), 67.

43. William Kempe, *The Education of Children in Learning: Declared by the Dignitie, Vitilite, and Method Thereof,* in *Four Tudor Books on Education*, ed. Robert D. Pepper (Delmar, N.Y.: Scholars' Facsimiles, 1977), 233.

44. Quoted in Wilbur Samuel Howell, *Logic and Rhetoric in England, 1500–1700* (New York: Russell & Russell, 1956), 141.

45. A critique of the inductive method is beyond the scope of this study, but for more detailed discussion of this point I would refer the reader to the section "Validity" under the topic "Modern Logic" in *The Encyclopaedia of Philosophy*, vols. 5/6, 13.

46. See Howell, *Logic and Rhetoric,* 25–6.

47. Bacon, *The Philosophical Works of Francis Bacon*, ed. John M. Robertson (1905; reprint Freeport, N.Y.: Books for Libraries, 1970), 202.

48. That Bacon could not have been wholly unconscious of his own skilled use of a rhetoric far beyond the formal in the case of the *Advancement* is pointedly attested to by the fact that among the King's many gifts that he sets himself to praise, he deliberately singles out the King's mastery of the art of *artless eloquence*:

> And for your gift of speech, I call to mind what Cornelius Tacitus saith of Augustus Caesar: *Augusto profluens, et quae principem deceret, eloquentia fuit.* For if we note it well, speech that is uttered with labour and dif-

ficulty, or speech that savoureth of the affectation of art and precepts, or speech that is framed after the imitation of some pattern of eloquence, though never so excellent; all this hath somewhat servile, and holding of the subject. But your Majesty's manner of speech is indeed prince-like, flowing as from a fountain, and yet streaming and branching itself into nature's order, full of facility and felicity, imitating none, and inimitable by any. (2–3)

49. The two dialogues in which Plato's distrust of rhetoricians is expounded at length are the *Gorgias* and the *Phaedrus*. Later students of both Plato and the art of rhetoric, among them Aristotle, Cicero, and St. Augustine, attempted to redeem rhetoric from Plato's charges. Aristotle, says Everett Lee Hunt, "unmistakably sides with Gorgias against Plato . . . , express[ing] his belief that rhetoric makes for the prevalence of truth and righteousness" (Hunt, "Plato and Aristotle on Rhetoric and Rhetoricians," *Historical Studies of Rhetoric and Rhetoricians*, ed. Raymond F. Howes [Ithaca: Cornell University Press, 1965], 58). Cicero is a Platonist clearly of the Renaissance stamp, adapting Plato's theory of ideas to "the image of perfect eloquence in the mind," in Erwin Panofsky's translation from *The Orator* (Panofsky, *Idea: A Concept in Art Theory*, trans. Joseph J. S. Peake [Columbia: University of South Carolina Press, 1968], 12). Augustine essentially follows Cicero; in the words of Mazzeo, he "brought rhetoric back to its ancient concern with truth by recreating a platonic view of rhetoric in the midst of fourth-century sophistic" (Joseph Anthony Mazzeo, *Renaissance and Seventeenth-Century Studies* [London: Routledge, 1964], 3). Howell develops the plausible theory that Bacon's triune division of the mind (reason, imagination, affection) in the discussion of rhetoric in *The Advancement of Learning* is an adaptation of Plato's myth of the charioteer in the *Phaedrus* (Howell, *Logic and Rhetoric*, 372).

50. Richard Sherry, *A Treatise of the Figures of Grammar and Rhetoricke* (London: n.p., 1555), fol. lx, a–b.

51. A. Bartlett Giamatti, "Proteus Unbound: Some Versions of the Sea God in the Renaissance," in *The Disciplines of Criticism*, ed. Peter Demetz, Thomas Greene, and Lowry Nelson, Jr. (New Haven: Yale University Press, 1968), 451.

52. J. B. Steane, *Marlowe: A Critical Study* (Cambridge: Cambridge University Press, 1964), 11.

53. Harry Levin, *The Overreacher: A Study of Christopher Marlowe* (Cambridge, Mass.: Harvard University Press, 1952), 2–5. The nondramatic postscript to the play, "*Terminat hora diem, Terminat Author opus*," makes the identification of Faustus with his creator explicit. For discussion of this point see Alvin B. Kernan, *The Playwright as Magician: Shakespeare's Image of the Poet in the English Public Theater* (New Haven: Yale University Press, 1979), 353. It is ironic, as Greg points out, that in all probability this line was inserted by the printer on his own initiative. (See W. W. Greg, *Marlowe's Doctor Faustus: 1604–1616*, ed. W. W. Greg [Oxford: Clarendon Press, 1950], 403.)

54. *Doctor Faustus*, 1.3.10, and 29–30. For the Raleigh "circle," on anagrammatizing the name of God, see Paul H. Kocher, "Marlowe's Atheist Lecture," *The Journal of English and Germanic Philology* 39 (1940): 98–106; reprint *Marlowe: A Collection of Critical Essays*. Ed. Clifford Leech (Englewood Cliffs, N.J.: Prentice-Hall, 1964), 165.

55. Quoted in Kocher, "Marlowe's Atheist Lecture," 164.

56. Quoted in Gray, "Renaissance Humanism," 207. For fuller discussion of rhetoric as a theme in *The Art of War*, see also E. Raimondi, "Machiavelli and the Rhetoric of the Warrior," *Modern Language Notes* 92 (1977), and William E. Wiethoff, "The Martial 'Virtue' of Rhetoric in Machiavelli's *Art of War*," *Quarterly Journal of Speech* 64 (1978).

57. Quoted in Kocher, "Marlowe's Atheist Lecture," 164.

58. Ralph Lever, *The Art of Reason, Rightly Termed Witcraft* (London: n.p., 1573), title page.

59. Bacon comes even closer to direct reference to his craft in things like his discussion of ciphers in book 6 of the *De Augmentis*, noting that besides the public there are secret and private alphabets, the use of which enables, in the words of James Stephens, "learned men to pass information without arousing suspicion" (Stephens, *Francis Bacon and Style of Science* [Chicago: University of Chicago Press, 1975], 72). And though no Bacon, Lever too has subtlety enough to know that "knowledge and diligence" alone will never achieve "witcraft," that "sleight, and cunning" (Lever, *Art of Reason,* dedication) are necessary to the discipline as well. Or a most memorable example of such a signal is found in one of the two principal works of one of the age's greatest rhetorical scholars, the person, according to Richard Foster Jones, than whom "no one has ever . . . sensed more distinctly the essential nature of a living language," Richard Mulcaster, headmaster of the Merchant Taylors' School and tutor to Edmund Spenser. In his discussion of what Jones calls "the law of mutation" in language, to which Mulcaster, with uncanny political as well as linguistic appropriateness, applied the term "'prerogative,'" Mulcaster talks about this feature of language as (in Jones' paraphrase) "spring[ing] from what he describes in quaint terms as a 'soulish substance,' 'a secret mystery,' and a 'quick-'ning spirit'" (Jones, *Triumph of the English Language,* 165), all of which expressions have far more meaning, in terms of Elizabethan rhetorico/political values, than clearly are dreamt of in Jones's "quaint" philosophy.

60. Stephen Gardiner, *A Detection of the Devils Sophistries, wherwith he robbeth the unlearned people, of the true byleef, in the most blessed Sacrament of the aulter* (J. Hereforde at the costes of R. Toye, 1546), fol. V[b].

61. Quoted in Frank L. Huntley, "*Macbeth* and Jesuitical Equivocation," *PMLA* 79 (1964): 393, 395.

62. For recent perspectives on this subject see Kenneth Burke, *A Grammar of Motives and a Rhetoric Motives* (Cleveland: Meridian, 1962), 573–79 and 688–704; also Paolo Valesio, *Novantiqua: Rhetorics as a Contemporary Theory* (Bloomington: Indiana University Press, 1980).

63. Streuver, *Language of History,* 33.

64. Hunt, for example, notes that Plato loads his argument in the *Gorgias* by setting up straw men: Polus, who "falls an easy victim to the Socratic dialectic"; and Gorgias himself, of whom Hunt observes, "it is difficult to believe that the real Gorgias would have been so easily entrapped" by Socrates's arguments (Hunt, "Plato and Aristotle," 40). Aristotle's ambitious attempt at a definitive rehabilitation of rhetoric from Plato's charges by "proving" its utility (i.e., its affinity for truth), the model for all later advocates of the art, fails similarly by reason of an inner contradiction. The fallacy of *Ignoratio elenchi* or irrelevance would appear to be the downfall of Aristotle's "proof" of the utility of rhetoric.

His syllogism may be reconstructed as follows: Premise: Rhetoric is defined as "the faculty of observing in any given case the available means of persuasion" (Aristotle, *The Works of Artistotle*, vol. 11, trans. and ed. W. Rhys Roberts [Oxford: Clarendon, 1959], 1355b). The same passage is translated by Theodore Buckley as the "faculty of considering all the possible means of persuasion on every subject.") See Aristotle, *Aristotle's Treatise on Rhetoric and Poetic*, trans. Theodore Buckley (London: G. Bell and Sons, 1914), 11. Premise 2: "things that are true and . . . just have a natural tendency to prevail [i.e., persuade] over their opposites" (Roberts, 1355a). In Buckley the same passage reads, "truth and justice are in their nature stronger [i.e., more persuasive] than their opposites"(7). Conclusion: "rhetoric is useful" (Roberts, 1355a).

The fallacy lies between the major and minor premises, the major referring to all the means of persuasion ("The modes of persuasion are the only true constituents of the art: everything else is merely accessory" [Roberts, 1354a]), means which must include irrational as well as rational means—i.e., emotional appeals, appeals to patriotism, false arguments and accusations, etc.—while the minor premise introduces the selective criterion of *truth*, thus falsely twisting the concept of *persuasion* into rational persuasion only.

65. See, e.g., Charles Sears Baldwin, *Ancient Rhetoric and Poetic* (Westport, Conn: Greenwood, 1971), 87 ff.

66. Aristotle, ed. Buckley, 8.

67. Quoted in Howell, *Logic and Rhetoric*, 117.

68. Sister Mary Geraldine describes sixteenth-century responses as follows:

Although it is unlikely that Erasmus, who was not modest about his achievements, underestimated the worth of his work, it is surprising to find his Renaissance admirers failing to recognize its difference from other paradoxes. To some the *Praise* seems little more than a merry commendation of folly; others consider it a Jeremiad attacking immorality and ecclesiastical abuse. Sir John Harington, for instance, in *The Metamorphosis of Ajax*, mentions the *Praise* as one of many such pieces, serious treatments of light subjects, of which he cites seven. (Sister Mary Geraldine, "Erasmus and the Tradition of Paradox," *Studies in Philology* 61 [1964]): 99)

69. John Jewel, "Oration Against Rhetoric," ca. 1548, trans. Hoyt H. Hudson, *Quarterly Journal of Speech* 14 (1928): 375.

70. By no means the only Mundayan "paradox" in Shakespeare, Parolles proving virginity a bad thing in *All's Well*, and Feste proving Olivia a fool in *Twelfth Night*, being two others that spring immediately to mind.

71. Seneca the Elder, *Declamations*, 2 vols., trans. M. Winterbottom (London: Heinemann, 1974), 2:7.

72. Quoted in C. S. Baldwin, *Ancient Rhetoric*, 88.

73. Seneca the Elder, *Declamations*, 1:121

74. E. F. Watling, introduction to *Four Tragedies and Octavia*, by Lucius Annaeus Seneca (Hammondsworth: Penguin, 1966), 9.

75. Quoted in ibid.

76. See, for example, Tacitus, *The Annals of Imperial Rome*, trans. Michael Grant (Harmondsworth: Penguin, 1956), 305 ff.

77. Cicero, *The Basic Works of Cicero*, ed. Moses Hadas (New York: Random, 1951), 182.

CHAPTER 2. RHETORIC, THEATER,
POETRY, AND SHAKESPEARE

1. A random culling of a few such studies from the shelves of any university library will confirm that, in discussions of Elizabethan drama, direct references to even the most popular of the classical rhetoricians, Cicero and Quintilian, are few and far between to say the least. In E. K. Chambers's classic *The Elizabethan Stage*, for example, the historical emphasis is entirely on the continuity of Elizabethan drama with the folk tradition: "At the close of the Middle Ages, the mimetic instinct, deep-rooted in the psychology of the folk, . . . reached the third term of its social evolution" (Chambers, *Elizabethan Stage*, 4 vols. [Oxford: Clarendon, 1923], 1:3). Chambers's four large volumes thus contain *not a single reference* to Cicero, Quintilian, or even Seneca. Ashley H. Thorndike's *Shakespeare's Theater* makes brief reference to the influence of classical drama in the Elizabethan theater, none whatever to classical rhetoric. He makes one reference to Seneca, none to Cicero or Quintilian. (See Thorndike, *Shakespeare's Theater* [New York: Macmillan, 1916], 17ff.) Glynne Wickham not only seconds Chambers's "continuity" thesis but goes him one further: where Chambers "dismiss[ed]" the records of civic pageantry as too ephemeral to warrant the tedium of full analysis," for Wickham it is this "failure to analyse [these records] which has deprived historians of the theater . . . of information in default of which any convincing connection between the ecclesiastical drama of the Middle Ages and the regular drama of Elizabethan times has been hard to establish" (Wickham, *Early English Stages 1300–1660*, vol. 1, 1300–1576 [London: Routledge, 1959], 63). Even contemporary criticism for the most part maintains this tradition; Louis Adrian Montrose, for example, places the "roots" of Elizabethan "professional drama" solely in its predecessor entertainments—"the late medieval religious drama; in the religiously and politically polemical drama of the turbulent mid-sixteenth century; and in the hodgepodge of popular entertainments—juggling and clowning, singing and miming, dancing and fencing, cockfighting and bearbaiting—from which it was still in the process of separating itself when Shakespeare began his theatrical career" (Montrose, "Of Gentlemen and Shepherds: The Politics of Elizabethan Pastoral Form," *ELH* 50 [1983], 19).

Esther Cloudman Dunn, in contrast to these, may be considered of the "miraculous birth" school of Elizabethan drama criticism, mentioning "the tremendous vitality of it, and the impression it gives of being sprung full-grown from barren ground" (Dunn, *The Literature of Shakespeare's England* [1930; reprint, New York: Cooper Square, 1969], 204). Among earlier critics coming at least a little closer to my position may be mentioned Alfred Harbage, in the key contextual observation that "one thing that *links the sixteenth century more closely to our own than to former times* is the importance allotted to persuasion" (Harbage, *Shakespeare and the Rival Traditions* [New York: Macmillan, 1952], 134; italics mine). A rare recent voice giving more explicit expression to the rhetoric/theater connection is Edward Burns:

> In so far as there is an emerging sense of 'the actor'[,] . . . it would seem to come out of the assumption, by the leading players on the Elizabethan professional stage, of that body of rhetorical skills which had,

since Aristotle, constituted the West's central discourse on the use and methods of writing and speaking. This kind of performer, then, is essentially a professional rhetorician, developing rhetorical skills . . . in order to present a theatrical performance.

. . . .

Acting and rhetoric are never seen as distinct entities[.] . . . The dramatic traditions of the universities, the Inns of Court and the choir schools had long explored acting and rhetoric as, essentially, the same. (Burns, *Character: Acting and Being on the Pre-Modern Stage* [London: St. Martin's, 1990], 10)

2. The beginnings of this secular and political trend may be spotted in details like Henry VII having in his employ, as John Payne Collier noted in 1831, "two distinct sets of players[,] . . . the Gentlemen of the Chapel, who appear to have performed always during the festivities of Christmas, and . . . the 'players of the King's interludes'," whose existence Edmund Malone discovered in a "remarkable and novel record" of 1494 (Collier, *The History of English Dramatic Poetry to the Time of Shakespeare and Annals of the Stage to the Restoration* [1831; reprint, New York: AMS, 1970], 36–37). T. W. Craik again confirms that "English secular drama virtually begins with the interludes performed at royal palaces and great houses at the . . . beginning of the Tudor period" (Craik, "The Tudor Interlude and Later Elizabethan Drama," *Elizabethan Theater*, ed. John Russell Brown and Bernard Harris [London: Edward Arnold, 1966], 37). The extent to which this alliance of drama and the court that developed during the Tudor epoch had political as well as social overtones is endlessly debatable, but the alliance itself is not. For discussion of some of its possible political ramifications, for example, see Conyers Read, "William Cecil and Elizabethan Public Relations," in *Elizabethan Government and Society*, ed. S. T. Bindoff, J. Hurstfield, and C. H. Williams (London: Athlone, 1961), 27–29, and Lawrence Stone, *The Crisis of the Aristocracy 1588–1641* (Oxford: Clarendon, 1965), 708–10.

3. Cf., for example, Felix E.Schelling, "If we consider now for a moment the men who wrote the earliest English plays, . . . we shall find their authors to have been either schoolmasters or courtiers. To the former belong Radclif, Rightwise, Palsgrave, . . . and Udall. . . . Among the courtiers were John Heywood, Gascoigne, and Sackville and Norton. . . . John Lyly was both courtier and schoolmaster" (Schelling, *Elizabethan Drama 1558–1642*, 2 vols. [New York: Houghton, 1908], 94).

4. Thomas Marc Parrott and Robert Hamilton Ball (*A Short View of Elizabethan Drama* [New York: Scribner's, 1943]), 35.

5. For brief discussion of the special *rhetorical* quality and appeal of Seneca's drama in the English Renaissance, see, for example, *The Reader's Encyclopaedia of Shakespeare*, s.v. "Seneca, Lucius Annaeus," 748. Lorraine Helms (*Seneca by Candlelight and Other Stories of Renaissance Drama* [Philadelphia: University of Pennsylvania Press, 1997]) provides an idiosyncratic viewpoint on several issues relevant here and earlier in this study on the influence of classical rhetoric in general and Seneca in particular on the rise of Elizabethan drama. She considers both essential, but distinguishes two classical traditions that correspond in several ways to Harbage's famous "rival" traditions of public and private theaters. She suggests first that the native folk tradition of drama

lives on in the public theaters (largely the domain of adult companies), and the Senecan dramatic traditions in the private, nurtured by the children's companies from the schools. She then finds correspondence in classical rhetoric itself to these two traditions, "the rival traditions in Rome" (25), as she calls them, the earlier Ciceronian, "'adapted to the ears of the multitude'" (quoted, 29), and the later Senecan, declamatory tradition, "the leisure discourse of the cultivated few" (29). The "elite tradition of Elizabethan Senecanism" is derived from both Senecas, father and son, who were considered a single person, author of both the *Controversiae* and, supremely, of the plays:

> The truly umbratical Roman drama is Senecan tragedy, in which the declamations live a lurid half-life. Like the rhetors, the tragedian privately offered *sententiae* and sensationalism to a coterie for whom the luxuries and terms of the Neronian court were the stuff of daily experience (28).

6. D. J. Palmer, "Elizabethan Tragic Heroes," in *Elizabethan Theater,* ed. John Russell Brown and Bernard Harris (London: Edward Arnold, 1966), 14. For further discussion of the political implications of *Gorboduc,* see A. M. Kinghorn, *The Chorus of History: Literary-Historical Relations in Renaissance Britain* (London: Blandford, 1971), 267–68.

7. G. Wilson Knight, "Lyly," in *Elizabethan Drama: Modern Essays in Criticism,* ed. Ralph J. Kaufmann (New York: Oxford University Press, 1961), 41.

8. For discussion of the popularity of Udall's text *Floures For Latine Spekynge* (1533) and of Shakespeare's exposure to it see T. W. Baldwin, *Shakespere's Small Latine,* 2:744–47. For the possible Udall-Shakespeare connection see William L. Edgerton, *Nicholas Udall* (New York: Twayne, 1965), 33. The connection is through Richard Mulcaster, pupil of Udall's at Eton, one of whose pupils at the Merchant Taylor's School in turn was Thomas Jenkins, who served as headmaster of the Stratford grammar school in Shakespeare's youth.

9. For a brief history of the children's companies, see, for example, Thorndike, *Shakespeare's Theater,* 253 ff. Among other significant points, Thorndike notes that "we have no extant plays before 1585 which we know were written primarily for professional adults" (249), indicating that it took more than twenty-five years for adult professional companies to displace the children's companies in popularity—companies like the children of the Chapel Royal, the children of Windsor, and the children of St. Paul's choir, which were well established at the beginning of Elizabeth's reign.

10. Elyot, *Boke Named the Gouernour,* 1:72–73. Italics mine.

11. T. W. Baldwin, *Shakespere's Small Latine,* 1:10.

12. Richard Mulcaster, *The Firste Parte of the Elementarie* (Np., n.p., 1582), 5. A number of pieces have recently appeared arguing that rhetoric's prominence in sixteenth-century English thought relates to the fact that political power was undergoing a shift from being the preserve strictly of the upper classes and the church into the hands of a new group whose claim to eminence was intellectual merit rather than either birth or position. Persuasion understandably figured prominently in the politico/social prescriptions of this group as being their only means of securing a place in the hierarchy of power in this transitional period. John D. Cox sees Elyot's replacement of Wolsey as Henry VIII's chief advisor as a symbolic moment marking this transition. Ciceronian rhe-

toric is upheld by this group as the model for the state because, as products themselves of this educational tradition, men like Elyot and Ascham invoke it to justify their own advancement. (See Cox, *Shakespeare and the Dramaturgy of Power* [Princeton: Princeton University Press, 1989], 41–60.)

Cox credits Frank Whigham with helping to form his views on these subjects. Whigham finds Thomas Wilson a particularly revealing source, quoting him to the unconsciously ironic effect that without being *persuaded* to do so, who would accept the place that he was born into?—thus persuasion becomes in effect the only thing holding the state together:

> Wilson makes possible a new conception of the hierarchical social order: not as a set of sealed ranks, not even as an order based on merit, . . . but as a system dominated by those who can convince others that they ought to submit. He effectively uncouples the existing order from transcendental authority and refounds it on the sheerly formal, learnable, vendible skills of persuasion. (Whigham, *Ambition and Privilege: The Social Tropes of Elizabethan Courtesy Theory* [Berkeley: University of California Press, 1984], 3)

Louis Montrose uses Puttenham, a nephew of Elyot ("Of Gentlemen," 437), to argue that the new courtierly group of the Tudor era sharpens the distinction between the "gentle" and the laboring classes in society *because* of their own origins in the latter, and that the pastoral convention both literary and social of the period—poetry and court masques—allegorize their transition from the one class to the other.

13. See Juan Luis Vives, *Vives: On Education. A Translation of the De Tradendis Disciplinis*, trans. Foster Watson (Totowa, N.J.: Rowman, 1971), 90–200, esp. 180–200. Ruth Kelso (*The Doctrine of the English Gentleman in the Sixteenth Century* [Gloucester, Mass.: Peter Smith, 1964]) has made an interesting comparison between Vives and Elyot as educators, showing that while their ideal of humanist education is similar, Elyot's is geared to state service, while Vives's is oriented more toward scholarship as an end in itself. This difference in approach, I suggest, is most striking in the strictness with which Vives adheres to the humanist ideal of virtue as the *sine qua non* of learning. As a teacher first and last Vives recognized no need for compromise, for example, on the principle of the use of rhetoric as an instrument of reason and truth: "[T]rue and genuine rhetoric is the expression of wisdom, which cannot in any way be separated from righteousness and piety" (*Vives: On Education*, 185). In calling Vives's educational theory dramatic, it must be understood, therefore, that theater per se at the same time is anathema to him, for the reason that its themes are imaginary and not based on life. As Foster Watson observes in comparing Bacon's boosting of the theater as an educational instrument with Vives's attitude:

> Bacon advocated stage plays [as] an educational method. . . . Vives in dealing with the *"Causes of Corruption of Rhetoric [Des Causis Corruptarum Artium*, bk 4 chap. 4], had urged the value of the declamation and had suggested the importance of oral repetition as an exercise for the memory, and had insisted on voice-training, and even required the student to regard gesture as a significant part of the oration. The training of the youth to "assurance and to being looked at," points which Bacon

considered the acting in stage plays would develop, . . . are not to be found in Vives. (Watson, introduction to *Vives: On Education. A Translation of the De Tradendis Disciplinis* [Totowa, N.J.: Rowman, 1971], cix–cx)

14. M. L. Clarke, *Rhetoric at Rome* (London: Cohen, 1953), 125.

15. B. L. Joseph, *Elizabethan Acting* (New York: Octagon, 1979), 10. And cf. also:

In Bulwer (J. Bulwer, *Chironomia* [1644] 24 ff.) we read: "The art was first formed by rhetoricians; afterwards amplified by poets, . . . but most strangely enlarged by actors, the ingenious counterfeitors of men's manners." He names Quintilian as the first Roman orator to collect "into an art" whatever his experience advised, including "so much from the theater to the forum as stood with the gravity of an orator." (*Elizabethan Acting,* 17)

Further elaboration of these principles, with respect especially to Quintilian's contribution, may be found in chapter 1 of Joseph R. Roach, *The Player's Passion: Studies in the Science of Acting* (Newark: University of Delaware Press, 1985), 23–57.

16. Cicero, *De Oratore*, 2 vols., trans. E. W. Sutton (Cambridge: Harvard University Press, 1959), 1:91.

17. Seneca, *Tenne Tragedies,* 197.

18. H. B. Charlton, *The Senecan Tradition in Renaissance Tragedy* (Manchester: Manchester University Press, 1946), cxli.

19. Eric C. Baade, introduction to *Seneca's Tragedies* (London: Macmillan, 1969), xx–xxi.

20. Norman T. Pratt, *Seneca's Drama* (Chapel Hill: University of North Carolina Press, 1983), 153.

21. Seneca, *Seneca's Tragedies,* ed. Eric C. Baade (London: Macmillan, 1969), 7.

22. See John W. Cunliffe, *The Influence of Seneca on Elizabethan Tragedy* (1893; reprint, Hamden, Conn.: Archon, 1965), 9–14.

23. Pratt, *Seneca's Drama*, 136.

24. Seneca, *Seneca's Tragedies*, 103. And cf. also B. L. Joseph's observations on the Elizabethans' awareness of the ironic tensions between the arts of oratory and acting:

In Shakespeare's day the difference as well as the similarity between the two was fully understood. Wright says that they "only differ in this, that these act feignedly, those really." The orators, "those" who act "really," express in action truly felt emotion to attain objectives by stirring up "all sorts of passions according to the exigencies of the matter." But "these," the players, who act "feignedly," use their action to communicate what they are experiencing within in order to represent an imaginary person, "only to delight." (*Elizabethan Acting,* 22)

25. Wilson, *Art of Rhetorique*, Fol. 3.

26. Allman, *Player King,* 10. Her suggestion that Shakespeare was personally exposed to these theories is based on T. W. Baldwin's speculation that Thomas Jenkins was Shakespeare's teacher at Stratford (Baldwin, *Shakespere's Small Latine*, 1:478–79). See note 6 above as well.

27. Bornstein, *Mirrors of Courtesy,* 115. In Bornstein's own note to this passage she cites Greenblatt's *Sir Walter Ralegh: The Renaissance Man and His Roles,* 52. Steven Mullaney takes a similar tack: his thesis is that the public theater was both a reflection and a critiquing of the theatricalization of culture under Elizabeth. He quotes Mulcaster in *The Queene's Majestie's Passage* that "he could not better terme the citie of London at that time, than a stage, wherein was shewed the wonderful spectacle of a noble-hearted princesse toward her most loving people" (Mullaney, *The Place of the Stage: License, Play and Power in Renaissance England* [Chicago: University of Chicago Press, 1988], 11–12). Montrose's chapter "The Power of Personation" (*The Purpose of Playing: Shakespeare and the Cultural Politics of the Elizabethan Theater* [Chicago: University of Chicago Press, 1996], 76ff.) explores several New Historicist perspectives on this subject, while Richard Grinnell adds further specifics on the threat to the social order many saw theater as representing at this time ("Witchcraft and the Theater in *Richard III,*" *The Upstart Crow* 17 [1977], 66–68).

28. For background on the cult of the queen, see, for example, Roy Strong (*The Cult of Elizabeth: Elizabethan Portaiture and Pageantry* [Wallop, Hampshire: Thames, 1977]), Frances Yates ("Queen Elizabeth I as Astraea," in *Astraea: The Imperial Theme in the Sixteenth Century* [London: Routledge, 1975]), and David M. Bergeron, from which the following is an example:

> Elizabeth's reign . . . is especially crucial in helping us understand the nature of the civic entertainments. The theme that binds all the pageants . . . together is the celebration of Elizabeth's power, her spiritual, mystical, transforming power. She is able to set men free, to still the voices of war, to provide a refuge for those who are distressed. Later pageants document and fulfill the hope implicit in the 1559 coronation royal entry, as the pageant-dramatists offer an apotheosis of Elizabeth. (Bergeron, *English Civic Pageantry, 1558–1642* [London: Edward Arnold, 1971], 11)

29. J. E. Neale, *Elizabeth I and Her Parliaments 1584–1601* (London: Jonathan Cape, 1957), 119.

30. Stephen Orgel notes that after Elizabeth, James I made this principle a "precept for his heir in his handbook of Kingship, *Basilikon Doron:* 'A King is as one set on a stage, whose smallest actions and gestures, all the people gazingly do behold'" (Orgel, *The Illusion of Power: Political Theater in the English Renaissance* [Berkeley: University of California Press, 1975], 42). For further background on the political implications of the theatricalization of Elizabeth's position see also Stephen Greenblatt, *Renaissance Self-Fashioning, From More to Shakespeare* (Chicago: University of Chicago Press, 1980), 168–69.

31. G. K. Hunter, *John Lyly: The Humanist as Courtier* (London: Routledge, 1962), 7.

32. Carolly Erickson, *The First Elizabeth* (New York: Summit, 1983), 153.

33. Greenblatt, *Renaissance Self-Fashioning,* 162.

34. Ascham, *The Schoolmaster,* 56. See also Daniel Javitch, "The Philosopher of the Court: A French Satire Misunderstood," *Comparative Literature* 23 [1971], 121.

35. Castiglione, *Book of the Courtier,* 7.

36. See note 34 above.

37. Javitch, *The Philosopher of the Court*, 104.

38. Ibid., 109.

39. Philbert of Vienne, *The Philosopher of the Court,* trans. George North (London: Henry Binneman), 13.

40. "This facilitie of the spirite is not therefore to be blamed which makes man according to the pleasure of others, to chaunge and transforme himself, for in so doing he shall be accounted wise, winne honour, and be free of reprehension everywhere: which Proteus knew very well, to whom his diverse Metamorphosis and oft transfiguration was verie commodious" (Ibid., 101).

41. Wilson, *Arte of Rhetorique,* Fol. 117.

42. Ibid., Fol. 83.

43. Quintilian, *The Institutio Oratoria of Quintilian,* trans. H. E. Butler, 4 vols. (London: Heinemann, 1958), 4:215.

44. Wilson, *Arte of Rhetorique*, Fol. 113.

45. Barbara Hardy, *Shakespeare's Self-Conscious Art* (Lethbridge: University of Lethbridge Press, 1989), 17.

46. Quoted in Cohen, *The Language of Power,* 18.

47. Puttenham, *Arte of English Poesie,* 158–9.

48. Ibid., 144.

49. Quoted in Alexander H. Sackton, *Rhetoric as a Dramatic Language in Ben Jonson* (New York: Octagon, 1967), 41.

50. Puttenham, *Arte of English Poesie,* 299–300.

51. Montrose, "Of Gentlemen," 442.

52. Frank Whigham's observations on Renaissance court life, though not applied specifically to Puttenham, complement his views:

> [T]o get at the typical character of the rhetorical life at the Renaissance court, we must work with [an] . . . elastic notion that includes the achievement of just such aspects of the good life as the courtly butterfly cherished: comfort, prestige, entertainment, a sense of personal superiority. . . . The motor of life at court was the pursuit of power and privilege, and we must be sensitive to the serious (not high-serious) privileges of this order. For these were goals shared by famous, infamous, and trivial courtiers alike, all of whom sought them by means of the same humanist rhetorical postures. . . . [W]e should reconsider these lives for what they tell us about the dialectical tensions of rhetoric. Such rhetoric both *maintained* and *altered* the status quo; it was at once conservative and disruptive. Life at the margins of power and privilege gave full scope to these various modes of rhetorical behavior, and so constitutes an unusually rich object for the study of shifting notions of social being. (Whigham, *Ambition and Privilege,* 20)

And cf. also Thomas M. Greene on the "game" of courtly conversation in *The Courtier*:

> We can follow the progress of the game in terms of the potentially threatening or divisive issues it raises, in terms of the doubts it flirts with, the embarrassments it skirts, the social and political and moral abysses it almost stumbles into, the dark underside of the authorized truth it sometimes seems about to reveal. This threat is really double:

there is an intellectual threat to the minds of the players, but there is also a social threat that the conversational surface might be ruffled irreparably; there is a threat that the talk might reach a point that would destroy its quality as game, as amusing conversation between ladies and gentlemen. . . . The game really becomes a contest between the community's will to understand itself, to examine and know itself, and conversely its will to protect itself from excessive knowledge, in order to function politically and socially. (Greene, "Il Cortegiano and the Choice of a Game," Renaissance Quarterly 32 [1979], 180)

53. James Henry Smith and Edd Winfield Parks, eds., The Great Critics (New York: Norton, 1951), xvi.

54. Sidney, An Apologie for Poetry, ed. Geoffrey Shepherd (1595; reprint London: Nelson, 1965), 101.

55. Ibid., 139.

56. Cicero's Latin "docere, . . . delectare, . . . permovere," comes from his De Optimo Genere Oratorum (Cicero, Opera, 12 vols.[London:1830], 2:1687). The English version of Horace (ll. 333–34 of the Ars Poetica) given here comes from I. A. Richards, Principles of Literary Criticism (London: Routledge, 1961), 68. For Scaliger's contribution see Smith and Parks, Great Critics, 159–60; on Minturno see Smith and Parks, Great Critics, 149. Wilson translates Cicero exactly in his "[t]hree thynges are required of an Orator [:] To teache. To delight. And to perswade" (Arte of Rhetorique, ai[b]), and Sidney echoes Horace again in making "to teach and delight" poetry's accorded "end" (An Apologie for Poetrie, ed. Evelyn S. Shuckburgh [1595; reprint, Cambridge: Cambridge University Press, 1951], 10). Kathy Eden traces Sidney's association of "dramatic poetry and forensic oratory" in the Apology (see Apology, ed. Shepherd, 124) to Aristotle's "explor[ation of] the similarities between tragic mimesis and rhetorical persuasion," as "fully reflected in his Poetics and Rhetoric, the oldest extant systematic discussions of these two related activities" (Eden, Poetic and Legal Fiction in the Aristotelean Tradition [Princeton: Princeton University Press, 1986], 4, 8). And cf. also C. S. Lewis: "Nearly all our older poetry was written and read by men to whom the distinction between poetry and rhetoric, in its modern form, would have been meaningless" (Lewis, English Literature, 61). For further general background on this subject as it pertains to the Elizabethans, see Neil Rhodes, The Power of Eloquence and English Renaissance Literature (New York: St. Martin's, 1992), 5ff.; also Rosemond Tuve, Elizabethan and Metaphysical Imagery (Chicago: University of Chicago Press, 1947), 180–91.

57. Puttenham, Arte of English Poesie, 8.

58. The distinction is implicit in the opening chapters of Clark's Rhetoric and Poetry in the Renaissance, with the emphasis here, however, more on "imitation" as "the distinguishing mark of poetry" (Rhetoric and Poetry, 6) than on the other side of the question, the so-called truth-bias of rhetoric. Ian Sowton quotes Leonard Cox's stricture that "it is of the nature of poetes to fayne and lye" (Sowton, "Hidden Persuaders as a Means of Literary Grace: Sixteenth-Century Poetics and Rhetoric," University of Toronto Quarterly 32 [1962], 59); and O. B. Hardison, while defending poetry on other grounds as "a higher form of eloquence," also makes the familiar Aristotelean claim for rhetoric that, "[r]hetorical skills being equal, the orator with truth on his side will be assured

of victory" (Hardison, "The orator and the poet: the dilemma of humanist literature," *The Journal of Medieval and Renaissance Studies* 1 [1971], 36).

59. Thomas O. Sloane, "The Crossing of Rhetoric and Poetry in the Renaissance," *The Rhetoric of Renaissance Poetry from Wyatt to Milton,* ed. Thomas O. Sloane and Raymond B. Waddington (Berkeley: University of California Press, 1974), 222.

60. Vickers, "'The Power of Persuasion:' Images of the Orator, Elyot to Shakespeare," in *Renaissance Eloquence. Studies in the Theory and Practice of Renaissance Rhetoric,* ed. James J. Murphy (Berkeley: University of California Press, 1983), 418.

61. See, for example, Charles G. Osgood, *Boccaccio on Poetry* (1930; reprint, Indianapolis: Bobbs Merrill, 1956), xli–ii, 115–16; also Jerrold E. Seigel, "Ideals of Eloquence and Silence in Petrarch," *Journal of the History of Ideas* 26 (1965), esp. 149–51, 169.

62. Puttenham, *Arte of English Poesie,* 4.

63. Quoted in Smith and Parks, *Great Critics,* 149.

64. Quintilian, *Institutio Oratoria,* 2:419.

65. Quoted in Smith and Parks, *Great Critics,* 153.

66. Ibid., 156–57. Cf. from John Rainolds, in reference to poetry: "This, this certainly is that famous Persuasion which spurs on the pleasure-loving to danger, the indolent to combat, and the cowardly to seek death boldly"; and "it is by far the greatest of the arts" (Rainolds, *Oratio in Laudem Artis Poeticae,* trans. Walter Aller, Jr. [Princeton: Princeton University Press, 1940], 47). And cf. also the following from William Webbe's *A Discourse of English Poetrie* (1586):

> Thus it appeareth that both Eloquence and Poetrie to have had their beginning . . . [in musical] exercises, beeing framed in such sweete measure of sentences and pleasant harmonie . . . drawing as it were by force the hearer's eares euen whether soever it lysteth, that *Plato* affirmeth therein to be contained . . . an inchauntment, as it were to perswade them anie thing whether they would or no.
> (quoted in G. Gregory Smith, *Elizabethan Critical Essays,* 2 vols. [London: Oxford University Press, 1904], 1: 231)

67. All Shakespeare quotations taken from the Tudor Edition of *William Shakespeare: The Complete Works,* ed. Peter Alexander (London: Collins, 1951).

68. George Brandes, *William Shakespeare: A Critical Study,* vol. 1 (1898; reprint, New York: Frederick Unger, 1903), 77.

69. See the chapter "Giordano-Bruno: Heroic Enthusiast and Elizabethan," in Frances Yates's *Giordano Bruno and the Hermetic Tradition* (London: Routledge, 1975), 275–90. Shakespeare's familiarity with Bruno is directly testified to, she suggests, in the character of Berowne in *Love's Labours Lost,* a Bruno namesake, and in Prospero, the "benevolent Magus" of *The Tempest.*

70. Puttenham, *Arte of English Poesie,* 303.

71. Ibid., 8.

Chapter 3. Shakespeare's Conscious Art

1. Ben Jonson, *Ben Jonson, vol. VIII, The Poems, The Prose Works*, ed. C. H. Herford Percy and Evelyn Simpson (Oxford: Clarendon Press, 1954), 583.

2. See Harold C. Goddard, *The Meaning of Shakespeare,* vol. 1 (Chicago: Phoenix, 1960), 19–20.

3. Goddard, *Meaning of Shakespeare,* 15.

4. L. C. Knights, *Some Shakespearean Themes and An Approach to 'Hamlet'* (Stanford: Stanford University Press, 1966), ix.

5. Washington Irving's words, written in 1819, may stand as representative of both German and British critical sentiments for most of the nineteenth century:

> There arise authors now and then who seem proof against the muta-bility of language, because they have rooted themselves in the unchang-ing principles of human nature. . . . Such is the case with Shakespeare, whom we behold, defying the encroachments of time, [and] retaining in modern use the language and literature of his day. . . . He is the faithful portrayer of Nature, whose features are always the same, and always in-teresting. (Irving, *The Sketch Book,* [1809; reprint, New York: New American Library, 1961], 136)

6. Quoted in D. Nichol Smith, (Smith, ed., *Eighteenth Century Essays on Shakespeare* [Oxford: Clarendon, 1963], 15.

7. James Joyce, *A Portrait of the Artist as a Young Man* (1916; reprint, New York: Viking, 1966), 215.

8. Northrop Frye, *The Anatomy of Criticism* (Princeton: Princeton University Press, 1957), 58.

9. Puttenham, *Arte of English Poesie,* 262, 263.

10. Annabel M. Patterson, *Hermogenes and the Renaissance: Seven Ideas of Style* (Princeton: Princeton University Press, 1970), 10.

11. See, for example, Gerald P. Mohrmann, "Oratorical Delivery and Other Problems in Current Scholarship on English Renaissance Rhetoric," in *Renaissance Eloquence: Studies in the Theory and Practice of Renaissance Rhetoric,* ed. James J. Murphy (Berkeley: University of California Press, 1983), 66; also Leon Battista Alberti, *Leon Battista Alberti on Painting and Sculpture,* ed. Cecil Grayson (London: Phaidon, 1972), 95; also Judith Dundas, *Pencils Rhetorique: Renaissance Poets and the Art of Painting* (Newark: University of Delaware Press, 1993), 56ff.

12. Leonard Mades, "Baltasar Gracián," in *Encylopedia Americana* (1978 ed.), 139.

13. Baltasar Gracián, *Baltasar Gracian's The Mind's Wit and Art,* trans. and ed. Hugh Chambers (Dissertation, University of Michigan, 1962; reprint, Ann Arbor: University Microfilms Inc., 1981), 80.

14. Quintilian, *Institutio Oratoria,* 3:189.

15. See Marion Trousdale, *Shakespeare and the Rhetoricians* (Chicago: University of Chicago Press, 1982), 162–69.

16. Castiglione, *Book of the Courtier,* 59.

17. M. Steven Guazzo, *The Civile Conversation of M. Steeven Guazzo,* the first three books translated by George Pettie, anno 1581, and the fourth by Bartholomew Young, anno 1586, with an introduction by Sir Edward Sullivan, 2 vols. (London: Contable, 1925), 1:123.

18. Peacham, *Garden of Eloquence,* A.B.iii.

19. Kenneth Orne Myrick, *Sir Philip Sidney as a Literary Craftsman* (Cambridge: Harvard University Press, 1935), 46.

20. Sidney, *Apology,* ed. Shepherd, 139.

21. Alvin B. Kernan, "The Plays and The Playwrights," in *The* Revels *History of Drama in English. Vol. 3. 1576–1613,* ed. Clifford Leech and T. W. Craile (London: Methuen, 1975), 255.

22. Mable Bruland, *The Presentation of Time in Elizabethan Drama* (New York: Haskell, 1966), 108.

23. Ibid., 135.

24. Jane Donawerth, *Shakespeare and the Sixteenth-Century Study of Language* (Urbana: University of Illinois Press, 1984), 7.

25. Trousdale, *Shakespeare and the Rhetoricians,* 17.

26. S. C. Sen Gupta, *The Whirligig of Time* (Calcutta: Orient Longmans, 1961), 15.

27. See Alfred Stern, *Sartre : His Philosophy and Existential Psychoanalysis* (London: Vision, 1968), 139. Sartre's original: *"La psychanalyse existentielle rejette le postulat de l'inconscient; le fait psychique est, pour elle, coextenif à la conscience"* (Jean-Paul Sartre, *L'être et le Néant: Essai d'Ontologie Phénoménologique,* [1943; reprint, Secaucus, N.J. : Citadel, 1965], 630). See also "Bad Faith and Falsehood" in Sartre, *Essays in Existentialism,* ed. Wade Baskin (Secaucus, N.J.: Citadel, 1965), 147–60.

28. Terry Eagleton, *Literary Theory: An Introduction* (Minneapolis: University of Minnesota Press, 1983), 133. See also discussion of Freud in Jonathan Culler, *On Deconstruction: Theory and Criticism after Structuralism* (Ithaca: Cornell University Press, 1982), 159–75 and 261–68.

29. See Leonard Unger, *The Man in the Name: Essays on the Experience of Poetry* (Minneapolis: University of Minnesota Press), 3–17.

30. Murray Krieger, "The Innocent Insinuations of Wit: The Strategy of Language in Shakespeare's Sonnets," in *The Play and the Place of Criticism* (Baltimore: Johns Hopkins University Press, 1967), 19.

31. Norman Rabkin, *Shakespeare and the Common Understanding* (New York: Macmillan, 1967), 2.

32. Jonathan Dollimore, *Radical Tragedy: Religion, Ideology and Power in the Drama of Shakespeare and his Contemporaries* (Chicago: University of Chicago Press, 1984), 277.

33. Ibid., 210.

34. Peacham, *Garden of Eloquence,* 137.

35. Quoted in Sonnino, *Handbook,* 54.

36. Peacham, *Garden of Eloquence,* 137.

37. James L. Calderwood, *Shakespearean Metadrama: The Argument of the Play in* Titus Andronicus, Love's Labour's Lost, Romeo and Juliet, A Midsummer Night's Dream, *and* Richard II (Minneapolis: University of Minnesota Press, 1971), 115.

38. William G. Crane, *Wit and Rhetoric in the Renaissance* (1937; reprint, Gloucester, Mass.: Peter Smith, 1964), 138.

39. See Patterson, *Hermogenes and the Renaissance: Seven Ideas of Style* 22. See also Crane, *Wit and Rhetoric,* 138ff.; Burns, *Acting and Being,* 6–16; and Sherry, *Schemes and Tropes,* 66. Desmet's book explores in exhaustive detail the extent to which Shakespeare's characters spring directly from the rhetorical tradition.

Chapter 4. "Invisible" Rhetoric
and the Shakespearean Allegory

1. Aristotle, *Treatise on Rhetoric and Poetic,* 13.

2. George Williamson, "The Poetry of the Storm in *King Lear,*" *Shakespeare Quarterly* 2 (1951), 11.

3. Erasmus, *Collected Works,* 28:423.

4. Bacon, *Advancement,* 1:27.

5. Peter Alexander, introduction to *William Shakespeare: The Complete Works,* (London: Collins, 1951), xxiii–iv.

6. E. K. Chambers, *William Shakespeare,* 1:182.

7. Braunmiller discusses the Jacobean dramatists' clear awareness of the difference between reading and performance, that this is frequently noted in the prefaces to their published texts, and that they "almost unanimously prefer performance" (Braunmiller, "Art of the Dramatist," 60). Harry Berger misses the rhetorical aspect of the question of publication as Shakespeare might have seen it, but he explores in depth the practical constraints that writing for the theater imposed on an author, as well as the further complications that the availability of printed texts brings in. See Berger, *Imaginary Audition: Shakespearean Stage and Page* (Berkeley: University of California Press, 1989), 9–24.

8. Neil Rhodes, *The Power of Eloquence and English Renaissance Literature* (New York: St. Martin's), vii.

9. See *Reader's Encyclopedia,* 668–69, 844.

10. Alvin B. Kernan, *The Playwright as Magician: Shakespeare's Image of the Poet in the English Public Theatre* (New Haven: Yale University Press, 1979), 32.

11. Quoted in G. Gregory Smith, *Elizabethan Critical Essays,* 2: 201–2.

12. Ibid., 1:136. Northrop Frye concurs that "[t]he conception of major poetry as concealing enormous reserves of knowledge through an allegorical technique was widely accepted in the Renaissance." (Frye, *The Princeton Encylopedia of Poetry and Poetics* [Princeton: Princeton University Press, 1974], 14.)

13. Quoted in Carolynn Van Dyke, *The Fiction of Truth: Structures of Meaning in Narrative and Dramatic Allegory* (Ithaca: Cornell University Press, 1985), 25.

14. Puttenham, *Arte of English Poesie,* 38.

15. Ibid., 186. And cf. also Wilson, *Arte of Rhetorique*:

> The Poetes were wise men, & wished in harte the redresse of thynges, the whiche when for feare they durst not openly rebuke, thei did in coloures paynte them oute, and tolde men by shadowes what they shoulde do in good south: or els because the wycked were unworthy to heare the truth, they spake so, that none myghte understande, but those unto whom they pleased to utter their meaninge, and knew thẽ to be menne of honeste conversation. (Fol. 105)

Narrow definitions of allegory, usually implicit, of course abound in criticism. Indeed, most students of the subject seem to assume that allegory is of one kind, though they differ widely as to what that "kind" actually is. To Francis Fergusson, for example, "allegory" means the traditional four-level medieval scriptural interpretive system of which Dante spoke in his letter to Can Grande (Fergusson, *Trope and Allegory: Themes Common to Dante and Shakespeare,* [Athens: University of Georgia Press, 1977], 1–6). To David Bevington, on the other hand, the allegorical issue as far as Elizabethan literature was concerned was political in the narrowest topical sense, relating directly to specific political issues of the day, such as the question of Queen Elizabeth's marriage (Bevington, *Tudor Drama and Politics: A Critical Approach to Topical Meaning,* Cambridge: Harvard University Press, 1968], 6–8). Michael O'Connell also appears to view allegory in the Renaissance as having a predominantly political focus. See O'Connell, *Mirror and Veil: The Historical Dimension of Spenser's Faerie Queene* (Chapel Hill: University of North Carolina Press, 1977), 1–4. James L. Calderwood, on the other hand, in his discussion of *Titus Andronicus* as a metadramatic allegory, contrasts his approach with what he calls "conventional allegory," without, however, clarifying the distinction between the two (Calderwood, *Shakespearean Metadrama,* 17).

16. William Empson, *The Structure of Complex Words* (1951; reprint, Ann Arbor: University of Microfilms Inc., 1967), 346.

17. Paul Zumthor, "The Great Game of Rhetoric," *New Literary History,* 12 (1981): title. Zumthor's article is on the theme of the delicate balance of politics and art in the Renaissance world, and of the critical role of the poet, the *rhetoriqueur,* in holding that world together. Cf:

> That quintessential theater, the court, is the center and perennial emblem of the universe. Meticulously ordered according to the rules of a *re*presentation which is both pleasing and serious, it is staffed by nobles, loyal scribes dedicated to the expression of devotion to the prince, minstrels, ladies-in-waiting, maids, jesters, and household servants. . . . In this unique place, being is identified with appearing; having, with giving. But every manifestation is a dramatic one, in that it is a coded action, a narration revealed through predetermined actantial and functional structures. (Zumthor, "Great Game," 493)
>
> . . . .
>
> Although prisoners of courts where they were, for better or worse, dependents, these men [the *rhetoriqueurs*] had one place in which they could hide from this alienation–the inside of the poetic universe, i.e., the act of constituting the text. In the midst of an aristocratic world claiming for itself immutability but in which, beneath outward forms that had apparently gone unchanged for two hundred years, all of existence was becoming a rite and a spectacle, the *rhetoriqueurs* sought to make of language, and of language alone, the spectacle, the stage, and the actor. (Zumthor, "Great Game," 507)

18. Quoted in G. Gregory Smith, *Elizabethan Critical Essays,* 1:48.

19. Jackson I. Cope discusses Thomas B. Stroup's thesis that "there is an inherent relationship between the concept of the world as a stage and the construction of the Elizabethan stage as a little world" (Cope, "The Rediscovery of Anti-Form in Renaissance Drama," *Comparative Drama 1,* [1967]: 157). For wide-ranging discussion on the implications of this stage-reality metaphoric (allegorical) transformation in Shakespeare and in Elizabethan drama generally, see Angus Fletcher's discussion headed "Kosmos: the allegorical image"

(Fletcher, *Allegory: The Theory of a Symbolic Mode* [Ithaca: Cornell University Press, 1964], 108–17).

20. Michael Murrin, *The Veil of Allegory: Some Notes Towards a Theory of Allegorical Rhetoric in the English Renaissance* (Chicago: University of Chicago Press, 1969), 10–11.

21. For discussion of Sidney as allegorist, see for example J. G. Nichols, *The Poetry of Sir Philip Sidney: An Interpretation in the Context of His Life and Times* (Liverpool: Liverpool University Press, 1974), 38–42. For discussion of allegory in some of Jonson's plays, see, for example, James E. Savage, *Ben Jonson's Basic Comic Characters and Other Essays* (Hattiesburg: University and College Press of Mississippi, 1973), 27–44.

22. Edmund Spenser, *The Faerie Queen,* ed. A. C. Hamilton (London: Longman, 1977), 737.

23. Quoted in William Nelson, *The Poetry of Edmund Spenser: A Study* (New York: Columbia University Press, 1963), 129.

24. F. W. Bateson, *English Poetry and the English Language: An Experiment in Literary History* (Oxford: Clarendon Press, 1934), 39.

25. Puttenham, *Arte of English Poesie*, 148.

26. Murrin, *Veil of Allegory*, 171.

27. For Vives's comment, see Atkins, *English Literary Criticism,* 42. Robert Burton's expression was very much Puttenham's, but shorter: "It is most true, *stilus virum arguit*, our style bewrays us" (Burton, *The Anatomy of Melancholy,* 2 vols. [1621; reprint, London: G. Bell, 1923], 1:25). Trousdale further quotes Sturm's *Rich Storehouse* to the effect that "without Arte . . . the secret image of an Imitator is not perceived" (Trousdale, *Shakespeare and the Rhetoricians,* 87).

28. Wallace Stevens, *The Necessary Angel* (New York: Knopf, 1951), 45.

29. Montaigne, *The Essays of Montaigne Done Into English by John Florio* (1603; reprint, New York: AMS, 1967), 400.

30. I. A. Richards, *The Philosophy of Rhetoric* (1936; reprint, New York: Oxford University Press, 1965), 27.

31. Charles L. Stevenson, *Ethics and Language* (New Haven: Yale University Press, 1944), 210.

32. Ibid., 213.

33. It will not escape the reader's attention that Plato's ancient "rhetoric" vs. "dialectic" antithesis, like Bakhtin's contemporary "monologic" vs. "dialogic," both confront the same linguistic problem.

34. Alfred Harbage, *William Shakespeare: A Reader's Guide* (New York: Octagon, 1971), 5.

35. Hardin Craig, *The Enchanted Glass* (1935; reprint, Oxford: Basil Blackwell, 1960), 166.

36. Aristotle, *Treatise on Rhetoric,* trans. Buckley, 12.

37. Murrin, *Veil of Allegory*, 146.

38. Edgar Wind, *Pagan Mysteries in the Renaissance* (New York: Norton, 1968), 27.

39. D. W. Robertson reinforces the continuity of Renaissance with classical thinking in this regard, discussing "medieval aesthetics," with specific reference to St. Augustine's use of figurative language:

[I]ncoherence [in] the surface materials is almost essential to the formation of the abstract pattern, for if the surface materials . . . were consistent or spontaneously satisfying, there would be no stimulus to seek for something beyond them. (Robertson, *A Preface to Chaucer. Studies in Medieval Perspectives* [Princeton: Princeton University Press, 1963], 56)

And Maureen Quilligan makes a further interesting point about the allegorical genre, that it is always *about* language:

All true narrative allegory has its source in a culture's attitude toward language, and in that attitude, as embodied in the language itself, allegory finds the limit of its possibility. (Quilligan, *The Language of Allegory* [Ithaca: Cornell University Press, 1979], 15)

40. James Winny, *The Master-Mistress: A Study of Shakespeare's Sonnets* (New York: Barnes, 1968), 1.

41. E. M. W. Tillyard, *Shakespeare's Problem Plays* (London: Chatto, 1957), 2.

42. G. Wilson Knight, *The Wheel of Fire* (London: Methuen, 1959), 168.

43. J. W. Mackail, *The Approach to Shakespeare* (1933; reprint, New York: AMS, 1970), 16.

44. Arthur Quiller-Couch, introduction to *Measure for Measure* (Cambridge: Cambridge University Press, 1950), xvi.

45. See discussion of various of these points in, for example, G. K. Hunter's introduction to the Arden *All's Well that Ends Well* (London: Methuen, 1962), xxvi–xxviii. The play ends "honourably," conspicuously having failed, however, to deal in any way with the calculated offenses to "honour" perpetrated by the characters previous to the final scene. It is particularly flagrant, Hunter notes (xxvii), that *no expression* of regret or remorse regarding any of his previous actions is given to the Bertram character to utter, in spite of those actions' exaggeratedly dishonorable quality.

Chapter 5. Rhetoric and the Plays: An Overview

1. I count, for example, of 572 items under "Shakespeare" in PMLA's 1994 *International Bibliography*, ten of which may be considered as taking this approach. The ratio for 1995 is effectively the same, eleven out of 597.

2. See Milton G. Kennedy, *The Oration in Shakespeare* (Chapel Hill, University of North Carolina Press. 1942), 67–70.

3. Puttenham, *Arte of English Poesie,* 219.

4. Clarke, *Rhetoric At Rome,* 53.

5. Charles Sears Baldwin, *Renaissance Literary Theory and Practice* (Gloucester, MA.: Peter Smith, 1959), 46.

6. George Kennedy, *The Art of Rhetoric in the Roman World* (Princeton: Princeton University Press, 1972), 619.

7. Elyot's reference to Hermogenes has been quoted previously; for the reference to Vives see T. W. Baldwin, 2:28; for Sturm see Baldwin, *Shakespere's Small Latine,* 2:22–23. For detailed discussion of Sturm's grammar school curriculum, influential in the second half of the sixteenth century, see Baldwin, *Shakespere's Small Latine*, 1:285–91. Leonard Cox, author of the first English

vernacular rhetorical textbook, also recommends Hermogenes. See Baldwin, *Shakespere's Small Latine,* 2:31.

8. These words are translated from *Statutes of the Colleges of Oxford* (1853), 3:49–50. See Baldwin, *Shakespere's Small Latine,* 1: 106. It may be noted here also that the man who "introduce[d] the works of Hermogenes . . . into the humanist curriculum" (John O. Ward, "Renaissance Commentators of Ciceronian Rhetoric," *Renaissance Eloquence: Studies in the Theory and Practice of Renaissance Rhetoric,* ed. James J. Murphy [Berkeley: University of California Press, 1983], 131), called by Brian Vickers "the leading Renaissance rhetorician" (Vickers, "Book Review of John Monfasini's *George of Trebizond: A Biography and Study of his Rhetoric and Logic,*" *Quarterly Journal of Speech* 63 [1977]: 444), and by John Monfasini "an authority to be compared with Cicero, Quintilian, and Aristotle . . . into the late sixteenth century" (Monfasini, "The Byzantine Rhetorical Tradition and the Renaissance," in *Renaissance Eloquence: Studies in the Theory and Practice of Renaissance Rhetoric,* ed. James J. Murphy [Berkeley: University of California Press, 1983], 176), George of Trebizond, is named specifically by all of Cox, White, and Vives as a modern rhetorician especially worthy of study. See Baldwin, *Shakespere's Small Latine,* 1:106; and 2:28.

9. Kennedy, *Art of Rhetoric,* 621.

10. Ibid., 620.

11. Hermogenes, *Hermogenes' On Types of Style,* trans. Cecil W. Wooten (Chapel Hill: University of North Carolina Press, 1987), xvi.

12. Monfasini, "Byzantine Rhetorical Tradition," 176.

13. See Monfasini, "Byzantine Rhetorical Tradition," 176, 186; Patterson, *Hermogenes,* 45; Hermogenes, *On Types of Style,* 108; George Kennedy, *Art of Rhetoric,* 631.

14. Ong, *Ramus, Method, and the Decay,* 231.

15. Kennedy, *Art of Rhetoric,* 620.

16. Monfasini, "Byzantine Rhetorical Tradition," 183.

17. Patterson, *Hermogenes,* 33.

18. In addition to its purely stylistic implications, a possibility also exists that Hermogenes's "speed" had some influence thematically in Renaissance poetry, another way that it may have touched Shakespeare. While any thematic aspect must be considered implicit at best in Hermogenes himself, the thesis has been maintained that Renaissance poems on the subject of the transience of time show the specific influence of his idea of speed. Patterson cites Marvell's classic "To His Coy Mistress" as an example of this influence (169–73), and Thomas O. Sloane acknowledges the same possibility in Milton's "On Time" (Sloane, "Reading Milton Rhetorically," in *Renaissance Eloquence: Studies in the Theory and Practice of Renaissance Rhetoric,* ed. James J. Murphy [Berkeley: University of California Press, 1983], 397–400). Neither mentions Shakespeare, but it is no great conjectural leap to extend the thesis to his many ruminations/declamations on the same subject.

19. The quote from Aristotle is from Aristotle, *Aristotle's Theory,* trans. Butcher, 290. Regarding the exactness of the unity of time in *Comedy,* in Shakespeare's addition to the original of the framing device of Aegeon's search for his son, the Duke decrees the "limit [of] this day" allowed to Aegeon to raise his ransom.

20. In 1.3.239–40, the time of day is "past the mid season . . . [a]t least two glasses"; act 5 then begins (5.1.3) "[o]n the sixth hour." The interval from some time after 2:00 P.M. to 6:00 P.M. would correspond very closely to the play's actual performance hours in an Elizabethan theater.

21. W. G. Boswell-Stone, *Shakespeare's Holinshed: The Chronicle and the Historical Plays Compared* (London: Chatto, 1907), 224.

22. See entries under *audacia* in Sonnino, *Handbook,* 272.

23. Quoted in Carpenter, introduction, *26.*

24. Quoted in Wayne A. Rebhorn, *The Emperor of Men's Minds: Literature and the Renaissance Discourse of Rhetoric* (Ithaca: Cornell University Press, 1995), 96.

25. Monfasini, "Byzantine Rhetorical Tradition," 186.

26. Hermogenes, *On Types of Style,* 109. And cf. also, from the opening paragraph of the section entitled "Pure Practical Oratory *(Haplōs Politikos)*":

The style that could be described as being purely practical is one that is produced by those types that create Clarity in the speech, as well as the types that reveal a modest and simple Character and the type that makes the style unaffected, because this is conducive to persuasion. All these styles should be understood as a unity: the purely practical style is created out of their mixture and combination into one. All the speakers whom we call practical orators use this style . . . which is why they are so persuasive.

27. Puttenham, *Arte of English Poesie,* 277.

28. Cf. from Joseph M. Williams:

The gentility consisted of two segments. One was a titled set ranging from the sovereign through his or her barons. In a population of 4 to 5.5 million at the end of the sixteenth century (estimates vary), they numbered no more than about 5000–6000; a century later, perhaps 7000–8000. . . . This gentry with their families and servants constituted perhaps 2–3 percent of the population, but they controlled 50 percent of the land; the nobility, a miniscule fraction of the population, another 15 percent. . . . Since the right to govern depended upon owning land, this minority governed the other 95+ percent of the Elizabethan population. (Williams, "'O! When Degree is Shake'd': Sixteenth-Century Anticipations of Some Modern Attitudes Toward Usage, in *"English in its Social Contexts: Essays in Historical Sociolinguistics,* ed. T. W. Machan and Charles T. Scott [Oxford: Oxford University press, 1992], 78)

29. Alvin B. Kernan first used the term *Henriad* for the second tetralogy. See Kernan, *"The Henriad:* Shakespeare's Major History Plays," in *Modern Shakespearean Criticism*, ed. Alvin B. Kernan (New York: Harcourt, 1970), 245.

30. Oscar James Campbell, "Comment," in *The Reader's Encyclopedia of Shakespeare*, ed. Oscar James Campbell and Edward G. Quinn (New York: Crowell, 1966), 338.

31. In each case the death is feigned (the "statue" trick of *The Winter's Tale* uses the same principle), which has the effect of eliminating the dramatic illusion between stage and audience. Juliet, having taken her sleeping potion, "acts" dead: no distinction as between on-stage and off-stage perceptions operates at this point, then, since both see the identical thing, a living person play-

ing dead. In Falstaff's and Hermione's cases the identity of feeling between off-stage and on-stage audiences is even greater because, like Hal and Leontes, we are surprised too when the "dead" come to life.

CHAPTER 6. "NONE ARE FOR ME THAT LOOK INTO ME WITH CONSIDERATE EYES": *RICHARD III* AND RHETORIC

1. "That it was instantly successful, whenever produced, allows of little doubt. And Crookback, which is known to have been one of Burbage's parts, is likely to have been that for which he was most famous in the middle nineties. The play's immense popularity is also attested by the fact that no fewer than six editions of it were published in quarto before a better text was included in the Folio of 1623, a record only equalled by the Quarto of *1 Henry IV* 'with the humorous conceits of Sir John Falstaffe'; while the number of contemporary allusions to it, or imitations of it, which have survived seems to be larger than that of any other Shakespeare play except perhaps *Hamlet*." (John Dover Wilson, introduction to *Richard III*, ed. John Dover Wilson [Cambridge: Cambridge University Press, 1968], x.)

2. Thomas F. Van Laan, *Role-Playing in Shakespeare* (Toronto: University of Toronto Press, 1978), 138.

3. Russ McDonald, "*Richard III* and the Tropes of Treachery," *Philological Quarterly* 68 (1989): 469.

4. A. P. Rossiter, *Angel With Horns and Other Shakespearean Lectures* (New York: Theater Arts, 1961), 6.

5. Paul Murray Kendall, *Richard III. The Great Debate* (New York: Norton, 1965), 35.

6. Anthony Hammond, editor of the Arden *Richard III*, wonders if Shakespeare's Richard "was in Bacon's mind when he penned" these words in his essay "Of Deformity":

> In a great Wit, *Deformity* is an Advantage to Rising . . . they will, if they be of *Spirit*, seeke to free themselves from Scorne; Which must be, either by Vertue, or Malice. (Hammond, introduction to *Richard III* [London: Methuen, 1981], 102)

7. Boswell-Stone, *Shakespeare's Holinshed*, 383.

8. The device employed to bring the citizens in has the technical designation *paralepsis*: "in pleading or perswasion to make wise as if we set but light of the matter, and . . . do passe it over slightly when in deede we do then intend most effectually . . . to remember it" (Puttenham, 232). There is a high probability that Shakespeare had Puttenham specifically in mind when he penned this scene. Puttenham's colorful illustration of the technique, that it "may be likened to the maner of women, who as the comon saying is, will say nay and take it" (232), is very nearly quoted directly in Buckingham's "be not easily won to our requests. / Play the maid's part: still answer nay, and take it" (3.7.50–51). Classic variations on the same device are played in at least two other memorable instances in Shakespeare, the pivotal first insinuations of treachery by Iago and Edmund, which Abraham Fraunce's definition of the trope exactly de-

scribes: "[A] kind of *ironia*, a kinde of pretĕded omitting or letting slip of that which we elegātly note out in the very shewe of praetermission . . . [a] denial or refusal to speake, as I will not say that which I might, I will not tell you, &c. when neverthelesse we speake and tell al" (Fraunce, *The Arcadian Rhetorike*, ed. Ethel Seaton [1588; reprint, Westport: Hyperion, 1979], 13).

9. The ambivalent "perhaps" in this sentence is deliberate, because although it *seems* that Richard has triumphed here, the Princess Elizabeth is pledged to marry Richmond at the end of the play. Shakespeare follows his sources exactly in reconstructing these events. Holinshed first says the courtship (Anne's death was in March 1485) was successful:

> insomuch that she [Queen Elizabeth] faithfullie promised to submit and yeeld hir selfe fullie and frankelie to the kings will and pleasure. . . .
> After she sent letters to the marquesse hir sonne, (being then at Paris with the earle of Richmond,) willing him in aniewise to leaue the earle, and without delaie to repaire into England, where for him were prouided great honours, and honourable promotions; ascertaining him further, that all offenses on both parts were forgotten and forgiuen, and both he and she highlie incorporated in the kings heart. (Boswell-Stone, *Shakespeare's Holinshed*, 400)

It is later stated, however, that a firm compact between Queen Elizabeth and Richmond had been in place since 1483, with Sir Christopher Urswick acting as go-between:

> So the mother, studious for the prosperitie of hir son, appointed this Christopher Urswike to saile into Britaine to the earle of Richmond, and to declare and reueale to him all pacts and agreements betweene hir & the queene agreed and concluded. (409)

Dorothea Kehler sees Elizabeth's rhetoric as superior to Richard's in this scene, as she "plays the fox, safeguarding the princess while using a sophisticated rhetorical figure—amphibology—to deceive Richard but not the alert playgoers" (Kehler, Shakespeare's *Richard III*, *Explicator* 56, [1997–98], 118). She also discusses Elizabeth's rehearsal for this triumph in the earlier scene of her courtship by Edward in *3 Henry VI*, who "wins his widow not on his terms but on hers" (118–19).

10. Ascham, *Schoolmaster*, 22. There is much also in Watson's *Vives: On Education* on the same subject; see esp. 75–80.

11. Clarence was jailed 21 May 1477 (Boswell-Stone, 342 n.3); he was put to death 18 February 1478 (Boswell-Stone, 348 n.1); Edward died 9 April 1483 (Boswell-Stone, 350).

12. The only possible break in the action here is between scenes 2 and 3 (in modern editions of the play–neither Folio nor Quarto texts indicate any break at this point), and if there is an interval we know it is short, Tyrrel's last words when he leaves the stage in 2 being "I will dispatch it straight" (1.84).

The Quarto text makes the linking explicit in two additional lines here that are missing in Folio:

> King.   *Shal we heare from thee* Tirrel *ere we sleep?*
> Tir.   *Ye shall my lord.*

That scenes 3 and 4 are also close in time is confirmed by Richard's "Now. . . / To her I go, a jolly thriving wooer" (3.40, 43), with reference to his marital scheme announced in 3, followed by his reference to being "in haste," presumably to broach his scheme to Queen Elizabeth, when "intercepted" by his mother in 4. Shakespeare even throws in a couple of gratuitous time-of-day reference points for us to ponder if we wish in 2 and 3; Buckingham noting the time as "upon the stroke of ten" (116) at the end of 2, Richard engaging to talk to Tyrrel again "soon at after-supper" (31) in 3; clearly signaling both Shakespeare's awareness of the absurdities he is perpetrating and of the impossibility of his being detected in them.

13. Inga-Stina Ewbank, "Shakespeare's Liars," *British Academy Shakespeare Lectures 1980–89* (Oxford: Oxford University Press, 1993), 106.

14. Robert Y. Turner, *Shakespeare's Apprenticeship* (Chicago: University of Chicago Press, 1974), 81, 82.

15. James Russell Lowell, "Shakespeare's *Richard III,*" in *The Complete Writings of James Russell Lowell,* vol. 8 (Boston: Houghton, 1904), 297.

16. I was made aware of the ironic implications of this passage by Murray Krieger, "The Dark Generations of *Richard III,*" in *The Design Within: Psychoanalytic Approaches to Shakespeare,* ed. M. D. Faber (New York: Science, 1970), 360. Roland Cotterill ("Shakespeare and Christianity," in *The Discerning Reader: Christian Perspectives on Literature and Theory,* ed. David Barratt, Roger Pooley, and Leland Ryken [Leicester: Apollos, 1995) and Anthony Hammond use the irony implicit here and elsewhere to reinforce a Christian interpretation of the play. Richard, though himself the epitome of evil, is nevertheless God's agent, like Milton's Satan, "whose free choice of evil is also (by the familiar Christian paradox) the means by which God brings about good" (Hammond, introduction to *Richard III,* 109).

17. "But I think this was no dream but a punction and prick of his sinful conscience" (Richard Hosley, ed., *Shakespeare's Holinshed* [New York: Putnam, 1968], 262).

18. Marjorie B. Garber, *Dream in Shakespeare: From Metaphor to Metamorphosis* (New Haven: Yale University Press, 1977), 21.

Chapter 7. "Much Like to Madness": *Measure for Measure* and Rhetoric

1. Brian Gibbons, introduction to *Measure for Measure* (Cambridge: Cambridge University Press, 1991), 28.

2. Mark Fortier, "'Mortality and Mercy in Vienna': *Measure for Measure,* Foucault and Marowitz," *English Studies in Canada* 21 (1995): 376.

3. L. C. Knights, "The Ambiguity of *Measure for Measure,*" *Scrutiny* 10 (1942), reprint, *Shakespeare: Measure for Measure. A Casebook,* ed. C. K. Stead (London: Macmillan, 1971), 141.

4. Richard S. Ide, "Shakespeare's Revisionism: Homiletic Tragicomedy and the Ending of *Measure for Measure,*" *Shakespeare Studies* 20 (New York: Burt Franklin, 1988), 123.

5. Brian Gibbons, introduction to *Measure for Measure* (Cambridge: Cambridge University Press, 1991), 51–72, discusses in some detail the variety of theatrical interpretations that have been offered of the play over the centuries, interpretations engineered by judicious cutting; the low-life parts were often left out in seventeenth-century productions to give one emphasis, in many twentieth-century productions presented in full to give another. Philip C. McGuire speaks of "a network of silences [in *Measure for Measure*] that has no equivalent in any other Shakespearean play" (McGuire, *Shakespeare: The Jacobean Plays* [New York: St. Martin's, 1994], 59), that suggest to him, among other things, an intention on Shakespeare's part that the actors must create their own meanings and interpretations at these points. The director Charles Marowitz, finally, one of the play's most radical modern interpreters, in spite of his personal strongly leftist bias toward it, has to concede that, however cut, its "irritating ambiguity" (quoted in Fortier, "Mortality and Mercy," 390) cannot in the end be fully excised.

6. For Johnson, Coleridge, and Swinburne, see C. K. Stead, *A Casebook,* 37, 45, 62. For "contradictions" see William Witherle Lawrence, *Shakespeare's Problem Comedies* (Hammondsworth: Penguin, 1969), 97; for "inconsistencies" see Clifford Leech, "The 'meaning' of *Measure for Measure,*" *Shakespeare Survey* 3 (1950): 68; for "incongruities" see Krieger, "*Measure for Measure* and Elizabethan Comedy," *PMLA* 66 (1951): 782. Jonathan R. Price's "*Measure for Measure* and the Critics," *Shakespeare Quarterly* 20 (1969), sketches the complete critical history of the play to 1969.

7. Oscar James Campbell, *Shakespeare's Satire* (New York: Gordian, 1971), 134.

8. Tillyard, *Shakespeare's Problem Plays,* 132.

9. Leech, "'Meaning'," 68.

10. Campbell, *Shakespeare's Satire*, 123.

11. Anthony Caputi, "Scenic Design in *Measure for Measure,*" *Journal of English and Germanic Philology* 60 (1961); reprint, *Twentieth Century Interpretations of* Measure for Measure (Englewood Cliffs, N.J.: Prentice-Hall, 1970), 88.

12. Margaret Webster, *Shakespeare Without Tears* (Greenwich, Conn.: Fawcett, 1963), 188, 189.

13. Northrop Frye, *Frye on Shakespeare* (Markham: Fitzhenry, 1976), 148.

14. Tillyard, *Shakespeare's Problem Plays*, 119.

15. Webster, *Shakespeare Without Tears,* 190.

16. Lawrence, *Shakespeare's Problem Comedies,* 97.

17. See, for example, Ernest Schanzer, "The Marriage Contracts in *Measure for Measure,*" *Shakespeare Survey* 13 (1960).

18. Arthur Quiller-Couch, introduction to *Measure for Measure* (Cambridge: Cambridge University Press, 1950), xli.

19. Quoted in Price, "Critics," 184.

20. S. L. Bethell, *Shakespeare and the Popular Dramatic Tradition* (New York: Octagon, 1970), 33.

21. Fergusson, *The Human Image in Dramatic Literature: Essays* (Garden City, N.Y.: Doubleday, 1951), 134, 133.

22. Ibid., 133.

23. Gibbons, introduction to *Measure for Measure*, 48.

24. Sketchy research into the history of English legal education under the Tudors turns up no reference specifically to Seneca Rhetor, but Harold Greville Hanbury notes that "it was Roman law and not English law which was studied at the Universities of Oxford and Cambridge" during the reign of Henry VIII (Hanbury, *The Vinerian Chair and Legal Education* [Oxford: Basil Blackwell, 1958], 5). Frederick William Maitland quotes from Richard Morison's *Tenures* (1540), a work honoring Henry VIII and written on the occasion of his endowment of a King's College of Law, that as a regular part of the course of study "one of excellent knowledge in the Latin . . . is to read some orator or book of rhetoric, or else some author which treateth of the government of a commonwealth, openly to all the company" (Maitland, *English Law and the Renaissance* [Cambridge: Cambridge University Press, 1901], 72). S. E. Thorne then continues the same quotation in his chapter "English Law and the Renaissance," "In the mean vacations, after two years passed, instead of moots there are to be daily declamations in Latin" (Thorne, *Essays in English Legal History* [London: Hambledon, 1985], 191).

25. Seneca the Elder, *Declamations,* 1:479.

26. Ibid., 2:235.

27. Ibid., 1:121. While in Senecan mode I cannot resist citing one more of the *Controversiae* for its strongly suggestive links to *Measure for Measure*. In pledging Isabella to a celibate sisterhood, and then introducing various erotic complications into her life, including possible marriage at the end, Shakespeare is covering very similar ground to that covered by Seneca in his "The Vestal's Verse":

> A vestal virgin wrote the following verse: "How happy married women are! O, may I die if marriage is not sweet." She is accused of unchastity. (1:523)

The arguments then used against Seneca's hypothetical virgin in this controversy are precisely those that could be brought out against Isabella *if* she were to accept the Duke's proposal of marriage!

A relevant article that came to my attention at a late stage in the preparation of this manuscript for publication is Neil Rhodes's "The Controversial Plot: Declamation and the Concept of the 'Problem Play', *Modern Language Review* 95 (2000). The article notes the same possible specific connection to the *Controveriae* cited here, as well as contributing considerable additional background on the importance of Greek and Roman declamation in English Renaissance education.

28. The best-known Christian interpretation of the play is probably G. Wilson Knight's often-reprinted *"Measure for Measure* and the Gospels" essay from his *The Wheel of Fire,* but Price notes that what he calls "the Christian school" of commentators has been around since at least Ulrici's *Shakespeares dramatische Kunst* of 1846 (Price, "Critics," 187).

29. *American Heritage Dictionary of the English Language* (New York: American Heritage, 1969), 369.

30. Caputi, "Scenic Design," 87.

31. Kenneth Muir, *Shakespeare's Sources* (London: Methuen, 1957), 108.

32. Quoted in Price, "Critics," 195.

33. R. W. Battenhouse, "*Measure for Measure* and the Christian Doctrine of the Atonement" *PMLA* 61 (1946): 1043.

34. For a psychoanalytic interpretation, see, for example, Hans Sachs, "The Measure in *Measure for Measure,*" *The Design Within: Psychoanalytic Approaches to Shakespeare*, ed. M. D. Faber (New York: Science, 1970), 479–97; John Vyvyan also speaks of the Duke's disguise as an "experiment in psychiatry," using "shock-therapy" as a means of "helping his subjects discover their true selves" (Vyvyan, *The Shakespearean Ethic* [London: Chatto and Windus, 1959], 64, 65). Malcolm Evans does not discuss *Measure for Measure* in detail, but the tone of his references to it as well as the general drift of his argument have a distinctly Marxist slant (Evans, *Signifying Nothing* [Athens: University of Georgia Press, 1989]; see in particular 147, 255). For Foucauldian interpretation, see Fortier, "Mortality and Mercy."

An interesting recent example of an interpretation containing both rhetorical and historical elements, and foregrounding as well the motif of contradiction as a central structural principle in the play, is Carolyn Harper, "*"Twixt will and Will Not": the Dilemma of* Measure for Measure (Boulder: University of Colorado Press, 1998). The rhetorical element is the concept of *paradigma* (exemplum), taking "a deed or a saying past and applying it . . . in a comparative form"—said to be "of great force to move, persuade" (Peacham, *Garden of Eloquence*, quoted in Harper, *'Twixt will and Will Not,'* 45). *Measure for Measure*'s particular *paradigma* then reflects contemporary history, implicitly comparing still-papist Vienna, where spiritual and secular law exist in separate and contradictory spheres, to James I's England, in which the person of the king embodies both, resolving all contradictions.

35. Kaori Ashizu has analyzed the Duke's questionable role in the nine-year history of the Barnardine case, demonstrating in detail the manifest inconsistencies that it involves, including its last act: "To pardon and release a convicted and unrepentanat murderer is at odds with any serious conception of justice" (Ashizu, "'Pardon Me?'—"Judging Barnadine's Judge" [*English Studies* 78, 1997]: 424).

36. Knight, *Wheel of Fire*, 85.

37. Webster, *Shakespeare Without Tears*, 189.

CHAPTER 8. SUPERSUBTLE SHAKESPEARE:
OTHELLO AS A RHETORICAL ALLEGORY

1. Coleridge, *Lectures and Notes on Shakespeare and Other English Poets*, ed. Thomas Ashe (London: G. Bell, 1908), 384. In the original lecture the word *unsuspiciousness* is, strictly speaking, applied only to Desdemona, but the implication is that it applies to Othello as well. In the report on Lecture 4, at Bristol (Coleridge, *Lectures and Notes*, 477), the word is applied to Othello.

2. A. C. Bradley, *Shakespearean Tragedy*, 2d ed. (London: MacMillan, 1949), 191.

3. Knight, *Wheel of Fire*, 107.

4. Bradley, *Shakespearean Tragedy*, 188, 191.

5. Elmer Edgar Stoll, *Othello: An Historical and Comparative Study* (1915; reprint, New York: Haskell House, 1964), 6, 5, 7.

6. John Munro, introduction to *Othello,* in the *The London Shakespeare,* vol. 5, ed. John Munro (New York: Simon, 1958), 723.

7. Quoted in Horace Howard Furness, *The Variorum Shakespeare: Othello* (Philadelphia: Lippincott, 1886), 435.

8. Knight, *Wheel of Fire,* 97.

9. Helen Gardner, "The Noble Moor," *Proceedings of the British Academy* 41 (1955; reprint, in *Othello: A Casebook,* ed. John Wain, London: Macmillan, 1971), 147.

10. Adding a further dimension of ambiguity to the light/dark issue in *Othello,* R. B. Graves observes that "Renaissance dramatists brought real or real-appearing lighting instruments on stage not to increase illumination, although they had that effect, but to indicate darkness: light paradoxically represented darkness, and as such must be accounted not illusionistic" (Graves, "Elizabethan Lighting Effects and the Conventions of Indoor Outdoor Theatrical Illumination," *Renaissance Drama* 12 [1981], 56).

11. Quoted in Furness, *Variorum Shakespeare,* 412.

12. Eliot's famous remarks on Othello are in his "Shakespeare and the Stoicism of Seneca." See Eliot, *Selected Essays* (New York: Harcourt, Brace, 1950). For Leavis see "Diabolic Intellect and the Noble Hero," in *The Common Pursuit* (London: Chatto & Windus, 1958). Stephen Rogers takes a stronger line yet on Othello's duplicity, for example, "The false music of his supposed eloquence is nothing but empty rhetoric, and takes us all in" (Rogers, "*Othello:* Comedy in Reverse," *Shakespeare Quarterly* 24 [1973], 211). Millicent Bell, noting both Leavis's and Stoll's reservations about the Bradleyan view of Othello, in the end is unable to find any satisfactory resolution of the character issue, concluding, typically, that "Shakespeare is shamelessly cavalier about this whole matter . . . , as though his mind is elsewhere" (Bell, "Othello's Jealousy," *Yale Review* 85 [1997], 125)[!]

13. And the only Concordance for really careful linguistic studies today is Marvin Spevack's computer-generated *A Complete and Systematic Concordance to the Works of Shakespeare,* 6 vols. (Hildesheim: Georg Olms, 1968–70).

14. *speech:* in *Hamlet* 16 uses, in *Othello,* 12; in *Lear,* 9; *speak:* in *Hamlet,* 63; in *Coriolanus,* 54; in *Othello,* 51; in *Lear,* 49; *say:* in *The Winter's Tale,* 73; in *Coriolanus,* 72; in *Othello,* 67; in *Shrew,* 63; *act:* in *Hamlet,* 14; in *Othello,* 11; in *King John,* 8. It is interesting that in every case but one of the above *Hamlet* is the closest play to *Othello* in terms of usage. This is perhaps an indication of certain thematic similarities between the two plays. For an examination of *Hamlet* as a rhetorical allegory, see Paul A. Jorgensen, "Hamlet's World of Words," in *Redeeming Shakespeare's Words* (Berkeley: University of California Press, 1962), 100–20. For analysis of *Hamlet* as theatrical allegory see Lionel Abel, "*Hamlet* Q.E.D," in *Metatheater* (New York: Hill and Wang, 1963), 41–58.

15. M. M. Mahood, *Shakespeare's Word Play,* 48.

16. Cohen, *Language of Power,* 30.

17. The Folio reading. Q 1 But what? Q 2 What?

18. It is with an appropriateness truly poetic, incidentally, that the *OED* chooses this line to illustrate a figurative meaning for the word *invest:* "3. *fig.* To clothe or endue with attributes, qualities, or a character." And cf. also, for a foreshadowing of the "It is not words" line in this speech, Brabantio's reply to the Duke in 1.3, who has attempted to "lay a sentence" as a "grise" to console Brabantio:

> But words are words: I never yet did hear
> That the bruis'd heart was pierced through
> the ear.

(1.3.218–19)

The meaning here is the same as Othello's statement; in effect, that it takes more than words to either create or to relieve the passions of the heart.

19. The thesis of Edward and Karen Jacobs's article is that Shakespeare does something similar in the earlier scene of the brawl (2.2.), in the line "'Tis monstrous. Iago, who began't ?" (209)—that if the punctuation is removed the question answers itself! They also say he does the same thing deliberately in Gloucester's line in *Lear* "Where is the villain, Edmund?" (2.1.41) (Jacobs, "'Tis Monstrous': Dramaturgy and Irony in *Othello*," *The Upstart Crow* 9 [1989]: 52–62).

20. *Sense*, like *honest* and *jealous*, has greater frequency of use in *Othello* than in any other of the plays; and like these words also, it is used in all its many possible meanings—ranging from roughly equivalent to psychology's *perception*, to nearly synonymous with *reason*.

21. Bradley, *Shakespearean Tragedy,* 182.

22. Not to crowd the text with a long explanation of what is essentially a technical matter, I would direct the reader to Furness (*Variorum Shakespeare,* 358–72) for background to this question. Furness gives a comprehensive history of the controversy up to the date of publication of his text in 1886, and modern editors have frequently rehearsed the arguments again since that time. Among those who discuss it are Harley Granville-Barker (*Prefaces to Shakespeare* [Princeton: Princeton University Press, 1952], 24–30), M. R. Ridley (introduction to *Othello* [London: Methuen, 1959], lxvii–lxx), and Kenneth Muir (introduction to *Othello* [Harmondsworth: Penguin, 1968], 26–28). There are some discrepancies in the various interpretations, even mechanical discrepancies. Ridley, for example, states (Ridley, introduction, lxix) that there could be a significant interval between acts 3 and 4. There could not; Bianca's line (4.1.146) "What did you mean by that same handkerchief you gave me even now?" negates this possibility. Muir, on the other hand, notes correctly that the only possible time lapse on Cyprus is between scenes 3 and 4 of act 3. It is true that definitive proof of direct continuity between these scenes is impossible, but even more than the "impression . . . that events are moving swiftly" (Muir, introduction to *Othello,* 27) that we have in these scenes, there is abundant textual near-proof of continuity. Almost Othello's last words in scene 3 are "I will withdraw / To furnish me with some *swift* means of death for the fair devil" (my italics), which is very nearly conclusive; almost his first words in scene 4, then, are "O, hardness to dissemble!," which as Furness points out (*Variorum Shakespeare,* 360) can logically only mean that this is his first attempt at dissembling. Likewise Desdemona's many references in scene 4 to her suit to Othello on Cassio's behalf (see 15–17, 29, 45–47), suggest a direct tie to scene 3, especially to 22–25: "My lord shall never rest; . . . / I'll intermingle everything he does with Cassio's suit." Cassio himself says in scene 4 (115), "I would not be delay'd," and his reference to the handkerchief here (189–91) implies clearly that it has *just* been found. It is worth noting as well that the Quarto versions of the play have no scene division here; only the Folio does.

23. Muir, introduction to *Othello*, 26.

24. Quoted in Furness, *Variorum Shakespeare*, 369.

25. Graham Bradshaw, "Obeying the Time in *Othello:* A Myth and the Mess it Made," *English Studies* 73 (1992), 215, 213. A particularly ambitious attempt to deal definitively with the issue is mounted by Emrys Jones, nine pages of question begging that concludes, as lamely as Bradshaw, that time is a problem only for those who demand that the play be "more naturalistic than it really is" (Emrys Jones, *Scenic Form in Shakespeare* [Oxford: Clarendon, 1971], 60), a conclusion no more rational than Muir's "the conventions of poetic drama do not require this kind of verisimilitude" (Muir, introduction to *Othello,* 28). If this is the case, we must ask, what *kind* of verisimilitude, or what *degree* of naturalism, then, do the "conventions" require and the play have?–with the implicit answer being, precisely the kind and degree *I* decide, and if you see it differently, you're wrong!

26. Desdemona's observation that "we must . . . not . . . look for such observancy as fits the bridal" (3.4.149, 150–51) when "men's natures" (145) are engaged with "great" (146) things hints at the same possibility. A number of recent articles touch this issue. The title of the Nelson and Haines essay (T. G. A. Nelson and Charles Haines, "Othello's Unconsummated Marriage," *Essays in Criticism* 33 [1983]), gives their stand, with which Andrew Sofer is in agreement (Andrew Sofer, "Felt Absences: The Stage Properties of *Othello's* Handkerchief," *Comparative Drama* 31 [1997–98], 380). Wayne Holmes (*"Othello:* Is't Possible?" *The Upstart Crow* 1 [1978]), on the other hand, follows Robert Speaight (*Nature in Shakespearean Tragedy* [London: Hollis, 1955], 75–76) in assuming that the marriage was consummated. He interprets the "nature would not invest herself in such shadowing passion without some instruction" line as Othello's reflection on Desdemona's performance the night before, that she must have had previous sexual experience, confirmation to him of her affair with Cassio back in Venice. The sticky issue of *virginity*, of the blood whose presence or absence would be definitive proof of her condition, is not raised by Holmes, however. Stanley Cavell suggests ("Epistemology and Tragedy: A Reading of *Othello,*" *Daedalus* 108 [1979], 39) that the description of Desdemona's handkerchief as "spotted with strawberries" is an indirect reference to her having lost her virginity, without specifying to whom she may have lost it. The Bradshaw article, finally, after looking at and dismissing Nelson and Haines's argument for its confusing of real and "accelerated time" (Bradshaw, "Obeying the Time," 223) concludes by saying that "textual evidence of whether the marriage is or is not consummated is uncertain" (Bradshaw, "Obeying the Time," 227).

27. *3 Henry VI* and *Troilus and Cressida*.

28. Leavis, "Diabolical Intellect," 152.

29. Maurianne S. Adams ("Ocular Proof in *Othello* and its Sources," *PMLA* 79 [1964]), discusses the "vision" motif in *Othello*, pointing out that the expression "ocular proof" (the only occurrence of the word *ocular* in all Shakespeare, incidentally) comes almost direct from Cinthio, and that Shakespeare has embroidered the one idea into the rich tapestry of vision metaphors that extend from beginning to end of the play.

With my ever-useful Spevack *Concordance*, I note that the words *seel, seem, seen,* and *sense* all have (with cognates), very nearly, their most frequent use in

Othello of all the plays; likewise the words *watch* and *proof.* The word *light* in *Othello* is third in frequency of use, after *Love's Labours Lost* and *Romeo and Juliet.*

30. Harry Berger makes the point that Othello, to be able to say "Your napkin is too little" (l. 291), must have seen it. It then follows in his naturalistic, *à la* Emrys Jones, interpretation, that he later, conveniently, "disremembers" having done so! (Berger, "Impertinent Trifling: Desdemona's Handkerchief," *Shakespeare Quarterly* 47 [1996]; 237).

31. 2.3.278; 3.3.362; 3.4.68; 4.1.42; 4.2.88. Also there are additional near repetitions at 1.3.9; 2.1.217, and 4.2.135.

CHAPTER 9. "NOTHING WILL COME OF NOTHING":
KING LEAR AND RHETORIC

1. Bradley, *Shakespearean Tragedy,* 249.

2. Leo Tolstoy, *Tolstoy on Shakespeare* (London: Everett, 1906), 43.

3. Allardyce Nicoll, *Studies in Shakespeare* (London: Hogarth, 1927), 154–55. Frank Kermode, obviously not wanting to condemn Shakespeare outright, nevertheless implies a Tolstoyan view of the first scene in noting the fact that "some critics, without going as far as Tolstoy, . . . have *openly admitted* that the anonymous author [of Leir] manages the opening scene better than his successor" (Kermode, introduction to *King Lear,* 1250, italics mine).

4. Edward Dowden, *Shakespeare: A Critical Study of His Mind and Art,* 16th ed. (London: Kegan Paul, n.d.), 257.

5. Quoted in John Dover Wilson and George Ian Duthie, introduction to *King Lear* (Cambridge: Cambridge University Press, 1960), xiv.

6. Jan Kott, *Shakespeare: Our Contemporary,* trans. B. Taborski (Garden City: Doubleday, 1964), 87.

7. Bradley, *Shakespearean Tragedy,* 256.

8. A. C. Swinburne, *Swinburne as Critic,* ed. Clyde K. Hyder (London: Routledge, 1972), 260.

9. Wilson and Duthie, introduction to *King Lear,* xix.

10. Muir, introduction to *King Lear,* xlviii–ix.

11. Ibid., li.

12. Maynard Mack, King Lear *in Our Time* (Berkeley: University of California Press, 1965), 29.

13. Ibid.

14. Daniel Cottom, *Text and Culture: The Politics of Interpretation* (Minneapolis: University of Minnesota Press, 1989), 41.

15. PaoloValesio, *Novantiqua: Rhetorics as a Contemporary Theory* (Bloomington: Indiana University Press, 1980), 60.

16. As regards the French invasion of England, Bradley has noted it as one of the play's absurdities, that it is impossible for word of the "hard vein which both [the Dukes], hath [sic] borne / Against the old, kind King" to have reached France, and for it thus to be a motive in mounting the invasion (Bradley, *Shakespearean Tragedy,* 210)—a serendipitous if inadvertent support for Vale-

sio. Muir's introduction reviews certain aspects of this issue as well (Muir, introduction to *King Lear*, xxxiii–iv).

17. In Holinshed's account the word *nothing* appears, though not as a word actually used by either father or daughter:

> The father being nothing content with this answer, married his two eldest daughters . . . betwixt whom he willed and ordeined that his land should be divided after his death, and the one half thereof immediatlie should be assigned to them in hand: but for the third daughter Cordellia he reserved nothing. (Boswell-Stone, *Shakespeare's Holinshed*, 3)

18. The exceptional instance is its use in the dedication of *Lucrece*, in which the third meaning is implied. The probables are *Merchant* 4.1.26 and *All's Well* 3.2.63; the definites are *Winter's Tale* 2.3.8, 3.2.37, and 4.4.800; *Henry V* 5.2.213; *Richard III* 1.2.249 and 2.2.60; *Henry VIII* 1.2.12; *Hamlet* 1.1.90; *Antony & Cleopatra* 5.1.19; *Cymbeline* 1.4.104; *Sonnets* 46.12.

19. Quoted in Muir, introduction to *King Lear*, xxvii.

20. It may be noted as well that the issue of possible preplanning of the division is in no way clarified by Burgundy's claiming to have been "offer'd" something more substantial as "dower" with Cordelia than the "curse" that is now "all her wealth." See 1.1.190–205.

21. John Higgins's *A Mirror for Magistrates*. See *King Lear*, ed. Muir, 239. Cordelia is speaking:

> Yet nathelesse, my father did me not mislike:
> But age so simple is, and easye to subdue:
> As childhode weake, thats voide of wit and reason quite:
> They thincke thers nought, you flater fainde, but all is true:
> Once olde and twice a childe, tis said with you,
> Which I affirme by proofe, that was definde:
> In age my father had a childishe minde.

22. Kenneth Muir, *Shakespeare's Sources* (London: Methuen, 1957), 145.

23. See Bradley, *Shakespearean Tragedy*, 256–57. Typically, Bradley, like Leech on *Measure for Measure*, can only call Shakespeare "exceptionally careless of probability . . . and consistency" in these "smaller matters," a view on which further comment from me at this point would be superfluous.

24. Kott's 1967 critique of *Lear* is a famous one, comparing it philosophically to the theater of Samuel Beckett; there are touches, he suggests, in *Waiting for God* that indicate he almost certainly had *Lear* near him during its composition. A point Kott does not make in the comparison, but one that is highly relevant in the context under discussion here, is that the absurdity in *Godot*, like the absurdity in the plot of *Lear*, is always extratheatrical. That is, given the parameters of Beckett's play world, the world in which the characters find themselves, their behavior is normal. They are real people caught in a nonreal, non-sense situation; the boundaries of the stage are now the boundaries of their world, and they behave exactly as real people, normal people, might well behave under such bizarre circumstances.

25. An observation on this speech by Terry Eagleton ("Language and Value in *King* Lear," in *King Lear*, ed. Kiernan Ryan [New York: St. Martin's, 1992],

86) complements my thesis on it neatly as well, that "to say 'ay' and 'no' to everything" is precisely to say *nothing*, an implicit absolute devaluation of language.

26. I have said that the "absurd exaggeration" of these speeches has a satirical point; in fact the degree of exaggeration over actuality they represent appears much *less* when they are set beside comparable contemporary examples, such as Bacon's encomium on King James, note 48, chapter 1.

27. Valesio, *Novantiqua*, 53.

28. The title of his classic text in Latin composition, *De Copia Rerum et Verborum*. The importance of the distinction is spelled out at the beginning of his text on methods published with it, and a standard introductory text in Elizabethan schools: "In principle, knowledge as a whole seems to be of two kinds, of things and of words. Knowledge of words comes earlier, but that of things is the more important" (Erasmus, *Collected Works*, 24:600).

29. Puttenham, *Arte of English Poesie*, 238.

30. Charles Lamb, *The Complete Works and Letters of Charles Lamb* (New York: Random, 1935), 298.

31. Webster:

> The arguments as to whether or not *King Lear* is an actable play center around the storm scenes. Can the cataclysmic convulsions of nature be reproduced in the theater? The answer, of course, is no. Thunder-sheets and wind machines, rain "effects" and stereopticon lightning, make a niggardly mockery of Lear's "cataracts and hurricanes," his "sulphurous and thought-executing fires." They succeed only in drowning out the actor's voice without arousing either pity or terror. Shakespeare must surely have relied on the actor to show us the tempest and convulsion of Lear's soul. Yet if he is called upon to do this while standing upon a stage where no wind stirs a hair of his wig, no drop of moisture falls upon his cloak, and the accompanying storm-sounds barely reach voice-level, he is asked to perform an almost impossible creative feat. Perhaps it can be done; I have never yet seen it. (Webster, *Shakespeare Without Tears*, 164–65)

See in Mack, King Lear *in Our Time*, 32–37, for example, his thoughts on Herbert Blau's staging of these scenes.

32. Granville-Barker, *Prefaces to Shakespeare*, 267.

33. Empson, for example:

> This speech to the heavens ["If it be you that stirs these daughters' hearts/Against their father, fool me not so much/To bear it tamely;"] has an important position because it touches off the storm; at least there seems no doubt that it would be taken so by the audience, who were accustomed to melodramas in which thunder comes as an immediate reply. The storm in Nature is no doubt partly the image of Lear's mind, but it is also an attack upon him, whether from the stern justice of God or the active malice of the beings he has prayed to. (Empson, *Structure of Complex Words*, 134)

Knight gives particularly close attention to the storm scenes and subsequent references to them in *The Shakespearean Tempest*, 194–99.

34. George Williams, "The Poetry of the Storm in *King Lear*," *Shakespeare Quarterly* 2 (1951), 65.

35. Tolstoy, *Tolstoy on Shakespeare*, 27.

36. John Greenwood, *Shifting Perspectives and the Stylish Style: Mannerism in Shakespeare and his Jacobean Contemporaries* (Toronto: University of Toronto Press, 1988), 8.

37. The rhetorical implications of the Dover episode and Edgar's "perspective on perspective" (Jonathan Goldberg, "Perspectives: Dover Cliff and the Conditions of Representation," in *Shakespeare and Deconstruction*, ed. David M. Bergeron and G. Douglas Atkins [New York: Peter Lang, 1988], 249) are linked suggestively with other significant rhetorical moments in the play in two recent articles. Jonathan Goldberg notes that Lear's earlier reference to the storm's "eyeless rage" anticipates Gloucester's condition at Dover, where "illusionistic rhetoric" (Goldberg, "Perspective," 145, 147) must serve him, and us again as well, for vision. Eagleton does not mention the episode itself, but notes that Regan's "let him / Smell his way to Dover" and Lear's "there I smelt 'em out" recognition of language's limitations, are complementary (Eagleton, "Language and Value," 86).

38. Ludwig Wittgenstein, *Philosophical Investigations*, trans. G. E. M. Anscombe (New York: Macmillan, 1953), sect. 110.

39. Wittgenstein, *The Blue and Brown Books. Preliminary Studies for the "Philosophical Investigations"* (New York: Harper, 1958), 41.

40. See, for example, Frank Whitehead, "The Gods in *King Lear*," *Essays in Criticism* 42 (1992). John F. Danby's lengthy examination of the issue from one perspective is also well known, of course. See Danby, *Shakespeare's Doctrine of Nature: A Study of* King Lear (London: Faber and Faber, 1949).

CHAPTER 10. "MURD'RING IMPOSSIBILITY":
CORIOLANUS AND RHETORIC

1. A. L. Attwater, "Shakespeare's Sources," in *A Companion to Shakespeare Studies*, ed. G. B. Harrison and Harley Granville-Barker (Cambridge: Cambridge University Press, 1966), 232.

2. Kermode, "Introduction to *Coriolanus*," in *The Riverside Shakespeare* (1392; reprint, Boston: Houghton, 1974), 1392.

3. G. B. Harrison was the first to point out this connection. See Harrison, *Shakespeare's Tragedies* (London: Routledge, 1951), 229–31, also E. C. Pettet, "*Coriolanus* and the Midlands Insurrection of 1607," *Shakespeare Survey* 3 (1950).

4. C. F. Tucker Brooke, ed., *Shakespeare's Plutarch*, vol. 2 (New York: Haskell, 1966), 154.

5. Ibid., 153.

6. Ibid., 196.

7. A. L. Rowse, *William Shakespeare: A Biography* (New York: Harper, 1963), 400.

8. See William Hazlitt, *Characters of Shakespeare's Plays: Lectures on the English Poets* (1817; reprint, London: Macmillan, 1908), 42ff.

9. Rowse, *William Shakespeare,* 395.

10. For background on this question, see particularly chapters 1 and 2 of Clifford Chalmers Huffman, *Coriolanus in Context* (Lewisburg: Bucknell University Press, 1971).

11. Thomas Heywood, *An Apology for Actors* (1612; reprint, Delmar, N.Y.: Scholars' Facsimiles, 1978), F3.

12. Brooke, *Shakespeare's Plutarch*, 138.

13. The ending of Menenius's fable of the belly (1.1.132–39) makes specific reference to the belly's distributing of food "through the rivers of your blood" (132) "to all parts of the body" (Livius, *The History of Rome*, vol. 1, trans. D. Spillan [New York: Harper, 1871], 136), an idea not found in Plutarch.

14. Anne Barton, "Livy, Machiavelli, and Shakespeare's *Coriolanus,*" *Shakespeare Survey* 38 (1985), 117.

15. Brooke, *Shakespeare's Plutarch,* 138–39.

16. Barton, "Shakespeare's *Coriolanus,*" 123.

17. Quoted in Barton, "Shakespeare's *Coriolanus,*" 124.

18. Peter Whitehorne's English translation of 1560 was reprinted in 1563, 1573, and 1588; English versions of the *Discourses* and *The Prince* did not appear until Dacres' editions of 1636 and 1640, respectively. See Felix Raab, *The English Face of Machiavelli* (London: Routledge, 1964), 52–53.

19. Weithoff, "The Martial 'Virtue' of Rhetoric," 310.

20. Brooke, *Shakespeare's Plutarch,* 148, 149.

21. Machiavelli, *The Art of War,* trans. Peter Whitehorne (1560; reprint, New York: AMS, 1970), 146.

22. Ibid., 160.

23. S. Visnawathan, "Some Uses of Topoi in Shakespeare's *Coriolanus:* An Approach to the Play," in *Renaissance Essays,* ed. Sukanta Chaudhuri (Calcutta: Oxford University Press, 1995), 138.

24. Coleridge, *Lectures and Notes,* 311.

25. Eliot, *Selected Prose,* 101.

26. Derek Traversi, *An Approach to Shakespeare* (Garden City: Doubleday, 1956), 216.

27. Ibid., 216, 217.

28. James E. Phillips, introduction to *Twentieth Century Interpretations of Coriolanus*, ed. James E. Phillips (Englewood Cliffs, N.J.: Prentice-Hall, 1970), 2.

29. Puttenham, *Arte of English Poesie,* 191, 192.

30. Peacham, *Garden of Eloquence,* 33.

31. Ibid.

32. Sherry, *A Treatise of Schemes and Tropes,* 34.

33. Visnawathan, "Some Uses of Topoi," 137.

34. Francis Barker's "Nationalism, Nomadism and Belonging in Europe: *Coriolanus*," in *Shakespeare and National Culture*, ed. John J. Joughin (Manchester: Manchester University Press, 1997), similarly sees Coriolanus as "quintessentially *Rome*," "the very embodiment of its values, its traditions, its national idea" (Barker, "Nationalism," 245, 246). He then argues, without discussing specifically rhetorical implications, that this embodiment "produces an

odd dislocation of the text from itself," in the later "nomadic anonymity" of his rejection of and by both patrician and plebeian Rome, epitomized in his repudiation of his name (Barker, "Nationalism," 251, 253). For further discussion of related questions see also Murray Biggs, "Naming in *Coriolanus*," *Notes and Queries* 45 (1998).

Works Cited

Adams, Maurianne S. "Ocular Proof in *Othello* and its Sources." *PMLA* 79 (1964): 234–41.

Abel, Lionel. *Metatheatre: A New View of Dramatic Form.* New York: Hill and Wang, 1963.

Alberti, Leon Battista. *Leon Battista Alberti on Painting and Sculpture.* Ed. Cecil Grayson. London: Phaidon, 1972.

Alexander, Peter. Introduction to *William Shakespeare: The Complete Works.* London: Collins, 1951, pp. ix–xxiv.

Allman, Eileen Jorge. *Player King and Adversary: Two Faces of Play in Shakespeare.* Baton Rouge: Louisiana State University Press, 1980.

American Heritage Dictionary of the English Language. New York: American Heritage, 1969.

Aristotle. *Aristotle's Theory of Poetry and Fine Art.* Trans. S. H. Butcher. 1902. Reprint, New York: Dover, 1951.

———. *Aristotle's Treatise on Rhetoric and Poetic.* Trans. Theodore Buckley. London: G. Bell and Sons, 1914.

———. *The Works of Aristotle.* Vol. 11. Trans. and ed. W. Rhys Roberts. Oxford: Clarendon, 1959.

Ascham, Roger. *The Schoolmaster.* 1570. Reprint, Ithaca: Cornell University Press, 1967.

Ashizu, Kaori. "'Pardon Me?'—Judging Barnadine's Judge." *English Studies* 78 (1997): 417–29.

Atkins, J. W. H. *English Literary Criticism: The Renascence.* New York: Barnes & Noble, 1947.

Attwater, A. L. "Shakespeare's Sources." In *A Companion to Shakespeare Studies,* Ed. G. B. Harrison and Harley Granville-Barker, 219–41. Cambridge: Cambridge University Press, 1966.

Bacon, Francis. *The Advancement of Learning.* 5th ed. Ed. William Aldis Wright. Oxford: Clarendon Press, 1963.

———. *The Works of Francis Bacon,* 1856. Ed. James Spedding, Robert Leslie Ellis, and Douglas Denton Heath. Vol. 13. St. Clark Shores, MI: Scholarly, 1976.

———. *The Philosophical Works of Francis Bacon.* Ed. John M. Robertson. 1905. Reprint, Freeport, N.Y.: Books for Libraries, 1970.

Baade, Eric C. Introduction to *Seneca's Tragedies*. London: Macmillan, 1969, pp. xiii–xxiv.

Bakhtin, Mikhail. *Rabelais and His World*. Bloomington: Indiana University Press, 1984.

Baldwin, Charles Sears. *Renaissance Literary Theory and Practice*. Gloucester, Mass.: Peter Smith, 1959.

———. *Ancient Rhetoric and Poetic*. Westport, Conn: Greenwood, 1971.

———. *Medieval Rhetoric and Poetic*. New York: Macmillan, 1928.

Baldwin, T. W. *William Shakespere's Small Latine & Lesse Greeke*. 2 vols. Urbana: University of Illinois Press, 1944.

Barker, Francis. "Nationalism, Nomadism and Belonging in Europe: *Coriolanus*." In *Shakespeare and National Culture*, Ed. John J. Joughin, 233–65. Manchester: Manchester University Press, 1997.

Barton, Anne. "Livy, Machiavelli, and Shakespeare's *Coriolanus*." In *Shakespeare Survey* 38 (1985): 115–29.

Bateson, F. W. *English Poetry and the English Language: An Experiment in Literary History*. Oxford: Clarendon Press, 1934.

Battenhouse, R. W. "*Measure for Measure* and the Christian Doctrine of the Atonement" *PMLA* 61 (1946): 1029–59.

Baumlin, James S. *John Donne and the Rhetorics of Renaissance Discourse*. Columbia: University of Missouri Press, 1991.

Bell, Millicent. "Othello's Jealousy." *Yale Review* 85 (1997): 120–36.

Berger, Harry, Jr. "Impertinent Trifling: Desdemona's Handkerchief." *Shakespeare Quarterly* 47 (1996): 235–50.

———. *Imaginary Audition: Shakespearean Stage and Page*. Berkeley: University of California Press, 1989.

Bergeron, David M. *English Civic Pageantry, 1558–1642*. London: Edward Arnold, 1971.

Bethell, S. L. *Shakespeare and the Popular Dramatic Tradition*. New York: Octagon, 1970.

Bevington, David. *Tudor Drama and Politics: A Critical Approach to Topical Meaning*. Cambridge: Harvard University Press, 1968.

Biggs, Murray. "Naming in *Coriolanus*." *Notes and Queries* 45 (1998): 347–50.

Blake, N. F. *Shakespeare's Language: An Introduction*. London: Macmillan, 1983.

Blank, Paula. *Broken English: Dialects and the Politics of Language in Renaissance Writings*. London: Routledge, 1996.

Bolton, Whitney French. *Shakespeare's English: Language in the History Plays*. Oxford: Basil Blackwell, 1992.

Bornstein, Diane. *Mirrors of Courtesy*. Hamden, Conn.: Archon, 1975.

Boswell-Stone, W. G. *Shakespeare's Holinshed: The Chronicle and the Historical Plays Compared*. London: Chatto, 1907.

Bradley, A. C. *Shakespearean Tragedy*, 2d ed. London: MacMillan, 1949.

Bradshaw, Graham. "Obeying the Time in *Othello*: A Myth and the Mess it Made." *English Studies* 73 (1992): 211–28.

Brandes, George. *William Shakespeare: A Critical Study*, vol. 1. 1898. Reprint, New York: Frederick Unger, 1963.

Braunmiller, A. R. "The Art of the Dramatist." In *The Cambridge Companion to English Renaissance Drama*. Ed. A. R. Braunmiller and Michael Hattaway, 53–90. Cambridge: Cambridge University Press, 1990.

Brooke, C. F. Tucker, ed. *Shakespeare's Plutarch*. Vol. 2. New York: Haskell, 1966.

Bruland, Mable. *The Presentation of Time in Elizabethan Drama*. New York: Haskell, 1966.

Burke, Kenneth. *A Grammar of Motives and a Rhetoric Motives*. Cleveland: Meridian, 1962.

Burns, Edward. *Character: Acting and Being on the Pre-Modern Stage*. London: St. Martin's, 1990.

Burton, Robert. *The Anatomy of Melancholy*. 1621. 2 vols. Reprint, London: G. Bell, 1923.

Calderwood, James L. *Shakespearean Metadrama: The Argument of the Play in* Titus Andronicus, Love's Labour's Lost, Romeo and Juliet, A Midsummer Night's Dream, *and* Richard II. Minneapolis: University of Minnesota Press, 1971.

Campbell, Oscar James. "Comment." In *The Reader's Encyclopedia of Shakespeare*. Ed. Oscar James Campbell and Edward G. Quinn, 338–39. New York: Crowell, 1966.

———. *Shakespeare's Satire*. New York: Gordian, 1971.

Caputi, Anthony. "Scenic Design in *Measure for Measure*." *Journal of English and Germanic Philology* 60 (1961): 423–34. Reprint, *Twentieth Century Interpretations of* Measure for Measure. Ed. George L. Geckle. Englewood Cliffs, N.J.: Prentice-Hall, 1970, pp. 86–97.

Carpenter, Frederick Ives. Introduction to *The Arte or Craft of Rhetoryke,* by Leonard Cox. New York: AMS, 1971, pp. 7–34.

Castiglione, Baldassare. *The Book of the Courtier*. Trans. Sir Thomas Hoby. 1561. Reprint, New York: AMS, 1967.

Cavell, Stanley. "Epistemology and Tragedy: A Reading of *Othello*." *Daedalus* 108 (1979). 3: 27–43.

Chambers, Hugh. Introduction to *Baltasar Gracián's The Mind's Wit and Art*, 1–77. Diss., University Microfilms, Inc., 1962. Ann Arbor: UMI, 1981.

Chambers, E. K. *William Shakespeare: A Study of Facts and Problems*. 2 vols. Oxford: Clarendon, 1930.

———. *The Elizabethan Stage*. 4 vols. Oxford: Clarendon, 1923.

Charlton, H. B. *The Senecan Tradition in Renaissance Tragedy*. Manchester: Manchester University Press, 1946.

Cicero, Marcus Tullius. *The Basic Works of Cicero*. Ed. Moses Hadas. New York: Random, 1951.

———. *Cicero's "Offices"; Essays on Friendship and Old Age and Select Letters*. Ed. Ernest Rhys. London: Dent, 1909.

———. *Opera*. 12 vols. London: A. J. Valph, 1830.

———. *De Oratore*. 2 vols. Trans. E.W. Sutton. Cambridge: Harvard University Press, 1959.

Clark, Donald Lemen. *Rhetoric and Poetry in the English Renaissance*. New York: Columbia University Press, 1922.

Clarke, M. L. *Rhetoric at Rome*. London: Cohen, 1953.

———. *Classical Education in Britain*. Cambridge: Cambridge University Press, 1959.

Cohen, Stephen. *The Language of Power, the Power of Language: The Effects of Ambiguity on Sociopolitical Structures as Illustrated in Shakespeare's Plays*. Cambridge: Harvard University Press, 1987.

Coleridge, Samuel Taylor. *Lectures and Notes on Shakespeare and Other English Poets*. Ed. Thomas Ashe. London: G. Bell, 1908.

Collier, John Payne. *The History of English Dramatic Poetry to the Time of Shakespeare and Annals of the Stage to the Restoration*. 3 vols. 1831. Reprint, New York: AMS, 1970.

Cope, Jackson I. "The Rediscovery of Anti-Form in Renaissance Drama." *Comparative Drama* 1 (1967): 155–71.

Cotterill, Roland. "Shakespeare and Christianity." In *The Discerning Reader: Christian Perspectives on Literature and Theory*. Ed. David Barratt, Roger Pooley, and Leland Ryken. Leicester: Apollos, 1995.

Cottom, Daniel. *Text and Culture: The Politics of Interpretation*. Minneapolis: University of Minnesota Press, 1989.

Cox, John D. *Shakespeare and the Dramaturgy of Power*. Princeton: Princeton University Press, 1989.

Cox, Leonard. *The Arte or Crafte of Rhethoryke*. Ed. Frederick Ives Carpenter. 1530. Reprint, New York: AMS, 1971.

Craig, Hardin. *The Enchanted Glass*. 1935. Reprint, Oxford: Basil Blackwell, 1960.

Craik, T. W. "The Tudor Interlude and Later Elizabethan Drama." In *Elizabethan Theatre*, Ed. John Russell Brown and Bernard Harris, 37–57. London: Edward Arnold, 1966.

Crane, William G. *Wit and Rhetoric in the Renaissance*. 1937. Reprint, Gloucester, Mass.: Peter Smith, 1964.

———. Introduction to *The Garden of Eloquence*, by Henry Peacham. New York: Scholars' Fascimiles, 1977.

Culler, Jonathan. *On Deconstruction: Theory and Criticism after Structuralism*. Ithaca: Cornell University Press, 1982.

Cunliffe, John W. *The Influence of Seneca on Elizabethan Tragedy*. 1893. Reprint, Hamden, Conn.: Archon, 1965.

Danby, John F. *Shakespeare's Doctrine of Nature: A Study of* King Lear. London: Faber and Faber, 1949.

Daniel, Samuel. *Poems and a Defence of Ryme*. Ed. Arthur Colby Sprague. Chicago: University Chicago Press, 1972.

Derrida, Jacques. "'To Do Justice to Freud': The History of Madness in the Age of Psychoanalysis." *Critical Inquiry* 20 (1994): 227–66.

Desmet, Christy. *Reading Shakespeare's Characters: Rhetoric, Ethics, and Identity*. Amherst: University of Massachusetts Press, 1992.

Dollimore, Jonathan. *Radical Tragedy: Religion, Ideology and Power in the Drama of Shakespeare and his Contemporaries*. Chicago: University of Chicago Press, 1984.

Donawerth, Jane. *Shakespeare and the Sixteenth-Century Study of Language.* Urbana: University of Illinois Press, 1984.

Dowden, Edward. *Shakespeare: A Critical Study of His Mind and Art.* 16ᵗʰ ed. London: Kegan Paul, n.d.

Dundas, Judith. *Pencils Rhetorique: Renaissance Poets and the Art of Painting.* Newark: University of Delaware Press, 1993.

Dunn, Esther Cloudman. *The Literature of Shakespeare's England.* 1930. Reprint, New York: Cooper Square, 1969.

Eagleton, Terry. *Literary Theory: An Introduction.* Minneapolis: University of Minnesota Press, 1983.

———. "Language and Value in *King Lear.*" In *King Lear.* Ed. Kiernan Ryan, 84–91. New York: St. Martin's, 1992.

Eden, Kathy. *Poetic and Legal Fiction in the Aristotelean Tradition.* Princeton: Princeton University Press, 1986.

Edgerton, William L. *Nicholas Udall.* New York: Twayne, 1965.

Eliot, T. S. *Selected Prose.* Ed. John Hayward. Harmondsworth: Penguin, 1953.

Elyot, Sir Thomas. *The Boke Named the Gouernour.* Ed. Henry Herbert Stephen Croft. 2 vols. 1531. Reprint, New York: Burt Franklin, 1967.

Empson, William. *The Structure of Complex Words.* 1951. Reprint, Ann Arbor: University Microfilms, Inc., 1967.

Erasmus, Desiderius. *Collected Works of Erasmus.* 86 vols. Toronto: University of Toronto Press, 1974–93.

Erickson, Carolly. *The First Elizabeth.* New York: Summit, 1983.

Evans, Malcolm. *Signifying Nothing.* Athens: University of Georgia Press, 1989.

Ewbank, Inga-Stina. "Shakespeare's Liars." In *British Academy Shakespeare Lectures 1980–89.* Oxford: Oxford University Press, 1993, pp. 85–116.

Fergusson, Francis. *Trope and Allegory: Themes Common to Dante and Shakespeare.* Athens: University of Georgia Press, 1977.

———. *The Human Image in Dramatic Literature: Essays.* Garden City, N.Y.: Doubleday, 1951.

Fleming, Abraham. *A Panoplie of Epistles, Or, A Looking Glasse for the Unlearned.* London: Ralph Newberie, 1576.

Fletcher, Angus. *Allegory: The Theory of a Symbolic Mode.* Ithaca: Cornell University Press, 1964.

Fortier, Mark. "'Mortality and Mercy in Vienna': *Measure for Measure,* Foucault and Marowitz." *English Studies in Canada* 21 (1995): 375–92.

Fraunce, Abraham. *The Arcadian Rhetorike.* Ed. Ethel Seaton. 1588. Reprint, Westport: Hyperion, 1979.

Frye, Northrop. *The Anatomy of Criticism.* Princeton: Princeton University Press, 1957.

———. "Allegory" In *The Princeton Encyclopedia of Poetry and Poetics,* 12–15. Princeton: Princeton University Press, 1974.

———. *Northrop Frye on Shakespeare.* Markham: Fitzhenry, 1976.

Fulwood, William. *The Enemy of Idlenesse. Teaching How to Indite Epistles.* London: Henrie Middleton, 1582.

Furness, Horace Howard, ed. *The Variorum Shakespeare: Othello*. Philadelphia: Lippincott, 1886.

Garber, Marjorie B. *Dream in Shakespeare: From Metaphor to Metamorphosis*. New Haven: Yale University Press, 1977.

Gardiner, Stephen. *A Detection of the Devils Sophistries, wherwith he robbeth the unlearned people, of the true byleef, in the most blessed Sacrament of the aulter*. J. Herforde at the costes of R. Toye, 1546.

Gardner, Helen. "The Noble Moor." In *Proceedings of the British Academy* 41 (1955). Reprint, *Othello: A Casebook*. Ed. John Wain, 147–68. London: Macmillan, 1971.

Giamatti, A. Bartlett. "Proteus Unbound: Some Versions of the Sea God in the Renaissance." In *The Disciplines of Criticism*. Ed. Peter Demetz, Thomas Greene, and LowryNelson, Jr., 437–75. New Haven: Yale University Press, 1968.

Gibbons, Brian. Introduction to *Measure for Measure*. Ed. Brian Gibbons, 1–72. Cambridge: Cambridge University Press, 1991.

Goddard, Harold C. *The Meaning of Shakespeare*. Vol. 1. Chicago: Phoenix, 1960.

Goldberg, Jonathan. "Perspectives: Dover Cliff and the Conditions of Representation." In *Shakespeare and Deconstruction*. Ed. David M. Bergeron and G. Douglas Atkins, 245–56. New York: Peter Lang, 1988.

Gracián, Baltasar. *Baltasar Gracian's The Mind's Wit and Art*. Trans. and Ed. Hugh Chambers. Diss., University of Michigan, 1962. Reprint, Ann Arbor: University Microfilms Inc., 1981.

———. *Oracle: A Manual of the Art of Discretion*. Trans. L. P. Walton. London: Dent, 1953.

Granville-Barker, Harley. *Prefaces to Shakespeare*. Princeton: Princeton University Press, 1952.

Graves, R. B. "Elizabethan Lighting Effects and the Conventions of Indoor and Outdoor Theatrical Illumination." *Renaissance Drama* 12 (1981): 51–69.

Gray, Hanna H. "Renaissance Humanism: The Pursuit of Excellence." *Journal of the History of Ideas* 24 (1963): 497–514.

Greenblatt, Stephen. *Renaissance Self-Fashioning, From More to Shakespeare*. Chicago: University of Chicago Press, 1980.

Greene, Thomas M. "*Il Cortegiano* and the Choice of a Game." *Renaissance Quarterly* 32 (1979): 173–86.

Greenwood, John. *Shifting Perspectives and the Stylish Style: Mannerism in Shakespeare and his Jacobean Contemporaries*. Toronto: University of Toronto Press, 1988.

Greg, W. W. *Marlowe's* Doctor Faustus: *1604~1616*. Ed. W. W. Greg. Oxford: Clarendon Press, 1950.

Grinnell, Richard. "Witchcraft and the Theater in *Richard III*." *The Upstart Crow* 17 (1977): 66–77.

Guazzo, M. Steven. *The Civile Conversation of M. Steeven Guazzo*. The first three books translated by George Pettie, anno 1581, and the fourth by

Bartholomew Young, anno 1586. With an introduction by Sir Edward Sullivan. 2 vols. Reprint, London: Constable, 1925.

Hammond, Anthony. Introduction to *Richard III*. London: Methuen, 1981, pp. 1–119.

Hanbury, Harold Greville. *The Vinerian Chair and Legal Education*. Oxford: Basil Blackwell, 1958.

Harbage, Alfred. *Shakespeare and the Rival Traditions*. New York: Macmillan, 1952.

———. *William Shakespeare: A Reader's Guide*. New York: Octagon, 1971.

Hardison, O. B. "The orator and the poet: the dilemma of humanist literature." *The Journal of Medieval and Renaissance Studies* 1 (1971): 33–44.

Hardy, Barbara. *Shakespeare's Self-Conscious Art*. Lethbridge: University of Lethbridge Press, 1989.

Harper, Carolyn. *'Twixt will and Will Not': The Dilemma of* Measure for Measure. Boulder: University of Colorado Press, 1998.

Harrison, G. B. *Shakespeare's Tragedies*. London: Routledge, 1951.

Hazlitt, William. *Characters of Shakespeare's Plays: Lectures on the English Poets*. 1817. Reprint, London: Macmillan, 1908.

Helms, Lorraine. *Seneca by Candlelight and Other Stories of Renaissance Drama*. Philadelphia: University of Pennsylvania Press, 1997.

Hermogenes. *Hermogenes' On Types of Style*. Trans. Cecil W. Wooten. Chapel Hill: University of North Carolina Press, 1987.

Heywood, Thomas. *An Apology for Actors*. 1612. Reprint, Delmar, NY: Scholars' Facsimiles, 1978.

Holmes, Wayne. "*Othello*: Is't Possible?" *The Upstart Crow* 1 (1978): 1–23.

Hoskins, John. *Directions for Speech and Style*. 1599. Reprint, Ed. Hoyt H. Hudson. Princeton: Princeton University Press, 1935.

Hosley, Richard, ed. *Shakespeare's Holinshed*. New York: Putnam, 1968.

Howell, Wilbur Samuel. *Logic and Rhetoric in England, 1500–1700*. New York: Russell & Russell, 1956.

Huffman, Clifford Chalmers. *Coriolanus in Context*. Lewisburg: Bucknell University Press, 1971.

Hunt, Everett Lee. "Plato and Aristotle on Rhetoric and Rhetoricians." In *Historical Studies of Rhetoric and Rhetoricians*. Ed. Raymond F. Howes, 19–70. Ithaca: Cornell University Press, 1965.

Hunter, G. K. *John Lyly: The Humanist as Courtier*. London: Routledge, 1962.

———. Introduction to *All's Well That Ends Well*, xi–lix. London: Methuen, 1962.

Huntley, Frank L. "*Macbeth* and Jesuitical Equivocation." *PMLA* 79 (1964): 390–400.

Hussey, S. S. *The Literary Language of Shakespeare*. London: Longmans, 1982.

Ide, Richard S. "Shakespeare's Revisionism: Homiletic Tragicomedy and the Ending of *Measure for Measure*." In *Shakespeare Studies* 20, 105–28. New York: Burt Franklin, 1988.

Irving, Washington. *The Sketch Book*. 1809. Reprint, New York: New American Library, 1961.

Jacobs, Edward and Karen. "'Tis Monstrous': Dramaturgy and Irony in *Othello*." *The Upstart Crow* 9 (1989): 52–62.

Javitch, Daniel. "*The Philosopher of the Court*: A French Satire Misunderstood." *Comparative Literature* 23 (1971): 97–124.

———. *Poetry and Courtliness in Renaissance England*. Princeton: Princeton University Press, 1978.

Jewel, John. "Oration Against Rhetoric." ca. 1548. Trans. Hoyt H. Hudson. *Quarterly Journal of Speech* 14 (1928): 374–92.

Jones, Emrys. *Scenic Form in Shakespeare*. Oxford: Clarendon, 1971.

Jones, Richard Foster. *The Triumph of the English Language: A Survey of Opinions Concerning the Vernacular from the Introduction of Printing to the Restoration*. Stanford: Stanford University Press, 1953.

Jonson, Ben. *Ben Jonson*. Vol. 8, *The Poems, The Prose Works*. Ed. C. H. Herford Percy and Evelyn Simpson. Oxford: Clarendon Press, 1954.

Jorgenson, Paul A. "Hamlet's World of Words." In *Redeeming Shakespeare's Words*, 100–120. Berkeley: University of California Press, 1962.

Joseph, B. L. *Elizabethan Acting*. New York: Octagon, 1979.

Joseph, Sister Miriam. *Shakespeare's Use of the Arts of Language*. New York: Hafner, 1966.

Joyce, James. *A Portrait of the Artist as a Young Man*. 1916. Reprint, New York: Viking, 1966.

Kehler, Dorothea. "Shakespeare's *Richard III*." *Explicator* 56 (1997–98): 118–21.

Kelso, Ruth. *The Doctrine of the English Gentleman in the Sixteenth Century*. Gloucester, Mass.: Peter Smith, 1964.

Kempe, William. *The Education of Children in Learning: Declared by the Dignitie, Vtilitie, and Method Thereof*. 1588. In *Four Tudor Books on Education*. Ed. Robert D. Pepper, 180–240. Delmar, N.Y.: Scholars' Facsimiles, 1977.

Kendall, Paul Murray. *Richard III. The Great Debate*. New York: Norton, 1965.

Kennedy, George. *The Art of Rhetoric in the Roman World*. Princeton: Princeton University Press, 1972.

Kennedy, Milton G. *The Oration in Shakespeare*. Chapel Hill: University of North Carolina Press, 1942.

Kermode, Frank. Introduction to *King Lear*. In *The Riverside Shakespeare*, 1249–52. Boston: Houghton Mifflin, 1974.

———. Introduction to *Coriolanus*. In *The Riverside Shakespeare*, 1392–5. Boston: Houghton Mifflin, 1974.

Kernan, Alvin B. *The Playwright as Magician: Shakespeare's Image of the Poet in the English Public Theatre*. New Haven: Yale University Press, 1979.

———. "The plays and the playwrights," In *The Revels History of Drama in English. Vol. 3. 1576–1613*. Ed. Clifford Leech and T. W. Craik, 237–465. London: Methuen, 1975.

———. "*The Henriad*: Shakespeare's Major History Plays." In *Modern Shakespearean Criticism*. Ed. Alvin B. Kernan, 245–75. New York: Harcourt, 1970.

Kinghorn, A. M. *The Chorus of History: Literary-Historical Relations in Renaissance Britain*. London: Blandford, 1971.

Knight, G. Wilson. "Lyly." In *Elizabethan Drama: Modern Essays in Criticism*. Ed. by Ralph J. Kaufmann, 41–59. New York: Oxford University Press, 1961.

―――. *The Wheel of Fire*. London: Methuen, 1959.

―――. *The Shakespearean Tempest*. London: Methuen, 1953.

Knights, L. C. *Some Shakespearean Themes and An Approach to 'Hamlet.'* Stanford: Stanford University Press, 1966.

―――. "The Ambiguity of *Measure for Measure*." *Scrutiny* 10 (1942): 222–34. Reprint, *Shakespeare: Measure for Measure. A Casebook*. Ed. C. K. Stead, 138–51. London: Macmillan, 1971.

Kocher, Paul H. "Marlowe's Atheist Lecture." *The Journal of English and Germanic Philology* 39 (1940): 98–106. Reprint, *Marlowe: A Collection of Critical Essays*. Ed. Clifford Leech, 159–66. Englewood Cliffs, N.J.: Prentice-Hall, 1964.

Kott, Jan. *Shakespeare: Our Contemporary*. Trans. B. Taborski. Garden City: Doubleday, 1964.

Krieger, Murray. "The Innocent Insinuations of Wit: The Strategy of Language in Shakespeare's Sonnets." In *The Play and the Place of Criticism*, by Murray Krieger, 19–36. Baltimore: Johns Hopkins University Press, 1967.

―――. "The Dark Generations of Richard III." In *The Design Within: Psychoanalytic Approaches to Shakespeare*. Ed. M. D. Faber, 347–67. New York: Science, 1970.

―――. "*Measure for Measure* and Elizabethan Comedy." *PMLA* 66 (1951): 781–83.

Lamb, Charles. *The Complete Works and Letters of Charles Lamb*. New York: Random, 1935.

Lawrence, William Witherle. *Shakespeare's Problem Comedies*. Harmondsworth: Penguin, 1969.

Leavis, F. R. "Diabolical Intellect and the Noble Hero." In *The Common Pursuit*, 136–59. London: Chatto & Windus, 1958.

Leech, Clifford. "The 'Meaning' of *Measure for Measure*." *Shakespeare Survey* 3 (1950): 66–73.

Lever, Ralph. *The Art of Reason, Rightly Termed Witcraft*. London: n.p., 1573.

Levin, Harry. *The Overreacher: A Study of Christopher Marlowe*. Cambridge, Mass.: Harvard University Press, 1952.

Lewis, C.S. *English Literature in the Sixteenth Century*. New York: Oxford University Press, 1954.

Livius, Titus. *The History of Rome*. Vol. 1. Trans. D. Spillan. New York: Harper, 1871.

Lowell, James Russell. "Shakespeare's *Richard III*." In *The Complete Writings of James Russell Lowell*. Vol. 8, 281–302. Boston; Houghton, 1904.

Machiavelli, Niccolò. *The Prince*. Trans. Robert M. Adams. New York: Norton, 1977.

―――. *The Discourses of Niccolò Machiavelli*. 2 vols. Trans. Leslie J. Walker. London: Routledge, 1950.

———. *The Art of War*. Trans. Peter Whitehorne. 1560. Reprint, New York: AMS, 1967.

Mack, Maynard. *King Lear in Our Time*. Berkeley: University of California Press, 1965.

Mackail, J. W. *The Approach to Shakespeare*. 1933. Reprint, New York: AMS, 1970.

Mades, Leonard. "Baltasar Gracián." In *Encylopedia Americana*. 1978 edition.

Mahood, M. M. *Shakespeare's Word Play*. London: Methuen, 1957.

Maitland, Frederic William. *English Law and the Renaissance*. Cambridge: Cambridge University Press, 1901.

Marlowe, Christopher. *Marlowe's Doctor Faustus, 1604–1616*. Ed. W. W. Greg. Oxford: Clarendon, 1950.

Mazzeo, Joseph Anthony. *Renaissance and Seventeenth-Century Studies*. London: Routledge, 1964.

McDonald, Russ. "*Richard III* and the Tropes of Treachery." *Philological Quarterly* 68 (1989): 465–83.

McGuire, Philip C. *Shakespeare: The Jacobean Plays*. New York: St. Martin's, 1994.

McLuhan, Marshall. *The Gutenberg Galaxy*. Toronto: University of Toronto Press, 1962.

Mohrmann, Gerald P. "Oratorical Delivery and Other Problems in Current Scholarship on English Renaissance Rhetoric." In *Renaissance Eloquence: Studies in the Theory and Practice of Renaissance Rhetoric*. Ed. James J. Murphy, 56–83. Berkeley: University of California Press, 1983.

Monfasini, John. "The Byzantine Rhetorical Tradition and the Renaissance." In *Renaissance Eloquence: Studies in the Theory and Practice of Renaissance Rhetoric*. Ed. James J. Murphy, 174–90. Berkeley: University of California Press, 1983:

Montaigne, Michel de. *The Essays of Montaigne Done Into English by John Florio*. 1603. Reprint, New York: AMS, 1967.

Montrose, Louis Adrian. "Of Gentlemen and Shepherds: The Politics of Elizabethan Pastoral Form." *ELH* 50 (1983): 423–59.

———. *The Purpose of Playing: Shakespeare and the Cultural Politics of the Elizabethan Theatre*. Chicago: University of Chicago Press, 1996.

Muir, Kenneth. *Shakespeare's Sources*. London: Methuen, 1957.

———. Introduction to *King Lear*. London: Methuen, 1964, pp. xv–lxiv.

———. Introduction to *Othello*. Harmondsworth: Penguin, 1968, pp. 7–44.

Mulcaster, Richard. *The Firste Parte of the Elementarie*. Np., 1582.

Mullaney, Steven. *The Place of the Stage: License, Play, and Power in Renaissance England*. Chicago: University of Chicago Press, 1988.

Munday, A. *The Defence of Contraries*. London: John Windet for Simon Waterson, 1593.

Munro, John. Introduction to *Othello*. In *The London Shakespeare*. Vol. 5. Ed. John Munro, 719–28. New York: Simon, 1958.

Murphy, James J. "One Thousand Neglected Authors: The Scope and Importance of Renaissance Rhetoric." In *Renaissance Eloquence: Studies in the*

Theory and Practice of Renaissance Rhetoric. Ed. James J. Murphy, 20–36. Berkeley: University of California Press, 1983.

———. *Rhetoric in the Middle Ages.* Los Angeles: University of California Press, 1974.

Murrin, Michael. *The Veil of Allegory: Some Notes Towards a Theory of Allegorical Rhetoric in the English Renaissance.* Chicago: University of Chicago Press, 1969.

Myrick, Kenneth Orne. S*ir Philip Sidney as a Literary Craftsman.* Cambridge: Harvard University Press, 1935.

Neale, J. E. *Elizabeth I and Her Parliaments 1584–1601.* London: Jonathan Cape, 1957.

Nelson, T. G. A. and Charles Haines. "Othello's Unconsummated Marriage." *Essays in Criticism* 33 (1983): 1–18.

Nelson, William. *The Poetry of Edmund Spenser: A Study.* New York: Columbia University Press, 1963.

Nichols, J. G. *The Poetry of Sir Philip Sidney: An Interpretation in the Context of His Life and Times.* Liverpool: Liverpool University Press, 1974.

Nicoll, Allardyce. *Studies in Shakespeare.* London: Hogarth, 1927.

O'Connell, Michael. *Mirror and Veil: The Historical Dimension of Spenser's Faerie Queene.*Chapel Hill: University of North Carolina Press, 1977.

Ong, Walter J. *Ramus, Method, and the Decay of Dialogue.* New York: Farrar, Straus & Giroux, 1979.

Orgel, Stephen. *The Illusion of Power: Political Theater in the English Renaissance.* Berkeley: University of California Press, 1975.

Osgood, Charles G. *Boccaccio on Poetry.* 1930. Reprint, Indianapolis: Bobbs Merrill, 1956.

Palmer, D. J. "Elizabethan Tragic Heroes." In *Elizabethan Theatre.* Ed. John Russell Brown and Bernard Harris, 11–35. London: Edward Arnold, 1966.

Panofsky, Erwin. *Idea: A Concept in Art Theory.* Trans. Joseph J.S. Peake. Columbia: University of South Carolina Press, 1968.

Parrott, Thomas Marc, and Robert Hamilton Ball. *A Short View of Elizabethan Drama.* New York: Scribner's, 1943.

Patterson, Annabel M. *Hermogenes and the Renaissance: Seven Ideas of Style.* Princeton: Princeton University Press, 1970.

Peacham, Henry. *The Garden of Eloquence.* 1593. Reprint, Delmar, NY: Scholars' Facsimiles, 1977.

Pettet, E. C. "*Coriolanus* and the Midlands Insurrection of 1607." *Shakespeare Survey* 3 (1950): 34–42.

Philbert of Vienne. *The Philosopher of the Court.* Trans. George North. London: Henry Binneman, 1575.

Phillips, James E. Introduction to *Twentieth Century Interpretations of Coriolanus.* Ed. James E. Phillips, 1–14. Englewood Cliffs: Prentice, 1970.

Plato. *Phaedrus and The Seventh and Eighth Letters.* Trans. Walter Hamilton. Harmondworth: Penguin, 1973.

Pratt, Norman T. *Seneca's Drama.* Chapel Hill and London: University of North Carolina Press, 1983.

Price, Jonathan R. "*Measure for Measure* and the Critics." *Shakespeare Quarterly* 20 (1969): 179–204.

Puttenham, George. *The Arte of English Poesie.* Ed. Gladys Doidge Willcock and Alice Walker. 1589. Reprint, Cambridge: Cambridge University Press, 1936.

Quiller-Couch, Arthur. Introduction to *Measure for Measure.* Cambridge: Cambridge University Press, 1950, vii–xliii.

Quilligan, Maureen. *The Language of Allegory.* Ithaca: Cornell University Press, 1979.

Quintilian, Marcus Fabuis. *The Institutio Oratoria of Quintilian.* Trans. H. E. Butler. 4 vols. London: Heinemann, 1958.

Raab, Felix. *The English Face of Machiavelli.* London: Routledge, 1964.

Rabkin, Norman. *Shakespeare and the Common Understanding.* New York: Macmillan, 1967.

Raimondi, E. "Machiavelli and the Rhetoric of the Warrior." *Modern Language Notes* 92 (1977): 1–16.

Rainolds, John. *Rainolds' Oratio in Laudem Artis Poeticae.* Trans. Walter Aller, Jr. Princeton: Princeton University Press, 1940.

Raleigh, Sir Walter. *The Works of Sir Walter Raleigh.* 1829. Vol. 8. New York: Burt Franklin, 1965.

———. Introduction to *The Book of the Courtier*, by Baldassare Castiglione. New York: AMS, 1967, pp. vii–lxxxviii.

Read, Conyers. "William Cecil and Elizabethan Public Relations." In *Elizabethan Government and Society.* Ed. S. T. Bindoff, J. Hurstfield, and C. H. Williams, 21–55. London: Athlone, 1961.

Rebhorn, Wayne A. *The Emperor of Men's Minds: Literature and the Renaissance Discourse of Rhetoric.* Ithaca: Cornell University Press, 1995.

Rhodes, Neil. *The Power of Eloquence and English Renaissance Literature.* New York: St. Martin's, 1992.

———. "The Controversial Plot: Declamation and the Concept of the 'Problem Play'." *Modern Language Review* 95 (2000): 609–22.

Richards, I. A. *The Philosophy of Rhetoric.* 1936. Reprint, New York: Oxford University Press, 1965.

———. *Principles of Literary Criticism.* London: Routledge, 1961.

Ridley, M. R. Introduction to *Othello.* London: Methuen, 1959, xv–lxx.

Roach, Joseph R. *The Player's Passion: Studies in the Science of Acting.* Newark: University of Delaware Press, 1985.

Robertson, D. W. *A Preface to Chaucer. Studies in Medieval Perspectives.* Princeton: Princeton University Press, 1963.

Rogers, Stephen. "*Othello*: Comedy in Reverse." *Shakespeare Quarterly* 24 (1973): 210–20.

Ronberg, Gert. "The Art of the Matter." In *A Way With Words: The Language of English Renaissance Literature,* 128–90. London: Edward Arnold, 1992.

Rossiter, A. P. *Angel With Horns and Other Shakespearean Lectures.* New York: Theatre Arts, 1961.

Rowse, A. L. *William Shakespeare: A Biography.* New York: Harper, 1963.

———. *Shakespeare's Sonnets: The Problems Solved.* New York: Harper, 1973.

Ryan, Kiernan, ed. *King Lear*. New York: St. Martin's, 1992.

Ryan, Lawrence V. Introduction to *The Schoolmaster*, by Roger Ascham. Ithaca: Cornell University Press, 1967, xi–xlii.

Sachs, Hans. "The Measure in *Measure for Measure*." In *The Design Within: Psychoanalytic Approaches to Shakespeare*. Ed. M. D. Faber, 479–97. New York: Science, 1970.

Sackton, Alexander H. *Rhetoric as a Dramatic Language in Ben Jonson*. New York: Octagon, 1967.

Sartre. Jean-Paul. *Essays in Existentialism*. Ed. Wade Baskin. Secaucus, N.J.: Citadel, 1965.

———. L'être et le Néant: Essai d'Ontologie Phénoménologique. 1943. Reprint, Paris: Gallimard, 1943.

Savage, James E. *Ben Jonson's Basic Comic Characters and Other Essays*. Hattiesburg: University and College Press of Mississippi, 1973.

Schanzer, Ernest. "The Marriage Contracts in *Measure for Measure*." *Shakespeare Survey* 13 (1960): 81–89.

Schelling, Felix E. *Elizabethan Drama 1558–1642*. 2 vols. New York: Houghton, 1908.

Seigel, Jerrold E. "Ideals of Eloquence and Silence in Petrarch." *Journal of the History of Ideas* 26 (1965): 147–74.

Sen Gupta, S. C. *The Whirligig of Time*. Calcutta: Orient Longmans, 1961.

Seneca the Elder. *Declamations*. 2 vols. Trans. M. Winterbottom. London: Heinemann, 1974.

Seneca, Lucius Annaeus. *Four Tragedies and Octavia*. Trans. E. F. Watling. Harmondsworth: Penguin, 1966.

———. *The Tenne Tragedies of Seneca*. 1581. Reprint, New York: Burt Franklin, 1967.

———. *Seneca's Tragedies*. Ed. Eric C. Baade. London: Macmillan, 1969.

Shakespeare, William. *The Complete Works*. Ed. Peter Alexander. London: Collins, 1951.

Shakespeare, William. *Measure for Measure*. Ed. Sir Arthur Quiller-Couch. Cambridge: Cambridge University Press, 1950.

———. *All's Well that Ends Well*. Ed. G. K. Hunter. London: Methuen, 1959.

———. *King Lear.* Ed. Kenneth Muir. London: Methuen, 1968.

———. *Love's Labour's Lost*. Ed. Richard Davis. London: Methuen, 1956.

———. *Othello*. Ed. M. R. Ridley. London: Methuen, 1959.

———. *Othello*. Ed. Kenneth Muir. Harmondsworth: Penguin, 1968.

Sherry, Richard. *A Treatise of the Figures of Grammar and Rhetoricke*. London: n.p., 1555.

———. *A Treatise of Schemes and Tropes by Richard Sherry* [1550], *and his Translation of the Education of Children by Desiderius Erasmus*. Ed. Herbert W. Hildebrandt. Reprint, Delmar, N.Y.: Scholars' Facsimiles, 1977.

Sidney, Sir Philip. *An Apologie for Poetrie*. Ed. Evelyn S. Shuckburgh. 1595. Reprint, Cambridge. Cambridge University Press, 1951.

———. *An Apology for Poetry*. Ed. Geoffrey Shepherd. 1595. Reprint, London: Nelson, 1965.

Sister Mary Geraldine. "Erasmus and the Tradition of Paradox." *Studies in Philology* 61 (1964): 41–44. Reprint, *Twentieth Century Interpretations of The Praise of Folly*. Ed. Kathleen Williams, 98–100. Englewood Cliffs, N.J.: Prentice, 1969.

Sloane, Thomas O. "The Crossing of Rhetoric and Poetry in the Renaissance." In *The Rhetoric of Renaissance Poetry from Wyatt to Milton*. Ed. Thomas O. Sloane and Raymond B. Waddington, 212–42. Berkeley: University of California Press, 1974.

———. "Reading Milton Rhetorically." In *Renaissance Eloquence: Studies in the Theory and Practice of Renaissance Rhetoric*. Ed. James J. Murphy, 394–410. Berkeley: University of California Press, 1983:

Smith, G. Gregory. *Elizabethan Critical Essays*. 2 vols. London: Oxford University Press, 1904.

Smith, James Henry, and Edd Winfield Parks, eds. *The Great Critics*. New York: Norton, 1951.

Smith, D. Nichol, ed. *Eighteenth Century Essays on Shakespeare*. Oxford: Clarendon, 1963.

Smith, Irwin. "Dramatic Time Versus Clock Time in Shakespeare." *Shakespeare Quarterly* 20 (1969): 65–69.

Sofer, Andrew. "Felt Absences: The Stage Properties of *Othello's* Handkerchief." *Comparative Drama* 31 (1997–98): 367–93.

Sonnino, Lee A. *A Handbook to Sixteenth-Century Rhetoric*. London: Routledge, 1968.

Sowton, Ian. "Hidden Persuaders as a Means of Literary Grace: Sixteenth-Century Poetics and Rhetoric." *University of Toronto Quarterly* 32 (1962): 55–69.

Speaight, Robert. *Nature in Shakespearean Tragedy*. London: Hollis, 1955.

Spenser, Edmund. *The Faerie Queen*. Ed. A. C. Hamilton. London: Longman, 1977.

Spevack, Martin. *A Complete and Systematic Concordance to the Works of Shakespeare*. 6 vols. Hildesheim: Georg Olms, 1968–70.

Spingarn, J. E. *A History of Literary Criticism in the Renaissance*. 1924. Reprint, Westport, Conn.: Greenwood, 1976.

Stead, C. K., ed. *Shakespeare:* Measure for Measure: *A Casebook*. London: Macmillan, 1971.

Steane, J. B. *Marlowe: A Critical Study*. Cambridge: Cambridge University Press, 1964.

Stephens, James. *Francis Bacon and the Style of Science*. Chicago: University of Chicago Press, 1975.

Stern, Alfred. *Sartre: His Philosophy and Existential Psychoanalysis*. London: Vision, 1968.

Stevens, Wallace. *The Necessary Angel*. New York: Knopf, 1951.

Stevenson, Charles L. *Ethics and Language*. New Haven: Yale University Press, 1944.

Stoll, Elmer Edgar. Othello: *An Historical and Comparative Study*. 1915. Reprint, New York: Haskell House, 1964.

Stone, Lawrence. *The Crisis of the Aristocracy 1588–1641*. Oxford: Clarendon, 1965.

Streuver, Nancy S. *The Language of History in the Renaissance*. Princeton: Princeton University Press, 1970.

Strong, Roy. *The Cult of Elizabeth: Elizabethan Portaiture and Pageantry*. Wallop, Hampshire: Thames, 1977.

Stroup, Thomas B. *Microcosmos: The Shape of the Elizabethan Play*. Lexington: University of Kentucky Press, 1965.

Sweeting, Elizabeth J. *Early Tudor Criticism, Linguistic and Literary*. New York: Russell, 1964.

Swinburne, A. C. *Swinburne as Critic*. Ed. Clyde K. Hyder. London: Routledge, 1972.

Tacitus. *The Annals of Imperial Rome*. Trans. Michael Grant. Harmondsworth: Penguin, 1956.

The Encyclopedia of Philosophy. Ed. Paul Edwards. 4 vols. New York: Macmillan, 1967.

The Reader's Encyclopedia of Shakespeare. Ed. Oscar James Campbell and Edward G. Quinn. New York: Crowell, 1966.

Thorndike, Ashley H. *Shakespeare's Theater*. New York: MacMillan, 1916.

Thorne, S. E. *Essays in English Legal History*. London: Hambledon, 1985.

Tillyard, E. M. W. *Shakespeare's Problem Plays*. London: Chatto, 1957.

Tolstoy, Leo. *Tolstoy on Shakespeare*. London: Everett, 1906.

Traversi, Derek. *An Approach to Shakespeare.* Garden City: Doubleday, 1956.

Trousdale, Marion. *Shakespeare and the Rhetoricians*. Chapel Hill: University of North Carolina Press, 1982.

Turner, Robert Y. *Shakespeare's Apprenticeship.* Chicago: University of Chicago Press, 1974.

Tuve, Rosemond. *Elizabethan and Metaphysical Imagery*. Chicago: University of Chicago Press, 1947.

Unger, Leonard. *The Man in the Name: Essays on the Experience of Poetry*. Minneapolis: University of Minnesota Press, 1956.

Valesio, Paolo. *Novantiqua: Rhetorics as a Contemporary Theory*. Bloomington: Indiana University Press, 1980.

Van Dyke, Carolynn. *The Fiction of Truth: Structures of Meaning in Narrative and Dramatic Allegory*. Ithaca: Cornell University Press, 1985.

Van Laan, Thomas F. *Role-Playing in Shakespeare*. Toronto: University of Toronto Press, 1978.

Vickers, Brian. "Book Review of John Monfasini's *George of Trebizond: A Biography and Study of his Rhetoric and Logic*." *Quarterly Journal of Speech* 63 (1977): 443–48.

———. "'The Power of Persuasion': Images of the Orator, Elyot to Shakespeare." In *Renaissance Eloquence. Studies in the Theory and Practice of Renaissance Rhetoric*. Ed. James J. Murphy, 411–35. Berkeley: University of California Press, 1983.

———. *The Artistry of Shakespeare's Prose*. London: Methuen, 1968.

Visnawathan, S. "Some Uses of Topoi in Shakespeare's *Coriolanus:* An Approach to the Play." In *Renaissance Essays*. Ed. Sukanta Chaudhuri, 132–41. Calcutta: Oxford University Press, 1995.

Vives, Juan Luis. *Vives: On Education. A Translation of the De Tradendis Disciplinis.* Trans. Foster Watson. Totowa, N.J.: Rowman, 1971.

———. *Tudor Schoolboy Life: The Dialogues of Juan Luis Vives.* Trans. Foster Watson. London: Cass, 1970.

———. "A Fable About Man." Translated by Nancy Lenkieth. In *The Renaissance Philosophy of Man.* Ed. Ernst Cassirer, Paul Oskar Kristeller, and John Herman Randall, Jr., 387–93. Chicago: University of Chicago Press, 1998.

Vyvyan, John. *The Shakespearean Ethic.* London: Chatto and Windus, 1959.

Ward, John O. "Renaissance Commentators of Ciceronian Rhetoric." In *Renaissance Eloquence: Studies in the Theory and Practice of Renaissance Rhetoric.* Ed. James J. Murphy, 126–37. Berkeley: University of California Press, 1983.

Watling, E. F. Introduction to *Four Tragedies and Octavia*, by Lucius Annaeus Seneca. Hammondsworth: Penguin, 1966, pp. 7–39.

Watson, Foster. Introduction to *Vives: On Education. A Translation of the De Tradendis Disciplinis.* Totowa, N.J.: Rowman, 1971, pp. xvi–clvii.

———. Introduction to *Tudor School-Boy Life: The Dialogues of Juan Luis Vives.* London: Cass, 1970, pp. vii–li.

Webster, Margaret. *Shakespeare Without Tears.* Greenwich, CT: Fawcett, 1963.

Weithoff, William E. "The Martial 'Virtue' of Rhetoric in Machiavelli's *Art of War.*" *Quarterly Journal of Speech* 64 (1978): 304–12.

Whigham, Frank. *Ambition and Privilege: The Social Tropes of Elizabethan Courtesy Theory.* Berkeley: University of California Press, 1984.

Whitaker, V. K. *Shakespeare's Use of Learning.* San Marino, Calif.: Huntington, 1953.

Whitehead, Frank. "The Gods in *King Lear.*" *Essays in Criticism* 42 (1992): 196–220.

Wickham, Glynne. *Early English Stages 1300–1660.* Vol. 1. London: Routledge, 1959.

Williams, George W. "The Poetry of the Storm in *King Lear.*" *Shakespeare Quarterly* 2 (1951): 57–71.

Williams, Joseph M. " 'O! When Degree is Shak'd': Sixteenth-Century Anticipations of Some Modern Attitudes Toward Usage. In *English in its Social Contexts: Essays in Historical Sociolinguistics.* Ed. T. W. Machan and Charles T. Scott. Oxford: Oxford University Press, 1992.

Williamson, George. *The Senecan Amble.* Chicago: University of Chicago Press, 1951.

Wilson, John Dover. Introduction to *Richard III.* Cambridge: Cambridge University Press, 1968, pp. vii–xlv.

Wilson, John Dover and George Ian Duthie. Introduction to *King Lear.* Cambridge: Cambridge University Press, 1960, pp. ix–lv.

Wilson, Thomas. *The Arte of Rhetorique.* 1553. Reprint, Amsterdam: Da Capo, 1969.

Wind, Edgar. *Pagan Mysteries in the Renaissance.* New York: Norton, 1968.

Winny, James. *The Master-Mistress; a Study of Shakespeare's Sonnets.* New York: Barnes, 1968.

Wittgenstein, Ludwig. *Philosophical Investigations*. Trans. G. E. M. Anscombe. New York: Macmillan, 1953.

———. *The Blue and Brown Books. Preliminary Studies for the "Philosophical Investigations."* New York: Harper, 1958.

Woodward, William Harrison. *Desiderius Erasmus Concerning the Aim and Method of Education*. 1904. Reprint, New York: Burt Franklin, 1971.

Wright, Celeste Turner. "'Lazarus Pyott' and Other Inventions of Anthony Munday." *Philological Quarterly* 42 (1963): 532–41.

Wright, Thomas. *The Passions of the Minde in Generall*. 1604. Ed. Thomas O. Sloane. Urbana: University of Illinois Press, 1971.

Yates, Frances A. *The Art of Memory*. Chicago: University of Chicago Press, 1966.

———. "Queen Elizabeth I as Astraea." In *Astraea: The Imperial Theme in the Sixteenth Century*, 29–87. London: Routledge, 1975.

———. *Giordano Bruno and the Hermetic Tradition*. London: Routledge, 1964.

Zumthor, Paul. "The Great Game of Rhetoric." *New Literary History* 12 (1981): 493–508.

Index